Praise for *Napoleon and the Revolution*

"David Jordan has a clear thesis – that Napoleon not only inherited the political changes made possible by the French Revolution but inadvertently helped to make them permanent. The book is written with a certain panache, and Napoleon emerges as a more complex figure than has been suggested by many of his biographers."

– Professor Alan Forrest, University of York, UK

"The excellent *Napoleon and the Revolution* is an admirable synthesis, which, without doubt, will enrich the bibliography in English and continue to make better known the reality of the man and his epoch."

– Thierry Lentz, Director, Fondation Napoleon, Paris

"Through fresh readings of sources including Napoleon's own memoirs as well as his contemporaries' writings about him, David Jordan argues that, in spite of his authoritarian tendencies, Napoleon always remained a self-conscious child of the Revolution. At a time when many scholars have highlighted Napoleon's repudiation of revolutionary reforms such as the granting of increased rights to women and the abolition of slavery, Jordan offers a provocative case for considering him as the man who guaranteed the survival of the Revolution's most basic innovations. *Napoleon and the Revolution* shows why the Emperor's legacy remains controversial, almost two centuries after his death."

– Jeremy D. Popkin, University of Kentucky, USA

"Did Napoleon destroy the French Revolution? Or was he its heir? The distinguished historian David Jordan argues that Napoleon, a man of great complexity, saved the French Revolution from the fate of many subsequent revolutions. This elegant study is thought-provoking and is sure to generate vigorous debate."

– John Merriman, Yale University, USA

"Readers familiar with works about Napoleon will find *Napoleon and the Revolution* strikingly different, challenging, refreshing, and brilliant. Here is more than simply 'rattling good history.' David Jordan tackles head-on the complex relationship of Napoleon to the French Revolution, a topic too often consigned to periphery, prologue, or epilogue in Napoleonic histories. In so doing, Jordan leaves no stone unturned, exploring the words and deeds not only of Napoleon himself, but of contemporaries, historians, and philosophers from the Emperor's day to ours. The result is not a compilation of 'for and against,' but keen, thorough, and objective analysis."

– Ralph Ashby, Eastern Illinois University, USA and author of
Napoleon Against Great Odds:
The Emperor and the Defenders of France, 1814

"Reflecting a lifelong engagement with the French Revolution, Jordan's splendid book shows Napoleon as contemporaries understood him, as revolutionary actor par excellence, indeed the Revolution's improbable savior. Judicious, provocative, wonderfully told, the book is especially well-suited for upper division students of revolutionary Europe."

– John Abbot, University of Illinois, Chicago, USA

"Historians have long debated the question of Napoleon Bonaparte's relationship to the French Revolution. Was he the heir to the ideals of 1789, or did he betray them? David Jordan's answer to this question is bold and succinct: Napoleon saved the French Revolution. By that he does not mean that Napoleon embraced all that the Revolution stood for. The Empire was neither democratic nor a friend to civil liberties. But without Napoleon, Jordan argues, the French Revolution might well have suffered the fate of 20th-century revolutions in Russia, China and Cuba, all of which were isolated by the other great nations of the world and forced, by that isolation, to adopt authoritarian policies. It is a provocative thesis, presented with verve and flair in a highly readable prose. This book is a welcome addition to the literature on Napoleon Bonaparte, one that will inspire a new generation of students to join the debate over Napoleon's relation to the French Revolution and to the modern world."

– Prof. Paul Hanson, Butler University, USA

"A book that is thought-provoking and engagingly written."

– R.S. Alexander,
H-France

Napoleon and the Revolution

David P. Jordan
Distinguished Professor of French History,
Emeritus, University of Illinois at Chicago, USA

First published 2012
Published in paperback 2014 by
PALGRAVE MACMILLAN

Palgrave Macmillan in the UK is an imprint of Macmillan Publishers Limited, registered in England, company number 785998, of Houndmills, Basingstoke, Hampshire RG21 6XS.

Palgrave Macmillan in the US is a division of St Martin's Press LLC, 175 Fifth Avenue, New York, NY 10010.

Palgrave Macmillan is the global academic imprint of the above companies and has companies and representatives throughout the world.

Palgrave® and Macmillan® are registered trademarks in the United States, the United Kingdom, Europe and other countries.

ISBN 978–0–230–36281–9   hardback
ISBN 978–1–137–42798–4   paperback

This book is printed on paper suitable for recycling and made from fully managed and sustained forest sources. Logging, pulping and manufacturing processes are expected to conform to the environmental regulations of the country of origin.

A catalogue record for this book is available from the British Library.

A catalog record for this book is available from the Library of Congress.

Typeset by MPS Limited, Chennai, India.

Transferred to Digital Printing in 2015

For Sarah, who grew up with 'Poleon,
and Richard Levy, friend of a lifetime

Contents

Figures

Preface

A recent author calculates from an unattributed assertion that 'more books and articles have been written on the subject of Napoleon Bonaparte ... than days have passed since the ex-emperor's death ...' – some sixty thousand titles. Indeed, as Thierry Lentz points out, there is virtually nothing we do not know about Napoleon. His whereabouts on every day once he became important are chronicled. So too are the number of hats made for him (between 160 and 170), the number of *culottes* he brought to St Helena (19), the color of his eyes and hair as well as his height – either a bit over five-feet-five or five-feet-five and nearly a half (1.68–1.69 meters) – how many plays and operas he attended when in Paris (more than 700), and much much more. Anyone who would add to the still growing count owes readers some explanation.

Napoleon was, as many agree, the child and heir of the Revolution. I argue this is no metaphor. He was the self-conscious embodiment of the dreams, the anxieties, the social and political reflexes, the assumptions, the rhetoric, even the delusions of the Revolution. The Revolution made him to the same degree as did his Corsican beginnings and his family. The 16 years of his predominance is a continuation of the Revolution militant, an enormous and bloody attempt to realize the messianic and ideological zeal that declared war against the *ancien régime*.

I am not writing a life of Napoleon. There are already a number of quite good examples. Nor am I attempting a monograph on a particular aspect of Napoleon's career. Rather I want to follow the thread of an idea, Napoleon's relationship to the French Revolution. In the long period when Marxist or Jacobin-inspired historians dominated the study of the Revolution it was customary to see Robespierre's fall in 1794 as the end of the creative phase of the Revolution, the moment when *le menu peuple* were forcibly excluded from affairs. After 9 Thermidor (27 July), the date in the Revolutionary calendar when The Incorruptible was brought down and then guillotined, a bourgeois reaction set in. The people were excluded from participation in the Revolution, price controls were lifted and inflation ran wild. The bourgeoisie severely limited the franchise, assuring their control of a revolution of which they were the chief beneficiaries. The radicals were destroyed in a series of high-profile political trials, and an inept and corrupt republican government dismantled much of the work of the Jacobins and left unfinished all those tasks concerned with social justice. This reaction would continue and be solidified under Napoleon, this view insists. He was a military dictator whose only ideals were efficiency in government, glory in conquest, hierarchy and political and social conservatism. This explanatory skein, which I have drastically compressed but not caricatured, has been unraveled in the last quarter century, yet lingers in old texts and intellectual habits. The unraveling demands another look at Napoleon's place in the Revolution.

We have a tendency to see our great historical figures whose trade is war as men of relatively simple, single-minded characters. Their temperaments are stressed at the expense of their ideas. Think for a moment of the differences between literary biography and the biographies of generals. The former tease from texts and letters, diaries and reminiscences complex and subtle psychologies and motives. The latter distill from public acts not so much the inner life of their heroes as the springs of their deeds. Napoleon's deeds are there for all to see, unmatched in their grandeur, folly, tragedy, and impact. Unlike most public men Napoleon also talked incessantly about himself. This torrent of words, whatever we may think of their authenticity, sincerity, and many contradictions, form a vast personal archive of his opinions, thoughts, and motives. We have tens of thousands of his letters, numerous records of his table talk, and Emmanuel Las Cases's *Mémorial de Sainte-Hélène*, the most unique and bizarre book about and by Napoleon. In addition we have a vast memoir repository of impressions of the man – more than 1500 in French alone, according to Jean Tulard's calculation. We may not know his innermost thoughts but we do know a great deal. He was an opportunist, a cynic, a Machiavellian, an egomaniac, a man who refused all constraints on his will or his ambition. He was also deeply read, a passionate devotee of French classical theater, a voracious student of history, a man with convictions and ideas who saw himself as the apotheosis of the French Revolution. His personality intrigued all who met him. He was admired by philosophers (Hegel), poets (Heine and Goethe), and novelists (Stendhal and Balzac). His inner circle of collaborators includes any number of men with impeccable revolutionary credentials among whom were many republicans and a number of Jacobins. He was for all of these a revolutionary, a man bent on continuing the work begun in 1789, not a mere warlord. The Revolution dominated his thought. I have emphasized this component in his complex makeup. I want to push back against the still prevailing view that he was an unprincipled conqueror who willfully cast aside all restraints, violated all the historical conventions of his day, and spread fire and sword throughout the continent in pursuit of his own obsessive and destructive ends. I want instead to advocate a multi-dimensional appreciation of the man and his deeds. No man who has so passionately affected his contemporaries and stirred controversy for nearly two centuries should be seen as one-dimensional.

Napoleon saved the Revolution. By this I do not mean that he legislated work that was on the agenda of the Revolution but never completed or realized, which he did. Nor do I mean that he brought to fruition the longings of the Revolution, let alone the Utopian dreams of the radicals, for he did not. What he did do, although not deliberately, was spare the French Revolution the disasters of quarantine, dismemberment, and isolation both internal and external, brought on by forced autarky. This is the fate that befell so many subsequent revolutions that self-consciously claimed descent from 1789: most notably those in Russia, China, and Cuba. They were made into pariah states and became convinced, not without reason, that their neighbors would do anything to destroy their revolution. In self-defense they walled out the world and became permanent police states. These horrors did not overwhelm France. The reason is Napoleon. By the time the allies were able to hold together long enough to build a coalition strong enough to defeat him it was too late to do what they ardently would have done in the first dozen years of the French Revolution: restore the old monarchy, church, and nobility, and quarantine if not dismember France. They were unable or unwilling to root out the Revolution in France. Napoleon's domestic work remained in place.

Everything he did and was has roots in the Revolution. His own views of his life and achievement – long-winded, self-serving, given to myth-making, utterly devoid of self-criticism – are nevertheless compelling. He should not be taken at his word any more than any historical actor, but most of the time he saw clearly enough what he was doing: the work of the Revolution. He may have been myopic about the historical significance of his extraordinary deeds, although his more penetrating and profound contemporaries – Hegel, Chateaubriand, Mme de Staël, Stendhal, Balzac among them – corrected the parallax. He wrestled with the French Revolution throughout his life, always with the aim of bending it to his will. He failed, but along the way preserved much of the fundamental work of the Revolution and bequeathed to the 19th century a tradition that included the Rights of Man (albeit selective and emasculated), the end of feudalism, a secular state, equality before the law, a series of legal codes that still endure, religious toleration, and constitutionalism. Nor did he destroy the revolutionary tradition that had made his career possible. It was inherited, as François Furet has so eloquently demonstrated, and shaped French history profoundly at least until 1880.

The argument sketched here calls for an unconventional structure. There are two basic ways of writing about his fabulous career: one can proceed chronologically or thematically. The former imposes the obligation to guide the reader through as many of Napoleon's 60 battles as are feasible while the reader, if not passionate about military history, wearies. The latter approach disrupts with digressions the cadence of a life. I have opted for a theme, the *leitmotif* declared in my title, and a thesis. Borrowing the language of the theater I interject several *Entr'actes* between the narrative chapters. These break the chronological flow to consider thematic material that does not advance the story chronologically. This arrangement also permits me to be selective about just how comprehensive is my narrative.

The French remain ambivalent about Napoleon, which I discuss in the long struggle for a fit national memorial. Elsewhere in Europe there is also ambiguity, except perhaps in Russia and England. I consider the Russian reaction in the chapter on Napoleon's terrible invasion. Here I want to say a word about the English tradition and its historiographical expression, since the Anglophone world is so indebted to what English historians have written. All states have their myths and Napoleon's obsession with destroying England contributed mightily to that of 'this sceptered isle'. England saw herself, not unreasonably although with some exaggeration, as having again saved continental Europe from tyranny. English intervention in continental affairs in the wars against Louis XIV checked the Sun King's ambitions; opposition to the French Revolution delayed and then demolished Napoleon's ambitions. Again in World War II England was instrumental in destroying another would-be continental tyrant. This providential rhythm has regularly renewed English pride and national self-satisfaction, making it difficult for English historians to write about Napoleon as other than a national enemy whose destruction saved civilization. But Napoleon was not Louis XIV let alone Hitler. He was the sword bearer of the Revolution.

'What a novel my life has been (*Quel roman pourtant que ma vie!*),' he once said. He could easily have added it was a revolutionary life.

A Note on England and Britain

I realize there is an ongoing debate on the use of England/English vs Britain/British. I have opted for England and English because it is the more familiar form, it was Napoleon's usage, and because I hope my English/British readers will indulge an American habit.

Acknowledgements

Tennessee Williams's creation, Blanche DuBois, depended on the 'kindness of strangers'. I have been more fortunate: I depend on friends and colleagues as well and continue to be grateful for their generosity. Richard Levy and Jonathan Marwil have been reading everything I write for more than 40 years. They have often improved any work I impose upon them. Alan Forrest of York University gave me that most precious commodity for a scholar, his time. He saw what I was trying to do in this book, encouraged me, and helped me find a publisher. Michael Broers, of Lady Margaret Hall, Oxford, who did extend the 'kindness of strangers', found many a gaff and blunder in the manuscript, all of which I hope I have fixed. Those that remain are mine alone. Ralph Ashby, who had been my student, became my consultant on military history. Again what inaccuracies remain are mine.

The University of Illinois at Chicago where I taught for nearly 40 years was generous in its support. I was a fellow at the Humanities Institute in 1999 where I first presented some of my ideas about Napoleon. I also had the good fortune to be a fellow of the Great Cities Institute in 2004 and spent a year studying Napoleonic Paris, which research is scattered, in small bits, throughout this book. Dean Stanley Fish gave me access to a research fund that made trips to Paris possible. The History Department allowed me to teach a seminar on Napoleon for several years which also helped clear my head about things Napoleonic.

The late François Furet had just embarked on a Napoleon project when he died in 1997. He would, as he did for the earlier years of the French Revolution, have altered the way we think about Napoleon. As it is, we have only some very suggestive ideas in his great history, *La Révolution*, and an article in the *Dictionnaire critique*. He inspired my work.

My family has spent many years with 'Poleon, as my daughter first called him, and are doubtless as pleased to have him off my desk as I am.

Prologue
Napoleon and the French Revolution

In the beginning was the Revolution. And at the end as well. For contemporaries Napoleon was the militant Revolution incarnate, not another dynast aggrandizing his territory, capturing subjects to tax. The fear he instilled in the kings, the priests, and the elites of the *ancien régime* was not just that he would destroy their armies or make them vassals, although he certainly did so. The greater threat was that he would make their states into revolutionized France, destroy privilege, unleash the resentments of subjects long repressed. *Liberté, égalité, fraternité* would replace 'the king is dead, long live the king'. The will of the people would replace God's will. Those who were last would come first, centuries of social hierarchy marked and rewarded with privileges would disappear. Napoleon was the Revolution on horseback.

In practice he was far more socially conservative than the Jacobins, the radical political faction he had joined as a young man. He threatened to free Russia's serfs and let them topple the tsar's autocracy. The threat remained mere bravado: revolution from below was the last thing Napoleon wanted. He nowhere unleashed the dogs of social revolution but he did impose at bayonet point the reforms his enemies feared. His method was to compel uniform obedience to his legal codes, create a secular state, assure religious toleration, end feudal entailments and entitlements, and administer his conquests with an efficiency that would fill his coffers, swell the ranks of his armies, and assure that the benefits won by the French Revolution were forced upon the rest of Europe. Even without the Jacobins, the *sans-culottes* who were the shock troops of street politics in the Revolution, massive peasant rebellion, and the Terror he successfully turned the old world upside down. Napoleon's revolution from above stopped far short of 'root-and-branch' destruction and reform, but the *ancien régime* was fighting for its life.

The struggle was rhetorical as well as physical. The parvenu First Consul and later Emperor was anathemized with bell, book, and candle, cast out of traditional society. He was for the old elites the Corsican Ogre, a *condottiere*, a usurper, a half-African barbarian who had crashed the gates hedging civilization. Above all he was a ruthless egoist and warlord driven by ambition, a view that contradicted their counter-revolutionary fears, although the paradox did not trouble his enemies. The power he usurped was done in the name of the Revolution and his persistent assertion that all he did was for France is not without truth. He was a new kind of conqueror, a revolutionary conqueror.

His two most famous literary foes, Chateaubriand and Mme de Staël, brilliantly created the *légende noire* of a monster of egotism which has endured to our day. For Chateaubriand he carried the Revolution to its logical paroxysm. For Mme de Staël he betrayed the Revolution. Those he quarreled with and sacked, Talleyrand and Fouché (respectively his minister of foreign affairs and his chief of police), among others, never forgave him: nor did they keep their resentments to themselves. Both betrayed Napoleon and celebrated their treachery in their memoirs, adding anecdotes of his dangerous self-absorption. Neither denied Napoleon was a revolutionary, only that egotism, somehow different in kind from their own, corrupted him. Metternich, Pitt and Castlereagh wove their detestation and fear into elaborate and effective international politics whose pivot was counterrevolution. The kings he dethroned or humiliated also swelled the ranks of the vengeful. The lesser fry, too many to enumerate, cursed Napoleon's unbounded ambition that willfully sacrificed a nation and its people. His ambition is still regularly invoked to explain his fabulous career and taint his revolutionary credentials. Ambition is a commodity never in short supply in public life and there is no way to differentiate the quality or quantity among its acolytes. Some are forgiven (even celebrated) and others are damned. Horatio Nelson and the Duke of Wellington were as ambitious as Napoleon, and as ruthless. One did not rise to the top of society, especially a commoner like Nelson, without ambition. Both became national heroes, their apotheosis still unchallenged, their ambition muted or absorbed into patriotic fervor.

Napoleon was a child of the Revolution, his career is unimaginable without the greatest upheaval of the age. The French Revolution, the perfect and violent contradiction to the European *ancien régime*, offered Napoleon opportunities otherwise denied men of his origins. Part of the price he paid for his extraordinary success was the hatred of the toppled society during his lifetime, bequeathed to posterity.

The ambition of Nelson and Wellington, indeed of all those ambitious men who overthrew Napoleon, was honored as the defense of king and country, resistance to the tyranny and insatiable appetites of the conqueror, or patriotic zeal. Napoleon's every act was tagged naked self-aggrandizement. The fear of the Revolution was focused on Napoleon, its nightmarish incarnation. It was not Napoleon the man, the general, the First Consul or the Emperor who was loathed and feared so much as the French Revolution he embodied. The great conservative thinkers, principally Edmund Burke, Joseph de Maistre, and Chateaubriand were right. Theirs was an age of historic and cosmic struggle between the *ancien régime* and the Revolution. Napoleon, whom Burke abstractly predicted but did not live to see triumph, was a hateful, even diabolical, and inevitable spawn of the Revolution. For all his enemies his ambition was untempered by devotion to some higher cause. He was unconstrained by God, civilization, or historical habit. The Revolution, whose agent Napoleon was, represented debasement, destruction, barbarism, and savagery. His deeds could be driven or inspired by no honorable motives. Only the raw emotional force of egomania unbound could explain the man.

Napoleon realized the problem. He lamented on St Helena and long before his final banishment that he lacked the legitimacy of the kings. The half dozen families who sit on the thrones of Europe, he told Jean-Antoine Chaptal, his minister of the interior, cannot bear 'a Corsican' among their number. 'I maintain my place only by force.' The kings 'could live in indolence in their chateaux ... no one contested their legitimacy ... For me it is different. There is not a general who does not believe himself as entitled to the throne as I ... Within France and without I only reign by the fear I inspire.' When the Revolution replaced primogeniture and blood inheritance with the will of the people expressed in elections, sustained by a representative government, and enshrined in a constitution, it made Napoleon's career possible. The new political paradigm would supplant the old. But so revolutionary a change needs time, a commodity in exceptionally short supply in the twenty-five years of violent upheaval from the fall of the Bastille to Waterloo.

It was an age of constitutions. For centuries Europe had had none, although during the English Revolution the great parliamentary champions had successfully claimed the primacy of their unwritten constitution over the prerogatives and pretensions of the king, with the assistance of a victorious army. After 1789 in France no government could command legitimacy without a constitution, even when it was suspended (as was the so-called Jacobin constitution of 1793). From the fall of the Bastille to Napoleon's fall six constitutions were written as well as Napoleon's *Acte additionnel aux constitutions de l'Empire* (22 April 1815), and two Declarations of the Rights of Man. Even the restored Bourbon kings were forced to issue a constitution, euphemistically called a Charter. Tsar Alexander, who governed without any contract with his subjects, insisted on one. Three of these constitutions (and the *Acte additionnel*) are Napoleon's. The first (22 frimaire, an VIII – 22 November 1799) was to legitimate Napoleon's *coup d'état*; the second (20 floréal, an X – 10 May 1802) was to legitimate the Consulate for life bestowed on him; the third (28 floréal, an XII – 18 May 1804) was the imperial constitution; and the *Acte additionnel* (written by Benjamin Constant and edited by Napoleon) was to legitimate the reformed government of the Hundred Days. None contained a Declaration of Rights, thought essential since the first Declaration adopted on 26 August 1789. The first Declaration did not specify the form of government but proclaimed the new principles of the Revolution. The first four propositions were and remained fundamental, as did proposition ten which proclaimed religious liberty:

I. Men are born and remain free and equal in rights. Social distinctions may be based only on common utility.
II. The aim of all political associations is to preserve the natural and imprescriptible rights of man. These rights are liberty, property, security and resistance to oppression.
III. The principle of all sovereignty rests essentially in the nation. No body and no individual may exercise authority which does not emanate from the nation expressly.
IV. Liberty consists in the ability to do whatever does not harm another; hence the exercise of the natural rights of each man has no limits except those which assure to other members of society the enjoyment of the same rights. These limits can only be determined by law.

Napoleon was obsessed with legitimacy. He could not govern without a constitution, although he approved the abbé Sieyès's cynical aphorism that the document should be 'short and obscure'. The alchemy of legitimacy, enjoyed by the most dissolute and inept king, eluded him. He honored his constitutional obligations despite some notable lapses and always insisted he had been chosen not by the army but by the people from whom his authority derived. Discovering the will of the people proved problematic. He rejected democracy expressed in universal male suffrage, preferring an electorate circumscribed by wealth and property. Sieyès's 1799 constitution created a deliberately complex system of indirect voting that effectively disenfranchised the majority once they had cast the first round of votes. It proved unworkable. Napoleon's subsequent method was to depend upon plebiscites. The adoption of the constitution of 1799, and those consecrating the consulate for life and imperial heredity, were all sanctified by plebiscites. In theory this was an instrument of direct democracy. Voters did not choose electors or representatives, they either approved or disapproved of fundamental constitutional issues. Napoleon's plebiscites were manipulated and there were so many abstentions (or both simultaneously) that they served essentially a propaganda purpose. No reasonable person then or now is convinced Napoleon's plebiscites measured the will of the people. With an estimated electorate of between eight and nine million he never achieved 50 per cent participation. In the first plebiscite of 1800 an astonishing 80 per cent of the eligible voters abstained, although it is impossible to know if this was a deliberate political tactic or the result of an overwhelmingly rural population, both uninformed and uninterested, with little access to information or transportation.

More out of habit than close analysis Napoleon's rule is often characterized as a military dictatorship. This is true only in the narrowest possible sense. Napoleon did use the army, or more precisely the Paris garrison he commanded, to drive the senators out of St Cloud when he seized power, but 18–19 Brumaire was both a parliamentary and a military *coup d'état*. Thenceforth Napoleon went out of his way to keep the army out of politics. 'Bonaparte rigorously marginalized the generals who gravitated around the Directory in order to rest his government on the notables,' writes Jean Tulard. He was not sustained in power by the army, which was mostly excluded from domestic politics. Although Napoleon preferred to appear in uniform, his court was deliberately civilian. The army, throughout his reign, was troubled by ambitious and even treasonous generals. Moreau and Bernadotte were early and persistent rivals, and Malet briefly seized power while Napoleon was in Russia. Instead of political power the Emperor loaded loyal soldiers with honors: the légion d'honneur was top-heavy with army men, but among his important functionaries only the minister of war was a soldier. It is true Napoleon regimented society and all its institutions. He put his prefects in uniform as well as students at the new elite schools. But civilians ran the new state; and once the army had pacified the conquered territories, civilian administrators took over. Napoleon created 'a citizenry without democracy' in Pierre Rosanvallon's apt characterization. In terms of the

Revolution he had returned to the constitutional distinction formulated in 1791 that created 'passive' and 'active' citizens. The former could not vote or stand for office. They were only the recipients of the benefits of the Rights of Man and the authoritarian, paternalistic state.

*****

Napoleon had the illusions of a self-made man and brushed aside the fictions of his flatterers. He was the maker of his own destiny. He owed his greatness to his sword. When he invoked chance or *la force des choses* it was most often to explain away his failures by fixing the responsibility in the actions of others or the unpredictable maelstrom of contingencies, both human and natural. The list included the Moscow fire, 'generals' Winter and Danube against whom any commander would have been powerless, Marshal Ney's frenzied passion at Waterloo or General Grouchy's dogged determination to follow orders and not return to the gunfire. Tolstoy, in *War and Peace*, offered a more profound understanding of Napoleon's failure, certainly in Russia. He spoke of vast historical forces, sometimes incarnated, as in Marshal Kutusov at the battle for Moscow, driving men and their deeds, often heedlessly, certainly without the impulsion of a single will. The philosopher Hegel too peered beyond events and petty human foibles to explain the meaning of history. The 'cunning of reason', whose unpredictable sloppiness he lamented, for it operated through the passions of men, diverted human agency from its imagined goals to the unimagined realization of history's trajectory. There is explanatory value in all these views, but the French Revolution trumps them all. Had there been no French Revolution Napoleon Bonaparte would have been poorly pensioned off as an artillery captain living a life of forced simplicity bordering on misery somewhere in provincial France. His dreams, confined to his imagination, would have been filled with fantastic visions of conquering an empire and embitterment toward his adopted country that had destroyed Corsica's bid for independence and frustrated his own career.

The French Revolution was so huge, lasted so long, and so affected the European world and everyone in it that it transcended history itself and became a force of nature. For Napoleon's generation it was all they knew: a world turned permanently upside down. Long after the revolutionary convulsion was over, Europe directly, and then indirectly in all the places in the world touched by European expansion whether physical, intellectual, economic, or cultural, continued to feel its influence. Its after-shocks rumbled through the 19th and

20th centuries. The Revolution easily eludes our understanding. Its very size resists intellectual compression, magnetically repelling our partial explanations. We have theories aplenty, all seeking or imposing coherence, consistency, and pattern. We ignore or mute the contradictions of the Revolution in favor of an explanatory thread that runs, however crazily, from beginning to end. The French Revolution was indeed about democracy, the rights of man, the end of inherited privilege, the destruction of an intricate and complex fabric of social and economic relationships we call feudalism, the new principle of the sovereignty of the people expressed in the nation, the predominance of politics as the instrument of change, the subordination of the Church to the state, the culture of public opinion, and the rationalization of the state for the benefit (some said the happiness) of its citizens. It was about a great deal more as well. Each of these characterizations is general, potentially or actually ambiguous, and was variously understood (or misunderstood) during the Revolution. No one idea or ideal ran a straight course. Each metamorphosed as the Revolution lurched, not always forward.

The history of the Revolution is fraught with pieces that have no obvious place in the patterns and meaning imposed on the Revolution from its beginnings until now. Historians, following contemporaries, have divided the Revolution into phases with a common ancestry but often without much family resemblance. Robespierre and the Jacobins, for example, were the theoreticians and agitators for unencumbered democracy. Once in power they purged the Convention, imposed a dictatorship by committee, crushed the unruly democracy of the first Paris Commune, and governed by terror. They drifted farther and farther from the will of the people they rhetorically championed, substituting their vanguard faction. They shelved the constitution of 1793, which was to replace the generally despised constitutional work of 1789–91, one of the cornerstones of revolutionary hope, until the end of the war crisis that never came. Yet they continue to be treated as the most leftward movement of the revolutionary government, and Robespierre's fall in 1794 for many still heralds a right-wing, or at least conservative, reaction, if not a counterrevolution: the end of the people's participation in the Revolution. Paradoxically in the Revolution's march to the left democracy recedes, replaced by emergency government and utopian visions that remain paper schemes.

Because of its complexity the Revolution became all things to all men. Groups and individuals at the time, and for the last two centuries, have insisted theirs is the true Revolution, which has been betrayed by their foes. From the right to the left of the political spectrum, from Edmund

Burke's historical conservatism and Joseph de Maistre's theocratic ideology, to the *robespierristes* and beyond – the Babeuvists (the proto-Communists of the age), and the obsessed and isolated extreme terrorists whose anarchism fascinated Richard Cobb – the French Revolution has had advocates, apologists, and anathematizers. Napoleon occupies an important place in this spectrum. He is a revolutionary and was taken as one by his contemporaries, including many who were later disillusioned when he failed to realize the Revolution they desired. His impact on the Revolution, whether intentional or unintended, is among the most important. All the other soldiers who tried to impose themselves on the Revolution, to seize power and restore what they considered order, most notably generals Lafayette and Dumouriez in 1792 and 1793, failed. Both men were cast out of the body politic: the former endured an Austrian prison, the latter eventually took refuge in England. Even those generals who were loyal to the Revolution, willing to serve sometimes distasteful or despised masters, found themselves in dangerous circumstances. Several aristocratic generals became the victims of revolutionary suspiciousness bordering on paranoia and went to the guillotine (most notably Count Custine). The Revolution distrusted its generals, especially those from the nobility, and with reason. Officers who fled early – many were *émigrés* by 1792 when the war broke out and the king was dethroned – joined the counterrevolutionary armies and were tainted. Those who remained to serve the new France were problematic in a Revolution and a republic created by citizens at war with monarchical Europe. The wars of the Revolution, however, had made the military the single most important power in the revolutionary state by 1795. All the civilian leaders sought, many with distaste, an army *coup d'état* to save the Republic and their political careers.

Napoleon was a most improbable savior. He was an outsider, physically and intellectually unimposing, with a checkered revolutionary past and some dubious political affiliations. He came late to the Revolution, and when he did he was the protégé of a feared and eventually disgraced faction, the Jacobins. He had none of the skills traditionally associated with revolutionary leadership: parliamentary savvy, oratorical power, a gift for ideology or the willingness to work diligently at the mundane tasks of politics. He was obscure enough before the Italian campaign that no one feared his ambition or realized his ability. His republicanism was suspect, but more compromising were his links to Robespierre. There was no hint of royalism in his past, however, and his Jacobinism, such as it was, was set to rest by 13 Vendémiaire (5 October 1795) when he dispersed a Paris mob with grapeshot. Then his deeds in the Italian theater, commanding an army tinted by its Jacobin origins and attitudes, electrified France. General Moreau, who had republican sympathies at the time, would briefly support Napoleon at Brumaire when he seized power. Because he was largely unknown, had an inconsistent past and had not waded in the treacherous waters of Paris politics, those who sought his support imagined him in their image, a malleable weapon for their own ambitions. If he proved difficult he could be discarded, sent to an inglorious command. Public opinion, far less self-serving than the political elite, saw him as a savior.

It is difficult, perhaps impossible, to know what the Thermidorians (named for the month of Thermidor in the revolutionary calendar – roughly the second half of July and the first half of August) who had toppled Robespierre, or the French public expected from their soldierly Messiah. What they got had been imagined and feared for years by civilian revolutionaries. Although Napoleon carefully kept the military from running the government his power derived from his army. He was a revolutionary soldier who had violently seized power and then held it by replacing *liberté, égalité, fraternité* with glory, conquest, and careers open to talent in an increasingly expanding empire. His work was for a long time a broadly popular series of riffs on the Revolution. He emphasized the crusading zeal of 1792, the centralized state of the Jacobins, and the authoritarianism that characterized the Revolution from the summer of 1793 onward. His popularity only slowly soured as the benefits of his huge imperial Ponzi scheme disappeared into the maw of war. By 1809 and his victory at Wagram more money was flowing out of French coffers than was coming in, but until 1811 he was fighting only in Spain. Body counts, at least for French nationals, remained relatively low. This would soon change with the invasion of Russia and the long denouement of his empire. Yet even when he escaped from Elba after his forced first abdication he was able to march triumphantly to Paris, seducing the armies sent to capture him and gathering supporters as he went. The recently restored Bourbons fled Paris unlamented.

But France did not uniformly rally. Much of the country remained wary and prudent. Napoleon was enthusiastically welcomed back to the Tuileries in 1814 in the capital which only a year earlier had refused to sacrifice itself. His promise of salvation through glory could still work its magic, his charismatic powers remained intact. His cynical evocation during the Hundred Days of the ideals and symbols of the republican revolutionary past – he even encouraged the singing of the *Marseillaise* – was only sporadically embraced. Yet the man who had left an army stranded in Egypt and twice lost the Grande Armée was still able to raise new ones. None of this can be explained exclusively by invoking his charismatic mystique. Napoleon, for all his faults, all the misery and humiliation he had inflicted on France, was the embodiment, however imperfect, of the Revolution. The choice by 1814 was stark: Napoleon or the Bourbons, the Revolution or the counterrevolution. The few who harkened after the republic had been exiled or wandered in the political wilderness. From the top to the bottom of society Napoleon remained the only viable choice. The restored Bourbons, even in the person of the reasonable and compromising Louis XVIII, were one of the many aspects of the *ancien régime* the Revolution had fought to destroy. They were not, for significant parts of the population (and even the Allies), acceptable, until there appeared no other choice, no other end to war, no other bulwark against the Revolution militant.

Napoleon's relationship to the French Revolution is complex. On St Helena he explained himself with candor, clarity and much repetition. The contradictions, self-delusions, ambiguities, special pleading, along with his myopia about the immediate past, his fictions about his intentions, his unrealized schemes for a vast French imperium, provide the best guide we have to these complexities as he saw them. Napoleon's French Revolution, the elements and ideas from that enormous event he selected out and forged into a loose intellectual agglomeration we can only call Bonapartism, is unique. Even before he was sent to St Helena he was obsessively explaining his relationship with the Revolution. He was never a systematic thinker but growing adversity forced him to think things through. Before the Russian campaign there was little reason to explain his deeds or motives, certainly not to others, perhaps not even to himself. He had not lost a major battle, he controlled the greatest European empire in history, he made and unmade kings, reconfigured the political map of the Continent, and had domesticated the French Revolution at home. Money poured into French coffers (although never enough), the French became an imperial people administering much of Europe, and the state floated euphorically on a sea of glory. Then the Russian catastrophe called everything into question. Thenceforth the Empire contracted, the Revolution returned to its natal country, and the Allies slowly organized for the kill. But it had been long enough, Napoleon had given the Revolution time to take root in France.

I
Becoming a Revolutionary

Napoleon's Corsica was as far away from the world-historical stage of his fabulous career as it was possible to be and remain in Europe. He told General Bertrand in 1819 'this island of Corsica which is so distant from European civilization, so different from African barbarism' nevertheless 'opened the windows of my mind.'

The most beautiful and mountainous of the Mediterranean islands was shaped by nature over a vast geological time into an island of about 590 square miles divided into four distinct geological areas by its mountainous spine, with an average altitude of 2296 feet. Mount Cinto, the highest peak, rises to 8877 feet and is snow-covered year-round. Corsica is separated from the French and Italian mainland by 105 and 52 miles respectively. The Phoenicians established the first colony, followed by the Romans. Seneca had been exiled to Corsica, a distinction not celebrated in guides to the island. Corsica was converted to Christianity in the third century and invaded by the Vandals in the fifth, the first of a number of invasions that marked and determined the island's history. From the 11th to the 13th centuries Corsica was governed by Pisa. Genoa defeated Pisa in 1284 and took possession, holding the island until 1768, when they ceded it to the French. The next year Napoleon Bonaparte was born a French subject in Ajaccio.

In *Du Contrat social* (1762) Jean-Jacques Rousseau wrote:

> There remains one country in Europe capable of legislation, and that is the island of Corsica. The valor and the constancy with which that brave people have recovered and defended its liberty would well deserve that some wise man should teach them how to preserve it. I have a presentiment that one day that little island will astonish Europe.

Rousseau had no inkling or desire that it was the conqueror of Europe that would astonish rather than a tenaciously courageous people who fought first to free themselves from the Genoese and then the French. The philosopher's celebration of Corsica as a country on the cusp of civilization, untainted by the corruption and degeneracy of aristocratic Europe, caught the attention of Antonio Buttafoco, a distinguished Corsican, who invited Rousseau to visit the island. Rousseau declined but did provide a constitutional project (1765), an outline of what the Corsicans must do to preserve their freedom and happiness. In his lyrical and rhapsodic style Rousseau ranges over all the familiar topics of his political thought – population, animal husbandry, agriculture, climate, mores, civic morality, the inherent dangers of political power, the equally fatal dangers of commerce, the virtues of simplicity (of manners, living, and diet), the corruptions of urban life, and the necessary will to become 'a flourishing people' and hence free. None of the complex philosophical postulates of *Du Contrat social* are in this project, and much of the argument rests on assumptions about Corsica derived from books and his own myth-making imagination. For Rousseau Corsica was a place just emerging from the state of nature, populated by a brave and intrepid people whose few vices would vanish along with Genoan suzerainty and be followed by the implementation of good laws. Rousseau proposed a democratic republic for Corsica, in his view the best (and rarest) form of government.

Commerce, industry, and luxury, the agents of decline and decadence, must be kept off the island. 'We have no need of wood-carvers and goldsmiths, but we do need carpenters and blacksmiths; we need weavers, good workers in woolens, not embroiderers or drawers of gold thread.' Corsica's happiness lies in returning to an earlier economic and social state. 'Everyone should make a living, and no one should grow rich; that is the fundamental principle of the prosperity of the nation.' There must be no tax farmers who place 'unselfishness, simplicity, morality and all the virtues under a cloud of scorn and opprobrium'. Napoleon's own evocations of his natal island, all written when he was a young man, owe much to Rousseau's diction, which he emulated, and his romanticized vision of the Corsicans which he then shared.

The other 18th-century outsider intrigued with Corsica was an obscure Scot from Edinburgh, son of a judge in whose footsteps he eventually reluctantly followed: James Boswell. He had little interest in Rousseau's visionary proposals although he had visited the great man on his way to Corsica and obtained a letter of introduction. Boswell easily absorbed the philosopher's largely mythic picture of the place and its people, but he was principally interested in adventure. His genius lay in description. A gadfly who thrust himself upon the great writers of his day, beginning with Dr Samuel Johnson whose biographer he would become, Boswell craved literary fame. In 1765 he left the beaten path of the Grand Tour to visit Corsica which 'occurred to me as a place which no body [sic] else had seen, and where I should find what was to be seen no where [sic] else, a people actually fighting for liberty, and forming themselves from a poor inconsiderable, oppressed nation, into a flourishing and independent state'.

As with so many travelers, Boswell found what he was seeking. His successful book popularized the struggle of the Corsicans against Genoa and broadcast the flattering myth of a 'brave and resolute nation' led by a hero, Pascal Paoli. The poet Thomas Gray wrote to his friend Horace Walpole after reading Boswell's account that Paoli 'is a man born two thousand years after his time!'. Boswell's book, he adds maliciously, 'proves what I have always maintained, that any fool may write a most valuable book by chance, if he will only tell us what he heard and saw with veracity'.

Napoleon seems to have read Boswell carefully, probably in the Italian translation that was published in 1769. His own Corsican writings are a blend of Rousseau's rhetoric and Boswell's details.

Napoleon had spent the first eight years of his life on the island, heard from his parents stories of the struggle to liberate it from France, and had inculcated feelings for the place and its plight that would dominate his childhood, youth, and early manhood. But in the mid-1790s, having been driven out by political and clan rivals, inseparable on the island, aided by his own strategic missteps and political convictions that made his presence untenable, he came to loathe the place. He turned his back on the island and never returned. In exile on his last island, St Helena, he expressed only contempt for Corsica and its benighted inhabitants. His juvenilia – including an unfinished history of the island, letters addressed to the abbé Raynal, author of a celebrated *Histoire des deux Indes*, and a number of less ambitious pieces – belie his mature scorn. Napoleon did not become a disenchanted Corsican nationalist until the French Revolution.

What Boswell saw was a rugged, beautiful island with none of the amenities of mainland Europe, which is what Prosper Merimée also found nearly 75 years later. Keith Steward, an officer in the British navy whom Boswell met aboard the ship that brought him from the mainland, told him that he risked his life disembarking and 'going among these barbarians' who lurked, heavily armed, behind every bush. Once ashore Boswell crossed Corsica on foot. 'I got a man with an ass to carry my baggage,' he writes. 'But such a road I never saw. It was absolutely scrambling along the face of a rock over-hanging the sea, upon a path sometimes not above a foot broad.' At Corte he met Paoli, whose conversation he carefully records as he would later that of Dr Johnson. He also had 'a Corsican dress made' in the rough cloth and leather of the region. After returning to England he commissioned a portrait of himself, with a brace of pistols, a gift from Paoli, in his belt.

From Paoli's capital of Corte he went to Bastia, where he was introduced to Louis Charles René, the Count (and eventually Marquis) de Marbeuf, the French commander-in-chief on the island who from 1770 to his death in 1786 wielded autocratic powers. For the first time in his visit Boswell found himself back in Europe. 'The brilliancy of his levee,' he wrote of Marbeuf, was 'like passing at once from a rude and early age, to a polished modern age; from the mountains of Corsica, to the banks of the Seine.' Marbeuf was a flamboyant character. Descended from a distinguished old Breton family, he had deftly climbed the administrative ladder of the *ancien régime* as a courtier, simultaneously enhancing his personal fortune, which was huge by Corsican standards. He made a shrewd, if loveless, marriage to a superbly connected Breton widow, who insisted the marriage contract contain a clause permitting her to live where she pleased (obviously not with the Marquis). The match brought him considerable property and two chateaux in Brittany, as well as a life of his own. His chief opponent at Court was the Count de Narbonne, himself a dexterous courtier, the military commander in Ajaccio who possessed the skills Marbeuf lacked, and one of the few French heroes of the disastrous Seven Years' War.

It was quixotic, heroic, and suicidal for the Corsicans, who numbered around 100,000, to go to war with the richest and most powerful nation in Europe. Narbonne and Marbeuf easily and brutally destroyed Corsican independence and drove Paoli into exile. He took refuge in England, never forgave the French, and when he returned to take up once more the cause of Corsican independence, spurned Napoleon's pro-French politics. The cause of liberty, so exciting to Rousseau and Boswell, was dead in 1768. Narbonne left the island in 1775 leaving Marbeuf with unchallenged power. Carlo, later Charles, Bonaparte, Napoleon's father, first engaged in the independence struggle and then like many other ambitious Corsicans courted his French overlords when Paoli's cause collapsed. His wife, Letizia Ramolino, reputedly the most beautiful woman on the island, proved a major asset to his fortunes and those of their famous son. She never tired recounting her adventures as an Amazon in the fight for Corsican freedom. She was pregnant with her second son, Napoleon, when she and Charles, who had wandered in the mountains after the slaughter at Ponte Novo destroyed Paoli's forces, returned to Ajaccio where she gave birth on 15 August 1769. Marbeuf's infatuation with Letizia assured Charles's success which in turn launched his sons in France.

Once Charles and Letizia's second son became the brilliant young general who captured Italy for the French Republic and soon dropped the Italian Buonoparte for the French Bonaparte, and shortly thereafter for 'Napoleon', any number of genealogists discovered or invented a pedigree. Napoleon mocked these genealogical fictions: 'My titles are in my sword,' he said, or 'the house of Bonaparte dates from 18 Brumaire', or 'permit me to be the Rudolph of my line', alluding to the first notable Habsburg whose descendant, Marie-Louise, he married. In 1771 Charles obtained recognition of his family as noble, which led to his appointment as *assesseur* to the law court and election to the *Nobles Douze* of the Corsican Estates. Marbeuf, already taken with Letizia, sponsored Napoleon's application for a scholarship in France, which was granted on 31 December 1778. Charles had already sailed on 15 December with his two oldest sons, Joseph and Napoleon, who had just turned nine.

Charles had made a realistic calculation. A few followed Paoli into exile. Others took to the *maquis*, the trackless interior of Corsica and carried on their fight as bandits. Charles devoted himself to getting his children a French education. He was a man of great charm, some talent, and a love of extravagance which his sons inherited. Napoleon told Montholon on St Helena more than 40 years later that his 'father consumed his patrimony in Pisa'. When he himself set up his courts, first at Montbello in Italy and later at the Tuileries, he demanded a lavish representation of his power. He invaded Russia with an entourage worthy of a Persian satrap. The Bonapartes were not rich but they were comfortable by Corsican standards. Life in France, however, was beyond their means. Both Joseph and Napoleon had scholarships – Joseph to a seminary (he had been first educated by the Jesuits on Corsica), Napoleon to a military school – but Charles had to scrape and borrow to buy them the necessary uniforms and clothing.

Napoleon would make five trips back to his natal island. In all he spent, at different times, 47 months in Corsica between the ages of nine and twenty-four. He finally abandoned his dreams of liberating Corsica by tying the island to the French Revolution in 1793, definitively returned to France and threw himself enthusiastically into revolutionary politics on the mainland. He shed his parochial nationalist fervor and became a French revolutionary. He always spoke French with a Corsican accent and was much mocked for it at school. His Italian, although unaccented, was grammatically faulty, as was his new language. His youthful writings, Thierry Lentz points out, are dotted with Italianisms and grammatical mistakes. His French orthography was appalling. A wit quipped that he had never fully conquered the French language.

To *ancien régime* Europe he was the Corsican Ogre, an insult redolent of the popular view of Corsica as a barbarous land. What remained of his Corsican heritage was boisterousness, willfulness, intransigence, perhaps cruelty, and the ambitions and passions of his family. The younger children (Caroline, Pauline, Louis, and Jerome) knew little of Corsica. The older brothers made sure they had a thoroughly French, indeed Parisian, upbringing. Napoleon early became the arbiter of family tensions, except when overruled by Letizia. The Bonapartes remained a devoted clan but their willfulness, their jealousies, and their greed exasperated Napoleon. The ruler of the European world was not always successful imposing his desires on his siblings who squabbled and shouted, often publicly, reinforcing the cliché about Corsicans.

Napoleon attended two French schools, the first at Autun, the second at Brienne. The latter was one of twelve provincial military colleges founded in 1776 by the Count Saint Germain, this one under the patronage of the Brienne family of Toulouse, whose most famous son, Loménie, the archbishop of Toulouse, was the penultimate minister of the monarchy before the Revolution. Almost all the places in the school were reserved for the sons of French officers, but a handful were held back for the children of the 'indigent nobility'. Charles procured a 'certificate of indigence', one of several documents Napoleon had to produce to gain admittance. There were only 600 such free places in all of France and competition was fierce. Napoleon entered Brienne, at the age of nine, a poor boy and a foreigner in a privileged school. He long remembered the mockery of the others, who chanted that his sallow complexion came from his wet-nurse having suckled him on olive oil. His name, Napoleone, was not French (and the boy continued to pronounce it in the Italian manner). Louis Antoine Fauvalet de Bourrienne, Napoleon's first secretary and a fellow student at Brienne, recounts that one morning when he found ice in his water jug he demanded 'Who's put glass in my jug?' More ammunition for ragging.

The teaching at Brienne, as at all the military *collèges* at the time, was entrusted to religious orders. Brienne was the only *collège* run by the Minimes or Franciscans, not celebrated for their learning. The school itself was well down the list of prestigious *collèges*. The official inspection in 1785 reported carelessness and a repugnance for work among both students and teachers. The curriculum was unimaginative and the teaching uninspired, but the routines were rigidly maintained. From 6 a.m., when the boys were wakened, until 10 p.m. when they were locked in their individual cells for the night, their time was filled. The morning held religion, mathematics, Latin, German, history, geography, and drawing. Only mathematics and geography, in both of which he excelled, interested Napoleon. Then there was a two-hour break for lunch and recreation. The afternoon was devoted to fencing, dancing, music, and writing in which Napoleon showed little interest and less aptitude. There were no amenities at Brienne. Each cell contained a camp bed covered with a single blanket, a jug and basin with cold water, and a small table. The menu was Spartan: bread, water, and fruit for breakfast; roasts, salad, soups, and dessert for dinner. There were treats on feast days and Napoleon recorded on the flyleaf of his atlas that chicken, cake, cauliflower, beetroot salad, and a hot dessert with chestnuts was served on Epiphany. He spent five uninterrupted years at Brienne, for the boys were not allowed to return home except in family emergencies. From Brienne Napoleon took no fond memories and little learning. His ability in mathematics was judged such that he could have become a mathematician had he not been more interested in action than calculation. His voracious reading was exclusively in French. His Latin was never serviceable enough for him to read the classics he admired while his German was primitive at best. His tastes were perfectly conventional. He was very attached to Rousseau, he loved the French dramatic poets, and he read Plutarch avidly (in Amyot's translation).

Napoleon graduated from Brienne without great distinction, and went on to the École Militaire in Paris. Here he enjoyed luxury and attention. With generous funding from the royal purse the staff outnumbered the students who were waited on, served, and insulated from lesser beings not in the army. The food was good, as were the accommodations. Napoleon and his cohorts were treated as a pampered elite. He chose the artillery, the only branch in which his mathematical ability would be of use, and at the time the most respected (and reformed) branch of the army. It was also the most bourgeois. When he sat for the artillery exam he placed 42nd out of 58 candidates. Not a brilliant achievement, but he had done it in record time and had held his own with some of the brightest young men of the kingdom. He was the first Corsican to graduate from the École Militaire. His early years as a newly minted lieutenant gave no hint of the future revolutionary. As most of the young men of his approximate generation who would later achieve distinction in the Revolution, Napoleon was obscure, unremarkable, and his ambitions and expectations were narrowly confined by the rigid social structure of the day. His first posts were in boring provincial towns – Auxonne and Valence. It is here that he wrote his earliest, ardent evocations of Corsica.

The Seven Years' War (1756–1763) had been disastrous for France. A series of reforms, administrative, strategic, and tactical, responded to the military humiliation. Frederick the Great's victories, especially at Rossbach (1757) spurred re-evaluation. Jean-Baptiste Gribeauval, whose work led to making field guns sufficiently mobile to support an attack, and Jacques-Antoine, Count de Guibert, advocated and imagined national wars involving entire states rather than the smaller and circumscribed dynastic clashes of the *ancien régime*. When Napoleon assumed his first post in Valence the French army was sunk in indolence and still plagued by the humiliations of the Seven Years' War. His service was undemanding and allowed for regional sightseeing and as much reading as local sources could support. He easily got the extended leaves he requested, and first returned to Corsica on 15 September 1786, where he stayed for nearly a year. He returned to Corsica in January 1788, rejoining his regiment in Auxonne at the end of May.

He returned to revolutionary ferment. The monarchy, having ruled for 175 years without its interference, was forced by bankruptcy to summon the Estates-General. The writs for elections went out and censorship was simultaneously lifted. France found her voice just as she embarked on the road to revolution. There is little of any of this in Napoleon's letters, none of the excitement that seized his generation of young Frenchmen. He wrote his mother on 12 March 1789 describing without much comment the political struggle of 'doubling the Third', the first attempt of the Commons to dominate the Estates-General controlled by the privileged orders of Church and nobility, by having double representation and voting by head. Two weeks later (28 March), writing to his uncle in Corsica, Napoleon commented at some length on events. He is little interested in France and asks for news of Corsica. In mid-June, with the Estates-General already sitting at Versailles, he writes to Pascal Paoli:

> I was born when my *patrie* perished. 30,000 French troops, vomited onto our shores, drowning the throne of liberty in rivers of blood, this was the horrible sight that I first saw.

The French Revolution for Napoleon began as an opportunity for Corsican liberation (and overwrought rhetoric). He saw clearly enough that without outside interference the cause of Corsican independence was doomed. The French Revolution now reified his hitherto largely literary national feelings. He left Auxonne on 9 September 1789 for another extended leave, arrived in Ajaccio at the end of the month and threw himself into local revolutionary politics, which were a renewal of the struggle for Corsican independence. Napoleon at the outset of his public life displayed the same improvisational agility in politics he would keep until its end. Here was no theoretician. His views on Corsican liberation were at best illogical and half-baked. He sought to have the island declare itself for the Revolution, despite the widespread detestation of French rule during the previous nearly 25 years. The National Assembly on the mainland – thus did the transformed Estates-General, now dominated by the Commons or Third Estate, dub itself on 17 June 1789 – had proclaimed Corsica an 'integral part of the Empire' and Napoleon embraced the slogan 'Vive la nation! Vive Paoli! Vive Mirabeau!' Here was encapsulated the Corsican problematic: the French were, for Paoli and his followers, the hated occupiers of Corsica, the destroyers of independence. They had no intention of submerging themselves in the new revolutionary French state. 'Vive la nation!' was equally hateful. Whose nation? The majority of Corsicans did not consider themselves French, whose language they did not speak and whose occupation they resented. Those who had joined the French, as had Napoleon's father, were suspect. 'Vive Mirabeau!' was unambiguous, but irrelevant to Corsican concerns. The patriotic society of Ajaccio sent the great tribune a complete Corsican costume, identical down to the pistols and hunting musket that Boswell had years before ordered and wore in England. There is no evidence that Mirabeau took any notice of the island and its conflicting aspirations.

Napoleon's first political activities in Ajaccio were modest. In October he read an address to be sent to the National Assembly (soon called the Constituent Assembly to emphasize its democratic ambitions) asking them 'to reestablish the Corsicans in the rights they have received from nature'. Paoli returned to Corsica on 17 July 1790 and enjoyed a triumphal march through the major towns of the island. Napoleon was in charge of his reception in Ajaccio. The national hero brought with him an entourage of fellow exiles and sought out *les purs*, the Corsicans who had supported his hopeless struggle through 20 years of harsh French rule. Charles-André Pozzo di Borgo, a distant and soon detested cousin of the Bonapartes, was the leader of the Paolists in Ajaccio. The Bonapartes were not among *les purs*. Joseph could not even get on the ballot to stand for deputy. Jean Peraldi, the colonel of the National

Guard, and Pozzo di Borgo were elected for Ajaccio. The rivalry with Peraldi was long-standing, but until the election relations between Pozzo di Borgo and the Bonapartes were cordial. Now poisonous enmity took over. Napoleon's political debut had failed completely. At the end of January 1791 he returned to France with his youngest brother Louis, then 12-and-a-half; but not before he purchased, with his uncle Joseph Fesch, his mother's half-brother and eventually appointed a Cardinal, three parcels of *biens nationaux*, the ecclesiastical lands that were confiscated by the Civil Constitutions of the Clergy, a central piece of revolutionary legislation. Napoleon had invested in the Revolution. So had his uncle the priest, untroubled by acquiring nationalized Church property.

Back in Auxonne, and soon in Valence to reassume his duties, Napoleon did some writing and even contemplated a history of Corsica, asking Paoli for materials: 'History is not written in one's youth,' was the hero's blunt reply. Napoleon carried this rebuke to Valence where he again rented his old room and joined the Society of Friends of the Constitution, the original name of the Jacobins, the most successful and muscular of the radical political factions in the Revolution. Robespierre would become the ideological voice of the Jacobins who would govern France and direct the Revolution in 1793–94, the year of the Terror. Napoleon became secretary of the local club and was involved in revolutionary politics in a small and ambivalent way. He participated in a regional gathering of popular societies enraged over the king's flight to Varennes (June 1791) when he nearly succeeded in fleeing revolutionary France with his family. He was caught and returned to Paris a prisoner. Unlike the Paris radicals Napoleon did not call for Louis's abdication. He publicly swore the civic oath on 14 July, but two weeks later celebrated the birthday of the king with the officers of his regiment. His ideas, his convictions, his resolve were unsettled. France had not yet supplanted Corsica. A few days after drinking the king's health Napoleon wrote sardonically to his brother Joseph: 'Barnave and Cazalès have fought a duel with each other. Cazalès has been mortally wounded. That makes one less great aristocrat.' Joseph, and later Lucien, were more engaged in the French Revolution than their brother. Joseph wrote a pamphlet in 1791 that was savaged by Napoleon. 'There is much here that is good,' he wrote his older brother, 'but it is drowned in a confused mass of inanities and pedantic flowers.' He recommended reducing the four pages to a page-and-a-half and suppressing all the verbiage. For a model he proposed Talleyrand's *Adresse aux française*. Terse, concentrated argument, simply expressed, was (and remained) Napoleon's ideal of effective prose. He would later find Lucien's pamphleteering equally flawed:

> I have read your proclamation: it is worthless. There are too many words and not enough ideas. You chase after pathos. This is not how one speaks to the populace. They have more sense and tact than you think. Your prose does more harm than good.

This was the tone Napoleon took throughout his life with his brothers. His criticism reveals a man who is thinking about the Revolution and its consequences, perhaps searching for his own principles in the new era. He is drifting away, however slowly, from the politics he inherited.

Corsica still beckoned. He returned at the end of September 1791 and remained until May 1792. This is the period of his *Lettres sur la Corse à M. l'abbé Raynal* [*Letters on Corsica addressed to the abbé Raynal*], and the end of Napoleon's brief quest for literary fame. He again threw himself into Corsican politics. He sought the rank of adjutant-major in a battalion of volunteers. This fourth trip to Corsica was as fruitless as the others. He made no headway with the local military, left the island and went to Paris. In France he had a problem about his military appointment when he sought to have himself reinstated with his unit. While waiting for the Committee of Artillery to decide he attended some sessions of the Legislative Assembly, the first elected under the new constitution. He wrote Joseph on 29 May that he had made his first visit, but left no detailed record of the tumultuous spring and summer of 1792 when France declared war on much of monarchical Europe, the Paris sections – the city had been divided into 20 sections, not unlike our precincts – issued an ultimatum that the king be removed, and then forcibly did the deed on 10 August 1792, successfully attacking the Tuileries where the king was a virtual prisoner. Napoleon watched the fighting from a friend's shop windows. More than 300 Parisians and at least as many Swiss mercenaries died in the assault. Afterwards Napoleon descended to the cobbled courtyard where most of the killing had taken place. It was his first battlefield and he later told his brother Joseph that the carnage he saw that day affected him more profoundly than did any of the subsequent killing fields he witnessed. The tenth of August, often called the Second French Revolution, launched France on her republican course which would only end more than a decade later when Napoleon crowned himself Emperor in Notre Dame cathedral.

Napoleon's direct experience of the French Revolution, although almost exclusively as a spectator in Paris, made a deep impression, but not the familiar one of celebrating the people's entry into politics. He had seen the mob in action, *'le peuple'* as they were reverently invoked in Jacobin oratory and the radical press, and did not like what he saw. Most of the Swiss guards killed at the Tuileries on 10 August had been massacred by the mob after the chateau was taken. Those who managed to escape the palace grounds were hunted down, killed, and their corpses stripped and mutilated. He was also in Paris when the hideous September Massacres broke out, raging for five days during which about half the prison population of the capital, perhaps as many as 1400 men, women, and children, were hacked to death in the streets after being condemned by ad hoc juries. Napoleon is silent on the episode. The murders went on in public, and it would have been impossible to avoid knowing what was happening. Whether this was the catalyst for his fear of the mob, an episode that set in motion his thinking about the possibility of having the Revolution without the people, is impossible to say. It is not impossible to imagine.

Napoleon remained unconverted to the Revolution in France. He had yet to work through his Corsican nationalism. In October he returned to Corsica for what proved his last visit. The time of proclamations and petitions was over. The struggle for the island had turned to arms. The tangled allegiances and antagonisms between Paolists both *pur* and compromised, supporters of the French Revolution and annexation to the mainland, and the many motivated by local and longstanding grievances, gave him his final taste of Corsican politics. Napoleon commanded six companies of volunteers in Corte which were involved in an expedition against the island of Maddalena that ended in retreat. Napoleon narrowly escaped a lynching at the hands of the mutinous Marseilles sailors. He accused his troops of treason, and the affair petered out amid mutual recriminations. In March 1793 he was back on Corsica and escaped an attempted assassination. There is some suspicion, never proved, that Paoli was behind the attack. What is true is that Napoleon had become disillusioned with Paoli and broke with him when the hero made it clear, by his avoidance, that Napoleon was not his protégé and would never enter the inner circle of Paolists. Corsican memories were intense, enduring, and unforgiving. He had no future there. Paoli was banished from Napoleon's personal Pantheon. Napoleon returned to France and a revolutionary destiny. If this was his revolutionary epiphany he left no record of his feelings or reasons.

Napoleon's nationalist ardor cooled slowly until he was left little choice by circumstances. Paoli, to avoid aligning himself with the detested French, was willing to throw himself into the arms of the

English, detested by Napoleon. The thought of English ships in Corsican harbors was equally intolerable to France. On 18 April 1793 news of the decree issued by the National Convention declaring Paoli an outlaw reached Corsica. The lines were drawn. In the midst of the French Revolution Corsica could not have stood unaligned: neither the French nor the English would tolerate it. Rousseau's dream of a simple, free, uncorrupted Corsica evaporated into fantasy with the Revolution. So too did Boswell's equally visionary view of a Corsica ruled by a benevolent Plutarchian hero. Both had enthralled the young Napoleon: now both were abandoned. Napoleon had failed to lead the island into the French Revolution and when Paoli marginalized the Bonapartes he had no choice but to flee. The passion he felt for liberation was effectively transferred to France. He had been educated in France, he had spent more time there than on his natal island, and the Revolution proved not only a comfortable vessel for his enthusiasm, his ambition, even his inchoate and haltingly enunciated need for *liberté, égalité, fraternité,* his desire for an end to the *ancien régime,* it was irresistible. Napoleon's failures on Corsica completed his conversion. The revolutionary that struggled for expression in Corsica found full scope in France.

The clan politics of Corsica completed the first phase of Napoleon's political education. The people of Corsica proved hopelessly incapable of moving beyond the parochial and traditional world of the island, where the old elites, untouched by the Enlightenment and spurning the Revolution, struggled to hold on to their privileges. Napoleon was stifled on Corsica, his ambition unfulfilled. His dreams of a new Corsica proved utopian. He left behind his natal island, along with much of his enthusiasm for Rousseau and ideological politics. The philosophers, to echo Karl Marx, had only imagined the world – the point was to change it. His future, as the future of Europe, lay in France. The French Revolution, which Napoleon now joined, would complete his political education and prove the most profound experience of his life. When Charles Bonaparte went over to the French and gave his children a French education he set in motion a new history for his family. Napoleon became a Frenchman and a revolutionary soldier. He had learned, by observation in France and by direct involvement in Corsica, to prefer revolution from above. In Corsica he held the people at bay. Later, on the continent, he had only contempt for the masses. His experiences of the people up in arms had frightened him and nearly got him killed. It served only to reinforce his fear of *le peuple*. He fled Corsica forever on 11 June 1793, setting sail for Toulon.

When Napoleon landed in France he was a man without a country. His years of absence from Corsica had made him an outcast of the patriot party. In France he was in the same position. He had no friends of consequence. He was an unimportant Corsican who could not make up his mind about when and whether to join the Revolution. He had again to make his way unaided in a precarious world now in full upheaval. The one great advantage France had was that the Revolution came to Corsica second hand, it had not been made there. On the mainland all of France, in the spring of 1793 before the unity of France and her new government was fragmented into the greatest crisis of the Revolution, choices seemed clear, the path of patriotism obvious. Napoleon found and followed it.

The *ancien régime* was dead, and with it any embarrassing compromises with the defunct government and society. All men were new men who saw the Revolution as a rupture with the past; even an obscure Corsican captain of artillery who had so far failed in all his political and military ventures had a chance. He plunged into the fray.

II
First Revolutionary Steps

'I would add to the list of patriots,' Augustin Robespierre wrote to his brother Maximilien from the Midi, 'the name of citizen Buonaparte, general in chief of the artillery, an officer of transcendent merit. He is ... a man who resisted Paoli's caresses, and who saw his property ravaged by this traitor.' Napoleon had found the patronage he needed, as he thrust his way into the history of the Revolution with a brilliant victory: the only time he would triumph over Horatio Nelson.

Toulon, the Mediterranean base of the French fleet, had been betrayed to the British. General Elzéar Auguste Dommartin, an old royal artillery officer who would die of tetanus from wounds received in Egypt after a loyal and successful military career in the Revolution, had been unable to drive the British out of the town and the harbor. Napoleon, then an acting lieutenant-colonel but officially still a captain, participated in the siege. Dommartin had been wounded and could not fight. This chance injury began an incredible run of luck for the young Corsican, just turned 24. He had begged the Committee of Public Safety, the emergency government of the Revolution, to send a general of artillery to replace Dommartin: someone who would 'destroy their prejudices [he thought little of the officers currently besieging Toulon] and execute what theory and experience have shown to be the axioms of every enlightened officer'.

Antoine-Christophe Saliceti, a Corsican deputy to the National Convention who had befriended Napoleon on Corsica, was *en mission* from the Committee of Public Safety. He too was impressed with Napoleon. When the Committee wrote they had no artillery general to send, Saliceti immediately promoted Napoleon to brigadier-general, gave him command of artillery, and watched as he brilliantly bombarded the British ships and then took the town by assault. 'Words fail me,' wrote du Teil, the brother of Napoleon's commander at Auxonne, to the Minister of War,

> to describe Bonaparte's merits. He has plenty of knowledge, and as much intelligence and courage: and that is no more than a first sketch of the virtues of a most rare officer.

Napoleon was equally taken with himself: 'I promised you brilliant successes, and, as you see, I have kept my word,' he wrote the Minister. He had become, literally overnight, a Jacobin general and a revolutionary hero. But he had little enthusiasm for Jacobin ideology. Less than a year after Toulon, he wrote a letter to General Jacques-Louis-François, Count de Tilly, then serving as representative in Genoa, upon learning of the deaths of the *robespierristes* in the purge that followed 9 Thermidor: 'I have been somewhat affected by the catastrophe of [Augustin] Robespierre whom I loved and who I believed pure. Were it my own father, I would myself kill him if he aspired to tyranny.' Once he came to power he hounded the Jacobins into exile or impotent retirement, but his purge was selective. A great many former Jacobins served in the police, the army administration, and the army itself, especially the Army of Italy which was resolutely Jacobin. The Jacobins who rallied to him, particularly the more moderate, were welcomed and rewarded.

His Jacobinism is usually dismissed as opportunism, an insincere expedient in a career driven by an insatiable craving for power. Maybe, but it is not implausible that he believed a good deal of what he embraced. His early writings, with their Rousseauian fervor, his Corsican idealism, and even the fervid love letters to Josephine, reveal a man of passion and enthusiasm. He admired Jacobin toughness, efficiency, patriotism, even their ruthlessness, qualities he himself possessed. If his Jacobinism was mere opportunism it could have proved fatal: there were enough examples of seemingly solid Jacobin patriots purged that Napoleon would have had to play a game of extraordinary duplicity and danger to remain in favor. He may have been a bully and a cynic in politics, but he was neither Iago nor Tartuffe. He was a man with strong convictions, not the caricature opportunist and egomaniac of his enemies. After Maximilien Robespierre's fall, in July 1794, the Thermidorians, who had destroyed Robespierre, imprisoned Napoleon as a Jacobin and he barely escaped the scaffold.

Napoleon adhered to the Jacobins because they were ferocious patriots, utterly devoted to preserving and winning the Revolution; and they had discovered him. They alone appeared willing to fight to the death if need be. Hardly the affiliation of a trimmer. Following the crisis of the summer of 1793 Jacobin leadership gave France the strong government she needed to survive. This is not insincerity or opportunism: it is practical politics informed by conviction.

Men in Napoleon's generation were educated and grew to young manhood in the last decades of the *ancien régime*. With Napoleon they embarked on their careers in the turbulent 1780s when so many of the verities of the French monarchy and society were being challenged or coming unraveled. They were old enough to vote in the first elections in living memory, in 1789 – although Napoleon himself just missed the age requirement – and they witnessed the heady history of the first years of revolution. The bulk of their public and political lives were lived under the First French Republic, established in September 1792, and their political education was shaped by the Revolution in its republican manifestation, including the year of the Terror. Napoleon's public life follows this trajectory after his definitive return from Corsica.

The Revolution, between Thermidor year II (July–August 1794 in the officially abandoned Gregorian calendar) and Napoleon's *coup d'état* on 18 Brumaire year VIII (18 November 1799) has had a bad press. The Thermidorian governments have been sometimes seen as little more than preparation for the advent of Napoleon, which is his explanation. Historians who share Napoleon's view emphasize the political corruption and ineptitude of the Thermidorians, incapable of any policy except perpetual war. They have also been seen as the bourgeois betrayers of the Jacobin Republic and *le peuple*, the liquidators of the Terror, the people's justice. This is the view favored by the Jacobins, given its classical expression by arguably the greatest historian of the Revolution, Jules Michelet, who interrupts his *Histoire de la Révolution française* at Robespierre's death to anathematize his conquerors:

> We recoil from recounting what follows, the blind reaction that seized the Assembly ... Horror and ridicule struggled with equal force ... an execrable comedy began, lucrative assassinations committed in the name of humanity, the vengeance of sensible men who massacred patriots and then continued their work ... Paris regained its gaiety. There was famine, it is true, but the staircase of the Elysée Palace was radiant, the Palais-Royal was full, the theaters were at their height. Then there were the 'balls of victims' where impudent debauchery enveloped the orgy of fake mourning.

For those more favorably disposed to the Thermidorians they are treated as moderate republicans and liberals overwhelmed by the challenges, from Jacobins and Royalists, from left and right, who turned first to civilian and then military *coups d'état* for survival. All of these views have distinguished defenders, all have some truth.

The conspirators of Thermidor could agree upon little beyond their fear of Robespierre; his death proved the only way to end the Terror. In the days after his fall the Convention hunted down the *robespierristes* and executed hundreds. This is the purge Napoleon narrowly escaped. Then they dismantled the machinery of Terror: the Committee of Public Safety was reorganized, the frightful Law of 22 Prairial which intensified the already horrific Law of Suspects (17 September 1793) was repealed. The Revolutionary Tribunal was reorganized, the *maximum*, the chief economic legislation of the Terror, was abolished, and the Jacobin Club closed. Then the Thermidorians went after the terrorists: Carrier, the terrorist of Nantes, the sadistic inventor of the *noyades* or drownings in the Seine, was tried and executed. Fouquier-Tinville, the equally sadistic public prosecutor of the dreaded Revolutionary Tribunal, suffered the same fate. Disarming the so-called terrorists in Paris, who increasingly were defined as all those opposed to the Thermidorians, began and a new constitution was written.

The winter following Robespierre's destruction was exceptionally bitter. Prices, unchecked by the *maximum* laws, rose inexorably, frozen bodies were regularly collected every morning from the doorways of Paris, as well as from the Seine where a record number of suicides sought escape. The remnants of the popular movement in the capital were starved into submission by the spiraling price of food and the dearth of work. The White Terror of retribution directed against all who had supported the Jacobins and many who had bought Church lands (*biens nationaux*) raged in the countryside. The central government was powerless to stop it nor did the Thermidorians object to the open season declared on rural and provincial radicals. Pushed to the wall by cold and the free market, the Paris poor, the *sans-culottes* who had been the motor of the Revolution and the Terror in year II (September 1793–September 1794), broke. Those who recalled the days 'when the guillotine smoked and we had bread' took to the streets in desperation. They were crushed by the authorities and the few remaining Jacobins in the Convention were purged.

On 12–13 Germinal (1–2 April 1795) Paris rose in what was to be the most feeble of the urban insurrections of the French Revolution. Without Jacobin support, without the support of the Commune of Paris, without adequate leadership in the streets or in the Convention, the *sans-culottes* were doomed and easily crushed. Three of the remaining Jacobin leaders who had served on the Committee of Public Safety and not been *robespierristes* – Billaud-Varenne, Collot d'Hérbois, and Bertrand Barère – were expelled. Billaud and Collot were sent to die on Cayenne island, colorfully called the 'dry guillotine'. Barère went into hiding and lived on well into the 19th century. On 1–2 Prairial (20–21 May 1795) came another feeble and desperate Parisian uprising which resulted in further repression of the Jacobins and the *sans-culottes*, and the purge of several members of the National Assembly, including the astronomer Gilbert Romme who had done the calculations for the new revolutionary calendar, assuring its accuracy well into the 21st century. This marked the end of popular insurrection from the left in the French Revolution. The royalists took heart from the political chaos in France and with British backing and ships, landed at Quiberon in Brittany. The inept invasion was quickly crushed. Attacks from right and left exposed the precarious balance of the Republic and explained the oscillation of Thermidorian politics. Napoleon would inherit these polar politics: his attack on the right gave him the credentials he needed to gain the trust of the republican political elite; those on the left convinced the Jacobins there was no hope for an ongoing social revolution.

The Convention Assembly was dissolved on 26 October 1795, to be replaced by a new constitution that established a Republic with a bicameral legislature (a Council of Elders and a senate of Five Hundred). Five directors comprised the new executive branch. To insure the perpetuation of a majority of the members of the old Convention, thus guaranteeing a continuity in the government while eliminating the extreme Jacobins and their sympathizers, the new constitution included a two-thirds rule. Two-thirds of the members of the old assembly would continue in subsequent assemblies, carrying with them the rancor, the divisions, and the frustrations of the Convention. To inoculate the government against the Jacobins and keep the royalists at bay, the new electorate was heavily restricted. A mere 30,000 males, only a proportion even of the local notabilities who met the property qualifications, now had the vote. The same combination of manipulation and restriction marked the selection of the directors. A list of 50 names deliberately included 45 nonentities, which constrained the Elders to choosing a Directory composed of the desired men. The fundamental flaw in the new Republic was not so much that the elections were rigged, albeit legally, but that the Republic rested on a very narrow social and economic base which none of the elite was willing to expand lest the Jacobins or the royalists again assert themselves.

What almost all the political elite shared, in addition to their regicide and *terroriste* past, was intransigence and a lack of magnanimity. They had survived the storms of year II and wanted no more. The new Directors were themselves not notoriously dishonest (with the exception of Paul Barras, Napoleon's patron), nor were they incompetent. All were sincere republicans; but they disliked and distrusted each other. The new constitution under which they governed was a document of self-defense to insure political and social stasis. It was by law unalterable until the early years of the next century. The irony was that the ideological basis of the Revolution had originally been the need for a constitution to make French government responsive to the people, a contract between the people and the state. Now constitutions came and went. That of 1791, France's first, lasted less than a year. The so-called Jacobin Constitution of 1793 was shelved until the end of the war, which never came. The Constitution of Year III, that of the Directory, allowed no political change short of a *coup d'état*.

The finances of the Republic rested on impending bankruptcy. The Revolution and the collapse of the paper currency had reduced France to economic ruin. Despite the victories of 1794 and the diplomatic successes of 1795, the Convention had not given France peace. The Revolution had paid for itself partly with booty but mostly with inflation. Some quipped that the government was hard pressed to print during the night the paper money it would need to sustain itself the next day. When the new regime of the Directory began, the *assignat* of 100 francs was worth less than 20 *sous*, slightly more than 1/100 of its printed value. The Directors were desperate and sold off all the national assets they could, but they had to accept *assignats*, their own legal tender, in partial payment. Massive woods and forests, ponds and chateaux, everything that had not been auctioned off earlier in the Revolution, now disappeared into private hands at bargain prices, as did the crown jewels. The struggle to stay financially afloat conveyed more power into the hands of the generals, among whose most important responsibilities was filling the empty coffers of the state with booty. Napoleon had been told upon his appointment to command the Italian army that he was expected to raise substantial sums.

This buccaneering society offered fabulous wealth to many. Joseph Fouché, in minor orders in the Oratorians before the Revolution, became an Hébertiste, a terrorist, a dechristianizer, and a conspirator against Robespierre. He emerged from 9 Thermidor in disgrace and penniless. He set up a company to supply the military, with two other ex-terrorists, Pierre-François Réal and Jean-Lambert Tallien, the 'butcher of Bordeaux'. By 1799 he had a chateau and an income of 20,000 francs. The characters in so many of Balzac's novels could be and were drawn from life. The financial vertigo of the Directory had to be stopped. In September 1797 the most drastic financial measure of the entire Revolution was enacted. One third of the state debt was consolidated and registered as a sacred charge upon the nation. The other two-thirds were converted into bearer bonds reissued to the stockholders as securities and were acceptable as part of any payment for the purchase of national property. The interest on the state's debt immediately dropped about 240 million francs while those whose debts were revalued suffered catastrophic losses as the new bonds collapsed in value. The estimate is that some 368,000 families were seriously compromised if not ruined. This was a repudiation of the National Debt.

The other major piece of legislation that would determine France's future and sustain Napoleon's wars was the Jourdan Law (approved on 5 September 1798), which systematized the existing practices of the Revolution, the *levée en masse* that introduced the first modern universal conscription. The new law established compulsory military service for all unmarried men between the ages of 20 and 25. They were to be called up according to their annual class, determined by when they came of age. Enforcement was the responsibility of the local administrations in France and was carried out by the *gendarmerie*, a national police force, and the National Guard of the larger towns. Both enjoyed exemption from the draft and were resented for it. There was an initial levy of 200,000, which produced immediate and widespread national hostility to the law. The official figures were not even approximately met. 'Of the first class of 203,000 conscripts,' writes Sydenham, '60,000 were declared unfit by local medical boards which were often scandalously lenient; of the remaining 143,000, only 97,000 presented themselves for service; and of these, thanks to desertion, only 74,000 finally reached the armies.'

The Thermidorian governments survived three uprisings in Paris of various degrees of intensity and purpose, and held on to power with two successful *coups d'état*. The third *coup*, led by Napoleon, ended the Directory. On 13 Vendémiaire (5 October 1795) the Convention crushed a royalist uprising in Paris. Napoleon was sent by his patron Paul Barras to put down the riot. For only the second time in the Revolution – the first was at the Champ de Mars in 1791, when another general, Lafayette, proclaimed martial law – government troops fired on the demonstrators. Barras gave the command to fire and was the nominal commander, but Napoleon set the guns and ordered grapeshot, a particularly murderous charge at close range, not unlike buckshot. It was not his brutality that was significant, but the transformation of his reputation. In one afternoon he successfully repudiated his Jacobin past and made himself acceptable to the governing republicans. He still had no substantial reputation or popularity but he was no longer seen predominately as an ex-*robespierriste* general.

18 Fructidor (4 September 1797) was the most serious of the *coups* in the sense that it profoundly changed the nature of the Directory and hence the Republic, while fully exposing the defects in the Constitution of year III. At dawn on 18 Fructidor soldiers occupied the legislature, closed the gates to Paris, and arrested the heads of the legislative majority who had not fled. The walls were placarded with posters denouncing 'a royalist plot financed by England'. The following day those deputies sympathetic to the conspiracy voted the law of 19 Fructidor. This quashed the local and national elections in 49 of France's 98 departments. Fifty-three deputies (soon the number had swollen to 65) and two directors were proscribed. Of those captured, 16 were sent to the penal colony on Guyane in the Caribbean, where half of them soon died.

What made this *coup* so significant was not the proscriptions, a common practice in all the *coups* of the Revolution and Directory, but the fact that for only the second time in the Revolution – the first was on 2 June 1793 when the Jacobins purged the Convention – duly elected representatives had been purged, this time by the army. The directors who seized power, Paul Barras, Jean-François Reubell, and Louis-Marie de La Revellière-Lépeaux, reintroduced censorship of the press, arrested a number of editors, and left the Republic more authoritarian, militarized, and far less representative. They had successfully frustrated a royalist project for restoration of the Bourbons, but the price paid was enormous and not refundable. They forcibly undid the results of an election. The long dialectic between the civil rights in a liberal democracy and the felt need to survive and stay in power whatever the cost, had been decided in favor of expediency using military repression. The way had been paved for a future military *coup* that would complete the political logic of Fructidor, replace the directors, and sweep aside an increasingly fictive republic. Napoleon was not the only eligible applicant for the job, nor the only man who realized Fructidor was the beginning, not the end of another phase of the French Revolution. He was the most successful.

Of the three new directors who benefited from Fructidor, Barras was the most important and the least attractive. Born in 1755 into the minor nobility of Provence, he became an officer in the Royal Army in a regiment commanded by a family member, and fought at Pondicherry (now Puducherry) in India. He resigned his commission in 1783 and moved to Versailles where he led a life so obscure its details remain impossible to reconstruct. The Revolution offered a new life. He was elected to the Convention in 1792, voted for the king's death, and was sent with Stanislas-Louis Fréron, the editor of the scurrilous *Orateur du Peuple* during the Revolution as well as a ferocious terrorist, *en mission* to the departments of the Alps. In 1793 he joined the deputies sent by the Committee of Public Safety to Toulon to drive the English out. Here, thanks to Napoleon's friend, the deputy Saliceti, they met the young captain. Barras was as impressed as all the others who saw Napoleon in action and approved his promotion to general. After the English evacuated Toulon, on 18 December 1793, Barras launched a terrible series of reprisals. Between 800 and 900 English 'collaborators' were killed in Toulon. His credentials as a terrorist were established. From Toulon he was sent to Marseilles. He proposed to the Committee of Public Safety that the city be renamed 'Sans-nom' (nameless) and, thus humiliated, removed from the map of France. The Committee sensibly declined the proposal and recalled its representatives, whom they, and especially Robespierre, received coldly in Paris. Barras joined other former terrorists who had become conspirators who feared Jacobin retribution and he was instrumental in Robespierre's overthrow. As a reward he was given command of the Army of Paris and sent to capture Robespierre, his brother Augustin, Georges Couthon, Philippe Lebas, and Saint-Just. After he was named commander of the Army of the Interior he took Napoleon as his adjutant: 'General Bonaparte will be employed in the army of the Interior under the orders of Barras, the representative of the people and general in chief of this army,' read the official appointment. He was also promoted to Division General.

A contemporary and rival, the director La Réveillière-Lépeaux, described Barras as 'tall, vigorous, and powerfully built, but with a hard air about him. Despite his masculine figure and height he had a striking lack of physical dignity'. He was the only one of the important Thermidorians to remain in power from Robespierre's fall to Napoleon's *coup d'état*. It is difficult to know his precise machinations in all the insurrections and *coups* of the Directory but he was always a direct beneficiary, until that of 18 Brumaire. He was also a man whose personal corruption, cynicism, self-indulgence, unscrupulousness, licentiousness, and treacherousness have been unfairly taken as representative of the Directory. Barras became enormously rich during the Revolution, bought himself a gorgeous chateau, Grosbois, in the

Brie, and introduced Napoleon to Josephine, whom the gossips (and historians) insist was Barras's discarded mistress. Five days before the wedding (2 March 1796) Barras appointed Napoleon commander of the Army of Italy. He expected after Brumaire to be recalled by his protégé: he waited unsummoned and bitter at Grosbois.

The Directory, which completed Napoleon's political education begun on Corsica, was no school of republican virtue, moral rectitude, or civic honor. Napoleon thought it a living example of bad government, made even more so by hypocrisy and republican pretensions. Whatever scruples of legality he may have had were easily discarded in a world with so few, where the directors connived at almost any illegality to stay in power, transferred enormous power to the army, and where republicanism became increasingly an article of blind faith or cynicism, a metaphor rather than a lived experience. Just when Napoleon decided to seize power cannot be known, but certainly by the time he took command of the Army of Italy he knew he had no interest in confining his ambition to propping up a government that could not support itself. Those who sought to overthrow the Directory needed none of the arts of political seduction to attract Napoleon. He welcomed their overtures.

III
Italy: The Imperial Revolution

Napoleon's was not the first brilliant military career of the Revolution, but it was the most dazzling, not least because he made sure that his deeds (and indispensability) were broadcast. Toulon, when he successfully recaptured the port from the British, gave him his first victory. Vendémiaire, when for the first time he dispersed a revolutionary crowd with cannon fire, certified the end of his Jacobin past. But it is Italy that made him Napoleon. As Jean Tulard writes, 'The Napoleonic legend was not born on St Helena but on the plains of Italy'.

The Italian command was not sought by any of Napoleon's rivals. It was the least desirable theater in a war whose center of gravity was the Rhine. Italy was a sideshow designed to draw Austrian troops away from the German theater. The army in Italy had been neglected: there were not enough boots to shoe the soldiers, nor money to pay them, few bayonets, muskets, or sabers, and even fewer horses to mount an adequate cavalry. The army was thought still to be infected with the Jacobin virus. General Barthelémy Louis Schérer (1747–1804), of whom Napoleon spoke well, was a man whose capacity for alcohol exceeded his military talents. He was bogged down after a mildly successful winter campaign. When Shérer ignored the Directory's order to be more aggressive he was replaced by the 26-year-old Napoleon, who would sink or swim in Italy.

By the time Napoleon received his first command the fervent crusading zeal proclaimed by the war party of the Revolution in 1792 had been eclipsed by the need for money. The Convention Assembly had decreed (15 September 1793) that

> the general commanding the forces of the Republic on land and sea, renouncing from henceforth every philanthropic idea previously adopted by the French people with the intention of making foreign

nations appreciate the value and benefits of liberty, will behave towards the enemies of France in just the same way that the powers of the coalition have behaved towards them; and they will exercise with regard to the countries and individuals conquered by their armies the customary rights of war.

The adage 'war must pay for war' had been amended to war must yield a profit. The goal of the Directory was clear: squeeze the most money out of Italy in the shortest time by concentrating on the richest part, Lombardy, held by the Austrians. Napoleon modified, then ignored, and finally rejected the constraints imposed by Paris. He refused to be 'a kind of conquistador, a Cortez, a Pizarro, charged to amass gold rather than win friends'. Once at the head of an army Napoleon became his own man. His scorn for the Directory was clear. So was his ambition.

The veterans, many of them older than their new commander, focused their grousing on the inexperienced, young, and physically unimpressive general, who, thanks to his patron Barras leap-frogged over more conventionally deserving men. He had secured the support of Lazare Carnot, 'the organizer of victory', a member of the great and now defunct Committee of Public Safety, and currently a minister in the Directory. Napoleon's situation was unpromising, but he had inherited a formidable weapon, despite its neglect and demoralization. His soldiers, whose core had been blooded in the revolutionary wars and retained much of its Jacobin faith and idealism, had fought in Italy and the Pyrenees. Their *esprit*, dormant before Napoleon arrived, proved crucial. The government was so strapped for cash that it could give the general a mere 2000 gold Louis, a laughable war chest. The army itself had an effective force of 38,000 and faced the same number of Austrians, plus 25,000 Piedmontese. The French were hopelessly outnumbered and outgunned. But the Austrian forces were scattered, the best troops were fighting in the Rhine theater, and the Piedmontese were poorly equipped. What had to be done was clear: split the armies and fight each separately. Between 10 and 15 April he fought (and won) at Montenotte, Dego, and then Mondavi. On 10 May he nearly got himself killed at Lodi where he personally serviced the artillery as the French stormed the single bridge to the town, tenaciously defended by the Austrians. It is here, legend has it, that he was dubbed the 'Little Corporal' by his troops, although this is not the only explanation. Lodi, a small town on the west bank of the river Adda, about 20 miles southeast of Milan, would become the first Bonapartist legend. It was, as battles go, minor; but it served to make Napoleon appear, to friend and foe alike, an irresistible leader. His own later account of the engagement also credits Lodi with instilling in him self-confidence and revealing his potential greatness:

> It was only on the evening of Lodi that I believed myself a superior man, and that the ambition came to me of executing the great things which so far had been occupying my thoughts only as a fantastic dream.

Carl von Clausewitz, then a subaltern in the Prussian army and years away from writing the most renowned study of war – *Vom Kriege* (*On War*) – wrote his first military history on Napoleon's Italian Campaign. 'Never, without question,' he writes, 'did a feat of arms inspire such astonishment as did the crossing of the Adda.' He goes on:

> He [Napoleon] was drunk with victory by which I mean he was in that elevated state of hope, courage, and confidence by which the soul raises itself above the mundane calculations of reason – he sees his opponent running away in a state of confused terror – and in that moment there is almost nothing he cannot do!

This episode would soon be conflated with the bridge attack at the Battle of Arcole (15–17 November 1796) into a great narrative of personal heroism commemorated in Antoine Gros's painting, *Bonaparte at the Bridge of Arcole*. The canvas established Gros as a supreme historical painter. Lest there be any confusion or misunderstanding of his role at Arcole, Napoleon wrote the Directory a long account that was published in the Paris press:

> This village [Arcole] stopped the avant-garde of the army the whole day.
> In vain all the generals, recognizing the importance of time, rushed to the front to compel our columns to cross the little bridge of Arcole: too much courage hurt them – they were almost all wounded; Generals Verdier, Bon, Verne, and Lannes were knocked out of action. Augereau grabbed a flag, carried it to the extremity of the bridge ... and stayed there several minutes without producing any effect. It was imperative, however, to cross the bridge, or make a detour of several leagues, which could have ruined our entire operation. I went up myself: I asked the soldiers if they were still the victors of Lodi. My presence produced a reaction in the troops that convinced me to

attempt the crossing again [in which two generals fell]. We had to abandon the idea of a frontal assault on the village.

This gift for personal celebration and propaganda would continue throughout his life. Napoleon instinctively understood not only the political theorem that what is thought about an event, a man, or a deed is often more potent than the truth. He had mastered the culture of the democratic politics of the Revolution: public opinion not only ruled, but it could be shaped. His account of what happened at Arcole so glorifies his role that it becomes a fiction. Those who were there tell a different story. Napoleon led a charge which was stopped well short of the bridge. In the confusion of retreat he was knocked into a narrow, deep ditch by the side of the road. Several officers pulled him, covered with mud, out of his inglorious situation. He borrowed a horse and left to change his clothes.

It had taken Napoleon two weeks to defeat the Piedmontese. He imposed a huge indemnity which he demanded in specie. With this money he paid his troops in hard currency 'for the first time since 1793', wrote General Rouget (then a captain). The Italian army, hitherto bedraggled and neglected, became the most privileged in the French army. They alone were paid in cash. If the soldiers were not already devoted to him, and Napoleon made a point of demanding their personal allegiance rather than a more abstract attachment to the Republic, their wages accelerated conversion. The string of victories continued against the Austrians, now fighting without their allies. He beat them at Castiglione (5 August), at Bassano (8 September), at Arcole, at Rivoli (14 January 1797), and from 10 March to 6 April he successfully fought Archduke Charles, the only one of the Austrian commanders equal to facing him. He then headed towards Vienna and was within 75 miles of the capital when the Austrians sued for peace.

It was a fabulous campaign, all the more heady for a struggling Republic bogged down on the Rhine. By the end of May there were no Austrian soldiers on Italian soil, with the exception of the troops locked in Mantua where Napoleon successfully besieged them (2 February 1797). But it was not as fabulous as Napoleon later remembered; the spoils of war he extracted from Italy to enhance his glory ultimately tarnished it. Now was the time to 'squeeze the Italian lemon', as Carnot put it. Florence was the most important source of purloined art, Genoa was the entrepôt of money, but the entire peninsula was mulcted. The dukes of Parma and Modena, along with the King of Naples, all hastened to sign an armistice with Napoleon, who demanded millions in silver, and precious paintings and manuscripts by the hundreds, sent to Paris to proclaim his victories. Parma was squeezed for 2 million francs in cash and 20 paintings, including Correggio's great *Madonna of St Jerome*. Milan was squeezed for 20 million francs, which represented five times the annual tax burden imposed before the French invasion, as well as 25 paintings. Bologna had to surrender Raphael's *The Ecstasy of St Cecila*. Venice, which had risen in revolt, was (along with the Papacy) squeezed especially hard, losing its famous bronze horses atop St Mark's, a valuable bas-relief and bust, an exceptionally precious cameo, 16 pictures (including Veronese's *The Marriage at Cana* and several Titians), 230 incunabula, and 253 manuscripts. The Pope had to pay 21 million *livres* in money and goods. The Treaty of Bologna of 23 June 1796, which reinforced the earlier Treaty of Tolontino, was brutally precise:

A hundred pictures, busts, vases or statues to be selected by the commissioners and sent to Rome, including in particular the bronze bust of Junius Brutus and the marble bust of Marcus Brutus, both on the Capitol, also five hundred manuscripts at the choice of the said commissioners.

The two busts, of the man who first drove out the kings and his descendant who assassinated Caesar, continued the regicide iconography of the Revolution.

Mantua and Modena were also looted by treaty or armistice. Napoleon's depredations were not just the spoils of war confiscated by the victor, hitherto taken for the personal use or collection of king or prince. Art was the cultural dimension of revolutionary war, designed to aggrandize and endow the new state with the artifacts of power, prestige, and legitimacy. During the invasion of Belgium in 1794 a commission had followed the army and selected the best paintings to send back to Paris. 'The fruits of genius are the patrimony of liberty,' declared the Jacobin Jean-François Barbier. Even more emphatic was the politically agile Boissy d'Anglas. He began his political career as a moderate (and prudently reserved) patriot, moved carefully away from the Jacobins in the Convention Assembly, then rallied to Napoleon, and deftly survived his fall to be made a peer under the Restoration. 'Let the entire world hasten to ... deposit its treasures ...' in the museum established by Napoleon, he declared. Plunder had become political as well as ideological.

The confiscation of the Old Masters, accelerated and rationalized by Napoleon, would present the Revolution as the legitimate inheritor of the European past, the apotheosis of the universal yearning for liberty. His commissioners, charged with deciding what would be sent to France, were carefully chosen in consultation with the distinguished mathematician Gaspar Monge, who accompanied Napoleon to Italy, as he would later to Egypt. The commissioners were painters (Jean-Baptiste Wicar, Carlo Giuseppi Gerli, and Antoine-Jean Gros, the only artist of genius of the three); musicians (Rudolf Kreutzer, the violinist and pedagogue whose *Etudes* are the Bible of all violinists); sculptors (Joseph-Charles Marin) and a number of lesser-known *savants* who would insure that the booty claimed by treaty was the best to be had. The great names were regularly included in Napoleon's lists of desired treasure: da Vinci, Michelangelo, Rubens, Raphael. The Commission spent two years in Italy overseeing the confiscations, crating and shipping the loot to France. Wicar made a fortune out of his appointment by rushing back to Paris to sell what he had expropriated for himself. A hollow intellectual justification for looting Italy, one that went beyond spoils for the victor, was already in place by the time Napoleon took the Italian command. The *Moniteur*, the semi-official newspaper of the Revolution, insisted that 'by virtue of its power and the superiority of its culture and its artists, the French Republic is the only country in the world which can provide a secure refuge for these masterpieces'. Napoleon sent the booty back to Paris with an army escort, and arranged for it to be publicly displayed so the people could see what their darling general had captured. Soon after the paintings from Turin and Florence were put on public display (19 March 1800). Napoleon inaugurated the galleries devoted to classical sculpture by placing on the socle of the Belvedere Apollo (wrenched from the Papal collection) a bronze plaque exalting the glory of the Army of Italy and the young general to whom France owed all these masterpieces.

'I am not their dupe,' he told Miot de Melito in Turin in the fall of 1797, referring to the Paris politicians, as a number of paintings were being assembled for shipment to France. 'I have tasted command and I cannot give it up ...' He told Melito later at Mombello, the palace just outside Milan where he held court amid pomp and luxury:

Do you believe that it is to increase the grandeur of the lawyers of the Directory, the Carnots, the Barrases, that I triumph in Italy? Do you believe that it is to found a Republic? What an idea! A Republic of thirty million citizens! With our mores, our vices! How would that be possible? ... What they need is glory, to have their vanity satisfied. But liberty, they don't understand the first thing about it.

He would not stray far from these still embryonic ideas for the rest of his career. It was a new view of the French Revolution: glory would replace liberty, Bonaparte would replace the directors.

The transfer of art from Italy to France represented the transfer of sovereignty and civilization from Rome, for centuries the historical epicenter of the empire from which Europe took its rise and in 1796 still the capital of international Catholicism. 'Rome is no more in Rome. It is now in Paris' was a popular chant of those who watched the procession of wagons laden with Italian spoils. The reference to the ancient Roman triumphs was not lost on contemporaries. Napoleon's plunder became the occasion for a revolutionary festival. The days of Robespierre's celebration of a new civic religion were supplanted with the celebration of national glory won on the battlefield and reified in booty.

The Directory marked five national celebrations: 14 July 1789 (the Fall of the Bastille); 10 August 1792 (the overthrow of the monarchy); 22 September 1792 (1 Vendémiaire in the revolutionary calendar, the declaration of the Republic); 21 January 1793 (the execution of Louis XVI); and 27 July 1794 (9 Thermidor, the overthrow of Robespierre). Of these 9 Thermidor, euphemistically dubbed the Fête de la Liberté, was the most important and significant: it commemorated the founding act of the renewed republic, the birth and *bona fides* of the Directory. The celebration lasted two days and the symbolism was carefully orchestrated to contrast the Thermidorians who had overthrown Robespierre to the anarchy, as they referred to the year of Jacobin domination of the Revolution, they replaced. On the first day of the Fête the entire Commune of Paris, marshaled by age, overturned and destroyed a gilded throne decorated with a crown and *fleur-de-lis* and bearing the inscription 'The Constitution of 1791'. On the second day of the festival – devoted to 10 Thermidor, the day Robespierre went to the guillotine – nothing remained of the throne but debris, upon which had been erected another throne, veiled in black cloth, decorated by swords and masks and bearing the inscription 'The Constitution of 1793'. This throne was in turn destroyed by fire, and a statue of Liberty emerged and filled the space. The ritual provided the context for Napoleon's parade of booty.

He put up the money to transport his depredations to Paris, and the triumphal procession of Italian art was hastily added to the program, shifting the focus from the traditional symbolic enactments of the Republic's foundation to the young general's glory. A cavalry detachment and a military band led the parade and each of the 250 wagons of art, decorated with garlands, bore a banner identifying its contents.

Most of the works, divided into three categories, were still in crates: Natural History, Books and Manuscripts, and Fine Arts, an arrangement that followed the Enlightenment taste for the encyclopedic categorization of knowledge. The *Gazette nationale* declared that all parts of the world have been made to contribute to enrich the most beautiful French festival and to make it as magnificent as the triumphal entry of Aemilius Paulus [the victor of the Third Macedonian War] into Rome. The fine arts wagons were led by one containing the four bronze horses taken from St Mark's. The banner provided a pedigree of pillage: 'Horses transported from Corinth to Rome and from Rome to Constantinople to Venice, and from Venice to France'. Twenty-five wagons of the most celebrated sculpture of antiquity followed, justifying Napoleon's boast that 'we will have everything beautiful in Italy'. After the sculptures came the paintings with various brash banners – 'Artists come running! Here are your masters!' was one. The bust of Junius Brutus came last and was placed on a pedestal with the inscription: 'Rome was first governed by kings:/Junius Brutus gave it liberty and the Republic.' 'Never,' wrote the Goncourt brothers a century later, 'has the Eternal City itself seen so tremendous a spectacle, and never did a victorious emperor pass through the streets so glorified, never did his triumph lead such an army of such captives!' Never, they might have added, had the Revolution's identification with antiquity been so literally presented.

Napoleon's politics of plunder was just beginning in 1797, along with the implied declaration that the militant Revolution would continue. Each subsequent shipment of stolen art was shown at a special exhibition at the Louvre which Napoleon intended would become the greatest art museum in the world; and so it has, even with much of his loot repatriated after his fall. The estimate is that only about half of the stolen art was restored to its original owners, and this does not take into consideration the lesser booty – books, manuscripts, and natural science collections – where the percentage that remained in France is much higher.

*****

The French Empire, *la grande nation* as Napoleon dubbed it, was just beginning. Italy, a unique distinction, was twice conquered: in 1796 and 1800. The first time the war was settled by peace preliminaries signed at Leoben (17 April 1797) when Bonaparte's vanguard was less than a hundred miles from Vienna. The dictated terms were revised but not substantially modified by the treaty of Campo-Formio six months later (17 October 1797). The main provisions of Leoben compelled Austria to surrender Lombardy, which would become a republic on the French model. Vienna received the mainland territories of the Republic of Venice in compensation. Venice in turn was compensated with the Papal Legations which Napoleon had taken from the Church. Austria thus retained a foothold in Italy, which guaranteed future war. The defeated Austrians reasonably assumed that the French, who already occupied much of Venetia, would find a pretext to overthrow the Venetian government. Campo-Formio additionally specified that Austria would give up Milan, and approve the creation of two republics carved out and created by Napoleon: the Ligurian Republic (centering on Genoa), and the Cisalpine Republic (composed of Milan and Milanese territory, Lombardy, the Duchy of Modena, and the Romagna). Napoleon also extracted the Ionian islands, lopping off a significant and strategically important chunk of Venetian territory. These are only highlights. The victorious Bonaparte, by conquest, had taken over French policy in Italy. Italian politics were no longer independent. His territorial and political arrangements were necessarily accepted by the Directory, which he scarcely consulted.

Between the two Italian invasions came the *triennio*, three years of attacks on French hegemony in the peninsula inaugurated when the Directory withdrew her armies. Napoleon returned to France, soon embarked on the bizarre Egyptian campaign, and Italy endured a series of uprisings, reprisals, vendettas, banditry, and near civil war that undid most of his work. At the end of May 1799 French troops held only Genoa and the Ligurian coast. Rome, which resisted until the end of September, was soon added, followed by Ancona (which held out until mid-November). On 9 November 1799 (18 Brumaire) Napoleon seized power. He prepared to recapture Italy, daringly crossed over the northern St Bernard passes, thought impossible in May, took the peninsula by surprise, and set about reconquest. He was victorious at Marengo on 14 June, largely because General Desaix disobeyed orders and returned to the battlefield when he heard the guns. He arrived around 3 p.m., declared the battle lost but insisted there was still enough daylight to launch a second battle and save the French cause. He led a cavalry charge against the Austrians on the verge of victory, and routed them. He was killed in the action. Napoleon would minimize Desaix's central role in the victory in his official communiqués to Paris, himself monopolizing the glory, but Desaix was the only general for whom the Emperor erected a monument in Paris, which still stands in the Place Dauphine, behind the law courts. By the end of June 1800 the French were again masters of much of Italy. The period of the 'thirteen months' (*treize mois*), marked by reaction, counterrevolution, and massacre, deportation or exile of the 'Italian patriots' who had fought the invaders, was over. French hegemony would last until Napoleon's fall.

Italy was Napoleon's first foreign conquest. In no other territory in his eventual empire were comparable reforms attempted. In Poland the political privileges of the nobility endured. In the German territories, despite the abolition of feudalism, the seigneurial order was untouched. In Italy he imposed the great reforms which had codified the French Revolution: the new administrative system of prefects, departments, and an all-powerful Council of State; legal reforms which, both procedural and philosophical, rested upon a system of professional, hierarchal tribunals and, after 1804 the imposition of the Civil Code and an Italian version of the religious Concordat. In France reform had been enacted by revolutionary governments after the *ancien régime* was destroyed by a series of vast popular uprisings first in Paris, then in the cities and countryside. In Italy revolutionary reform was imposed by the conqueror upon an *ancien régime* still partially intact, whose populace, whether elite or common, was still defined by habits, beliefs, and cultural assumptions and practices that were relatively untouched by the Enlightenment – in other words, a land that had not undergone a French Revolution. The reshaping and reform of Italy would become the pattern for all Napoleon's subsequent conquests. In a letter of 12 June 1805, he declared he wanted 'to Frenchify Italy'. This was no trope. Napoleon intended to impose the French Revolution on Italy in its Bonapartist form, with the people reduced to passive participation under an authoritarian, efficient government, set in motion and sustained by Paris.

Napoleon could not have attempted, let alone succeeded, had the Italian *ancien régime* not already been perforated, even hollowed out, by decay, changing attitudes, the intellectual corrosion of the Enlightenment, and indigenous reformers everywhere. Even the Italian church was cautiously modifying its Tridentine inheritance from the Counter-Reformation of the 16th and 17th centuries. Napoleon accelerated everything. He created three major geographical divisions. The kingdom of Italy, whose crown he assumed in 1805 and for which he made Eugène de Beauharnais his viceroy, stretched from the Alps in the north about halfway down the Adriatic coast, where it met the Kingdom of Naples, which was ruled first by his brother Joseph and then by his brother-in-law Marshal Murat. The so-called *départements réunis* (those attached directly to France and administered as French departments) were a string of principalities, republics, and monarchies – including Genoa, Parma, Florence, Rome, Trieste and their surrounding territories, as well as the Illyrian provinces (the Adriatic lands of the Balkans) – that were made into French departments. The three territorial blocs had, by 1814, nearly the same institutions, and economic and social structures, and were subject to the Napoleonic Codes and judicial practices (although jury trials were never introduced in Italy). There is an intense and enduring debate about the relationship between Napoleon's organization and reform of the Italian peninsula and the eventual nation of Italy forged in the later 19th century. Whatever the many details and nuances, the fact is that Napoleonic Italy provided not only a model of the new French state, but gave the peninsula the first secular unity it had enjoyed since the Roman Empire.

*****

Napoleonic nation-building did not come easily. The Italians were at best reluctant *administrés* (those administered), the contemptuous designation used by their French masters. Napoleon was neither a patient man nor one given to diplomacy, negotiation, or compromise. He made it clear to the Italians that he would brook no resistance. When counter-revolution flared up he replaced civilian authorities with the military: his satraps, generals Junot, Menou, and Miollis. They were tough, colorful, anticlerical, and utterly loyal soldiers who had embraced the French Revolution and then rallied to Napoleon. Their unique skills had been learned and honed first in the Vendée and the Midi in France where the counterrevolution resisted central control during the first years of Napoleon's Consulate, then in the first Italian campaign and in Egypt. Miollis and Menou were from aristocratic families, Junot was a Burgundian bourgeois. They were notorious for their tempers as well as for their flamboyant private lives and 'perfect for a certain phase of imperial expansion', when 'the mutinous truth of the *administré* is revealed in all its seeming savagery and guile,' writes Michael Broers, the historian of Napoleonic imperialism in Italy. They were given *carte blanche* to subdue resistance to Napoleonic rule, predominately in the hinterlands of the *départements réunis* where lawlessness prevailed, where there was literally no government and economic life was defined by smuggling and banditry. Broers has likened these regions and their mores to the American Wild West. Once order had been brutally established the military men departed and their civilian colleagues took over. Those with a republican or even a Jacobin past – Hugues Nardon, Luc-Jacques-Edouard Dauchy, and Antoine-Christophe Saliceti (Napoleon's Corsican patron from Toulon) – were a bit more austere in their personal habits than the satraps but yielded nothing to the generals in determination, ruthlessness, or even cruelty. The extirpation

PASSAGE DU MONT St BERNARD, LE 20 FLORÉAL AN 8, par ...

Figure 1 Napoleon Crossing the Alps, 20 May 1800, by Carle Vernet: Although Vernet did not accompany Napoleon he had earlier crossed the Alps and lived in Rome for a number of years. He broke with Jacques-Louis David during the Consulate over personal not political matters. This accurate depiction of the crossing stands in sharp distinction to David's famous and mythic portrait of the same event. It is probably Napoleon himself in the middle of the bridge in the foreground, with members of his staff behind.

of banditry in southern Piedmont was their most enduring achievement. It never returned. Of all the Napoleonic work in making Italy governable the conquest of the hinterlands and an efficient administration alone were welcomed by the landowners and retained.

Force had its limits. Nowhere was this more apparent than in the confrontation of Napoleon's revolution with the papacy. Napoleon shared Edward Gibbon's witty characterization of religion: 'The various modes of worship which prevailed ... were all considered by the people as equally true; by the philosopher as equally false; and by the magistrate as equally useful.' To this Enlightenment view was added the strident anticlericalism of the French Revolution and the conviction that the Church be returned to apostolic poverty by being stripped of its land and then kept firmly under the control of secular authorities. The French spurned any help from the Church, the best instrument of social control available in *ancien régime* Italy. Missions and the regular monastic orders were abolished. The practices and the moral and cultural allegiances wielded by the Church were anathema to the French, especially in their Baroque, Tridentine manifestation in Italy. The Pope responded with the only weapon he had: passive resistance.

Governments, particularly imperial and colonial governments, have proved inept and incapable when dealing with passive resistance, especially when leavened with religious conviction. Pius VII impressed all who tried to compel his submission, except Napoleon who raged about his stubbornness and guile. Even those sent to arrest Pius were struck by his highly principled and spiritual character. He wielded a unique authority, derived from God, and used it brilliantly. The passive resistance he asked of his followers disrupted the French administration of justice, undermined the imperial regime throughout the Papal States, denied Napoleon the collaborators he needed, and reached into the furthest corners of Italy. The Pope's imprisonment only strengthened the resolve of the non-violent movement. The city and *département* of Rome proved the most recalcitrant of all. The Baroque piety of Italian Catholicism, with its emotive public displays, its festivals, and the still fresh memories of the Inquisition whose authority depended on denunciation, torture, and secret proceedings which spilled over into all the legal practices in Italy, were detested by the French as superstition and tyranny. The revolutionary mission was to bring to benighted Europe the light of reason that already shone in France. Catholicism, for the French, infected important facets of Italian legal culture which 'were genuinely alien ... and utterly inadmissible in an imperium rooted in the legal precepts of 1789, reinforced by the binding focus of the Civil Code after 1804'.

Less obvious but equally obnoxious to the new rulers were Italian social mores. The public sphere, the direct concern of administration, was riddled for the French occupiers with behavior, beliefs, and habits that they found detestable: Italian frivolity, sexual laxity, and cruelty. We are here speaking only of the elites. Even those who wanted to collaborate, who saw the French as the only force that could compel Italian reform, break the power of the nobility and patriciate, and check the authority of the Church, found themselves spurned. The overwhelming majority of the prefects and their staffs were French. The new judges appointed from the local legal elites were thought mostly incompetent and needed to be carefully monitored. The elites who had rallied to the French were kept at a safe distance from positions of power. They too were only *administrés*. French imperialism in Italy centered on two principles: *raillement*, rallying to Napoleon, and *amalgam*, integration into the French system. There were many who rallied but only the French enthusiasts were able successfully to integrate. Those in the conquered lands were effectively excluded by distrust, bias, chauvinism, and the arrogance of the victors. The French Revolution was the determining factor. From the first days of the Revolution there were nobles and churchmen who joined the Revolution. A number of them later became Jacobins. Some were later purged. Napoleon inherited many rallied nobles, generals Miollis and Menou, already mentioned, among them. The Italians who rallied appeared opportunists, men infected with the same disabilities, superstitions, and mores as were the more repellant *administrés*. It was not, Michael Broers argues, the Italian elites who sought to rally to Napoleon who were at fault, but their French masters who would not embrace them. In these circumstances integration became impossible.

Officially the French had no desire to create a subaltern Italian colony. Until he was overthrown Napoleon's policy remained inclusiveness, a sharp difference from the imperialisms of later empires. He wanted to transform, to revolutionize Italy. Taxes and troops would continue to be extracted. In all else, at least in theory, the *départements réunis* and their citizens would be equal partners of the Napoleonic empire. The work of the French Revolution remained to be finished. Old battles had still to be fought, but now on foreign soil. The weapons would not be those that made the Revolution, popular insurrection, unruly representative bodies, street politics, emergency governments, and the Terror. The past would be undone by fiat, the *ancien régime* replaced by new machinery: the laws and procedures embodied in the Civil Code and sustained by a tight regulation of society. Given time the laws, as Lycurgus had insisted and Napoleon believed, would change men's mores. Laws would regenerate Italy. Napoleon ran out of time. He also launched a process that was inherently flawed. Whatever were the advantages and benefits of *raillement* and *amalgam* they were the spawn of force. Once French force, maintained by occupation, was removed, those who had rallied and tried to integrate found themselves exposed as collaborators who paid the traditional price of clients abandoned by their patrons. The old elites resumed power and carefully cut away the gangrened flesh of innovation and reform; but not entirely. The Ligurians kept the justices of the peace, civil tribunals, and criminal and appeal courts. They made sure that these structures were manned not by professionals but by 'the most distinguished citizens'. Even a good deal of the Civil Code was retained, with all the French legislation on marriage and divorce excised. So too was the equal division of property among heirs. The reactionary monarchy of Savoy, 'even in its most virulent, early moments', retained French tax officials and replaced the French Gendarmerie with their own version of provincial police, the Carabiniere Reale. The Revolution was rejected, efficiency was retained.

IV
Egypt

Napoleon's imperiousness and cultural politics did not allow for nicely nuanced political alliances with Directory politicians. When the hero returned from Italy all the lawyers he despised courted him. La Réveillière-Lépeaux invited him to an intimate family dinner to discuss his future. Napoleon later told Las Cases he found the three members of the family 'masterpieces of ugliness'. Barras and Sieyès also sought to charm (and use) him. All miscalculated his political savvy. Soon after his appointment as commander of the army assembling at Boulogne to invade England, a project many knew to be impossible, Napoleon wrote the Directors: 'To attempt an invasion of England without mastery of the sea is the most challenging and difficult undertaking that has ever been done.' He went on to detail all the resources he would need, and if his ample list could not be fulfilled 'we should abandon any expedition to England, contenting ourselves with maintaining the appearance of [an invasion] ... and fix all our attention on ... the Rhine'. Then he proposed, almost in passing, the possibility of an expedition to Egypt. A few weeks later he sent the Directors a detailed breakdown of the men and matériel he would need, and by the end of March he was making comprehensive plans, including gathering and packing moveable type (in Arabic characters, as well as Greek). Propaganda was always part of Napoleon's war train.

The constitution of 1795 stipulated that one be 40 to be a Director. An attempt to revise it to make room for Napoleon, who was only 28, had failed. The constitution further stipulated that it could not be changed without overcoming insuperable barriers. Any revision had to be ratified by both legislative chambers three times, at intervals of three years. After this nine-year period if revision was again voted by a majority it had to be ratified by a special assembly called for this purpose, and approved

CONQUETE DE L' ÉGYPTE, PAR LES FRANÇAIS.
en Messidor, an 6°

Figure 2   Napoleon's Ships in the Alexandria Harbor. A contemporary anonymous lithograph of Napoleon's armada soon after its arrival in Egypt and before anchoring in Aboukir Bay. The celebrated lighthouse is clearly visible and the details of rigging as well as the long boats ferrying soldiers ashore are accurate.

by the thousands of primary electoral assemblies. This left only two options: graceful withdrawal or a *coup d'état.* Napoleon was not ready for the former and judged, correctly, that the time was not yet ripe for the latter. He had backed the *coup d'état* of Fructidor (4 September 1797), sending General Augereau, who had excellent republican *bona fides,* to Paris as his proxy. He had also played a leading role in the Congress of Raastat, demonstrating his diplomatic and political skills. But he still had his way to make in the world. Even with the brilliant Italian victories he was not supreme in the army, where generals Moreau and Masséna remained more influential. He had turned down command in the Vendéan civil war, which he rightly saw as a potential graveyard for his ambitions. Killing domestic rebels was inglorious. He turned his back on Parisian politics for the more agreeable life of the camp.

With Talleyrand he proposed a bold, unconventional plan. The invasion of Egypt would disrupt Britain's lifeline to India as well as control the eastern Mediterranean. The conventional view is that the Directory readily granted Napoleon's request for an expedition to Egypt in order to be rid of the hugely popular and ambitious general. The Directory may have been filled with greedy, unscrupulous, and intransigent men but they were not so foolish as to deprive France of a substantial army at a critical time in their war with Europe to humor a threatening general bent on a romantic quest for more glory. The Directory demonstrated surprising vitality in raising an army for conquest, assembling the armada that would carry it to Egypt, and paying substantial sums for scientific instruments that were the best then available for the nearly 150 *savants* who would accompany the expedition. By Napoleon's count they provided 24,300 infantry, 4000 cavalry, 3000 artillerymen, and 1000 non-combatants, which included the *savants*. His reckoning was a bit low: 38,000 men sailed from Toulon. The Directors prepared the Egyptian expedition in record time, outfitted the troops and the fleet according to Napoleon's desires, and assembled them all in Toulon with remarkable efficiency and relative secrecy. The English had only the vaguest suspicion of what revolutionary France would do next. However encumbered by the contradictions of their republican and revolutionary faiths and a desperate need of money the Thermidorians were capable of mounting a major military expedition.

The French fleet – 13 warships, six frigates, one corvette, and 35 additional ships of various descriptions and tonnage, plus over 300 transports – eased out of Toulon harbor on 19 May 1798, several days behind the original timetable. Napoleon blamed General Bernadotte for the postponed start but the delay proved a blessing. The following day the flagship, the mighty *l'Orient* carrying 118 guns, set sail with Admiral Brueys d'Aigalliers and Napoleon aboard. Admiral Horatio Nelson was searching the Mediterranean for the French. The enemies literally passed in the night off Toulon. Vivant Denon, who would become Napoleon's commissar of art, described how he stood silently on the deck, with many of his compatriots, as the British sailed past them in the fog. The crossing, first to Malta and then Egypt, proceeded without a hitch. The French reached Alexandria on 1 July, having paused long enough to seize Malta from the knights of St John, a medieval military order. Admiral Brueys, who did not like the look of the Egyptian coast, advised they disembark the following day. Napoleon dismissed these reservations, as he would all Brueys' counsel. The admiral, so the story goes, prophetically said as he parted from Napoleon: 'Fortune has abandoned me.'

In Egypt as in Europe Napoleon posed as a liberator, the agent of the French Revolution that had broken the chains of the *ancien régime*. His assertions resonated quite differently on the other side of the

Mediterranean. Napoleon declared he had come to liberate the Egyptians from the corrupt and despotic rule of the Mamelukes, originally kidnapped Christian slaves who were made into a warrior caste by the Ottoman Turks. He proclaimed his tolerance of Islam, insisted he meant the Egyptians neither harm nor persecution. He assured the Sultan in Constantinople that his sovereignty over Egypt would not be compromised. None of this was believed. The Egyptian chronicler Al-Jabarti analyzed the first French proclamations of liberation carefully. A member of the patriciate, the sophisticated and well-educated Al-Jabarti found the French command of Arabic pitiful. The original French had been translated into Arabic by a Maltese whose dialect was despised by classically educated Arabic speakers. Not only were the proclamations full of grammatical gaffs that a modern orientalist has likened to the contrast between Oxbridge English and Cockney, but much was unintelligible to the Egyptians. Worse yet, the proclamations were theologically dubious and impolitic. 'As for his statement, "and destroyed the Papal See",' Al-Jabarti wrote:

> ... by this deed they have gone against the Christians as has already been pointed out. So those people are opposed to both Christians and Muslims, and do not hold fast to any religion. You see they are materialists, who deny all God's attributes, the Hereafter and Resurrection, and who reject Prophethood and Messengership.

The invaders 'had rebelled against their sultan six years ago and killed him'. Revolutionary France's achievements were anathema to the Muslims.

Napoleon made every effort to win the support of the Egyptians. He established the *Diwan* as a new court system administered by Egyptians, but then used it to examine titles of property and assess new taxes. He had ignorantly assumed that Egypt would be an even richer Italy systematically to be extorted. In fact, as Pierre Branda has shown, the country was not even able to sustain the costs of Napoleon's army let alone provide the fabulous wealth he imagined. 'The cost of the Army of the Orient,' he calculates, 'was about 22 million francs a year. The net revenue of Egypt under the Mamelukes probably did not exceed 10 million. They had to innovate.' Innovation is a euphemism for legal rapine. Far from winning the hearts and minds of the Egyptians Napoleon forced them, under the tutelage of French bureaucrats, to extract every *sou* that could be found. He refused to believe, as later in Spain he refused to believe, that the country was not rich. The Egyptians were deviously, cunningly, even criminally denying the French what they needed. The cultural imperialism of the conqueror was as resented as his fiduciary tyranny. The French world of rationalism, scientific faith, secularism, technological superiority, and the Rights of Man, along with distrust of religion and metaphysics, held no attraction for Islamic Egypt. The invader was a layman and an Infidel. Napoleon's opinions about the Arabs were generally those of the Enlightenment. They were the transmitters of the knowledge of antiquity to Renaissance Europe which was now being returned with interest. The Egyptians saw their history as genealogy, the filiation of the various tribes as they descended from The Prophet. Their beliefs, their laws, their glorious past and their language, the language of the Koran which was the word of God, needed no European intermediary. In a short time negotiations broke down and the French resorted to force and oppression. Here was the true face of France and the Revolution: infidel extortion by force, a modern-day version of the Crusades.

Napoleon first saw the great pyramids on 20 July. His *Campagnes d'Egypte et de Syrie* is strangely silent. He detailed over many pages the Egyptian irrigation system, the annual flooding of the Nile, the possibilities of a canal across the isthmus, but one of the wonders of the ancient world remains uncelebrated. The next day Napoleon faced Ibrahim Bey with 100,000 men to the latter's 25,000. He easily won the fabulous Battle of the Pyramids where the brilliantly caparisoned Mamelukes fatally charged a modern European army:

> The sun, reflected off the helmets and mail of the Mamelukes [he later wrote] made this handsome army glitter in all its *éclat*. ... The Mameluke displays all his imposing self and his courage and excites our admiration. He is bound to his horse which appears to share all his passion. His saber hangs from the pommel, he fires his carbine, he launches his hand bomb, fires his four pistols, and after having discharged his six firearms he rides through his troops with marvelous dexterity.

All the glory of his brilliant victory at the Pyramids could neither erase nor blunt the personal misery that overwhelmed him when on 19 July he learned, from General Junot, of Josephine's flamboyant affair with Captain Louis-Hippolyte Charles. He was crushed and in despair:

> I am overwhelmed with domestic sorrow because the veil has been completely lifted [he lamented to his brother Joseph]. Only you, on

the entire earth, remain for me. Your friendship is so dear to me. For me to become a misanthrope all that is needed is to lose you and see myself betrayed! ... I hope to pass the winter buried in the country-side ... I need solitude and isolation. Grandeur bores me, emotion is dried up, glory is insipid. At 29 I am worn out. All that remains for me is to become a complete egoist ... Adieu, my only friend. I have never been unjust to you.

The letter never reached Joseph. It was intercepted by the English who captured the French ship carrying Napoleon's correspondence along with a treasure-trove of intelligence. They immediately published his *cri de cœur* to the world.

There are few glimpses of Napoleon's inner life. He did not much dwell in introspection. He almost immediately began an affair with the wife of one of his officers out of jealousy and spite, posting the cuckold miles away. He loved Josephine, as his extravagant and often vulgarly explicit love letters testify. There would be a reconciliation upon his return to France, but something had broken and his unedited passion would never again be expressed to her. Jean Tulard has suggested, perhaps a bit cynically, that the world of the Directory was dominated by women. Napoleon needed her and she proved invaluable. Josephine knew the powerful political personnel as her husband did not. She correctly analyzed Barras's reactions to Napoleon's *coup d'état* and neutralized Louis-Jérôme Gohier, the director who was most hostile to Napoleon's ambitions. Josephine's betrayal was a shock, a deep disillusionment. The possible loss of her political connections probably played a small part in his pain. The external manifestation of his anguish, Henry Laurens speculates, may have been an increase in cruelty. Henceforth the Egyptian campaign would be punctuated with acts of extreme and willful cruelty. Here, directed against an alien culture and religion, was a release of the misanthropy he confessed to Joseph.

He had not much time to surrender to misery. On 1 August Nelson and the English fleet found the French at Aboukir Bay, after four months of searching. They were anchored in a line close to shore, under the protection of the guns in Aboukir Castle and the dangerous shoals that created a defensive pocket where the fleet had safely and complacently harbored for weeks. When Nelson's ships came into view, at 4 p.m., many French crews were ashore getting water. Admiral Brueys was taken by surprise but he thought it too late in the day for action. He ordered his ships to be ready to weigh anchor on a moment's notice and to remain where they were. Nelson, audacious, self-confident, unorthodox, the Napoleon of the sea, had no intention of waiting till the next day when the French could position themselves for attack. His brilliantly executed plan was to sail directly at the French squadron, deftly skirting the shoals that provided protection for Napoleon's fleet – the *Culloden* ran aground making the turn – and then, dividing his warships into two main lines, begin at the head of the French line, taking on the ships one at a time, from both sides, as he made his way down the line. Nelson's plan called for exact maneuvering on the English side, exceptional self-confidence to fight from dusk into darkness – the attack began at 6:30 p.m. and lasted till midnight – and precise gunnery. The fight raged on until sometime after 9 p.m. when the *Alexander* and the *Swiftsure* set the massive *Orient* afire. It became a floating inferno endangering all the ships downwind. Admiral Brueys had his legs taken off by a cannon ball when his flagship was attacked. His sailors propped him up against a bag of barley, tied tourniquets around his legs, and Brueys, in surgical shock, fought on with two pistols. The fire on the *Orient* burned its way down to the ammunition magazine and blew the ship to smithereens. Napoleon's stateroom, containing the gilded billiard table which the old Jacobins in the expedition mocked, along with all the scientific instruments of the expedition, was destroyed. The British rescued only 14 French survivors. Another 50 or so reached shore. More than 1000 went down with the ship, including the mortally wounded Brueys. Witnesses described the grisly flotsam and jetsam of body parts, torn limbs sticking out of the sand, and pieces of bloody clothing strewn across the beach. The British triumph went beyond victory, which 'is not a name strong enough for such a scene', said Nelson. He had obliterated the French Mediterranean fleet. Napoleon was marooned in Egypt.

By any military measure the Egyptian campaign was a failure. Napoleon lost the Mediterranean fleet at Aboukir Bay, his army could neither be reinforced nor evacuated. When he returned secretly to France the army, filled with veterans of the Italian campaign and riven by plague, was abandoned and not repatriated until 1801. The catastrophe additionally signaled the end of any serious French challenge to English superiority at sea, definitively sealed at Trafalgar a few years later. The destruction of his fleet sent Napoleon into the Biblical lands. He was thwarted at the siege of Acre, which he lifted in humiliation after 63 fruitless and deadly days, marked by eight failed assaults. The suffering of his troops, beyond their defeat, surpassed anything they had previously endured. Napoleon's forced marches across the desert, which displayed the force of his will, were achieved at terrible cost. The great confrontation between revolutionary France and the declining

Ottoman Empire left no significant legacy. The Mamelukes were driven from power, but the Ottomans, with whom France was officially at peace when Napoleon invaded, held Egypt until 1918. Napoleon accelerated Egyptian political disintegration by sweeping away the ruling Mameluke beys, demonstrating how ineffectual were Egyptian and Ottoman forces in a battle with a European army. He showed Egypt, in the most brutal manner imaginable, that profound changes were needed: he did nothing to achieve those changes. Measured as an episode in carrying the Revolution outside Europe, the Egyptian campaign was also disastrous. The Napoleonic imperial model, first tried in Italy, failed completely in Egypt. He would tolerate no social dislocation and had no more interest in freeing the *fellahin* than he would later show in breaking up the Spanish latifundia or liberating the Russian serfs. The Egyptian local elites would be empowered, under French guidance and supervision, to provide an interface with the local population. Muslim law would be allowed and administered so long as it did not interfere with French dominance. Such, at least, was the theory. It all came to naught. Napoleon's reforms derived from the Revolution worked only in France, for the simple reason that only there had there been a revolution from below driving reform articulated and instituted by the bourgeoisie. Only in France had there been social upheaval, new fault lines created, old habits and institutions destroyed. Everywhere else, whether in Europe or North Africa, Napoleon's transformations, applied, enforced, and sustained by the army, remained dependent upon force. Once removed the reforms collapsed. Muslim society retained no traces of the French Revolution.

*****

Napoleon blamed Admiral Brueys for the loss of the fleet, although he had forced the admiral to anchor at Aboukir Bay. On 19 August when he understood the scope of the Aboukir disaster he wrote to the Directory. On 18 Messidor (6 July) he had told them 'I left Alexandria' and 'I wrote to the Admiral telling him to enter the harbor within twenty four hours; and if his squadron could not anchor there to unload promptly all the artillery and all the supplies for the army, and to sail to Corfu'. The Admiral would need only six hours, Napoleon mistakenly insisted, to sail into Alexandria's harbor. None of this was true. Napoleon did not leave Alexandria until 7 July and there were no orders sent to Brueys. Napoleon goes on: 'I received several letters from the Admiral, where I saw with astonishment that he was still at Aboukir Bay. I immediately wrote him to impress upon him that he could not lose another hour to enter the harbor or sail to Corfu.' This too is false.

Napoleon included Vice-Admiral Villeneuve in his accusation. Villeneuve had stood aside from the battle awaiting orders from Brueys, which never came. When, on St Helena, Napoleon dictated his *Campagnes d'Egypte et de Syrie* he added the detail that Brueys disobeyed a direct order by remaining at anchor in Aboukir Bay. He elaborates that he immediately sent a Captain Julien with orders to board the flagship, and not leave until he had personally seen the fleet enter Alexandria harbor or set sail for Corfu (or Toulon). Julien, alas, was captured and killed by a party of rogue Arabs near the town of Al'qâm and never reached the fleet, nor have his supposed orders survived. The battle of Aboukir Bay was lost in Napoleon's account 'by the negligence of the captains of the *Guerrier* and the *Conquérant* and the accident [the explosion] of *l'Orient* and the bad conduct of Vice Admiral Villeneuve. Brueys,' he continues, in a moving eulogy, 'showed the greatest courage. Wounded several times, he refused to go below. He died on his quarter deck, and with his final breath ordered an attack.' This part of the account, however gallant, reports facts Napoleon could not have known. He disparages Nelson's 'desperate plan of action' that would not have succeeded had the French squadron not shown so much 'ineptitude and pusillanimity'. Later, as First Consul, Napoleon edited the official record by inserting the fabricated direct orders to Brueys later reported in *Campagnes d'Egypte et de Syrie*. This was the first of several Napoleonic exculpatory exercises by a man who could not accept blame for his mistakes: he also commanded Clio.

News of the French defeat stirred up a restless Cairo to rebellion. This was not the first or the last conquered city to resist revolutionary 'liberation'. When Milan rose in rebellion Napoleon took severe measures. He summarily shot anyone taken with arms, stormed the city and turned it over to his troops for six hours of uncontrolled pillage, which General Marmont described as 'complete'. Venice was similarly punished for rebellion, as would be Madrid (although Napoleon himself was not present). In Cairo too Napoleon was pitiless:

> Shall we be the playthings of some hordes of vagabonds, of these Arabs whom one barely counts among the civilized peoples, and of the populace of Cairo, the most brutish and savage rogues who exist in the world?

His vehemence knew no check when he called down damnation on any who would thwart his will. The street fighting began on 20 October and lasted two days. The French gave no quarter. Artillery, loaded with grapeshot and canister (a smaller and more lethal version of grapeshot) for its murderous impact at close range, was especially deadly in the narrow streets of Cairo. Mobile columns drove the rioters into the mosques, where they were captured or slaughtered. If Al-Jabarti is accurate, the uprising was popular in nature, involving only a few Sheikhs (whom the French executed out of public view). The patrician author was horrified at the desecration of the great mosque of Al-Azhar. The French rode into the sacred building and tied their horses to the *qibla*. The foot soldiers behaved 'like mountain goats':

> They sacked the rooms, smashed the lamps and destroyed the lamp posts, they smashed the cases that held the books of the students, the pensioners of the mosque, and the public scribes. They carried off everything they found – plates, vases, and whatever was in the cupboards. They scattered the pages of the Koran and tramped them underfoot. They befouled the mosque with their excrement, urine, and phlegm. They drank bottles of wine which they smashed when empty .... if they ran into anyone they stripped him and chased him.

Hundreds of prisoners were taken. Any Arab captured with weapons was summarily condemned to death. In the citadel the prisoners were shot by firing squad. For more than a week after the insurrection, as many as 30 a day were still being executed. Overall more than 3000 Egyptians died in the uprising by Napoleon's 'rigorous justice'. General Charles Dugua, in charge of the executions, persuaded his commander that it would be economical to replace the firing squads with decapitation. The French used the local hangman for the work – they had not brought a guillotine with them – and the bodies were dumped into the Nile. This grisly evidence was the only information the Cairenes had of the extent and savagery of Napoleon's 'rigorous justice'. The Egyptian campaign was not different in kind from the Italian. French (and European) armies of the day were brutal and Napoleon was uninterested in moderating this aspect of war. Yet some of the episodes in Egypt starkly stand out for their savagery. At Jaffa, where he arrived on 3 March 1799 and met stubborn resistance, he laid siege to the town. After three days of careful preparations General Lannes led a successful assault. Three thousand Turks in the citadel surrendered to Napoleon's *aides de camp* (including Eugène de Beauharnais, his stepson) who granted them quarter. Napoleon ordered the Turks massacred along with an additional 1400 prisoners, some of them taken at El Arish.

In his own account of the massacre he argues 'they had thus violated their sworn oath' by again taking up arms. As for the defenders of the town, who had violated no oaths, Napoleon offered the sophistry that his *aides de camp* had no authority to grant quarter. Besides, duping the defenders into surrender saved numerous French lives by avoiding a street fight. He would later add that the killing was necessary because he had no food for the hapless victims. He then turned the town over to his troops for a day of riotous looting, which added considerably to the body count, not to mention a catalogue of rape, terror, and arson.

It was at Jaffa that the French army first became exposed to the plague. There were 300 cases of the dread disease, and when Napoleon left Jaffa only 36 men remained alive. These poor wretches were left behind with enough opium to take their own lives. Napoleon later explained the euthanasia as a defense against the torture the Turks were believed to inflict on the wounded and dying. General Bertrand records his master's *apologia*, and adds that had it been 'my wife or my son, I would have acted the same way'. The horrors of the plague, not seen in Europe for nearly a century, stirred the same fear in the French army the disease had caused since its 14th-century appearance in Europe. Napoleon, in a brilliant and foolhardy gesture that proclaims his conceit of immortality as well as his genius for the stunning gesture, tried to banish fear by exposing himself to the disease. He visited the plague victims in Jaffa and even touched an exploded buboes – the pustules that formed in the lymph nodes under the arm or in the groin – without contracting the fatal disease. The episode would be painted some years later by Baron Gros. It was presented at the Salon of 1804 and Napoleon paid a record price for the canvas celebrating his courage. The horrors of the Jaffa massacres, he hoped, would vanish behind the powerful image of the general as healer, a kind of later-day thaumaturgic king whose touch could cure. The pity and benevolence he displayed in the pest house of Jaffa did not long endure. 'The Turks,' he lectured General Menou as he ordered him to take over the port city of Rosetta, 'can only be led by the greatest severity'. 'Every day I cut off five or six heads in the streets of Cairo. We had to manage them up to the present in such a way as it is necessary to take a tone that will cause them to obey; and to obey, for them, is to fear.' By Turks he meant all Muslims. He had resorted to the politics of the Mamelukes.

On the eve of the land battle of Aboukir, his most important Egyptian victory, he told General Murat he had decided to return to France. Miot de Melito was a witness to this conversation and vouches for its accuracy. He did not discuss what might happen if he lost at Aboukir.

Victory would assure France the possession of Egypt. His first boast proved correct, the second mistaken. The land battle of Aboukir gave the French a respite but capitulation was inevitable unless the British blockade could be broken: impossible without his navy. At best the battle at Aboukir spared Napoleon the humiliation of signing the eventual surrender. Within days he transferred command to General Kléber, the most republican of French commanders, who did his duty with diligence and reluctance, until he was assassinated by a Muslim fanatic. Kléber learned of Napoleon's departure and his own elevation by letter. His known distaste for the savage work in Egypt had kept him out of Napoleon's confidence. Flushed with victory, Napoleon arranged to send a messenger to France to carry the news, which reached Marseille on 25 September. The victory at Aboukir was everywhere known by 4 October. Napoleon was once again the victorious general, the hero. Less than a week after the news of victory Napoleon himself landed at Fréjus, with his entourage and a number of *savants*. He disdained quarantine and immediately set out for Paris, where he arrived on 16 October, enthusiastically cheered all along the route. The Directors continued to misread the man they thought would save them by serving them. 'I will arrive in Paris,' he told General Menou, before he left Egypt, as they walked along the beach 'soaked by the splashing sea', and 'I will chase out this bunch of lawyers who mock us and who are incapable of governing the Republic, and I will put myself at the head of the government'. He was as good as his word.

'Great reputations,' Napoleon once remarked, 'are made only in the Orient; Europe is too small.' The lure of a great Oriental empire was an illusion that stayed with him for a lifetime. Like a catch in a rhyme Egypt and the Orient reappeared in his conversations. 'I was truly free only in Egypt,' he later told Jean-Antoine Chaptal, his minister of the interior. When he dictated his *Campagnes d'Egypte et de Syrie* on St Helena he included a careful enumeration of just how many troops, what kinds of troops, what kind of weaponry, how many animals – horses, mules, camels – he would need to conquer sub-Saharan Africa then march through the Biblical lands to Constantinople, and on to the Indus valley of India, following in Alexander the Great's footsteps. He had originally thought of Egypt in terms of a colony of France, an outpost of the French Revolution, although this is not his vocabulary. The French would occupy the country, rule it, impose the achievements of the Revolution, establish a religious rapprochement with the Muslims, rationalize the tax and legal systems, establish schools, and permanently disrupt British trade in the Levant and with India. He achieved none of this. When he first contemplated the invasion of Egypt he rightly concluded that there was ferment in the Middle East, specifically in Egyptian society, that the hold of the Ottomans was feeble, and that a French invasion, bringing the benefits of the Revolution to the region, would be relatively easy. Egyptian society was indeed fraught with clamor for change, but no infidel was wanted to effect this change. Egypt's problems and those of the Middle East immediately dropped from Napoleon's concern once he sailed for Europe. Egypt returned to his fantasy life, his imagination of things he would do if he had time. Later, on St Helena, Egypt provided a return to the hopefulness and illusions of his young manhood, an increasingly important refuge from the miseries and despair of his island imprisonment.

V
Power

'What I find difficult, even impossible,' Roederer, a shrewd contemporary observer, told Napoleon when asked about the plans for a *coup d'état*, 'is that it will not succeed, because it is already three-quarters accomplished.' He was right: circumstances made another *coup* inevitable. Only the personnel and timing remained unfixed. By 1799 the army, as Howard Brown has shown, was entrenched in the political life of the Republic. The statistics are impressive. Not since the early years of Louis XIV's reign had the army been so important in imposing the state's authority. They had dramatically intervened in the Paris uprising of Prairial (20–21 May 1795), the destruction of a royalist mob attack on the Convention Assembly on 13 Vendémiaire (5 October 1795), the *coup d'état* of 18 Fructidor (4 September 1797) with its bloody aftermath, and then on 18 Brumaire. Napoleon was instrumental in the last three of these actions.

All of France was divided into military districts and there were some 70 generals, about a fourth of those on active duty, who commanded. Each had the authority to proclaim a state of siege and take over an unruly town or district. By the time of Napoleon's *coup d'état* 40 per cent of the country was under the jurisdiction of generals and more than 200 communes saw the civilian police power pass to army commanders. Robespierre had always distrusted and feared the generals. He was a suspicious man and his politics pivoted on his cast of mind. As with much else his suspicions proved correct; only his timing was off. The generals were a threat to the Revolution. From the debates on declaring war in early 1792, till the end of his revolutionary career he warned against giving power to the generals of the *ancien régime*, nobles from military families great and small whose allegiance to the Revolution was suspect. From May 1793 to July 1794 20 generals were executed, some with cause, some not. Robespierre was not alone in his suspicions or his fears of the military in politics. Well before 18 Brumaire the two most celebrated and important generals of the Revolution, Lafayette and Dumouriez, had fled after they failed to seize power. By Napoleon's day the generals were being courted by civilian leaders.

The Thermidorian governments inherited a war and the contradictions it posed for a government whose legitimacy rested uneasily on a parliamentary *coup d'état* against an emergency government (the Committee of Public Safety dominated by Robespierre) operating under a suspended constitution. The overthrow of Robespierre and the eventual abolition of the Terror, the Committee of Public Safety, and much of the machinery of emergency government, as well as the punishment of several notorious terrorists, did not create the long-desired republic of liberal ideas and democratic practices. In theory the Thermidorian government was civilian and constitutional. In practice the generals were given or took more and more power. The militarization of the Republic was not dramatically accomplished through an army *coup*. From 18 Brumaire until 1802 Napoleon carefully presented himself as head of a civilian government, despite his repression in the countryside. After 1802 he kept the army and the generals away from the levers of power. Their irresistible power lay outside France and Napoleon was careful to keep it there. The soldiers and generals were amply rewarded but it was the 'masses of granite', Napoleon's metaphor for the civilian notables upon whom he rested his government, who ruled. His was not, in any meaningful sense, a military dictatorship. Before Napoleon, however, a concatenation of crises, exacerbated by the war and internecine political strife, made it impossible for the Thermidorian governments to let their new constitution function without exceptional military interference. The grain harvests could not be protected from pillage without army escort and the rule of law could not prevail until substantial areas of France were subdued. Efficient centralization eluded the government. The roads, where brigandage flourished, often on a huge scale, were unsafe. Even when free of danger travel was maddeningly slow. It took 15 days to go from Paris to Pau, in the Pyrénées, for example. The country had to be conquered. The savage mopping up of the rebellion and civil war in the Vendée was the most blatant policing Napoleon launched. Elsewhere he strove to camouflage the naked face of military might. The *gendarmerie*, a national police who were a branch of the army, was under partial civilian command. The National Guard, which dated back to the first years of the Revolution, was still intact, although its strength and effectiveness varied from place to place. The military courts were very complex but much used because of their efficiency achieved by shortcuts through civilian procedure. They often deferred to civilian courts rather than supplant the rule of law and bully local notables. Napoleon made sure the generals did not use their courts as a springboard for political ambitions, but civilian authorities had increasingly to negotiate with the military over jurisdiction. Nearly a quarter of the generals on active duty held domestic postings and *de facto* often governed the provinces. Paris too felt the ubiquity of the army. Soon after the rioting of 12–13 Germinal year III (1–2 April 1795) came the insurrection of 1–2 Prairial (20–21 June 1795). The line army was permanently brought back to the city.

When Louis XVII, the young son of Louis XVI, died in custody (8 June 1795) politics abruptly changed. The remaining Bourbons, the future Louis XVIII and his more reactionary brother the Count d'Artois, were intransigent and would accept no compromise with the revolutionary Republic. They had, as a wit said, 'learned nothing and forgotten nothing'. But theirs was more than ideological stubbornness. The majority of the Thermidorians, who had sat in the Convention, voted for the king's death, and had Louis XVI's blood on their hands. Napoleon was untainted. The royalists sounded him out. Would he be the French General Monk, the soldier who had returned the Stuarts to the English throne in the 1660 revolution? If so Louis XVIII would consent to reign under the white Bourbon flag: not otherwise. Briefly, with the royalist victories in the elections of Fructidor, it looked as if the Bourbons needed no counterrevolutionary general. They might legally come to power. Then, with Napoleon's aid, the elections were quashed by a *coup d'état* and the royalist deputies expelled. The surprising popular strength of the Bourbon cause initiated a purge of administrative personnel, especially in the provinces. Many knelt before military firing squads in the Fructidorian Terror. Jacobin challenges to the Republic were also destroyed and two state trials – of the Babouvists, the conspiratorial followers of Gracchus Babeuf, and the so-called Martyrs of Prairial, the remaining radical Jacobin deputies in the Convention – deprived the extreme left and the Jacobins of their leaders. The Thermidorians, challenged from right and left, instinctively treated criticism as the foreshadowing of rebellion, or the renewal of *chouannerie*, the guerrilla war in the west. The sporadic but chronic violence in the southeast caused the government to turn increasingly to the army. Preserving the Republic trumped constitutionalism. The dilemma of the Thermidorian governments, as Howard Brown points out, was that 'continued aggression abroad spelled continued coercion at home' which in turn increased hatred of the government and reliance on the army. When the first Directory assumed office the Republic had suffered serious military reverses, the civil war in western France had reignited, and the financial crisis had brought the military supply system to near collapse. They responded with a series of fierce revolutionary exactions, including a huge forced loan and an equally huge levy on horses. Government resting on some kind of broadly embraced legitimacy and articulated in the rule of law remained out of reach.

The political clubs and revolutionary mobs that had dominated the Revolution were now gone. So too were the most notorious terrorists and the emergency government they had served. Conspiracy and factions were not. Elections had been ignored before Thermidor. Now they were quashed. Parliamentary oratory no longer determined who would lead the Revolution and the great factions, Girondins and Jacobins, were no longer either organized or coherent. A number of the former had returned to France after Robespierre's fall. A number of the latter remained, although frozen out of politics. The political world of the Revolution was contracted to a small republican elite which appeared increasingly unable to sustain itself. The Thermidorian Republic had become a government of the center, with increasingly less popular support. The *coups d'état* stood in for constitutional change. Each was followed by a shuffling of the directors and administrative and governmental personnel and some change in the political compass. The Second Coalition of France's enemies had driven them out of Italy, forced the army back from the Rhine, and General Masséna had had to evacuate eastern Switzerland. Victories in September momentarily gave the Republic breathing space, but the military situation was precarious when Napoleon landed from Egypt (9 October) and reached Paris (22 October).

The abbé Sieyès was there to stir the pot. Of the many significant men of the Revolution, a great event without great men (until Napoleon), as François Furet has said, the abbé Sieyès was the most durable but far from the most attractive figure. His pamphlet, *Qu'est- ce que le Tiers Etat? (What is the Third Estate?)* was the most cogent, most radical, and clearest articulation of the ideology of the Revolution. His call to exclude the privileged orders, the clergy and the nobility, from the new state had some responsibility for the ideology of the Terror. From political exclusion to Terror proved a short step, although it took nearly four years to take. He was also the man who convinced the Third Estate, in the first weeks of the Revolution, to transform itself into a body to be called the National Assembly and thus assume representation of the entire nation, with or without the privileged orders. Then his influence waned. His laconic explanation of what he did during the Terror – 'I survived' – is often quoted, as is his chilling vote in the king's trial: 'Death. Without more words' (*la mort, sans phrase*) but he played no major role in the nearly two years of the Jacobin Republic.

Sieyès survived more than the Terror. He is one of the few to have been present at the Revolution's birth and at the death of the Republic. For the Thermidorians he was the great constitutional expert, ever fruitful in creating documents that would sustain the wobbly government after each jolt of ambition or crisis, and give it paper legitimacy. His personality was without warmth. He might inspire admiration but never affection. Talleyrand, another ex-priest, was one of many who disliked Sieyès:

> What Sieyès calls a principle [he wrote] is in his hands an iron scepter which yielded neither to the imperfections nor the weaknesses of human nature ... In his eyes men were pieces on a chess board ... When he made a constitution he treated the country for which it was destined as a place where the inhabitants had never felt or seen anything before.

Marie-Antoine Baudot, an old regicide who lived long enough to see the Revolution of 1830 and the first seven years of Louis-Philippe's reign, was similarly hostile:

> He [Sieyès] seemed to be uttering a confidence when he said hello. His obscure sentences had to be thought about to be understood, and because he was glacial to his auditors they themselves had the impression that they were in a state of being contemplated.

Complementing his icy reserve was a suspicious nature bordering on paranoia and occasionally crossing that permeable frontier. He ended his days in retirement and instructed his servant to refuse admittance to Robespierre, then long dead, should he come calling. To his penchant for sibylline utterances was added notorious avarice and an exceptionally thin skin. When Napoleon, making the rounds of the aspiring conspirators upon his return, encountered Sieyès at Gohier's house, the abbé said, as soon as the general was out the door: 'Did you see how this impertinent little man behaved toward a member of a government that could have him shot?' As a Thermidorian politician Sieyès was very effective. Deviousness was in his nature, he was a born plotter whose skills years in the Church had honed. Earlier than most he saw that only another *coup* could save the Republic and his own career. Once again, as in Fructidor, the army needed to play a direct role. He bluntly expressed his needs: 'a sword' to secure himself and his friends in power. He would have preferred another general for he rightly distrusted Napoleon's ambition, but all his rivals were disqualified, some for their political leanings, both left and right, or by an untimely death (General Hoche). Napoleon, whose triumphal return from Egypt provided significant political capital in the form of popularity, could pose, alone among the contenders, as a savior. It was with Napoleon's landing that the Brumaire crisis began, long before it culminated in the *coup d'état*. The *coup*, as Roederer implied, required only the all-important missing piece, Napoleon.

Since returning from Egypt Napoleon had met with all the would-be conspirators, presenting himself as a republican general, the least military of soldiers, a man of simple republican manners and convictions. Seemingly more interested in the meetings of the Academy than in politics, he persuaded some he would preserve the faltering Republic not for himself but for France and the Revolution. In public he appeared a hero redolent of the exotic orient. He wrapped around his waist the colorful cummerbund he had acquired in Egypt, carried an Egyptian scimitar, and was sometimes accompanied by his Mameluke Roustan. The conspirators saw what they wanted to see: themselves sustained in power by a simple if vain soldier willing to share in the spoils but uninterested in the lion's share.

Brumaire, like so many of the great days of the Revolution, is filled with ambiguities, fraught with confusion and contradiction, which culminates in a tragic-comic denouement. Tocqueville thought the *coup* was the most ill-conceived and executed plot imaginable. Napoleon himself proved an inept conspirator. It only succeeded because of the powerful forces that drove the faltering Republic to desperate measures, the fact that the army was already the most formidable element in the state, public opinion was passive, Lucien Bonaparte kept a cool head, and Napoleon's soldiers were personally loyal. Brumaire is made up of two *coups*: the first a political attack on the Directory, engineered by Sieyès with some help from Napoleon; the second within the ranks of the conspirators themselves when Napoleon shunted all his fellow schemers into secondary roles while he himself assumed supreme power in the state. The Directory may have been corrupt and without a gyroscope, but it remained a formidable government that could marshal armies, as the Egyptian expedition proved, and retain the loyalty of most of its troops as well as the commitment to civilian government by almost all who remained after Robespierre's fall. It had to be defanged, and Paul

Barras, the most powerful and militarily capable of the directors, the 'king' of the Directory, had to go. He fixed the time of the expected *coup*, though not its outcome, by removing himself from the Directory. His resistance could have presented serious problems. His fellow directors refused to follow suit and on 18 Brumaire were kept from events by Napoleon's soldiers. There was much talk at the time and afterwards about two million francs, supposedly loaned to Napoleon and given to the notoriously venal Barras, perhaps with perhaps without the promise that he would be recalled to power. We shall never know where the two million went, nor even if the huge sum existed outside Fouché's *Mémoires*. Barras himself said in his *Mémoires* that he received no money for his demission and accused Talleyrand of spreading the slander. With Barras out of the way the *coup* could go forward.

The plan was simple and flawed. Not unlike the improvised *coup* that toppled Robespierre on 9 Thermidor, Sieyès and Napoleon hoped to seize power by acclamation once they had warned the Elders and the Five Hundred of an impending crisis. If panic failed there was the army. Napoleon had just had himself appointed commander of Paris. The elusive question of legitimacy had haunted the Revolution from its beginning, and would trouble Napoleon until his fall. If the two chambers, the Council of Five Hundred and the Council of Elders, proclaimed Napoleon by giving him emergency powers in the midst of the state crisis, confected but plausible, he would have at least some claim to election and legality. But unlike Thermidor when the majority of deputies jumped on the juggernaught crushing Robespierre and his friends, those deputies who might be expected to rally to Napoleon in Brumaire, even those who supported Sieyès, remained silent and impassive. Those who opposed him, most particularly the Left, the neo-Jacobins, were vociferous with calls of 'tyrant', and 'outlaw': the very cries that had brought Robespierre down and stirred the supine and intimidated Convention into rebellion. Those responsible for the *coup* were a mixture of intellectuals, soldiers, and revolutionary veterans from the Estates-General of 1789. Conflicting interests had driven some ex-nobles and clergymen, as well as constitutional royalists and ex-members of the Convention into the loose coalition. The 19th-century historian Edgar Quinet was to call Brumaire the alliance of fear and glory.

Among the many anomalies of 18 Brumaire was that the actual *coup* took place on the 19th. The conspirators played on a genuine fear of a Jacobin revival, and with it a return to the Terror of year II. The Directory assemblies had to be moved out of Paris, away from potential mob support. This was done on the 18th when the Ancients denounced a Jacobin plot, a fiction crafted by Sieyès, and voted to reassemble at the chateau of St Cloud the following day. Away from the Paris population, the grounds at St Cloud could accommodate the army, which Napoleon held in readiness. The first act concluded successfully.

When addressing his troops Napoleon had oratorical genius. He could always strike the right tone, find ringing phrases to pump up his soldiers. But he was no orator in an age that followed men who could speak compellingly. He had never sat in a deliberative assembly and he despised politicians. Almost alone among revolutionary leaders he did not, could not, command by ideas, ideology, or persuasion. He was a charismatic leader with an army at his back. Although possessed of considerable political ability he seemed constitutionally unable to operate at the level of the give and take, the compromise and cajolery of mundane politics. He dealt from strength. Much that he did in Italy, not least the creation and leadership of the Cisalpine Republic, revealed remarkable political intelligence, but he achieved his considerable successes through bullying. Thus would he soon govern France, whether as Consul or Emperor. He had bungled his appearance before the Ancients in Paris on 18 Brumaire with hesitation, inarticulateness, and indecision; now he repeated his ineptitude before the Council of Five Hundred at St Cloud. His lack of skill was accentuated by the blunder of bringing armed men into the Council chambers, strictly forbidden by the constitution. When he tried to speak of the dangers to the country and the need for an emergency government he became flustered, was shouted down, and a number of deputies called for a vote on *hors la loi*, the dreaded declaration of outlawry. His brother, Lucien, was president of the Assembly that day, which determined the timing of the *coup*. He refused to bring a motion of *hors la loi* to a vote. Instead he harangued the chaotic Five Hundred while his brother fled the hall in confusion, and then himself went outside to inspire the waiting soldiers:

> I convey to the soldiers [he concluded his harangue], the responsibility of saving the majority of the representatives. Generals, soldiers, citizens, you should only consider those who adhere to me as French legislators. As for those who will persist in remaining in the Orangerie [where they were meeting], they must be expelled. They are no longer representatives of the people but representatives of violence.

It is Lucien, not his older brother, who kept his head that day and rallied the waiting troops. Napoleon's solicitous care for his soldiers in Italy now bore fruit. They obeyed orders, chased the deputies from the hall, many of them jumping out of windows, an exit that delighted General Murat. Lucien subsequently served his brother as a minister and manipulated the first referendum of the Consulate, but he had rendered Napoleon a service on 19 Brumaire that could never be forgotten and in many ways never forgiven. Napoleon owed him a place in the succession, which he was denied. He left France and settled permanently in Rome, immune to his brother's brow-beating, enticements, cajolery, and expectations.

18 Brumaire was a *coup* that stirred no enthusiasm: not in the Directory, not in the nation, not among those who described and analyzed it at the time. For contemporaries Brumaire was of minor significance. The non-action of the majority of the deputies who stood aside and let events unfold is a perfect metaphor. So too is popular Parisian quiescence. The city and its suburbs did not budge. They would not rise again until 1830. The *coup* was an insider's enterprise. The roles allotted to senators and people alike were passive. It became clear only in retrospect, as Napoleon carefully ousted Sieyès and his friends over the next months, that when he drove the senators from the hall at bayonet point the servants had displaced the masters. So shrewd an observer as Mme de Staël, who came to detest Napoleon, later wrote that between the Jacobins and Bonaparte she would have chosen the latter, 'as did France, which did not love him but preferred him'. Antoine-Claire Thibaudeau, an old *conventionnel* who was sympathetic to the left wing of the Jacobins although he never formally joined the Club but voted for the king's death and early rallied to Napoleon, had a similar response:

> Although 18 Brumaire was a *coup d'état* carried out by bayonets, the overwhelming majority of the nation and the most distinguished men of the Revolution adhered to the Consulate. He had against him the royalists, who didn't amount to much, the most ardent Jacobins, a few malcontent generals and troublemakers [*frondeurs*], and some sincere republicans who thought themselves Bonaparte's equals because of their services (to the Revolution).

Brumaire for most was but another internecine struggle among the political oligarchs to keep themselves in power. The *coup* would bring forth yet another shift in power retrospectively justified in a constitution by Sieyès. The Republic would be saved, at least nominally, and would limp along, it was widely thought, to the next *coup*.

Napoleon, Sieyès, and Roger Ducos were immediately declared provisional consuls since the new constitution of the year VIII would not be promulgated for a month. Napoleon, ever aware of the power of words, affirmed, 'I am the Revolution', which he immediately contradicted by adding 'the Revolution is over', an ingenious formula, powerful in its ambiguity. The first assertion is pure Robespierre. The second is the familiar language of the moderate Revolution and had punctuated politics since 1789. At the inception of the Consulate in 1799 Napoleon and the other two Consuls, Régis Cambacérès and Charles Lebrun, both moderate revolutionaries, issued a proclamation reiterating and modifying the formula: 'Citizens, the Revolution is established on the principles with which it began. The Revolution is realized.' The French word is *finie*, which we now understand as finished. Thierry Lentz argues that it did not have this meaning in 1799. Rather it meant perfected, as a work of art, or finished with care. I have translated it in this sense. How many had tried to stop the juggernaut of revolution by a similar proclamation, insisting their views were the fulfillment of the Revolution? The *Feuillant* faction in 1791 who wanted a constitutional monarchy, Barnave's triumvirate that sought a *rapprochement* with the court in 1792, the Girondins, who hoped a messianic war would destroy the monarchy in their favor, generals Lafayette and Dumouriez who tried to seize the government, the so-called 'Indulgents' who gathered around Danton and hoped to begin peace talks in 1794, Robespierre who destroyed his rivals and promised an end to Terror but offered no timetable, the Thermidorians who overthrew him, and the several incarnations of the Directory had all proclaimed the Revolution realized. And now Napoleon. It remained only to formalize the work of the Revolution, and there was considerable disagreement over just what was to be preserved, which Revolution would be enshrined, and lead the new France away from violence, into the promised future. The problem, however, was not merely political, not merely the triumph of one faction over another and the insistence that their victory was the true Revolution realized. At issue was the Revolution itself.

Whatever else may have been asserted in the turbulent years of the French Revolution, it was a desired democratic revolution that soon became demonically driven. The difficulty lay not in nomenclature nor in the persistent declaration of the primacy of the will of the people as the guarantor of government and legitimacy, but in the realization of the goal and the various available definitions of democracy. One man one vote had been rejected in the constitution of 1791 that distinguished citizens by wealth. The principle was proclaimed in the 1793 constitution, but that document was never ratified. The principle was again rejected in 1794 when the *robespierristes* were toppled. They had insisted the people were sovereign yet *de facto* governed in the name of a vanguard faction. The creation of a government and society that was by the people and for the people, finding some machinery that would assure and articulate these democratic ideals proved elusive. Who were the people? There were a number of definitions offered. How were they to be represented? Again there were conflicting proposals and theories. Could a minority represent the people, as the Jacobins insisted? When did crisis trump democracy, when was it necessary to institute emergency government, suspend the constitution, abridge legal procedures, and overawe the nation's representatives? When was the crisis over? In a decade of revolution none of these questions had been answered to the satisfaction of a majority.

Paradoxically the French Revolution, which created democracy and a democratic culture in France, experienced very little democracy. In a long revolutionary quest for democracy and legitimacy Napoleon's declaration is neither surprising nor unexpected. His first government, the Consulate, was an expression of the militant, authoritarian side of the French Revolution, not its long-ignored, debased, or manipulated democratic ideology. From the beginning of the Revolution oligarchies had wielded authority. They were tolerated so long as they delivered security, cemented the gains of the Revolution for the peasantry and the bourgeoisie, successfully fought the war, and steered a course between the extremes of left and right. The personnel of these groups or factions was changed periodically, but the principle of oligarchic dominance was not lost. Oligarchy, defined by a political elite and not money, stood in for representative government. Each successful clique insisted it represented or was the embodiment of the people. So long as it had the will and authority to enforce this assertion it governed until supplanted. Now Napoleon reiterated the claim.

What revolutionary politics had in place of a functioning democracy was embodiment. All the major parliamentary leaders of the Revolution, culminating in Robespierre, insisted they spoke for the people. In the Incorruptible's case he declared he *was* the people. In the French Revolution the realization of principles – liberty, equality, fraternity – was primary; all else would follow, including a democratic government. How one achieved these ideals, or how the Revolution responded when *la force des chose* demanded the sacrifice of liberty, equality, and fraternity along the way, in the name of security or survival, became secondary. Part of the millenarian quest of the Revolution was the faith that the achievement of liberty would, by some murky alchemy, create a free government. Napoleon too governed by embodiment. He had been chosen by the people, although he was remarkably vague about how and when. The idea that dominated his assertions of revolutionary legitimacy was acclamation. The ardent reception he received when he returned from Egypt, and later when he escaped from Elba, were offered as a kind of direct democratic affirmation. There was no need regularly to consult the nation. He abolished the Tribunate he had at first made a part of the Consulate. This instrument for articulating the will of the nation was not replaced. Henceforth Napoleon declared that he embodied the will of the nation because he perpetuated the ideas and policies of the Revolution, had been 'elected' by the people, and was the heir of the Revolution. In 1801 when four departments on the Rhine's left bank were incorporated into France, Napoleon as first Consul described for them the benefits of joining the Grande Nation, and asked 'what reasonable man could ignore these advantages':

> Odious privileges will no longer check the industry of workers; the hunting laws will no longer ravage the fields of the farmer nor devour the fruits of his labor. Degrading forced labor will cease for all, as will the degradation of feudal servitude.
>
> The *dîme* [a Church tax on the harvest] is abolished, contributions of whatever kind are made lighter, direct taxes are equally borne by seigneurial and ecclesiastical lands previously exempt ... interior customs duties ... are suppressed; there is free trade in France ... no longer restrained by the obstacles of old frontiers.

He says nothing about democracy, representation, or the will of the people. The revolutionary benefits are economic and social, not political. A few years later when he crowned himself Emperor he swore a not dissimilar oath:

> I swear to maintain the integrity of the territory of the Republic, to respect and cause to be respected the laws of the Concordat and freedom of religion, to respect and cause to be respected the equality of rights, political and civil liberty, the irrevocability of sales of *biens nationaux*, to raise no levies or establish any tax except by law, to maintain the institution of the Legion of Honor, to govern with the sole purpose of the interest, the happiness, and the glory of the French people.

Contemporaries estimated the French electorate had about five million eligible voters. Three million votes, representing a clear majority (about 60 per cent) of the eligible voters, thus became the official target.

In 1800 Lucien Bonaparte had falsified the returns to get the results he wanted, ignoring the vast number of abstentions. In 1802 Napoleon had no difficultly garnering 60 per cent of the vote. This plebiscite on the Consulate for life thus gave him the legitimacy Brumaire had not provided.

As he embarked upon his personal rule Napoleon appeared about to fulfill the revolutionary longings for peace, security, institutionalized reforms (the promises of the Revolution made permanent), and efficient, honest, reasonable, and responsible government. No other figure of the day was applauded both by the peasantry of the Rhône valley as he made his way to Paris following his return from Egypt, and the Parisians when he arrived in the capital. He was careful to present himself as a military hero but not a military man. He carefully restrained the extravagance and luxury he had enjoyed at Mombello during the first Italian Campaign, now presenting himself as a soldier given to austerity, a man who never lingered at the table with sybaritic pleasure. His astonishing capacity for work impressed the bourgeoisie; his escutcheon with bees, an emblem borrowed from the Merovingian kings of a thousand years earlier, declared his industriousness not his victories. Here was no military grandee, no warlord, and no democrat. Lest there be any doubt about his intention to rule without interference, he immediately shut down 60 of the 73 newspapers published in Paris, swept those deputies who had opposed the *coup d'état* from office, gave his two colleagues as consuls largely decorative roles to play, and replaced two-thirds of the municipal administration of Paris. In the provinces only a few dozen functionaries were removed from office. Most of the men in power and administration before Napoleon's *coup* remained to serve him. All the factional fights of the Revolution had culminated in purges and a long line to the guillotine or the firing squad. But Napoleon was the beneficiary of the 'Fructidorian Terror' when repression, not carried out by him personally, was ruthless. In the first couple of years of the Consulate military courts sentenced more than 1600 civilians to death and executed 'a staggering fivefold increase (at least) over' what the old monarchy had done at the height of its repressive powers. 'In other words,' Howard Brown concludes, 'an extraordinary level of quotidian repression lay at the heart of the Consulate's return to law and order'.

The draconian justice in the countryside was tempered by carefully orchestrated clemency. Napoleon's important political opponents were forced into retirement not killed. The non-juring priests, those who refused to swear an oath to the constitution, who were held on the islands of Ré and d'Oléron, were liberated. There was a suspension of arms in the still-smoldering Vendéan civil war. The émigrés who awaited execution at Calais for having returned to France without permission were set free and expelled from the country. These gestures were effective propaganda. More substantial was the general clemency of his first months in office. The laws against the relatives of émigrés were abrogated, opening the way for 300,000 refugees of the Revolution to return. A number of proscribed political opponents and some terrorists from year II were pardoned. Priests were no longer required to swear an oath to the state and Mass could be said in private houses. Most symbolic was the declaration that henceforth only two national *fêtes* would be celebrated: 14 July and 22 September, the Fall of the Bastille and the declaration of the Republic. The execution of Louis XVI, the purge of the Girondins, and the fall of Robespierre were eliminated from the patriotic calendar. Revolutionary vengeance seemed at an end.

'The failure of the Revolution,' Napoleon wrote some years earlier, 'was to have destroyed much and built nothing. Everything remains to be done.' He set to work forging what would be the weapons not only for governing France and domesticating the Revolution, but creating the 'Grande Nation' he had envisioned and christened when he left Paris to command the Army of Italy. This arsenal would be revolutionary in content and application.

Entr'acte
Revolution and Empire

'The dynasty of Naples has ceased to reign.' So declared Napoleon from Schönbrunn (27 December 1805) where he was basking in the glory of his victory at Austerlitz (2 December, the anniversary of his coronation as Emperor in Notre-Dame a year earlier). His nephew, Louis Napoleon, would honor the auspicious day for his own *coup d'état* in 1851.

1805 had been an exceptionally busy year, containing both Napoleon's most perfect victory and the destruction of the French fleet. Napoleon learned of Lord Nelson's annihilation of the Franco-Spanish fleet at Trafalgar a few days after receiving the surrender of General Mack at Ulm. The British victory fixed the nature of his obsessive struggle with England. A long chain of consequences followed: the imposition of the Continental System, the invasion first of Spain and then Russia to stop the leakage of British goods onto the Continent, the invasion of the kingdom of Naples as part of his never abandoned obsession to thwart England by controlling the eastern Mediterranean, and his creation of the kingdom of Italy, the first of his imperial acquisitions. The prologue to all this was the Battle of Marengo (14 June 1800).

More than his seizure of power in Paris, Marengo solidified Napoleon's authority. There was no reason to think the *coup d'état* of Brumaire would do more than had its predecessors: rearrange the leadership, further exclude the people from governing, and be only a temporary solution. Marengo removed whatever skepticism or prudence kept many from choosing sides. Opposition to Napoleon now appeared hopeless. What little lingered was drowned in nationalistic enthusiasm. The pattern of foreign triumph propelling domestic change was established. The victory at Marengo had been close but it gave Napoleon undisputed control of Italy and provided the *imprimatur* of victory and glory to an extraordinary burst of energy, even by Napoleonic standards. He had

Figure 3 Joseph Bonaparte (1808), by José Flaugier. A portrait of Joseph as the King of Spain, here presented without the usual royal pomp. Joseph is painted uncrowned and without the symbols of royal power, although the crown is curiously resting on a cushion. He is depicted as a grandee rather than an anointed monarch. The painting was created at the outset of Joseph's reign.

put the finishing touches of drilled discipline on the first (and best) Grande Armée at Boulogne, he set in motion his great reforms (of the law, the administration, the educational system), he signed a Concordat with the Papacy that returned Roman Catholicism to France, fixed his attention on imposing a definitive settlement on Italy, and above all he worked a miracle: he made peace. First came the Treaty of Lunéville (9 February 1801) and a year later the Treaty of Amiens (27 March 1802), the former signed with Austria, the latter with England. Together they ended an endless war; but only temporarily. After a decade of war France had regained a preponderant role in European affairs, of necessity accepted by the other powers. The distribution of power in Europe appeared to create a plausible balance that looked potentially durable. France was dominant in Western Europe, England on the seas, and Russia in Eastern Europe. But contemporaries were too optimistic. The settlements unraveled quickly. The treaties proved only an armistice. Those who blame England and those who blame France for destroying the fragile peace are approximately equal in number. There is enough blame to be generously shared by Napoleon and Addington's government. Mediterranean politics broke the peace neither side was devoted to perpetuating. Malta, captured by Napoleon on his way to Egypt, was to have been returned to the French. The island would give him a presence in the Eastern Mediterranean he had long sought. England could not tolerate such a presence and refused to turn the strategic island over to France. The treaty of Amiens collapsed, all the English visitors who had flocked to the Continent to see the new France returned home. Napoleon's strategic planning shifted to southern Italy and the Ionian Islands, where he would continue to seek a foothold to check British sea power.

Italy had long been special for the Bonapartes. Napoleon's father had been educated there, the entire family spoke Italian without the Corsican accent Napoleon and Joseph brought to their French, and Joseph, Lucien, Elisa, and Pauline all eventually chose to live in Italy. Napoleon had first tasted the delights of glory there and his name was everywhere warmly spoken and celebrated, at least until he began remaking the Italian map, forcing reforms, and imposing military quotas on the population. The Papal States and the kingdom of Naples feared his return to Italy. Their fright was well founded. In March 1805 Napoleon had given his sister Elisa the principality of Piombino. In May he had himself crowned king of Italy in the Milan cathedral. Eugène de Beauharnais was named viceroy of the newly created kingdom in June, after Joseph Bonaparte refused the honor. 'My intention,' he wrote to Joseph on the last day of 1805,

> is to seize the kingdom of Naples. Marshal Masséna and General St-Cyr are marching there with two army corps. I am naming you *my lieutenant, commander-in-chief of the army of Naples.* Leave within 48 hours of receiving this letter ... and let your first dispatch announce your entry into Naples, and tell me that you have broken this perfidious court and subjected southern Italy to my laws.

The city and the kingdom, including Sicily, was an irresistible prize. The promise of wealth, a stronghold in the Mediterranean, and control of the entire peninsula all marched together. Naples itself was one of the largest cities in Europe, with a population of 550,000 souls, nearly equal to Paris. It was also thought one of the richest. Napoleon shared the unexamined assumption of its wealth: 'the beautiful country of Naples where there is bread, wine, oil, linen-making, bed-clothes in all the houses, society, and even women.' The illusion of Neapolitan riches remained compelling at least until 1809. A report prepared by the *Council for Trade and Industry* in Paris described Naples as 'the promised land ... unlike Peru where you have to dig for gold in the bowels of the earth in Naples it lies glittering on the surface'. A junior branch of the Spanish Bourbons, in the person of Ferdinand IV, sat upon a throne they had held only since 1735. Ferdinand, in the eyes of the English colony at Naples, was fit to be a country gentleman with a passion for hunting and fishing. His sporting obsessions and his detestation of the French Revolution submerged the needed discipline for ruling his kingdom. He was at his best peaceful, indolent to the point of finding work repugnant, perfectly willing to be influenced by others, most particularly the unimpressive Englishman Sir John Francis Acton who was the de facto ruler of the kingdom, and Marie-Caroline, his wife (as well as the sister of Marie-Antoinette). There was general agreement about Ferdinand's mediocrity. The well-born deplored his familiarity with the low-born. The more outspoken privately called him 'this stupid king' (*ce roi stupido*). He was, unfortunately for the Neapolitans, also despotic and unwilling to check his queen's passion for revenge or her taste for cruelty, which he shared.

Marie-Caroline, for her apologists, had some of the talent of her mother, Empress Marie-Theresa, and the beauty of her sister, whose execution she included in her detestation of Napoleon: 'That ferocious animal, that ferocious beast ... that Corsican bastard, that *parvenu*, that dog!' Her enemies were legion, including Neapolitan patriots and reformers, the French, and even her allies, the English. The secretary of the French embassy in Naples thought Marie-Caroline 'all powerful, a mad woman, an abhorrent fury'. An inveterate plotter, whose schemes included an assassination attempt against Joseph Bonaparte, as well as her dependence on those of low birth and often a criminal past, made her much feared. Among her enemies she enjoyed, with her dead sister, the special scorn reserved for women who meddled in politics. She and Ferdinand were a prodigal pair. 'If mount Etna was made of gold,' wrote Admiral Collingwood, 'the court would be no less poor.' They skimmed money from funds set aside for public works, plundered the bank of Palermo, sequestered land from political opponents, and were utterly dependent upon English subsidies. When they fled Naples for Palermo they took 50,000,000 gold francs worth of valuables and sailed to Sicily in Horatio Nelson's ships. The palace was stripped to the bare walls. Joseph found not a stick of furniture, no sheets for the beds, and no firewood, which he could not have burned anyway because the andirons had been purloined.

The kingdom of Naples in 1806 presented Napoleon the opportunity for a recapitulation of the French Revolution: a Bourbon king with a meddlesome Austrian wife, a prodigal court, a legal system hopelessly complicated, inept, and arbitrary, a tangle of feudal arrangements and exactions, a wretched and illiterate populace, financial anarchy abetted by a government that had no idea of how much money it had or owed, rapacious ministers, a priest-ridden countryside – it was estimated that there were 100,000 ecclesiastics or one for every 50 subjects – a restless peasantry, and profound social resentments at every level of society. Napoleon could not resist imposing the achievements of the French Revolution on this relic of the *ancien régime*. The kingdom had also become a miniature Koblenz, the Rhineland city where French *émigrés* gathered. They gravitated to Naples, where they easily mingled with the British colony. Nearby, quite coincidentally, was the English governor of Capri, (then colonel) Hudson Lowe, who would become Napoleon's jailer. But that is a story for later.

If the lure of reenacting the French Revolution, without the unpredictable participation of the people, was not enough, Naples was, in 1806, almost a protectorate of the British. Nelson, fresh from destroying the French fleet at Aboukir Bay, docked in Naples on 23 September 1798. There he encountered not only Emma Hamilton, whose lover he became, but a kingdom already flush with Englishmen. Nelson and the English colony persuaded Ferdinand to force a confrontation with the French in northern Italy. General Mack, on loan from Austria, invaded Rome. He was soon put to flight by the French general, Championnet, whose army entered Naples in January 1799. The king and queen fled, becoming wards of the British. The reformers and republicans of Naples, virtually all of high social standing, welcomed Championnet's army as liberators and protectors. They abolished feudalism, did away with primogeniture and entail, and though the republic did not last long enough for these reforms to take hold, prepared the way for Joseph Bonaparte's revolutionary government. The fledgling republic was soon undone with British aid and Nelson's ships. A bloody counterrevolution put Ferdinand and Marie-Caroline back on their throne. Their barbarous revenge was sanctioned by Nelson, Acton, the British colony, and Cardinal Maury, all of whom abhorred the infection of the Neapolitan elite by republican principles. The royal couple executed 119 'Jacobins' including two princes, four marquises, a count, and a bishop. Marie-Caroline was consumed by vengefulness: 'At last, my dear Milady,' she wrote to Lady Hamilton, 'I recommend that Milord Nelson treat Naples as if it was a vile rebel in Ireland.' So he did. The republican prince and former admiral Caracciolo was hanged, on Nelson's order, from the yardarm of the warship *Minerva*.

Nelson proved himself in Naples as much a satrap as had Napoleon in Italy and Egypt. He committed his ships to the Bourbon cause and imposed his political views on Ferdinand and Marie-Caroline without consulting London. The ship of state was more than a metaphor for Nelson. He believed states were best run as he ran a British warship. Rewards and punishments were meted out by the admiral with complete self-righteousness. The British government had little choice but to accept all their hero had ordered or condoned.

Napoleon's Italian revolution had already begun when, as king of Italy, he inaugurated the new year (1806) with the promulgation of the Civil Code. On 19 January 1806 he offered his brother the Neapolitan throne:

> Tell him [Napoleon instructed Miot de Melito] that I am making him King of Naples and a Grand Elector of the Empire ... but tell him also that the slightest hesitation, the slightest indecision and he will lose everything ... I am determined to nominate someone else if Joseph refuses. All feelings of affection must now give way to *raison d'état* ... It is not with the thing in my breeches that I make sons, but with my fingers. Joseph must forget all the bonds of childhood and make himself worthy of my esteem.

The counterrevolutionary savagery of Ferdinand and Marie-Caroline, abetted by British muscle, engendered a warm welcome for the new king. The Bonaparte name did the rest. Joseph inherited a troubled, precarious, and structurally unsound kingdom. The seemingly impregnable fortress city of Gaeta remained in the hands of the Bourbons and in the toe of Italy Calabria was in open revolt. Ferdinand and Marie-Caroline had again fled to Sicily, and British ships not only controlled the Straits of Messina – Joseph was never able to invade Sicily – but sailed unopposed in and out of the Bay of Naples. There was not much Joseph could do until he controlled his kingdom. He was ill-prepared to be a warrior king. He had spent some months at the camp in Boulogne, as a colonel of the Fourth Line regiment, but had seen no action. He had the good sense to take the advice of Masséna and St-Cyr. He also had the good sense to lean heavily on his talented advisers, all of whom had excellent revolutionary credentials and had served Joseph's brother loyally. Antoine-Christophe Saliceti was a Corsican and an ex-Jacobin who had rallied to Napoleon. He was tough, smart, loyal, austere, considered incorruptible, and completely dedicated to the Revolution. An *homme de poing*, he was one of Napoleon's favorites. 'It seems to me [he wrote

Joseph] that your confidence in Saliceti has completely diminished.
I cannot conceive of anything more disastrous for you than to alienate
so important a man.' When Saliceti died under mysterious circumstances that many believed indicated poisoning, Napoleon lashed out at
his brother's release of a suspected conspirator who in fact had nothing
to do with Saliceti's death. 'Since when do you grant a pardon to a man
who has conspired against you, and set him free in the capital?'

Joseph preferred Pierre-Louis Roederer, a much more circumspect man,
whom Napoleon thought too devious, intellectual, and soft. Besides, he
carried a grudge. In 1805 after Austerlitz the *Journal de Paris*, edited by
Roederer, harshly criticized the treaty. 'Those who today bemoan the
peace are blaming the conditions I accepted,' wrote Napoleon. 'I am
especially very displeased,' he continued, 'with the articles in the *Journal
de Paris* ... It is only intriguers or imbeciles who can think and write
thus.' Napoleon never forgot a slight. Roederer was no Jacobin and had
little sympathy with the popular politics of the Revolution. He had
gone into hiding during the Jacobin ascendancy, emerging only after
Robespierre's fall. Napoleon's advent moved Roederer to the forefront of
politics. He rallied early and was useful. His *Journal*, vivid and concrete,
is invaluable. 'Certainly,' Napoleon told him,

> there are men I esteem equally, even more than him [he's speaking
> of Joseph]! It is not because of my esteem that I am determined to
> put him on the throne ... I have made him king because my family
> was essential to secure my dynasty. I have made him king because
> of my system.

The others who served Joseph in Naples were devoted and able. They were
also, to a man, freemasons and several were Corsicans and/or Jacobins.

The new regime was launched amid disarray. Ferdinand had governed
badly and fled ignobly, but he had a sense of dignity, expressed in his
parting manifesto:

> We protest before the whole world that we consider the usurpation
> of our kingdom of Naples as an act of the most execrable violence,
> done by the emperor of the French.

'Never,' wrote Pietro Colletta, a Neapolitan general who joined Joseph,
'has society undergone political convulsions comparable to those experienced in the Kingdom of Naples at the start of the 19th century.' But
first the kingdom had to be subdued. Joseph simultaneously attacked

the civil war in Calabria and besieged the fortress of Gaeta. Both proved more difficult than imagined. Napoleon's barrage of letters to his brother are filled with advice, badgering, and impatience.

Calabria was among the poorest parts of Europe, whatever fables of Neapolitan wealth Napoleon believed. A wretched peasantry struggled with little arable soil badly irrigated, a harsh climate, and an enormous burden of feudal exactions. Primitive farming methods characterized the region. The wheeled plow was here a rarity. The land itself, so hostile to cultivation, was as if fiendishly created for guerrilla warfare. There was easy access to the sea controlled by the British navy. The region was mountainous with only primitive footpaths winding through a landscape cut by deep ravines and ambuscades masked by thick foliage or dense forest. Villages were perched like eagles' nests: their inaccessibility exacted an exorbitant price in blood from attackers. It was difficult to move troops and impossible to move artillery. Calabria defied any regular army. The first attempt made to subdue the Calabrians was led by General Jean-Louis Reynier and failed. His colleague, General Jean-Maximilien Lamarque – who had the honor of receiving Hudson Lowe's capitulation on Capri – correctly analyzed the situation. Calabria was unlike any other region of Europe. 'Here those who have absolutely nothing outnumber the haves by ten to one ... here when someone cries for help the population comes to the aid of the thief.' Calabria was 'a war of the rich against the poor'. It was civil war complicated by the impossibility of distinguishing bandits from rebels and both from the general population. Joseph's troops, especially the Poles in his army, killed Calabrians indiscriminately. New tactics were needed after Reynier's defeat, tactics learned in the Vendée. The rebels had to be flushed out of hiding, cut off from their supplies of food and intelligence provided by the peasantry and the villagers, kept on the run by mobile troops who tracked them relentlessly, and denied the protection of the population. Terror was the principle weapon. Villages were systematically burned, anyone caught bearing arms was summarily shot, and many knelt before Joseph's firing squads just because they were Calabrians. Despite the savagery of this war of intimidation and annihilation it took years to succeed. The partisans of Calabria were not finally crushed until General Manhès, during Joachim Murat's reign (1808–15), led a ferocious, merciless, and inexorable campaign.

Joseph likened the Calabrians to Corsicans: 'they are very susceptible to violent emotions, they have been completely neglected by the court (the king has never visited their region).' They 'know their government only by the taxes and exactions they pay'. He told a few atrocity stories to show Napoleon what he was up against. 'In the village of Nicastro,' he wrote, 'the commander ... was crucified after being blinded. He was a prince who had welcomed me in his house.' Napoleon responded with criticism of Joseph's character, and some familiar advice:

> You do not change and reform states with moderation. You need extraordinary and vigorous means. Since the Calabrians have assassinated my soldiers, I will myself issue the decree that confiscates half the revenues of the province ... your good will can be seen only as weakness and timidity. It will be disastrous for France. Your friends themselves say it: you do not inspire confidence, you are too good.

Napoleon monotonously accused his brother of goodness, softness, and dangerous sensibility.

Napoleon was not much interested in the Calabrian war. He held the guerrillas in contempt, as he would later in Spain. He was itching to invade Sicily and flush out Ferdinand and his court. He was impatient of Joseph's progress and his persistent complaining. Despite the evidence he never conceded that an irregular war, fought by the *canaille*, could hold his army and his generals at bay. Although he misread the situation he did send Joseph several good generals. Masséna and Reynier were already there and were joined by Jourdan and Berthier. 'The war is as murderous today as it was in the summer,' wrote Joseph in January 1807. 'In a country of high mountains cut by torrents at every step, the soldiers are always in the water. They are always on the march. No matter what efforts are made they lack clothing and shoes. In ten days a pair of shoes are worn out, and the regiments are short of officers.' Napoleon was unimpressed.

The siege of Gaeta was a more conventional military undertaking. Here Napoleon's attention was engaged and he sent and received a flurry of letters to manage the siege from afar. The town, perched atop a double summit, lay at the end of an isthmus. The chateau was on the lower of the two peaks. The other held the enormous first-century mausoleum of the Roman general Lucius Munatius Plancus. Gaeta itself had 5000 to 6000 inhabitants, and was one of the most impregnable natural fortresses in Europe, often compared to Gibraltar. Like Gibraltar it commanded the harbor below, where British ships sailed unmolested. The garrison was larger than the town's population and when Joseph began his siege it was commanded by Louis, the son of the landgrave of Hesse-Philippsthal, William II. He was courageous, energetic, and obstinate, ideal characteristics for withstanding a siege. His detractors quipped that 'his ignorance equaled his bravery'. Widely and mistakenly underestimated by the French, he proved a fierce and tenacious foe. His older brother, Frederick, while in Dutch service was killed by the French, a death Louis hoped to avenge. 'Gaeta is not Ulm, Hesse is not Mack!' he once taunted the French from the ramparts.

Hesse prepared carefully for the siege, stocking the town with food, water, money, and ammunition. It is reported that he gave the town's prelate the keys to his cellar with orders not to give the count more than one bottle of wine per day. The British, commanded by Sir Sidney Smith, who had thwarted Napoleon at the siege of Acre in the Biblical lands, controlled the sea. Gaeta, like Acre, could be reinforced. Hesse's troops were mediocre but he inspired by example and terrified his men into bravery. Joseph could attack only by land and the besiegers were always in the sights of the surprisingly competent gunners of Gaeta, who had 140 pieces and an abundance of shot and powder. They were also under fire intermittently from the British and Sicilian ships in the harbor. The barren rock resisted siege works, which had to be hacked out in sight of the besieged for there was no cover. Throughout the siege Joseph would send letter after letter to his brother begging for more men, more artillery, more powder and shot. Taking Gaeta was central to Joseph's ability to reign. It became, in the words of one of the besiegers 'the thermometer of public opinion'.

Joseph poured into the siege all the resources he could spare from the Calabrian campaign and preparations to invade Sicily. When the fortress finally fell there were 10,000 men involved, commanded by 14 generals, all under Masséna. The summer heat was unbearable on the naked rock. Dysentery was the affliction of the spring, fever that of summer. As many as 30 soldiers a day fell to disease, many more than were claimed by enemy fire. The soldiers slept fitfully in the trenches. Supplies arrived irregularly. Most serious was the lack of ammunition. Joseph had to go as far afield as Rome to beg, borrow, or steal powder; his soldiers collected the cannon balls lobbed by the enemy in order to reuse them. By mid-May the besiegers had held out for five months. On 28 June Masséna arrived to take charge. Within a week he had hauled 107 field guns into place and was able to keep the enemy ships at bay. Bombardment from the sea ceased. On 7 July, at 3 a.m., 'amid complete silence' Joseph gave the signal to start the bombardment. The defenders, seemingly paralyzed by so much shot, did not respond for two hours. When they did return fire 'the entire mountain was lit up' according to Rambaud. The French continued firing until the 11th. On the 10th Hesse was seriously wounded by a piece of flying masonry and was evacuated. He had been the very soul of resistance, which now collapsed. The French bombardment was relentless. All the parapets were destroyed, as were the artillery platforms, and two breeches were punched in the walls. As the French prepared their final assault the white flag appeared, on 18 July. Joseph and Masséna were lenient in victory, granting the honors of war to the defenders.

Joseph now seemed secure on his new throne. But it was a close call. 'The Gaeta ulcer' – the same metaphor would be used to characterize the war in Spain – had drained Neapolitan resources and pushed Joseph's army to the edge of endurance. Salerno was in insurrection and Naples itself poised nervously on the brink of riot. The capitulation of Gaeta came none too soon. The war in Calabria would smolder on for years, but its fights were far from public scrutiny and the numbers of troops involved was relatively small. By mid-1807 Joseph had reduced the Calabrian war to the methodically murderous pursuit of scattered bands of guerrillas or bandits. Now Joseph could turn his attention to more gratifying work.

******

Joseph was a reluctant soldier but a passionate reformer. Formed by the Enlightenment he was secular in his convictions, a devotee of rationality and reform, a man of urbane and literary sensibility, and a child of the French Revolution. He had inherited the Bonaparte gifts: the common touch, an instinctive feel for public opinion, and devotion to public works, along with a love of luxury, pomp, and pageant. It is to her French kings, Joseph and Murat, that Naples owes her transformation into a modern state. Joseph inherited economic and social conditions that reached far back into the Neapolitan past and were deeply rooted. The structural deficits of the kingdom had only been exacerbated by the earlier Bourbon reform failures, the inept and irresponsible rule of Ferdinand and Marie-Caroline, and the savage destruction of the brief republic. The Neapolitan Bourbons had, under Charles who founded this branch of the family, and the early rule of his son, Ferdinand, introduced some of the reforms of the so-called Enlightened Despots. The republican revolution of 1799 did not last long enough to extend and continue this work; and the counterrevolution turned Ferdinand deeply reactionary. There remained a significant residue of reforming zeal among the Neapolitan elite, many of whom rallied to the Bonapartist cause. There was no better example than Giuseppe Zurlo, 'the key figure in the final season of Bourbon reformism after 1799'. After Joseph's departure he became Murat's interior minister and continued his work. Joseph successfully tapped into native sympathy for his cause. Reform that had been tentative, partial, and intermittent under the Bourbons now became focused, forceful, and radical under the Bonapartes.

Joseph traversed what he governed. For the first time the Calabrians saw their king. Joseph intended to be a king whose authority derived from and rested upon the people rather than God and a tiny noble and clerical coterie. He would be accessible and sensitive to public opinion. His failure, and it proved the fatal vulnerability of all Napoleon's Italian and imperial reforms, was the narrowness of popular support. As in the *départements réunis* the Revolution Napoleon exported to Naples was based solely on the bureaucracy and the army. The masses never rallied and the indigenous reformers were not successfully amalgamated. Despite what the Emperor and most commentators have said, Joseph was willing to work hard at being king. 'He showed energy in all his important undertakings and consistency in everything he undertook,' wrote his friend and minister Roederer. General Mathieu Dumas, who served as Joseph's minister of war, praised his master's 'clarity of mind, vigor, [and] indefatigable activity'. In his *Précis des événements militaires* (*A Summary of Military Events*) published long after Joseph had retired and could not further his career, Dumas was even more flattering: Joseph was 'very capable', and had 'the unswerving will to reform abuses'. He had 'an ardent will for justice and the public good'. The Neapolitans, not noted for their tolerance, celebrated 'the good and paternal government of the best of sovereigns' and praised Joseph's intelligence, affability, and eloquence in both French and Italian, all of which contrasted with the ignorance of his predecessor.

We are accustomed to a pattern of imperialism and colonialism different from Joseph's. In Naples there was no attempt to destroy or utterly devalue the local cultural habits and practices. Government offices were not monopolized by Frenchmen. Nor was a police state established. The new king and his chief ministers spoke the language and were fond of the country. Joseph's Bonapartism was a revolution from above, but unlike that of his brother he did not model Naples on the army. Government and administration were not regimented. No Napoleonic state better preserved its individuality than Naples. Of the ten ministers appointed at the outset of Joseph's reign six were Neapolitans. The personnel of local courts and the supreme court was entirely Neapolitan. Joseph closed the tribunals of the *ancien régime*. The old magistrates were bitterly resentful and staunchly opposed him. Along with the clergy they resisted reforms, especially the introduction of the Civil Code so long as it sanctioned divorce. In all the branches of the administration Neapolitans predominated. Even in the army, and more especially in the navy, Neapolitans were in the majority. Joseph also had the good fortune to find and cultivate considerable sympathy among the upper levels of society. The Neapolitan elites, having paid the blood-tax imposed by the ousted Bourbons and Lord Nelson, were committed to reform.

Just as the structure and institutions of Naples before 1806 resembled France before the Revolution, so too did Neapolitan feudalism. Roederer told the Council of State in 1806 that 'of the 4,578,894 ducats paid each year in taxes on property, only 589,934 ducats were paid on feudal property'. He counted 102 different levies that varied from province to province, and since no property survey had ever been made, taxes were imposed differently in almost every town and feudal properties were exempt. The *banalités*, a vast and often arbitrary accumulation of petty exactions that regularly reminded the peasantry of their subservience, had grown unchecked. There were numerous personal exactions, the most resented being free labor and the forced loan of animals. There was a tax, the hated *taille*, levied on each house with a hearth. One of Joseph's officials counted 1400 different kinds of exactions, in one of the poorest agricultural regions of Europe. Feudalism in Naples had lost its significance as a political system, but it remained 'a monstrous assemblage' of privileges and monopolies for which there was no service delivered.

The law of 2 August 1806 abolished feudalism 'with all its attributions'. This law, Joseph proudly declared, will be 'the keystone of all the beneficial establishments' envisioned. Two additional pieces of legislation, the law of 1 September 1806, and the decree of 8 June 1807, completed the legal work. Taken together these laws and decrees accomplished the work of the night of 4 August 1789 in the French Revolution. The fisc, a hodge-podge of habit, special interests, and ineptitude, had been habitually raided by the Bourbons. It was reformed by Roederer, and restocked with land confiscations that resulted from the end of feudalism, the sequestration of all the lands abandoned by the nobility who fled to Palermo with Ferdinand, and most particularly by Joseph's attack on the extensive church holdings.

The debt Joseph inherited from the Bourbons had to be made good. The feudal lands taken from the Church and the *émigré* nobility became the *biens nationaux* of Naples. Confiscated land now belonging to the state was sold off to raise cash, secularize the kingdom, bind the new owners to his throne, and plug the holes in the state's finances. On 3 July 1806 he suppressed the Jesuits and confiscated their holdings. On

13 March 1806 he cancelled the debts owed to those who had fled, to the tax farmers, and even to some banks. He suppressed 33 monasteries and added their revenues to those taken from the Jesuits. The Neapolitan elites welcomed these assaults on the Church and the *émigrés*. So too did they welcome Joseph's abolition of the salt tax. Not so his brother:

> If you have abolished the salt tax you have made a mistake. With this kind of management you will lose your kingdom; with this kind of management you will take neither Sicily nor Gaeta and you will lack the most necessary things.

'I cannot believe you had the stupidity [*sottise*] to abolish the tax on salt,' he later added. In fact Joseph managed his state very well. The finances of the kingdom were put in respectable order. No mean achievement in two years. Never was Naples better governed.

The courts presented a special problem. The Napoleonic Code had been imposed on Italy, excluding Naples, in 1806. Joseph was extremely reluctant to introduce it in his kingdom without some serious editing. Napoleon demanded the Code, the whole Code, and nothing but the Code. 'Everything that is not attached to you will atrophy in a few years and what you want to conserve will be consolidated. That is the great advantage of the Civil Code.' Joseph always dealt with his brother obliquely, deflected his scolding, his insults, and his bullying with politeness laced with flattery and obsequiousness. He successfully parried Napoleon's thrusts about imposing the Code until he left Naples for Spain. On 22 June 1808, from Bayonne and about to depart for Madrid, Joseph signed a decree introducing the Code the following January. It was left to Murat, who was equally unhappy about the Code, to be the midwife of a new legal system.

Divorce was the stumbling block. The Church opposed it for obvious reasons. The conservative magistracy, driven into opposition by the loss of power and prestige, opposed divorce for less ideological reasons, but with equal fervor. The landowners were hostile because divorce played havoc with their traditional marriage strategies, designed to keep ancestral lands and family power intact. Once introduced the divorce provisions were simply ignored. The first divorce was granted in 1810, the second and last in 1814. In June 1815 the first legislative act of the restored monarchy was to abolish civil divorces. During the whole of Napoleonic rule in Italy – including the two satellite kingdoms and the *départements réunis* combined – there were only 19 divorces, even though the Code was everywhere in force.

When Joseph left for Spain, Murat inherited an unrealized ambitious agenda and problems both petty and profound. Roederer had left no accounts and D'Aubusson de la Feuillade, the French *chargé d'affaires*, reported Joseph had made generous settlements on his ministers, favorites, and mistresses. Maria Giulia Colonna, the Duchess of Atri, who bore him two children, received a gift of 5000 ducats. D'Aubusson estimated that Joseph had disbursed as much as 11,000,000 francs from the treasury, according to Davis. Murat, who was widely regarded in imperial circles as 'the pillaging cavalier' and 'an administrator of exceptional ineptitude' was ill-fitted to fix things, however much he loved being king. In addition, by the treaty of Bayonne, he was ordered to supply the Grande Armée with 16,000 infantry, 2500 light cavalry, and 20 pieces of field artillery, a levy he was never able to meet.

Napoleon was not a patient man nor was he gentle. His bluntness and his tantrums were legendary. Soldiering fit him perfectly. He and Nelson were not that different, but the admiral had been spared a boisterous, greedy, and insistent family. Napoleon's system required not only a supply of dynasts but their complete obedience. Here was the problem. His pedagogical methods with both his family and his generals was to load them with abuse so they might curry favor by doing his bidding. Much of his badgering was irrational, designed to compel obedience through intimidation, undermine personal initiative, stifle argument, and bamboozle rather than instruct. In the army hammering away at a subordinate's judgment, criticizing his every act, would eventually inculcate unquestioning acceptance of orders. These tactics worked much better with those who were not his siblings. The Bonapartes were not a submissive bunch. Each developed his or her own technique for dealing with Napoleon. Lucien had early on had enough and retired into private life. Louis was driven from the Dutch throne and he too left his brother's court. Jerome was the only brother who managed to run his satellite kingdom if not to Napoleon's satisfaction at least well enough so that money, men, and matériel flowed as the Emperor demanded. Eugène was the most obedient, but he was not born a Bonaparte. Of the sisters Pauline was fiercely confrontational and Napoleon's intellectual match. Caroline preferred to obstruct through her husband, Murat. Elisa seemed content as Grand Duchess of Tuscany and stayed away from her overbearing brother, although she was intensely jealous of Pauline. Joseph was a special case. Not only was he seemingly not cut from the same cloth as the others, he was the oldest; the early death of Charles Bonaparte had made him the nominal head of this noisy clan.

The Neapolitan correspondence between Joseph and Napoleon comprises 711 letters. They provide a running commentary on Neapolitan affairs. Napoleon demanded of all his subordinates a steady stream of information to which he responded with an equally steady stream of advice, information, and rebuke. These letters also contain a collection of Napoleon's thoughts about governing and politics. Unlike most of his thousands of letters to subordinates, where blunt commands and equally blunt criticism predominate, his letters to Joseph have a pedagogical dimension. He has taken it upon himself to instruct his brother in statecraft and the art of war yet the central thread running through the letters is Napoleon's disapproval.

'Disarm this *canaille*,' he told his brother. Assemble a guard 'of four regiments of *chasseurs* and *hussars* and form two battalions of grenadiers ... and a company of light artillery'. These arrangements will be essential since 'in two weeks, more or less, you will have an insurrection. This is something that always happens in a conquered country'. Napoleon despised the *lazzaroni*, the unruly urban poor of Naples, who had been so important in destroying the republic and bringing back the Bourbons. Only through 'salutary terror can you control the Italian populace'. 'I have seen the Vendée ... I have seen the Bedouins spook and snipe at my troops. A few bold strokes put an end to such things and led to tranquility.' But Joseph has surrounded himself with advisers 'who do not understand men. You refuse to listen to a man who has done much, seen much, thought much [Napoleon] ... Naples is a country of intrigues ... you do not understand men'. 'You gain nothing,' he lectured in another letter, 'in caressing the people of Italy. In general the people, if they do not constantly see their masters, are prone to rebellion and mutiny.' What is needed are severe public examples: 'In a conquered country,' Napoleon offered a dictum: 'benevolence is not humane.'

Joseph responded to this hectoring with politeness and flattery:

I hope that Your Majesty [thus did he always refer to his brother] will not take what I say as flattery, but it is true that I never fail to repeat, and above all to remind myself, that you were born with an astonishing superiority of mind. I today realize that men are what you have so often said they are.

And:

I recognize the justness of the principles I have often heard from ... Your Majesty and I swear that the experience of things has proved to me how true it is that I must see things for myself ... that I cannot count on others. I say to myself ten times a day: The Emperor is right.

He goes on to assure Napoleon that the Neapolitans consider themselves fortunate to be governed by a man who is so close to 'Your Majesty and who bears a name that you have made illustrious before becoming emperor, and who has the additional advantage of being Italian'. Despite this epistolary flattery and admission of failure, much of it genuine, Joseph went on doing what he had always done: rule without terror, intimidation, and bluster, and keep in place those advisers Napoleon disliked, particularly Roederer.

No one was long immune to Napoleon's abuse. Joseph knew that it was tactically useless to snap back, trading insults with a master of the *genre*. He defended himself, and, like a child, struck an attitude of contrition and sulkiness. 'I cannot hide from Your Majesty,' he wrote,

> that for some time I have received from Your Majesty and His ministers letters that make me believe that Your Majesty is not content with me. Nevertheless, I make every effort to merit His esteem and I do not believe I merit being chewed-out [*gourmandé*] by General Dejean.

The French in Naples, as Napoleon correctly saw, were divided into two camps. The moderates whom Joseph favored supported gradual reform and the merciful treatment of opponents. Napoleon wanted him to give all the moderates the boot. 'I am vexed that you do not think as I do,' he wrote Joseph. 'I consider savants and intellectuals as coquettes. One must see them, chat with them, but don't take one for a wife or a minister.' Coquettes is a term of scorn, not a turn of wit. Joseph's advisers are leading him to ruin: 'Your finances, and this is public knowledge, are horribly managed.' This was the work of Roederer and was draining money from Napoleon's treasury. By the time Joseph departed for Spain the imperial treasury had sent him 7,500,000 francs in specie.

Napoleon's scolding diminished when he lectured about military matters, although the occasion for his remarks was dissatisfaction with Joseph's handling of the army. He cautioned against 'listening to those who would have you far from the fighting. You have to show your courage'. 'The art of war,' he wrote – and the phrase occurs frequently in these letters – 'of which the world speaks, is a difficult one. You have not a single man on your council who has an inkling of what is involved.' Or, he says aphoristically, 'the entire art of war consists in a reasoned and circumspect defense and an audacious and rapid offense'. The excellence of his armies exists because 'I give one or two hours a day' to them, and when the reports on the army and fleet arrive each month, filling 20 thick notebooks, 'I stop whatever I am doing and read them closely in order to see what differences there are from month to month. I take more pleasure,' he adds, 'in this reading than a young girl does in reading a novel.' In another letter he expresses the same aesthetic pleasure differently: 'The reports on my armies are for me the most agreeable books of literature in my library, and are what I read with the greatest pleasure during my moments of leisure.'

Napoleon's passion for detail is everywhere in these letters. 'I have told you a hundred times,' he writes, 'that you have to have four brigade generals at Gaeta. There must always be one who spends 24 hours in the trenches, wrapped in his cloak.' A king must take precautions: 'Your valets, your cooks, the guards who sleep in your apartment, those who come to wake you in the middle of the night, the aide de camp who should sleep in your antechamber' must be trustworthy:

> Your door should be locked from the inside and you should never open it unless you recognize the voice of your aide de camp, and he should knock on your door only after he has taken care to close that of his own room, making sure he is alone, and that no one has followed him.

He need not have worried about Joseph's chef. Méot, the famous Parisian *traiteur*, was one of his most fervent admirers. One court wag quipped that all that was missing was a Homer to sing this hero's praises. His stationery featured the title '*Contrôleur* of His Majesty's mouth'.

*****

In Naples we see clearly not only the temperamental contrast between the brothers. Saliceti the Jacobin is Napoleon's man, not Roederer the man of the center. Napoleon liked none of the gradualists, none of those who sought some accommodation with the Neapolitans and advised caution, circumspection, and discretion. He has the impatience of the revolutionary, although he is no ideologue. It is the *ancien régime* itself that is the enemy, and there can be no compromise with such an opponent. He wants to confront the Church head-on, hasten the confiscation of Church property, break the reactionary mobs of Naples, destroy the hornet's nest of the Bourbons and their supporters in

Palermo. He is furious that Joseph cannot invade Sicily. It is the same frustration he himself faced contemplating an invasion of England. He wants Naples to resemble France because of his 'system'. The *ancien régime* must disappear and be replaced by secular institutions and laws, new men devoted to radical transformation, and the efficiency that he equated with good government.

The kingship would be retained, but everything else would vanish. The speed at which his reforms were to be imposed was itself revolutionary. All of Napoleon's brothers and subalterns were more cautious and careful than was he. The man who carried the French Revolution on horseback was incapable of walking. At every turn Naples offers an uncanny foreshadowing of the Spanish disaster: the same Napoleonic personnel, an unexpected early battle lost that then inspired a tenacious resistance, a stubborn Catholic culture the revolutionary French found repulsive, the Bourbons on the throne, a tiny native elite who welcomed the French as the bringers of change, the active and decisive interference of the English, a land made for guerrilla fighting, and a bitter guerrilla war. The difference is one of scale. Joseph was successful in Naples and failed in Spain. All that was missing in Naples was a Goya to record the disasters of war in all their darkness.

Napoleon has often been blamed for all the mistakes he made in Spain, which begin when he decided to remove the Bourbons. This is a retrospective judgment. Naples appeared a success and Napoleon had every reason to believe he would be equally successful in Spain. He failed to appreciate the structural problems which would have taken decades to overcome and he fatally disregarded the scale of the Spanish enterprise. Napoleonic rule transformed Italy. The ideological reaction against French rule was uncompromising. So too were the purges of those who had held office or supported the Napoleonic administrators. But if the Revolution in its Napoleonic version never took root in Italy, the storm that crossed the Alps with Napoleon did far more damage that contemporaries could assay.

VI

The Weapons of Revolution

Napoleon was a soldier, the most obvious fact about his life. We have an abundance of books on his battles and all the details of weaponry, uniforms, strategy, staff work, and tactics. Not one of the 60 battles he fought, by his own count, has gone unstudied. Fundamental to the new state, to Napoleon's rule, and to the revolution he claimed to embody is the army. The birth of the Grande Armée may be set on 18 May 1803, when England repudiated the Treaty of Amiens (signed on 27 March the previous year) and declared war on France. Napoleon devoted himself, during the hiatus of hostilities, to creating 'the finest army that has ever existed'. In August 1803 the *Armée des Côtes de l'Océan* gave way to the Grande Armée. It would not be tested in battle for another two years.

French armies were traditionally named for their region of operations. Napoleon broke with the practice. The Grande Armée, originally intended to be the invading force for England, would soon be led into Germany. Napoleon knew before he left for Egypt that only if he could 'be master of the Channel for six hours' could France triumph. Even before the catastrophe of Aboukir Bay there were structural reasons that prevented building a French fleet that could hold the Channel. Napoleon was able to mobilize and train the largest armies yet seen in Europe. His inability to do the same for the navy did not rest on a shortage of manpower but on a lack of skilled manpower of a particular sort. Deep-sea fishing, sea-borne commerce, and an overseas empire (mostly gone since the Seven Years' War) had played a relatively small part in the French economy since the late 18th century. The great ports – Marseilles, Bordeaux, Nantes – flourished but their economic success remained local, the great merchant families parochial. Louis XVI's fleet that had successfully bedeviled the Royal Navy in the American war still remained and could be the basis for a revivified navy but its expansion was vastly outpaced by the British with an empire to maintain and guard. Napoleon had at best, it is estimated, 50,000 competent seamen to draw upon, far too few for his purposes. The French fleet, bolstered by the addition of Spanish ships, fought well at Trafalgar, but between 1801 and 1813 Napoleon's naval budgets were two-thirds less than those of England. He was unable to spend more. The Grande Armée proved a bottomless money pit, even when the forced exactions of most of Europe were cast into it. He soon abandoned building an amphibious invasion force. The barges for carrying his men across the Channel rotted on the beach. With his usual energy and attention to detail Napoleon threw himself into creating the Grande Armée. The intense training that made his best armies, those of 1805 and 1806, was not lost. With relative ease his amphibious force became a land army.

Napoleon inherited a system of conscription, the *loi Jourdan*. It permitted him to take 30,000 men from each class as it became eligible, and an additional 30,000 in time of war. He found pretexts that swelled the number of conscripts. Between May 1802 and 1805 he raised more than 210,000 men. He had, for the only time in his career, the leisure to shape the recruits into a formidable army, the best of its time, the best he would ever command. The atrophy of armies, if not a law of nature is certainly a law of war. By the Battle of Wagram (1809), the historian of Napoleon's soldiers, Jean Morvan, argues the Grande Armée was in steady, probably irreversible decline. Napoleon himself dated the decline to the Battle of Friedland (1807): 'Since Austerlitz,' he lamented on St Helena, 'my armies declined in quality, although at Jena [1806] I still had good troops. [...] At Friedland there were already too many new soldiers.' There were other causes than the steady attrition of increasingly murderous battles. The enormous number of men sent to Spain removed them from the European theater and proved the immediate cause of the Austrian War that culminated at Wagram. The bulk of these men were seasoned troops, the absolutely essential leaven of veterans needed to incorporate new recruits into the Grande Armée. The regular and intense training Napoleon insisted upon at the depots he established fell off sharply as he was forced to move veteran instructors into the line. His elite corps, the Old and especially the Young Guards, regularly skimmed the best men from the ranks, co-opting the natural leaders. Napoleon's brothers and marshals insisted upon emulating their master, demanding an honor guard for prestige more than protection, drawing off even more seasoned soldiers. Napoleon railed against these multiplying Praetorian Guards, but without effect. 'You have taken elite companies of cavalry for your personal guard,' he snapped at Joseph in

Naples. 'My intention is that not a single drum be taken from my army without my order.' Inexorably the Grande Armée lost its veterans and incessant warfare meant new recruits were incompletely trained.

In 1802 glory and decline both lay in the future. The Grande Armée being created was not a newly invented war machine. It rested upon the practices and theories of the 18th century brought to their highest pitch, first in the crucible of the revolutionary wars and then the reforms imposed by Napoleon to perpetuate those wars. Napoleon continued to issue the 1777 musket, modified in 1801, to his infantry but not to the *voltigeurs* (light infantry units) and the Old Guard. All the muskets carried by Napoleon's troops were flintlocks requiring an elaborate routine to load and fire. Trained soldiers could fire four balls in three minutes, but after 60 rounds they had to clean the weapon. In high humidity, let alone precipitation, the so-called Charleville musket often misfired, but Napoleon thought it reliable in the field. The cannons he used had been designed by Jean Gribeauval and had been in service since before the Revolution. In 1805 the four-pounder, the principal artillery of the infantry divisions, was partly replaced by captured six-pounders. Napoleon persistently pressed for heavier artillery – the French also made eight-pounders and the Imperial Guard later had twelve-pounders – but the six-pounder had the advantage of allowing more shot in the ammunition cases and his horse artillery could pull them.

Part of Napoleon's genius lay, in Jacques Godechot's judgment, in 'using everything better than anyone had before'. A number of his reforms were cosmetic but important. He designed distinctive uniforms in brilliant colors, especially those of the cavalry. These sumptuous, even gaudy uniforms proclaimed the military glory upon which his government depended. No drab colors, no camouflage for Napoleon's army which emulated the appearance of the old royal army but was made up of citizens and not peasant conscripts pressed into service. Each soldier was to have at least two uniforms, one for the field, the other for parade. Napoleon himself made a point of wearing the green uniform of an Imperial Guard (the *1er chasseurs à cheval*), a gray redingote that became ratty with the years, and a cocked hat, an affectation he declined to alter. He liked the contrast of his own simplicity and even shabbiness amid the dazzling dress of his army. He made himself unique by dressing below his deeds and power. The conqueror presented himself as a soldier of the Revolution. He also gave his legions eagles atop their regimental flags, institutionalizing the revolutionary passion for ancient Rome. The new martial splendor was brilliantly depicted in painting, nowhere better than in the work of Théodore Géricault and

Jacques-Louis David's *le Serment de l'Armée après la distribution des Aigles* [*The Oath of the Army upon the Distribution of the Eagles*].

His major organizational innovation was to make the corps the standard unit of all branches of the service, replacing the division. The key advantage of the new organization was its strategic flexibility. Corps commanders had, in addition to their dominant infantry component, small contingents of cavalry and artillery. Military historians point to General Davout's victory at Auerstädt, and Lannes's holding action in the early phase of the Battle of Friedland as examples of this successful innovation. The new corps, commanded by a general, were self-contained and could give battle at any time, under any circumstances.

Each corps numbered 20,000–30,000 men, consisting of at least two infantry divisions (8,000–12,000), a brigade of light cavalry, generally three regiments (2000–3000), six to eight companies of artillery, engineers, medics, bridging and siege trains, and headquarters staff. The bulk of the cavalry were for the first time formed into separate corps, complete with contingents of horse artillery (*artillerie-à-cheval*). Most of the heavy cavalry, cuirassier, and carabinier regiments were in separate corps. The infantry brigades were composed of two regiments (3500 men or more), with two or more brigades to a division, and two or more divisions in a corps. Artillery contingents were at corps level, and heavier artillery, especially twelve-pounders, were at army-level command. Napoleon put his artillery on wheeled carriages accompanied by caissons that could be pulled by horses into the line, and he made the carters members of the army rather than civilian contractors. The total artillery support averaged about two guns per 1000 troops.

The Imperial Guard, both an elite army with many privileges and a special corps to which some were promoted and many aspired, grew out of the Consular Guard of 1800–1804 and was honed at Boulogne. The Guard was small and self-contained, with its own artillery, cavalry, engineers, siege and bridge trains, and headquarters. By the time the Grande Armée marched out of Boulogne on its way to Austerlitz it had grown to 8000 men and would reach ten times that number on the Russian Campaign. There were three distinct components of the Guard. The Old Guard was composed of combat veterans of three or more campaigns and was fully formed by the time the new army went into combat in 1805. The Middle Guard, formed between 1806 and 1809, had the same admission requirements as the Old Guard. The Young Guard, formed after 1809, had a good many veterans but also significant numbers of young, promising soldiers. The different categories of Guard are sometimes confusing. The Young Guard was used extensively in virtually all the 1813–1814 battles. Although the Old Guard and the Old Guard cavalry fought in more battles overall than did the other two elite units, beginning against the Russian Imperial Guard Cavalry at Austerlitz, they were rarely used in these crucial years, and, along with the Young Guard they had not fought at the Battle of Borodino in 1812, nor had their cavalry. This decision remains controversial, but it was always Napoleon's choice whether or not to commit them to battle.

Uniforms and organization are but the external wrap for what mattered in Napoleon's first Grande Armée. It was training and discipline that shaped the army and it continued, with diminishing intensity, until 1814 when he ran out of time and fought predominantly with raw recruits. The Grande Armée was trained with a thoroughness and to a standard no army of the day could match. His letters, especially those written between 1802 and 1805 when the Grande Armée was created, are dominated by demands that the recruits be drilled regularly, rigorously, and precisely as he demanded. With time and the pressures of war his epistolary commands fell off, but he never ceased badgering his commanders and military instructors. Armies were made and maintained by training, élan was inculcated. The conscripts who would become the Grande Armée were scattered up and down the Atlantic coast from 1802 to 1805. Not much of the army of the 1790s was left. Napoleon built almost from scratch. He drilled the new men, or more accurately Marshals Ney and especially Soult drilled them, incessantly. Nicolas Jean de Dieu Soult (1769–1851), the son of a Gascon notary, enlisted in the infantry in 1785 rather than becoming a baker. His brilliant career is a history of the Revolutionary and Napoleonic wars and one of the few examples of the popular cliché that every soldier carried a marshal's baton in his kit. With the Revolution Soult rose quickly in the ranks. In 1791 he was a sergeant. The next year he was commissioned. In 1794 he was promoted to general. He fought everywhere with distinction, and was loaded with honors. Despite being badly battered by Wellington in the French retreat from Spain he managed to hold off the Allies for ten months after the debacle of Vitoria (21 June 1813), which definitively lost Spain. He was legendary for his excessive ambition and unbounded avarice. He was loyal to Napoleon until the end, refused to serve the restored Bourbons, yet had a distinguished career long after the Empire was gone. He represented France at Queen Victoria's coronation (1838) – the first time he met his nemesis, the Duke of Wellington – and was the youngest of the still living Imperial marshals to welcome the return of Napoleon's remains to France in 1840.

Soult was a demanding and severe commander, never having lost his skills as a sergeant. Along with Marshal Davout's 3rd corps Soult's 4th corps was the only one to arrive at Ulm in 1805 without having suffered desertions or trailed by a string of laggards. Except for a few hours of relaxation he worked the recruits relentlessly at the St Omer camp. Every day they marched with full pack, drilled on the parade ground, and took target practice. Three times a week Soult himself took his men through maneuvers, which often lasted 12 hours. Observers thought 'that at no other time or place has there been such an excellent military school'. He was not alone in rigor. The major of the 20th *chausseurs* hung lanterns in the riding stable and had his troops out with their mounts from 4 a.m. until 8 p.m. Every day in the harbor at Rochefort there was gunnery practice. Every other day the men had to fire mortars and practice with *boulet rouge*, shot heated red-hot before being launched. To hone their skill the gunners fired at old hulks towed into the harbor. The teams received 12 francs for each successful shot, and six for *boulet rouge*. These exercises lasted 20 days. Training also included teaching every man to swim, and those who were illiterate were taught enough so they could pick their way through written orders and sign their names.

No one was spared Napoleon's hectoring instructions He wrote to Cambacérès to order General Junot to inspect the troops 'three days running: one day to inspect their arms, their equipment, and make a note of those missing; the second day to see that they maneuver by regiment; the third day to see they maneuver by division'. He was to visit the forts and camps and 'send me a daily account, in a detailed report, of the troops, their instruction, their health, and their *esprit*'. Eugène de Beauharnais, whom he considered a 'real stubborn cuss' [*un vrai tête carrée*] was regularly lectured on the art of generalship:

> My intention is that the Verona and Brescia divisions be quartered in neighboring villages and constantly exercised with line maneuvers and target practice. An army is not an assembly of men. Exercise drill gives them their character.

Drill was the technical dimension of an army. Napoleon was equally concerned with its spirit. He welded the army to himself, a link earlier generals, especially Lafayette and Dumouriez, had failed to forge. Here he broke with the tradition of a citizen army loyal to the Revolution. He received their devotion as commander and after Brumaire as head of state. The Grande Armée was Napoleon's army, owing its allegiance personally to him. It was shaped with the utmost secrecy, although the English ships blockading the channel harbors daily saw Napoleon's men taking target practice and easily inferred he was preparing an amphibious invasion. So many men – by the time the army marched into Europe it was 200,000 strong – and so much concentrated ship and barge construction could not go unnoticed. There was not much the English could do except monitor from a distance, beef up their garrisons, and patrol off the channel ports until the French made their move. For more than two years the enemies faced each other and prepared for an attack that never came.

Boredom is the chief condition of any army not in a fight. The *Armée des Côtes de l'Océan* drilled daily and then was bored. Then, on 27 August 1805 Napoleon changed gears. He definitively abandoned an amphibious assault on England and turned his new army into a land force. Roughly half of all the effective soldiers in France, assembled in the channel ports, began an immense march to Eastern Europe. It would be the first of many such marches to battle and announced the capacity of the French military administration to move vast numbers across Europe in record time. There was little time left in the campaigning season in 1805 and the Grande Armée had to move fast and with precision. Each soldier carried a 58-pound pack. Among the Guard's many privileges was a gorgeous ceremonial uniform, which added seven pounds to their load. The standard pack contained 60 rounds of musket ammunition, a spare pair of trousers, two shirts, two extra pairs of boots, and rations for a week. This last burden speaks volumes about Napoleon's dependence upon swift victory. Years later his army would carry only three weeks' worth of food into Russia. His need to travel light, coupled to his maxim that war was to pay for war became a license to plunder.

The march from France's Atlantic coast to Austerlitz in East Central Europe, about 1000 miles across the continent, was 'one of the most brilliantly conceived, and speedily executed, of all time' in Alistair Horne's judgment. No other state achieved such coordination and commanded such capacity during the Napoleonic wars. Not until the age of the railroad could any European state move so many men so efficiently in so short a time. Napoleon's staff and administration retained this ability until the end of his career. He could ask more marching of his exceptionally well-trained soldiers than could any other commander. Most importantly he had superb staff work and gifted men willing to labor long and unnoticed in the inglorious duty of caring for the army. Napoleon appreciated their labors but military advancement in the Grande Armée came quickly only through courage in battle.

Who today could name the head of Wellington's quartermaster corps? Pierre Daru, Napoleon's military major-domo, was a significant figure in Napoleonic France. There is a street bearing his name in Paris, an honor bestowed by Napoleon's nephew. Daru was principally in charge of the stunning feats of military logistics, assembling the mountains of matériel the army would carry, and providing the transportation to move everything by a strict timetable, long before railroads taught civilization punctuality. Daru was born in Montpellier in 1767, the son of a minor royal functionary. He was a brilliant student of the classics at the Royal Military College in Tournon, and upon graduation climbed slowly up the ladder of preferment in the *ancien régime*. He served in the armies of the Revolution but got into trouble for 'an epistolary imprudence' as his biographer coyly puts it without giving any details. After Thermidor his career resumed and in 1796 he was named division chief in the Ministry of War, where he would spend the rest of his military days. Daru prudently stood aside during the Hundred Days and went on to serve the restored Bourbons until his death in 1829.

For those less interested in military matters, Daru was also distinguished by being the cousin of Henri Beyle (Stendhal), whose military career he launched. Daru thought or wished himself a man of letters. He wrote a *Histoire de la République de Venise*, now thoroughly forgotten, and translated Horace. Stendhal, for many the greatest of French novelists and one of the master spirits who shaped the Napoleonic myth, considered himself a man of action, although he passed much of his military career doing numbing administrative work in the Empire. He had marched with Napoleon to Moscow, but his chief renown was his incomparable creation, Julien Sorel, the hero of *The Red and Black* (*Le Rouge et le Noir*). Julien's ambitions to live the life of a soldier during the Restoration when the Church, not the army, was the preferred career and Napoleon was officially anathemized, is the greatest of Napoleonic novels.

*****

War, not horse-racing, is the sport of kings: even the greatest cannot afford it for long. The budgets of the Consulate and the Empire ran deficits more often than not. The first three budgets of the Consulate were balanced, the last of these thanks to the forced contributions of the conquered. For the remainder of Napoleon's rule it was his conquests that kept the annual deficits to a moderate level. The problem was both structural and willful. It is clear from the rapid recovery the French economy made in the early years of the Restoration, despite an enormous burden of reparations imposed by the Allies, that the economy was basically healthy, growing, and the state was able to pay its bills; so long as it was not engaged in perpetual war. This is precisely the relief that Napoleon was unable to provide.

Napoleon's regimentation of the state, the imposition of uniforms, hierarchy, and ceremonies throughout government and the schools as well as the army, was assured by the law of 16 July 1804. All the graduates of Napoleon's new schools, along with the École Polytechnique, the great engineering school created by the Revolution in 1794, were trained to serve the state. The Minister of War controlled the new schools, and at graduation the majority were commissioned junior lieutenants and posted to the artillery or the *corps de Génie* (the engineering corps), stationed at Metz. The Napoleonic state was not a barracks as Mme de Staël insisted, but it resembled one. The system of *préfets* (prefects) and an updating of the *Intendant* system of the *ancien régime* – the 13 royal appointees charged with the administration of the kingdom divided into as many provinces – centralized the state. Appointed by Napoleon himself, the *préfets* were directly answerable to the central government. They had below them sub-prefects for smaller towns, and for those too small to merit a resident representative there was a system of *piétons* (meaning messengers in this case) who physically connected the dispersed bureaucracy. It is this system, military in conception (with uniforms to match), that allowed Napoleon to reach into the most obscure corners first in France and then in the Empire. The prefects, at least in the large cities connected to Paris by a visual telegraph that was moderately efficient in clear weather and worthless on cloudy days, were the most typical and efficacious instruments of Napoleonic centralization.

Along with prefectoral and educational centralization went financial centralization and the reimposition of some of the most hated taxes of the *ancien régime*. After his glorious victory at Austerlitz Napoleon felt confident enough to levy the *gabelle*, the detested salt tax, along with the 'cellar rats', agents of the government sent out to search for hidden food and cross-examine citizens about the wealth of their neighbors. There is a memorable passage in Rousseau's *Confessions* where his host snatches away the simple spread of milk, cheese, and ham they had offered him, while sounding the alarm '*des rats-de-cave*'. The hated practice had been suppressed during the Revolution.

There was no state or society of the *ancien régime* that would not have benefitted from legal reform, but revolutionary France was the first. The French kings had now and again attempted codification and control of a sprawling assortment of laws, decrees, proclamations, precedents, courts both lay and ecclesiastical, and the difficult and contentious marriage of Roman and Germanic law, which prevailed, roughly and respectively in southern and northern France. Sweeping legal reform, desired, imagined, but barely begun by the Revolution, was realized by Napoleon in the first four years of the 19th century. Jean-Etienne-Marie Portalis (1746–1807) was the central figure, as he had been in achieving a Concordat with the Church. After a conventional and brilliant legal career before the Revolution Portalis failed to get elected to the Estates-General in 1789 and remained outside revolutionary politics. Soon after his electoral defeat he moved from his native Provence to Lyons. When that city, after seceding from the Republic, came under siege by a Jacobin government determined to compel obedience to Paris, he managed to escape. Portalis fled to the capital where the Terror was the order of the day. He stayed far from public life and its dangers. Through obscurity and extreme caution he rode out the storm. His political career did not begin until after Thermidor and Robespierre's fall.

Portalis was chosen by Napoleon, who sought talent whatever one's political opinions: Portalis repaid him with devotion. Thibadeau, an old revolutionary and one of Napoleon's *préfets*, describes Portalis as grateful that his patron had returned France to monarchical principles. He had an imagination that worked on a large canvas which was congenial to Napoleon's own grand designs. He was a gifted orator both in court and at the tribune, despite his southern accent. He united in his ideas and personality philosophy and religion, *bonhomie* and elegance, the emotional simplicity of a child with the gravity of a man of state, the independence of a citizen with the suppleness of a courtier. He was an 'instrument of great usefulness when in strong hands' in Thibadeau's judgment. He proved the ideal man to direct both Napoleon's *rapprochement* with the Church and his codification of the laws. Portalis was a religious man but a Gallican, a believer in a national Catholic Church relatively free of Papal interference and Papal exactions. If Catholicism was to be again legalized in France the Church had to accept the supremacy of the state, a cause to which Portalis was passionately devoted, as was his master. If the rule of law, which he described as 'acts of wisdom, justice, and reason' was to prevail it needed the work of a 'legislator who functioned less as an authority than as a quasi-religious figure'. The need for a legislator, a supra-historical law-giver, was one of the few Rousseauian ideas he embraced. The *philosophe* himself had celebrated Lycurgus, the mythic law-giver of Sparta. Portalis found his Lycurgus in Napoleon.

Portalis's *Discours préliminaire au premier projet de Code civil* [*Preliminary Discourse to the First Proposal of the Civil Code*] is a superb introduction to the *Code Napoléon*. It is closely argued, filled with learning both philosophical and legal, and informed by the clarity of a first-class legal intelligence. 'Uniformity,' he writes, expressing one of Napoleon's cherished convictions, 'is a genre of perfection which, according to a celebrated author, *sometimes inspires the greatest minds, and unfailingly impresses the petty.*' It was to be one of the master principles of the new Code. Portalis had no illusions about either the perfectibility of man or his laws. 'History,' he writes, 'offers us little more than the promulgation of two or three good laws in the space of several centuries.' He warned against seeking perfection 'in things that are susceptible only to relative excellence'. Laws, necessarily riddled with imperfections, are the best that men can do in ordering their societies.

Portalis was far more restrained than Napoleon in imposing the uniformity of the Code on other states. His affection for Montesquieu's insistence on difference and diversity made him sensitive to historically and culturally generated mores which had to be expressed in the laws of any society. He certainly would not have given Europe laws at bayonet point, which was Napoleon's preferred practice. The law, for Portalis, was not a weapon of empire, a powerful corrosive of old institutions, a revolutionary leaven to undermine the *ancien régime*, which is precisely how Napoleon used his new Code. Nowhere was his revolutionary use of law more obvious than in the provisions governing the family, which proved the most hated aspects of the Civil Code and one in which Napoleon himself took a keen interest. Whether it was his Corsican heritage, with its misogyny, traditional family hierarchy and constraints, and the power of the *pater familias*, or some residue of his Rousseauian urge to force his subjects to be free, or only the need of a general to impose order on his subordinates, we cannot know. But the Code, along with his administrative reforms, became the vanguard of Napoleon's revolution from above. All who forcibly received the new legislation detested it as the spawn of the French Revolution and repulsed it when Napoleon fell. The administrative reforms, which taught the restored *ancien régime* efficiency, especially in tax collection, were maintained.

Marriage and divorce, Portalis was aware, as was his master, were the most vexing of all the laws. The new Code was far more restrictive than had been revolutionary experiments, but stopped well short of returning to the practices of the Catholic *ancien régime*. 'The question of divorce,' Portalis writes, 'is a pure civil question whose answer must be sought in weighing the inconveniences and the advantages that can result from divorce, considered from a political point of view.' The Code would allow divorce only 'for civil death [as punishment for some crimes], which imitates natural death, and for the crimes and misdemeanors one spouse can charge against another. We do not believe it would be tolerable to render divorce easier that it has previously been for separations.' 'Private virtues alone,' Portalis continues, 'can guarantee public virtues ...' There is no mention of a sacrament or priest. An *officier de l'état civil* [a kind of Justice of the Peace] presides and his function is confined to purely civil matters: verifying and recording the names, ages, place of birth and residence of the couple, their parents, and their witnesses, a request for any opposition to the marriage, and signing the official documents. Divorce is treated with the same dry precision. The causes allowed are the wife's adultery (#229), the husband's adultery if committed in the marital home (#230), mutual consent in the case of 'excessive brutality or grave injuries of one partner by the other' (#231), a criminal judgment against one of the partners (#232), and by mutual consent 'when it can be legally determined that a life together is unsupportable' (#233). All of these requirements, it has been often pointed out, favor the husband.

Marriage and divorce may have been the focus of political as well as ecclesiastical outrage, but the bulk of the Civil Code concerned property: 1570 of its 2281 articles to be precise. All feudal distinctions, whether of property, service, or privilege, had no legal standing in the Code. The intermediary institutions that had grown up in the *ancien régime* and were swept away in the French Revolution were formally deprived of legality by the Code. In its French setting the *Code Civil* essentially codified what the Revolution had reformed, promised, or practiced. When the Code was imposed on states that had not undergone a revolution it became a revolutionary weapon. Napoleon made no allowances for local traditions, habits, or history. He demanded the Code *en bloc*. All those who were given satellite kingdoms saw the impact the Code would have on their kingdoms and sought, with limited success, to moderate both its clauses and Napoleon's impatience.

Every aspect of Napoleon's state emanated from his will. Even more than Louis XIV – despite the unverified attribution of his boast – he could say *l'État c'est moi*, I am the state. 'I alone arrange the finances,' he lectured his treasurer, Mollien. He did not embody the state symbolically or mystically as had the kings. He embodied the people, a revolutionary principle. By his orders he caused the state to run which then filled the conduits of administration he had created. Prince Metternich would argue that it is this willfulness that defined Napoleon as a revolutionary, a man oblivious to the constraints of custom and habit, unwilling to conform his power to the example of an orderly, predictable nature. There is truth here. In diplomacy Napoleon broke all the rules by which Metternich and his class lived. He lacked the social standing, the conventional finesse and fine manners that defined the diplomatic corps of the *ancien régime*. Most of all he lacked the temperament for negotiation, which he despised. He took a childish delight in behaving badly in the midst of studied and traditional decorum. He was a new man, made by the Revolution and not by generations of breeding and a code of behavior. His dealings with ambassadors and plenipotentiaries are marked by temper tantrums, rudeness, vulgarity, and imperiousness. The anecdotes of his undiplomatic behavior are many and amusing. One will suffice.

Talleyrand tells the story of Napoleon receiving Louis de Cobenzl, the Austrian plenipotentiary. Napoleon scheduled the meeting for 9 p.m. so he could use the darkness as part of the staging of the interview. He carefully arranged the room in the Tuileries for the reception. He had a small table and chair placed in the corner of a long room. Here he sat. All the other chairs were removed. The table contained some papers and an escritoire. There was a single lamp but it had not been lit. Cobenzl entered, ushered in by Talleyrand. 'The darkness of the room, the distance he had to cross to reach the table where Bonaparte sat' were calculated to make Cobenzl uneasy. He scarcely saw Napoleon sitting in the far corner. 'Bonaparte got up and sat back down. It was impossible for M. de Cobenzl not to remain standing ... in the place the First Consul had assigned him.' The arrogant Cobenzl was kept uncomfortable and awkward while Napoleon held forth.

With the Empire a complex court etiquette replaced the more informal practices of the Consulate. After 1804 Napoleon took refuge in the heady ceremonials of the imperial court, considered by many a distasteful reenactment of the Byzantine court of the Late Roman Empire. The pompous titles of *monseigneur, altesse sérénissime, excellence* were made mandatory, and *monsieur* was reinstated in place of the revolutionary and democratic *citoyen*. It became more difficult to see Napoleon, although etiquette did not improve his manners, refine his language, or soften his bluntness. Nor was his diplomatic conduct improved. He was a bully, and even when he turned on his considerable personal charm the sub-text of any Napoleonic negotiation was the chilling fact of the Grande Armée. In diplomacy as on the battlefield Napoleon believed in taking the offensive. At the bargaining table he wanted a clear victory and preferred to dictate his terms in the captured capital of the enemy in the palace once occupied by the vanquished king. The reality or looming threat of invasion and defeat was more compelling than the imperial smile.

Napoleon was the most conservative of revolutionaries. He expanded, recentered, extended, and refined what he had inherited after he curtailed democracy and shelved all the utopian schemes of the Jacobins. He did not begin from original premises or build anew. His genius was in rearranging and fully realizing what he found to hand. His military innovations rest upon using the technology and military theories of the 1780s. The Civil Code is above all a codification of laws, not a new approach to a legal system. The Concordat harkens back to Louis XIV's Gallican liberties. The same is true of his empire. He did not invent any new war aims for the French nor, in coining his ambition the 'Grande Nation' do anything more than expand, rationalize, and intensify the geopolitics of the Revolution. Even the Continental System, so apparently novel, is the mercantilism of Louis XIV and Colbert reimagined and writ large. Napoleon did not invent economic warfare, but he practiced it on so grand a scale, even without a navy, that it appears new. It has been rightly remarked that the theoretical underpinning of the Continental System took no account of the new economic world gestating in industrial England. The blockade failed not because it was theoretically old-fashioned but because he needed a navy to blockade the enormous coast of his empire. Lacking ships, he needed the cooperation of other rulers (the Tsar, his German allies, the Spanish Bourbons) to close the Continent to British commerce. Cooperation was a skill he utterly lacked.

At Tilsit, after having administered a drubbing to the Russian army at the Battle of Friedland (14 June 1807), he tried through the art of conventional diplomacy to intensify the economic war against England and stabilize his recent conquests. Napoleon could have imposed a humiliating peace, but he had more grandiose plans. He set out to seduce the Tsar to do his bidding. Although the settlements reached at Tilsit were short-lived it remains Napoleon's most complex and visionary exercise in geopolitics. For the occasion he had a special raft built and anchored in the middle of the Niemen where he and Tsar Alexander would deliberate. Napoleon's tripartite division of the world into English, French, and Russian interests merely formalized what existed. The agreements he made with Alexander, including their secret clauses, was to insure the complete isolation of England that Napoleon sought. We do not know what happened on the raft in the Niemen, but the Tsar's concessions and promises convinced Napoleon that his charm had worked. Alexander's concessions, however, were repellant to his court. For a few years he turned a blind eye even to flagrant violations of the blockade while his official policy was compliance. Then in 1810 he issued an *ukaz* that formally maintained his official policy yet heavily taxed imported French products.

About a year after Tilsit Napoleon staged another piece of diplomatic theater, in Erfurt in central Germany. Alexander, who had not yet veered away from policing the Baltic, was again the guest of honor. It was a summit meeting between the two emperors. Unlike Tilsit, little of significance was done. Erfurt was a theatrical representation of French power and culture, warfare by other means, to echo Clausewitz. All who had business or came to pay court to the new Caesar assembled. 'Every day someone left for Erfurt,' Talleyrand reports. 'The roads were covered with baggage trains, saddle horses, four-wheeled carriages, and liveried servants.' Napoleon's preparations were careful. He brought his favorite actor, François Joseph Talma, to Erfurt, and he himself chose the plays to be presented. The Revolution had officially spurned the culture of the court and the *ancien régime*. But if the great tragic poets were not presented on the stage they remained loved by the political elite. Robespierre and his close friends declaimed Racine's plays, but he never thought of high French culture as a revolutionary weapon. Napoleon shared Robespierre's love of classical tragedy and marshaled French culture to do battle. The ideas of immortality, glory, valor, and fatality were central to Racine's *Iphigénie*, while Voltaire's *Mahomet* best expressed the source of Napoleon's power:

> Mortals are equal, it is not by birth,
> It is only virtue that makes the difference.
> It is these being favored by the heavens
> Who owe everything to themselves and nothing to their ancestors.
> Such is the man, in a word, whom I have taken for my master;
> He alone in the universe is worthy to be such;
> Every moral has his one day laws to be obeyed, ...

Napoleon brought with him his secretaries, several of his ministers, and a number of generals and prefects. One of his entourage was specially assigned to see to the needs, including French actresses, of the Grand Duke Constantine, Alexander's cruel brother. Napoleon arrived on 27 September 1808 at 10 in the morning. 'A huge crowd gathered along the route to his palace. Each one, Talleyrand continues, 'wanted to see, wanted to approach he who dispensed all: thrones, misery, fear, hope'. With an acidity that came naturally Talleyrand describes the hierarchy of sycophancy among the German princes. 'The powerful princes wanted ... [to give] an idea of the grandeur of their Empire. The petty princes, on the contrary, wanted their court to hide the narrow limits of their power.' In the various courts, he continues, there is

> another way of aggrandizing oneself: by bowing. The petty princes only know how to abase themselves on the ground. There they remain until fortune should come and raise them up. I have never seen anyone pass a single ennobling morning under the mane of a lion.

Napoleon also enhanced his reputation as a civilized man, a friend to literature and the arts, reprising the role he had played soon after his return from Egypt. The great Goethe had been specifically invited. Every morning Napoleon glanced at the list of those who had arrived and when he saw Goethe's name ordered the poet immediately summoned. On Sunday, 2 October 1808 Napoleon, along with Talleyrand and Daru, had a long interview with Goethe. Talleyrand made a record of the meeting which he showed Goethe to be sure it was 'perfectly exact'.

Napoleon was at his most ingratiating, Goethe was the practiced courtier:

> Monsieur Goethe, I am charmed to see you.
>
> – Sire, I see that when Your Majesty travels he does not neglect to cast his glance on the smallest things.
> – I know that you are the first tragic poet of Germany.
> – Sire, you do an injustice to our country. We believe ourselves to have several great men: Schiller, Lessing, and Wieland should be known to Your Majesty.

Napoleon said he had read Schiller's *Thirty Years' War* and found it only furnished tragic matter 'for our boulevards'.

> – Sire (Goethe deftly responded), I do not know your boulevards, but I suppose that it is there that are presented plays for the people, and I am saddened to hear you so severely judge one of the great geniuses of modern times.

Napoleon changed the subject to matters where conflicting aesthetic judgments were not involved, or so he thought.

> – While you are here, he told Goethe, you must go in the evenings to see our plays. There you will not be sorry to see some fine French tragedies.
> – Sire, I will go with the greatest pleasure.

Napoleon then told Goethe he should write his impressions of the great things the French presented at Erfurt.

- Ah! Sire, one would need the pen of a writer of antiquity to undertake such a work.
- Are you among those who admire Tacitus?
- Yes, Sire, a great deal.
- Aha, not me. But we will speak of this on another occasion.

Tilsit and Erfurt are the last times we will see Napoleon in so light-hearted a mood, so deliberately charming, orchestrating the riches of French culture for political ends, behaving like a diplomat of the *ancien régime*. The line that divides Napoleon's years of success from those of gradual and then precipitous decline is difficult to draw with precision. He was still full of self-confidence, not entirely merited by reality, in 1808; the next year, at Wagram, he would demonstrate that his military mastery remained intact. He continued to rule his massive empire himself, but it not only taxed even his stupendous capacity for work, but he became increasingly dependent upon others. This was a role he played badly. The empire had become a vast juggling act, and the juggler appeared to be tiring.

Entr'acte
A Sighting in Jena

The first fights of the Grande Armée were in many ways their most glorious. Austerlitz (2 December 1805) is often thought the most perfect Napoleonic battle. He split the armies of the three emperors, beat them *seriatim* and executed his preferred *manoeuvre sur les derrières*, an oblique attack to turn the enemy flank, perfectly. Jena-Auerstädt (14 October 1806) was his most devastating triumph. In a single blow he utterly destroyed Prussia. He later regretted he had allowed the mortally crippled state to survive. He appeared invincible. The armies of the French Revolution had never penetrated so deeply into Germany nor had they made kings and emperors tremble so uncontrollably on their thrones. Napoleon's lightning victories reified the nightmares of princes, potentates, and the elites of the *ancien régime*. They also heartened all those who sought reform and transformation. Much of the German intelligentsia embraced Napoleon.

The Emperor, less than a year after Austerlitz, arrived in Jena between 2 and 3 p.m. on Monday, 13 October 1806. The war against Prussia was under way. He stopped briefly at Grossherzoglich Schloss then rode out the Weimar gate toward the battlefield. He arrived at the Langgrafenberg at 4 p.m., made arrangements for his bivouac, then returned to Jena. He reached the chateau of the town a little before 6 p.m. and later that night returned to his camp to sleep before the battle. He checked the paths his artillery would use around 10 p.m., and then retired. The battle was fought the next day. He slept after his crushing victory in Jena and left on the 15th at 1 p.m. riding the 12 miles to Weimar. Before Napoleon departed Jena, Georg Wilhelm Friedrich Hegel 'saw the Emperor – this world-soul – riding out of the city on reconnaissance. It is indeed a wonderful sensation to see such an individual, who, concentrated here at a single point, astride a horse, reaches out over the world and masters it'. So complete was the victory and the rout of the Prussians that such deeds 'are only possible for this extraordinary man, whom it is impossible not to admire'. Hegel even forgave the French for trashing his rooms and scattering his manuscripts. The chance encounter, a moment unnoticed by history at the time, would have far-reaching consequences. Hegel's philosophy of history, the most influential and profound of the age, was inspired by the French Revolution and Napoleon. He became the first contemporary of the extraordinary events of the age to put them into a vast philosophical context whose impact, both in Hegel's version and in its Marxist elaboration, is still alive. His is also the most searching appraisal ever made of Napoleon's historical significance and his complex relationship to the French Revolution. Hegel's Napoleon, stripped of anecdote, physical details, and personal description is the embodiment of the French Revolution, its unwitting agent, and by inference its savior.

A few years later, in Düsseldorf, the nine-year-old Heinrich Heine also saw Napoleon ride into his town in his pale green uniform and 'world-famous little hat'. He rode through the park where horses were strictly forbidden. The penalty was ten thalers, payable on the spot. No Prussian policeman enforced the rule:

> A smile that warmed and reassured every heart played over the Emperor's lips, yet everyone knew these lips had only to whistle and Prussia would cease to exist. These lips had only to whistle and the clergy was finished. These lips had only to whistle and the entire Holy Roman Empire of the German Nation would dance to his tune.

Neither would ever forget seeing Napoleon on horseback. Nearly a year after the battle Hegel described it as 'that all-too-great event that was the Battle of Jena, the sort of event which happens only once every hundred thousand years'. It coincided with a personal triumph for the philosopher every bit as cosmic in his own mind as Napoleon's victory. On the eve of the battle he had entrusted the sole copy of his major philosophical work the *Phenomenology of Spirit* (*Phänomenologie des Geistes*) to a postal courier riding through French lines from Jena to Bamberg. A remarkable and foolish act: perhaps the philosopher's disdain for the real world.

Hegel's reputation among German philosophers, then as now, is as the maker of a profound, abstruse, often obscure, sometimes impenetrable, and always difficult philosophical system that permanently altered how we think about the world and its meaning. His thought is made even

Figure 4   Georg Friedrich Wilhelm Hegel (1831) by Johann Jakob Schlesinger. Painted in the year of Hegel's death, when he was the most celebrated philosopher in Germany, this is a haunting portrait. Hegel's gaze, dominated by his blue eyes, is penetrating. The painting has the immediacy of a photograph. The artist, known mostly as a restorer and copyist, has given us, in his most celebrated work, a face much lived in.

more daunting by his deliberate use of an original vocabulary which he believed would compel the reader to think for himself, and perhaps befuddle the censors. He avoids conventional philosophical language lest the reader be lulled into acceding uncritically to past conceptions. 'I am sorry there are complaints about the ponderousness of the presentation,' he wrote to a Dutch pupil, Peter Gabriel van Ghert:

> It is, however, the nature of such abstract subjects that treatments of them cannot assume the ease of a common reader. Truly speculative philosophy cannot take on the garb and style of Locke or the usual French philosophy.

The French philosopher, Victor Cousin, when he first met Hegel, was invited to tea at the sage's home where he interrogated him about his

Encyclopedia. Hegel 'himself was not always very intelligible to me,' Cousin confesses. But things went better when the philosopher talked of art, religion, history, and politics: 'On these subjects he was much more accessible to me, and we more easily fell into agreement ...' Hegel's love of words and metaphor enrich his thought but make it no more lucid. He brilliantly exploited the genius of the German language to make new words by putting old ones together. Some of his most characteristic tropes – the world-spirit for example – are of this kind. He transformed the philosophical school of German Idealism: virtually no subsequent thinker remained immune to his ideas.

Hegel's philosophy, for all its knottiness, is grounded in the reality of his day. The French Revolution and Napoleon play an enormous role in his thought and are correctly seen as the seismic creation of a new world. History is in Hegel's thought the central concern of philosophy, and he was remarkably well-informed about the past and the events of his own time. He read several newspapers every day, including those from France and England when he could get his hands on them. He was obsessively interested in the French Revolution, both as history and a spawning ground for the future. He looked to Napoleon as the savior of Germany, based his apotheosis of the Prussian state on the work done by the French Revolution, not least the defeat at Jena, and he remained throughout his life a partisan of the Revolution. He was, with many German intellectuals, enthralled by the actual and the possible trans- formative power of the Revolution. When he was not philosophizing he was a hard-headed, practical, well-informed radical. When he wrote or lectured he transmuted the mundane concerns of contemporary Germany into a form that can only be called Hegelian. He hoped to revolutionize Germany and early came to the conclusion that there was no indigenous mechanism for doing so. The Germans were incapable of getting rid of or even modifying their *ancien régime.* Only some outside force could accomplish the needed purge. He welcomed the destruction, in 1806, of the Holy Roman Empire, a historic dinosaur that stood in the way of German renewal, and he welcomed the French Revolution.

In a controversy with Karl Moser, a conservative legal scholar and apologist for Austria, Hegel argued that the Holy Roman Empire, unable to enforce laws or defend itself according to its laws, was not an *actual* state. It existed only in thought. Austria itself he consid- ered a pernicious power preventing the reforms he craved. It could only be removed by Napoleon. 'In the first place,' he wrote his friend Friedrich Emmanuel Niethammer following Napoleon's victory over the Austrians at Regensburg (19–23 April 1809), 'nobody can more eagerly congratulate you on your deliverance from the enemy forces than I'. He similarly welcomed the reforms in Württemberg undertaken by the Duke of Saxony, recently made a king by Napoleon. Frederick II (1754–1816) abolished medieval privileges, confiscated the property of the clergy, and secularized the University of Tübingen. The professors might devote their energies to justifications of princely power in Germany, but, Hegel wrote, 'the great professor of constitutional law [Napoleon] sits in Paris' and would decide Germany's future.

As a young man Hegel had joined a political club at Tübingen which discussed the Revolution as partisans, and he regularly read and applauded Johann Wilhelm von Archenholz's journal *Minerva*, which was passionately pro-Revolution. These enthusiasms stayed with him; an unusual constancy not shared by his intellectual peers, most of whom fell prey to German chauvinism once Napoleon had been defeated. Early impressions turned sour for many with the French occupation. In 1820, on a trip to Dresden, in the midst of a long mood of strident German nationalism and Metternichean repression, Hegel offended some friends by ordering the most expensive champagne on the menu, Sillery, which subsequently became Moët after 1848, and is happily still with us. The toast, which he renewed every year, was even more offensive: 'This glass is for the 14th of July, 1789 – to the storming of the Bastille.' On a trip to Magdeburg in 1822 he skipped the sights and visited Lazare Carnot, a Jacobin, a member of the Committee of Public Safety who ran the revolutionary wars and was gratefully dubbed the 'organizer of victory'. His support was crucial in Napoleon's rise to power. He was forced into exile in 1816, along with all the remaining regicides, by the restored Bourbons. 'But of all that I saw,' Hegel wrote to his wife 'the most treasured sight was General Carnot, a kind old man and a Frenchman. It was the famous Carnot. He took it kindly that I looked him up.' His attachment to the Revolution was not unconditional. Hegel abhorred the Terror. 'You probably know that Carrier [the notorious terrorist of Nantes] has been guillotined,' he wrote to Friedrich Wilhelm Joseph von Schelling before their philosophic break. 'Do you still read the French papers?' They had been banned in Württemberg. 'The trial is very important, and has revealed the complete ignominy of Robespierre's party.' Jean-Baptiste Carrier was guillotined on 16 November 1794 after a stormy trial. His death was a public repudiation of the Terror after Robespierre's fall.

Hegel followed Napoleon's meteoric career and after his death sought all the memoirs of the great man he could find. He wrote his pupil, van Ghert, from the University of Berlin where he had assumed the most important chair in philosophy in the country, asking for Las Cases's

Mémorial de Sainte-Hélène, whose publication in 1822 provided the gospel for the Napoleonic myth. He also ordered 'Napoleon's *Mémoires* edited in four volumes by Gourgaud and Montholon, and the memoirs of Barry O'Meara, an Irishman and Royal Navy surgeon who was one of Napoleon's doctors on St Helena. The books were not only hard to find but often banned in the German states. They were considered intellectual contraband: their price was steep and the cost of shipping equally so.

As the editor of the *Bamberger Zeitung* in 1807–08 Hegel had been pro-Napoleon and strongly supported virtually all the reforms forced upon the German states. He reported that the French army was behaving in an exemplary way toward the populace, and contrasted them to the barbarism of the Russian troops, who, although they were the allies of several German states, behaved like Cossacks, a contemporary metaphor for oriental savagery. Germany's rebirth, in a notice he published, could not depend on 'imitating the ethos, laws, politics, and humanity of a superstitious people' such as the Russians. He celebrated the Russian defeat at Friedland, as a 'glorious victory'. He approved of Napoleon's creation of the kingdom of Westphalia for his brother Jerome, cobbled together from lands confiscated from several German states, and praised its constitution, the first given to a German state. It embodied the promises of the Revolution: civil equality and religious liberty, the abolition of guilds, serfdom, and aristocratic privilege, the introduction of the French legal code, open courts, and trial by jury. Napoleon, he wrote, 'has not only opened to our eyes new views into inaccessible worlds, but rather, what is more, he has disclosed and completed a view into a new world here at hand for our gaze'. He got away with these opinions because Bavaria was an ally of the French.

Hegel was not a democrat. He disliked the Jacobins for their brutality, and feared the mob – he made a clear distinction in his letters between the people (*Volk*) and the dumb and dangerous masses (*Pippel*), who habitually supported reaction. Describing a torchlight ceremony that closed the Congress of Vienna, of which he disapproved, he wrote sardonically of the order of the procession:

> Behind Pippel there follow, as valets and attendants, a few tame house cats, such as the Inquisition, the Jesuit Order, and then all the armies with their absurdly commissioned, princely, and titled marshals and generals.

He desired the social and political changes wrought by the French Revolution, but without the violence. 'Thanks to the bath of her

Revolution,' he wrote his friend, Christian Gotthold Zellman, 'the French Nation has freed herself of many institutions which the human spirit had outgrown like the shoes of a child ... This is what gives this Nation the great power she displays against others.' France, liberated by the Revolution, 'weighs down upon the impassiveness and dullness of these other nations, which, finally forced to give up their indolence in order to step out into actuality, will perhaps – seeing that inwardness preserves itself in externality – surpass their teachers.' Here is Hegelianism applied to contemporary Germany. He is arguing for the complete realization of the French Revolution, which will be the historical task set for Germany. As he puts it, 'the world spirit has given the times the command to advance, and the command is being obeyed'. Hegel's views on the heritage and benefits of the French Revolution closely parallel those of Napoleon, who also wanted none of the dangerous disruptions of social revolution, no loosening of the constraints of class and habits of hierarchy, let alone democracy. Napoleon's revolution was to be accomplished from the top by an authoritarian imposition of legal, political, educational, and governmental reforms but without the participation of the *pippel*.

Hegel's philosophy is about the realization of human freedom, uniquely defined and understood. His historical thought is focused on a vast movement of civilizations toward freedom. World history began with the orientals, 'who knew only that *one* is free, then that of the Greek and Roman world, which knew that *some* are free, and finally our own knowledge that *all* men are free, and that man is by nature free'. This is his celebrated formulation from *Philosophy of History*. The French Revolution in this scheme has completed a long development and set men, all men, socially and politically free. The remaining task is to set their minds free and make them aware that they are free. This great, final liberation, the liberation of the human spirit, is the work reserved by history for German philosophy and its expression in the German, that is Prussian, state. The story of freedom in history is the story of Hegel's quest for the *logos* of history. The '*novel* of the Revolution', as he put it, would not be finished in France, but in Germany. Napoleon, coincidentally, had spoken of his life as a wonderful novel. What the French lacked philosophically, according to Hegel, was self-awareness, the great inner moral and ethical strength that characterized German idealistic philosophy, and revealed the essence of the world beyond mere appearances. French philosophy was materialistic, pragmatic, it described the surface of things, the manifestations of an underlying reality which it left unexplored. French philosophy could create the

modern state, it could centralize and rationalize state power, and liberate men from the shackles of accumulated privilege and exploitation.
It could not free their minds from the remaining shackles of conventional thinking, in Germany best expressed by the 'boneheadedness'
of German officialdom that Hegel deplored. Only German philosophy
could teach self-consciousness, make men aware of the new moral
spirit made possible by the Revolution, turn the inner moral world
outward, where it would infuse all. Hitherto this self-consciousness
of the realization of freedom in the world had remained unexpressed.
Men's thoughts might be free, but in a world where power and privilege conspired to make only a few free, the necessary final stage of
freedom remained unrealized. Once the freedom of the mind is made
external, *actual* in Hegelian language, when the ideal and the real
become one, mankind could be free. Once Germany, because of the
French Revolution and Napoleon, was forced to give up her 'indolence'
she had the possibility of expressing her 'inwardness' externally. Then
she will surpass her teachers. History will have fulfilled its goal. This
is all very abstruse, but it is Hegel's philosophical expression of the
history he lived: that of the French Revolution and Napoleon. When
he set about systemizing his thoughts on history, when he set himself the task of explaining the course of history and the place of the
Revolution and Napoleon in history, he provided the best contemporary explanation we have of Napoleon's relationship to the French
Revolution and its meaning.

Hegel was a year younger than Napoleon. Not unlike Corsica,
Stuttgart, where he was born, was far from the intellectual and political
centers of his world. He always spoke German with a thick Swabian
accent and self-deprecatingly told a friend going to Stuttgart that he
'at first will doubt whether [the inhabitants] actually speak German'.
As a young man in his twenties he was shaped and excited by the
French Revolution. When the revolutionary wars came to the Rhine
frontier and then to Jena and all of Germany, world history imposed
itself on Hegel. Despite his capacity for obfuscating the mundane and
enveloping his thought in philosophical abstraction – *Hegelei* is the
German word for abstruse and impenetrable prose – the Revolution and
Napoleon were at the center of his thought. There they would remain.
Hegel's lectures on history, delivered in the winter of 1822–23 at the
University of Berlin, were widely attended, profoundly influential, and
posthumously published in his collected works with the simple title *The
Philosophy of History* (*Philosophie der Geschichte*). Hegel himself did not
prepare the manuscript for publication, and some have quipped that

this is why the lectures on history are his most widely read and accessible work. They present Hegel at his least obscure and most dazzling. The premise of the work is simple yet profound: the contemplation of history is the study of the progress of reason in the world. The philosophy of history is the history of philosophy is his well-known dictum. Because history is the embodiment of reason it is comprehensible. It is not a few fleeting dark glimpses of a hidden God who reveals Himself only obliquely and only fully at the end of history itself. Hegelian history, in the Judeo-Christian tradition, is teleological, but its purpose is known through reason not revelation. These fundamental propositions he expressed more obscurely (and characteristically) before he prepared the lectures that make up *The Philosophy of History*. Even before the years in Jena that produced his *Phenomenology*, he was working on the meaning of history, and the *Phenomenology* contains a number of suggestive *aperçus* later elaborated. If we consider history irrational, Hegel argued, a concatenation of events united only by time and place, we trivialize it, deprive it of meaning. We can understand nothing of history for there is nothing to understand, no underlying *logos*. We will marvel, he wrote to his student, Christian Gotthold Zellman,

> speechless at events, like brutes – or, with a greater show of cleverness, [attribute] them to the accidents of the moment or talents of an individual, thus making the fate of empires hang on the occupation or non-occupation of a hill ...

The endless flood of events is an illusion. In truth the purposefulness of history, he wrote Niethammer, the world spirit,

> proceeds irresistibly like a closely drawn armored phalanx advancing with imperceptible movement, much as the sun through thick and thin. Innumerable light troops flank it on all sides, throwing themselves into the balance for or against its progress, though most of them are entirely ignorant of what is at stake and merely take head blows as from an invisible hand.

History marches to a predestined goal, despite the actions and misconceptions of men, those 'innumerable light troops' that take 'head blows'.

Men, the historical actors, do what they do out of self-interest and egotism, which he calls passion: 'we may affirm absolutely that *nothing great in the World* has been accomplished without *passion*.' The vast 'congeries of volitions, interests and activities, constitute the instruments and means of the World-Spirit for attaining its object'. Individuals seek to satisfy their own purposes and are 'the means and instruments of a higher and broader purpose of which they know nothing'. He will later call transforming the passions of men into historical causation the 'cunning of reason'. In his mature philosophy he will attempt to eliminate the inherent messiness and danger of depending on the blind passions of men by enshrining the *logos* of history in the state. Here the final historical apotheosis of reason will take place, unencumbered by egomania. But when he developed his ideas on history it was the French Revolution and Napoleon, with all their chaotic turmoil, that was driving history.

'The History of the World', in Hegel's vision, 'is not the theater of happiness. Periods of happiness are blank pages in it, for they are periods of harmony'. It is struggle that moves history. The huge collisions between antitheses, a cardinal Hegelian term, are accomplished by 'Historical men – *World-Historical Individuals*'. The first example he gives, which is a model for all the others, is Julius Caesar. In danger of losing his position in the Roman world, denied the rightful rewards of his patrician birth and his military conquests, beset by enemies, enormously in debt, and absent from Rome where he was being slandered and undermined, Caesar acted boldly to save himself. He had no concerns beyond political survival, defeating his enemies, and imposing himself on the Roman world. He crossed the Rubicon, and brought his army with him, thus violating the sacred precincts of Rome. His enemies, similarly pursuing their personal aims, which included the destruction of Caesar, had the constitution of the Republic, the religious sanctions of the state, and the appearance of justice on their side. By marching against legality, opinion, religion, and convention he overturned the Republic and mastered the whole of the Roman Empire, which his actions had in significant part created. He made himself, seemingly by his own hand, the autocrat of the state. The parallels with Napoleon are obvious. Caesar inadvertently destroyed the Roman Republic and created the Roman Empire to save himself from political oblivion. The Empire in turn would spread first Roman civilization and then Christianity and create Europe. Caesar knew none of this. Nor did anyone else. It is doubtful he would have cared or behaved differently had he known the consequences, all unintended, of his passion. He was the unwitting tool of history. He destroyed the old and ushered in the new and next stage in the unfolding of the Idea.

In the Hegelian scheme there is an additional motivation for the acts of great men. 'It was not, then, [Caesar's] private gain merely, but an unconscious impulse that occasioned the accomplishment of that for which the time was ripe. Such are all great historical men – whose own particular aims involve those large issues which are the will of the World-Spirit.' Unaware that their actions so harmonize with the world spirit, they blindly act in their own self-interest. They are unconsciously driven by 'that inner Spirit, still hidden beneath the surface, which, impinging on the other world [of conventionality and regularity] as on a shell, bursts it in pieces, because it is another kernel than that which belonged to the shell in question'. These individuals, Caesar, Alexander the Great, Napoleon, these 'World-historical men – the Heroes of an epoch – must therefore be recognized as its clear-sighted ones; *their* deeds, *their* words are the best of that time'. Their achievements, however, can only be seen in retrospect. 'The owl of Minerva,' Hegel writes in another place, 'flies only at dusk.' I take this to mean that the *logos,* the meaning, of history is seen only long after the events in question are over, when a civilization, a society, a culture is in decline. The final historical tragedy, for Hegel, is discarding the Heroes:

> They attained no calm enjoyment; their whole life was labor and trouble; their whole nature was naught else but their master-passion. When their object is attained they fall like empty hulls from the kernel. They die early, like Alexander; they are murdered, like Caesar; transported to St Helena like Napoleon.

Napoleon's destruction by history and the ironies of his personal illusions, the inherent tragedy of history, weighed heavily on Hegel's mind. His hero's death came just as he was preparing the lectures of *The Philosophy of History* and surely played an important role as he thought about history. He speaks only fleetingly of Napoleon in his lectures, but these were delivered at the University of Berlin and Napoleon was officially fit only to be anathematized. For Hegel Napoleon was not the conqueror of foreign lands, a latter-day Attila, the scourge of Germany, the anti-Christ; he was the child of the Revolution, a kind of 'Washington as emperor', a partisan of a Europe united under the banner of the rights of man. The Washington comparison had occurred to Chateaubriand and Mme de Staël as well. They used it to accuse Napoleon. Hegel, by contrast, was a Bonapartist.

'It is a frightful spectacle,' he wrote to Niethammer soon after Napoleon's first abdication, 'to see a great genius destroy himself. There is nothing more *tragic*':

> The entire mass of mediocrity, with its irresistible leaden weight of gravity, presses on like lead, without rest or reconciliation, until it has

succeeded in bringing down what is high to the same level as itself or even below. The turning point of the whole, the reason why this mass has power and – like the chorus [in Greek tragedy] – survives and remains on top, is that the great individual must himself give that mass the right to do what it does, thus precipitating his own fall.

The inert weight of mediocrity inevitably destroys genius. Napoleon may have lifted the mass up to liberate Europe and spread the Rights of Man, but in the end it returned to its leaden essence. Hegel's deep pessimism is touched with irony: Napoleon liberated those very mediocrities who would destroy him. Napoleon would be the last of the heroes of history. Henceforth the state, in its ideal Prussian form, would become the world historical actor. Yet Napoleon's fall was not, for Hegel, the downfall of the ideals of the Revolution that inspired him and his generation and were necessary for German liberation. In the midst of German nationalist reaction he kept his revolutionary ardor. Visiting Carnot at the very time he was writing his lectures on history is no coincidence. The personal tragedy of a great man was the stuff of history, but only a small part of its ineluctable movement. Napoleon's destruction was only a necessary tragedy along the way.

What makes Hegel's understanding of Napoleon's place in history so profound and powerful is that it explains the paradoxes of his fabulous career. Napoleon's egotism, his manic drive for glory, his willingness to sacrifice hundreds of thousands of men in the process and open France to foreign invasion and occupation, all fell with him. It is striking how quickly his empire collapsed, and the map of Europe he had redrawn was soon redrawn by the Congress of Vienna. France herself was reduced to her pre-revolutionary borders. All Napoleon's conquests were wiped out and in the German states, reduced from hundreds to about 30 by the invader, things French were repulsed. It became a badge of patriotism. But the ideals of the Revolution, and the concretization of those ideals in the Napoleonic Code, the centralization and secularization of the state, the definitive end to feudal tenures and privileges, the enshrinement, if not often the practice, of the Rights of Man, government by constitution and the will of the people, and the transformations forced upon *ancien régime* Europe by a powerful revolutionary enemy, these were too deeply rooted to be ripped up. They remained in post-Napoleonic France and as ideals in the defunct Napoleonic Empire. Napoleon's personal passion, in Hegelian language, coming when it did, made him the embodiment of the world spirit which he imposed on Europe.

Hegel kept his revolutionary faith to the end, even as he lectured in Berlin, the new home of the European reaction against the French Revolution. He too suffered a personal tragedy. He was not destroyed but his philosophic vision of German idealist philosophy realizing the hopes of the Revolution, achieving the final triumph of freedom, ran into the sands of utopian thought. In the midst of a reawakened nationalism, the prospect of Prussian hegemony in Germany, and the triumph of the allies over Napoleon and the Revolution, Hegel's revolutionary thought was muted and overtaken by those noisy parts of his often obscure system that glorified the state and said nothing about freedom.

VII
Napoleon at Zenith

After crushing Prussia Napoleon moved eastward into the plains of Poland. At Eylau (7–8 February 1807), in a snowstorm, he fought the first of what would be a long series of bloody battles of attrition in which two armies bludgeoned each other until one was driven from the field. Firepower would become increasingly important, armies larger, and casualty statistics shocking. Napoleon was so stunned by the bloodletting at Eylau that he remained on the battlefield for an unprecedented eight days (8–16 February), to see to the cleaning up of the killing fields and tending to the wounded and dead. 'A father who loses his children takes no comfort from a victory,' he said of Eylau. 'When the heart speaks glory itself loses all its illusions.' He also published, completely unprecedented (although he disguised his authorship), a *Relation de la bataille d'Eylau par un témoin oculaire, traduite de l'allemand (An Account of the Battle of Eylau by an Eye-witness, translated from the German).* It was the first Napoleonic battle that defied heroic representation.

The French revolutionary armies had not penetrated deep into Germany let alone Eastern Europe, nor had they crossed the Pyrenees. Napoleon's early battles were focused on the Mediterranean world. Italy had first absorbed his attention, divided into two phases by the Egyptian adventure. Spain, whose siren song he found seductive, proved more disastrous than Egypt. The catastrophic campaign unfolded unplanned. The Iberian invasion was inaugurated by an attack on Portugal, the logical consequence of the Continental System. The fact that the Spanish Bourbon kings ruled, and so ineptly, proved an irresistible lure that drew him into Spain. Both Naples and Spain stirred the revolutionary urge to finish with the Bourbons, a task begun by the Revolution that Napoleon sought to complete. Louis XVI's brothers remained at large, a reminder of the illegitimacy of the *parvenu* emperor and a focus for counterrevolution.

Figure 5 *Sacre de Napoleon* (detail), by Jacques-Louis David. Part of an enormous canvas (32 feet by 20 feet) containing 200 figures, this great painting purports to be a record of the event (12 December 1804) yet it is inaccurate, akin to his mythic presentation of Napoleon crossing the Alps. David painted himself into the canvas sketching the scene, and inserted Madame Mère (either at Napoleon's insistence or an act of flattery), who did not attend. He also rearranged some of the figures, thus violating the strict protocol observed, and allowed himself a number of minor liberties, including a visual insult to the archbishop of Paris whom he disliked. The prelate's face is partly obscured by a large cross. David chose the episode of Napoleon crowning Josephine rather than crowning himself. Many of the great figures of the Empire are present in this detail. In the foreground, with their backs to us, are (from left to right): Charles-François Lebrun, the Third Consul. Next to him is Jean-Jacques-Régis de Cambacérès, the Arch-chancellor of the Empire. Next to him, with his leg on a step of the dais, is Louis-Alexandre Berthier, the Minister of War during the Consulate. Next to him is Talleyrand. Eugène de Beauharnais, without a hat, stands to the right, next to General Armand de Caulaincourt, the Master of the Horse and the memoirist of the Russian Campaign. Next to him, also without a hat, is General Jean-Baptiste Bernadotte. The Pope, Pius VII, is seated, his right hand raised unenthusiastically to bless the crowning. When Napoleon first saw the painting (at the salon of 1810) he exclaimed, 'How the figures stand out, what truthfulness! This is not a painting. One enters into this tableau'.

Ferdinand of Naples had been driven to Sicily but, with his French cousins, remained poised to remount his throne. Spain's internal malaise stirred these smoldering embers of resentment. As he later told Las Cases:

> The old king and queen ... had become the object of the hatred and scorn of their subjects. The Prince of Asturias was conspiring against them ... and had become ... the hope of the nation. At the same time [Spain] was ready for great changes ... while I myself was very popular there. With matters in this state ... I resolved to make use of this unique opportunity to rid myself of a branch of the Bourbons, continue the family system of Louis XIV in my own dynasty, and chain Spain to the destinies of France.

There is a large literature on the reasons Napoleon annexed Spain but no unchallenged consensus. The dominant views are economic and psychological. The former argue that the Portuguese invasion was necessary to keep British goods out of Europe. The bitter family feud in Spain only enlarged the expedition and Napoleon's ambitions. The aging, ill, and inept Charles IV was embroiled in struggles with his son Ferdinand, impatient for his inheritance. Domestic discord was intensified by the favorite, Manuel de Godoy, the *éminence grise* of the kingdom. Since the destruction of the Spanish fleet at Trafalgar the flow of silver from the New World had been crippled. Desperately in need of money Godoy had, by 1808, confiscated and sold off about a sixth of all Church lands. His Enlightened Despotism along with his close (and probably sexual) friendship with the queen angered the king and enraged the old nobility and the Catholic hierarchy. Napoleon already had garrisons in almost all the cities and communication centers of Northern Spain prior to Junot's invasion of Portugal in November 1807. They were still there in 1808. Gradually Napoleon had moved three additional weak corps into the country. The Bourbon armies were considered a joke, their inefficiency and corruption judged second only to those of Bourbon Naples. These military assumptions were unchallenged. It looked to many as if conquering Spain would be easy and cheap.

The psychological argument depends less on inferences from the facts than on theorems of Napoleon's ambition, greed, opportunism, and will to power which led him to misinterpret and misconstrue what he knew about Spain; as he had already done for Naples and Egypt. He correctly recognized that *la force des choses* had cast into his lap an unexpected opportunity. 'To choose the right moment is the great art of men,' he had written his brother Joseph. If his timing was excellent he completely, and disastrously, underestimated the latent francophobia of Spain, the enormous size of the country, and the willingness of the Spanish people to fight the invader. He overlooked the impotence of the French party. More understandable but more fatally he was surprised by the decision of Britain to put an army on the ground, led by commanders of genius. She had, after all, not done so since 1794.

Whatever most mattered – the hoary ambitions of Louis XIV or even Charlemagne now realized, the seduction of an easy, cheap, and profitable conquest – his fateful decision appears improvised. In 1808 Spain asked Napoleon to choose a French bride for Charles's heir, Ferdinand. He decided to gobble up the country itself. He had shown no earlier inclination to depose the king. Napoleon always deplored the execution of Louis XVI as one of the greatest mistakes of the French Revolution. After 1804 he was especially sensitive to the 'divinity [that] doth hedge a king' but the prize was irresistible. It is worth pointing out that he merely deposed and held under house arrest – at Talleyrand's estate – Louis's Spanish cousins.

There were serious warnings about his miscalculations, which Napoleon ignored. On 1 April an uprising took place in Madrid although order was quickly restored. A month later, however, on 2 May, Madrid rose in rebellion. Even when the dreaded Mamelukes of the Guard appeared, the mob was only dispersed by a full-scale charge of *chasseurs* and dragoons. Marshal Murat was in command and immediately imposed martial law, set up his batteries to sweep the main streets, and ordered courts martial to try those responsible. Day by day the executions continued, their horror captured by Goya, who was there. A city riot was one thing, a pitched battle another. On 16–19 July the French army, albeit made up mostly of raw unblooded troops and led by General Dupont, who was widely disrespected, was beaten at Bailén. It was the first time since 1801 a significant French force had laid down arms. The Convention of Bailén granted the senior French officers parole, but 18,000 French conscripts became prisoners of war. It was a stunning setback for French arms, even had thousands of the prisoners not come to a horrible end in the Spanish hulks.

Napoleon arrived shortly afterwards, in November 1808, exasperated with the inability of his generals and marshals to hold a country he thought contemptible. He spent a little more than two-and-a-half months in Spain, fighting and organizing. His energy was boundless and he infused the French with it, recaptured Madrid, led a brilliant and arduous march across the Guadarrama Mountains and almost succeeded in cutting off the fleeing English before they could reach the sea and safety. Had the French been able to outmarch the English in what has entered British military history as 'the retreat to Coruña', Sir John Moore's army would have been destroyed. As it was his battered, rag-tag troops reached the sea on 12 January, the French were held off at the Battle of Coruña on the 16th, most of the army was aboard ship by the following day, and they sailed on the 18th. The denouement unfolded without Sir John Moore, who died in the Battle of Coruña, and without Napoleon, who extricated himself from any association with failure. He reduced the size of the forces engaged 'so as to minimize the impression of Moore's Fabian victory', in David Chandler's nice characterization, and handed over command of the campaign. He left Spain on 17 January and reached Bayonne in 45 hours. Joseph Bonaparte returned to the Spanish throne on the 22nd. A day later Napoleon arrived in Paris.

He immediately busied himself by examining the work being done on the Louvre and the elegant yet strategic rue de Rivoli, the first major east–west street built in Paris, which he left unfinished. On 28 January he dismissed Talleyrand, a move he had long contemplated, with a famous public tantrum:

> You are a thief, a moral coward, a man without faith. You don't believe in God. You have shirked responsibility your entire life, you have betrayed and cheated everyone. There is nothing sacred for you. You would sell your father. I have heaped riches on you but there is nothing you are incapable of doing against me. For the last ten months you have had the indecency to say to anyone who would listen that you always disagreed with my handling of Spain, because you assumed things were going badly for me. It is you who first gave me the idea of taking over, it is you who incessantly pushed me. And what about the Duke d'Enghien? Who told me where to find him? Who urged me to act against him? What other projects do you have? What do you want? What do you hope will happen? You would deserve it if I smashed you like a glass! I have the power to do so, but I despise you too much to make the effort!

This is the version given by Etienne-Denis Pasquier, Napoleon's unimpressive chief of police (1810–12). Nicolas-François Mollien, Napoleon's minister of the treasury, also reports the rant and includes an unforgettable additional phrase:

> Why haven't I hung you from the gates of the Carrousel? There is still time. You are shit in silk stockings.

The following day Napoleon stripped Talleyrand of his functions as grand chamberlain and bestowed them on General Montesquiou-Fezensac. The disgraced ex-minister quickly sought out Metternich to offer his service to Austria.

Napoleon's personal success in Spain was complete. Not only had the English been driven out, although their battered army remained intact, but Madrid had been recaptured and Joseph again installed on the throne. From his camp at Charmartin he issued a series of revolutionary decrees, abolishing monopolies, internal tariff barriers, feudal dues and all rights of private jurisdiction. Two-thirds of Spain's religious communities were dissolved, monks were to be forcibly returned to civil life, nuns were given the right to secularize and new novitiates were banned. The Inquisition was abolished and all property confiscated from the suppressed religious institutions was offered for sale. The short time he spent in Spain only confirmed Napoleon's views: the once great Spanish were an unworthy, superstitious, priest-ridden, cowardly people. They should have welcomed French liberation from their benighted kings, their obscurantist Church kept in power by the Inquisition, and their rapacious feudal landlords. Napoleon set about bringing the French Revolution to Spain and imposing its achievements, without of course granting its people *liberté*. The guerrilla war that soon erupted was little more than a nuisance in his view. He had, in addition, given generals Soult, Masséna, and Junot, the three marshals originally charged with conquering the Iberian Peninsula, a lesson in how the war was to be won. All these assumptions and self-congratulations were not only premature but proved profoundly mistaken. For now, however, there were more pressing matters. As soon as Metternich learned of the Spanish invasion he prepared for war.

Prince Metternich, the Habsburg ambassador to Paris in 1808 and the very embodiment of an 18th-century *seigneur*, was just beginning what would become the most illustrious diplomatic career of the age. He was an urbane, clever, pleasure-loving, vain, and devious man. His mind had been shaped in and by the Enlightenment. The elegance, poise, and wit of the age informed his character as it sculpted his values. He was perfectly at home in French and may even have preferred it to his native tongue. In international politics he craved a balance of powers, a theorem underlying all his calculations. Austria had no natural defensive frontiers. The first battle in war, not the last, was most important to the Hapsburg empire, a patchwork quilt feebly sewn together by a venerable monarchy served by a cumbersome bureaucracy and compelled to function in a dozen languages and a tangle of local mores and habits.

Her security depended on countervailing states that would keep her enemies from joining forces, keep the French at bay, and if need be take the brunt of an attack. With Napoleon bogged down and overstretched in Spain, Metternich incorrectly calculated that the Ogre could muster no more than 206,000 men. It was an opportune moment to strike and erase the disgrace of Austerlitz.

In the new year of 1809 Napoleon had no fewer than 270,000 of his best troops engaged in some part of Spain. This was approximately three-fifths of his total military strength and well beyond the 80,000 he originally dispatched for the job. It was also useful to Metternich's bellicose purposes to argue, accurately in this case, that in Spain Napoleon had attacked an ally. He preached that no state, whether friend or foe, was immune from Napoleon's insatiable ambition, yoked to the French Revolution's messianic expansionism. For the second time in less than a year – the first had been the movement to Spain of a substantial army – the French military administration transferred a huge army across Western Europe to fight the Austrians. A large number of the troops consisted of the Imperial Guard, among whose many perks was the right to travel by horse cart. It was an impressive accomplishment, well beyond the ability of any other state at the time or for many years to come. The last Guards left Spain on 24 March 1809. They were in Paris on 30 April, and in Strasbourg, the staging-area for the Austrian campaign, on 11 May.

On 2 March 1809 Metternich told Jean-Baptiste Champagny, Talleyrand's mediocre replacement as foreign minister, that the presence of French troops in Austrian territory was a virtual declaration of war. On 23 March Napoleon closed the door on any negotiations. A few days later (on the 27th) Archduke Karl, the Emperor's brother who would have to fight Napoleon, issued a manifesto inviting all Germans to rise in rebellion against the invading French. War had begun. Napoleon left Paris on 13 April and joined his troops on the 17th. For the next month the French were victorious, but the campaign of 1809 was punctuated by miscalculation and more potentially catastrophic mistakes than Napoleon usually made. He suffered his first defeat at Aspern-Essling (21–22 May), which debunked the myth of the Emperor's invincibility but had no serious military consequences. The campaign concluded with the bloody battle of Wagram near Vienna (5–6 July), from which the defeated Austrians left the field with a pummeled but viable army. His victory was the high-water mark of the Empire. Thenceforth it would contract, and with contraction the French Revolution would gradually return to the geographic limits within which it was born.

As the French approached the Viennese made frantic efforts to improve the walls, clear the glacis, and dig fieldworks. Unlike in 1805, when Napoleon marched triumphantly and unopposed into Vienna after the Battle of Austerlitz, the city was to be defended. At least so Napoleon assumed when he wrote Eugène de Beauharnais on 10 May. But preparations for a siege were remarkably inept and unimaginative. The war council, headed by Maximilian d'Este, Emperor Franz II's younger brother, cautiously decided all the least important issues long before Napoleon got to Vienna: where to quarter the garrison, how much to pay workers to repair the defenses, the methods needed for collecting wood, and rules for the conduct of the city's firefighters. More important military matters were left to improvisation. When the gates were hastily barricaded they enclosed enough armed men to defend Vienna, whose decayed defenses were not negligible. Napoleon could have been made to pay in considerable French blood. But the Viennese, beginning with Maximilian himself, had no stomach for a siege. Marshal Lannes' advance corps reached the outskirts of the city and occupied Prater Island and the suburbs on 11 May 'without firing a shot', according to Baron de Marbot.

Vienna, on the right bank of the Danube, had more than 200,000 inhabitants and was the largest city in Central Europe. Part of the city – the Prater Park and the Leopoldstadt suburb – were separated from the main city by a small branch of the Danube. In contemporary representations Vienna looks like a giant starfish, its arrowhead-shaped bastions pointing out into the surrounding glacis, which was 1900 feet across at its widest, the range of a late 17th-century cannon. Vienna proper was divided into a walled inner city, with some 50,000 inhabitants, and a semicircle of suburbs outside the fortifications. The Viennese bastions were defended by only 48 guns. Vienna's once sturdy fortifications, moats, palisades, and contrescarpes had held off the Turks in 1683 for 69 days before the city was relieved and the infidel driven out of central Europe. It was the second time Vienna had saved Europe from the Turks; first withstanding a siege from Suleiman the Magnificent in 1529. By 1809 there were far too many houses outside the walls than could be evacuated, demolished or defended, and they provided substantial cover to the enemy. In addition the city had become notorious for its 'jovial ease'. The Viennese were widely thought, not least by their rulers, to prefer voluptuousness 'even to ambition, to money, to that national vanity which is a caricature of patriotism'. In the early hours of the French bombardment women 'in their best hats' were watching from the walls. It was the best show in town.

Napoleon established himself on 10 May in Schönbrunn, the summer residence of the imperial family, about two-and-a-half miles from Vienna. Begun by Leopold I, who had defended Vienna in 1683, the chateau was completed by Marie-Theresa in 1750. The conqueror found it comfortable. He always enjoyed living in the castles of his enemies. At dawn on the 11th Napoleon sent Maximilien a summons to surrender. There was no reply and he spent the rest of the day reconnoitering Vienna's defenses. He and his staff knelt over the map, 'like a father in the midst of his family' deciding where to place his main breaching battery. He chose a spot screened by the imperial stables that Kara Mustafa had also found strategically inviting, set the guns himself and prepared to bombard Vienna into submission.

The two greatest composers of the age, Franz Joseph Haydn and Ludwig von Beethoven, were in Vienna when it was besieged. There is no better metaphor of the passing of the old and the arrival of the new, within and without the walls. Haydn lay dying. He was 77 and for years had lamented his age and infirmities. He had returned to Vienna to die and went to his rest on 31 May 1809 with the sound of French howitzers still fresh in his ears. In the days before his death of old age, exhaustion, and apparent fright at the French assault and occupation, his servants carried him to the piano where he would play his Austrian anthem, *Gott erhalte Franz den Kaiser* (*God Save Franz our Emperor*). Franz had left the city before the French bombardment. French gunners, indifferent to the great composer's final agony, lobbed their missiles haphazardly, one landing not far from Haydn's house on Untere Steingasse (later renamed Haydngasse). Once Vienna capitulated, Napoleon himself ordered an honor guard for the composer's door. His friends and servants buried the great man on 1 June in occupied Vienna. Not a single Viennese *Capellmeister* paid his respects.

Beethoven tried to preserve what little of his hearing he still had – the poignant Heiligenstadt Testament of 1802 was his *cri de coeur* on encroaching deafness – by stuffing cotton in his ears against the cacophony of the French guns. Cannon balls fell in Kärnthnerthor and the Wasserkunst Bastei near Beethoven's lodgings. Years later his publisher, with the composer safely dead, nicknamed the last of his five piano concerti, begun in Vienna in 1809, 'The Emperor', a sobriquet Beethoven would have deplored. He remained a resolute Napoleon-hater. The Emperor made no attempt to visit and charm the composer, as he had courted Goethe at Erfurt in 1807. Baron de Trémont, a French officer who 'admired his genius' paid his respects to Beethoven, although Luigi Cherubini, who taught at the Paris Conservatoire and thought Beethoven an 'unlicked bear', did not. At 9 p.m. the French barrage began. It lasted four hours, panicked Maximilien, who had never experienced a bombardment, terrified the populace, and set significant parts of the city afire. On the 12th, at the other end of Napoleon's empire, Arthur Wellesley, the future Duke of Wellington, defeated Marshal Soult before the city of Porto, in Portugal. It was an ominous warning, redolent of Nelson's victory at Trafalgar just before Napoleon's triumph at Austerlitz. But Napoleon had turned his back on Spain to deal with Austria.

Capturing Vienna was easy. Defeating Austria was not. Wagram was the bloodiest Napoleonic battle to date. It was also the largest in the area of the fighting and the numbers of men and guns involved. The Marchfeld where the battle was fought is a huge open field 'as flat as a billiard table'. It is broken here and there by branches and small tributaries of the Danube. Vienna is within eyesight and earshot and the great battle was seen by any number of Viennese from the roofs and bell towers of the city as well as from the heights upon which the city sat. 'What a rare and magnificent panorama the spectators had spread before them,' wrote General Marbot, who was there. On the Bisamberg, a hill to the north, Emperor Franz also watched while Metternich, his eye glued to a telescope – he had a fine collection of optical instruments – described the action. For those who were not spectators the sights and sounds were much grimmer. By the afternoon of 5 July Napoleon had brought over the bulk of his forces from the island of Lobau, 135,000 infantry, 27,600 cavalry, and 433 guns, not including the formidable Lobau batteries. Yet another marvel of staff planning. The construction of new bridges, the massing of troops on Lobau, their successful movement across the Danube, their deployment and readiness to fight the same day, had never before been attempted. 'The crossing of such a river as the Danube,' Napoleon wrote boastfully and truly on 2 July in the Tenth Bulletin, 'in the presence of an enemy well acquainted with all the local circumstances, and who has the inhabitants on his side, is one of the greatest military enterprises that can be imagined. The Danube,' he boasted, 'no longer exists for the French Army.'

The Marchfeld offered clear fields of fire for both the Austrian and French guns, and the additional horror of ricochet, where a ball would bounce and career into massed troops, adding a few hundred yards to artillery range. The nature of Napoleonic warfare required close-order formations if the infantry was to have any significant firepower from their small arms. They thus presented a perfect target for artillery on a field where there was no cover. More French soldiers were struck by Austrian artillery on a single day than on any other field in the Napoleonic Wars. 'It would take the Battle of the Somme 107 years later to surpass their loss rate', according to James Arnold. In the two days of fighting about 60,000 soldiers on both sides had been wounded by lead, the majority of them by artillery fire. The Guards guns alone fired close to 15,000 rounds. The French gunners suffered terrible losses, but inflicted greater ones.

Archduke Karl had deployed his army in a vast arc 12 miles long. His left wing was on the Russbach Heights, where the most deadly fighting took place around the village of Wagram. A small brook, the Russbach, curves around the village and then meanders parallel to the Danube for about three miles before reaching the hamlet of Neusiedel. The depth of the stream is no more than three feet, but its steep banks prevented cavalry, artillery, and even infantry from crossing without terrible losses. Archduke Karl had adopted a sound and simple plan; his enormous front line could not be turned by French maneuver and his army would be able to envelope Napoleon's on both the right and left. The problem was that the 12-mile front was beyond the limits of a single commander to see his forces let alone control them. The two corps on the extreme right were the farthest from central command. A well-mounted courier could reach them in 20 minutes, far too slow to allow a coordinated attack. The French front was compacted into half that space.

These physical problems were enhanced by Karl's early indecision. He could not decide between a defensive or an offensive fight. When he finally made up his mind he issued vague orders to his forward elements – 'offer determined resistance'. This led to the near destruction of his advance guard and did not prevent the French from crossing from Lobau and deploying. Karl's circumspection, his chief weakness as a commander, was evident. The French did most of the attacking. By the end of the first day of the battle Napoleon had accomplished all his objectives. The next day, 6 July, the Emperor took up his command post on a small knoll, conspicuous on his white charger Euphrates. His presence on the battlefield could always inspire and terrify. Napoleon wanted to be visible: the commanding intelligence. His cherished Guards, in full uniform, were drawn up behind him. He issued his orders to a dozen ordinance officers standing in a row. He listened to every report delivered by riders and if he wanted to send a message summoned the next ordinance officer in line. His orders were delivered slowly and clearly and each messenger was required to repeat them once and then a second time if something was garbled. 'Va,' said Napoleon, and the officer rode off. All this was done with reassuring calm and composure under constant artillery fire: 26 headquarters officers were killed that day, several of them standing or mounted close to Napoleon. Witnesses describe Napoleon as serious, immobile, and perfectly calm.

Wagram was a battle of attrition. Despite French superiority in men and firepower it was a close thing. There was no rout. The Austrians inflicted terrible damage, and years afterwards when anyone in Napoleon's hearing mocked the Austrian soldier the Emperor would snap they should have been at Wagram. By noon on 6 July the entire 13-mile battlefront was in flames from more than a thousand guns. Grain was grown on the Marchfeld and much of the uncultivated parts was grassland, made combustible by the excessive heat and drought. The incessant artillery fire and discarded wadding lit the place on fire. The flames panicked the troops who fled from the fires, trying to pull their wounded out of its path. Those who could not move or be moved were burned alive. The racket of the guns, the screams of the wounded men and dying horses, were now accompanied by fire and the stench of burning flesh.

The breakthrough came late in the day. Napoleon himself set the guns on the Austrian center and literally blew a hole in their line. Karl ordered his withdrawal to begin at 2:30 p.m. The Battle of Wagram was over. It was a great victory but not a definitive one. Karl left the field with his army still intact although brutally mauled. Napoleon's army was too exhausted to pursue the Austrians. The Emperor himself lay down, covered himself with his cloak, and got his first rest in almost 60 hours. Napoleon always considered Wagram one of his great victories. Especially remarkable was his recovery from the setback at Aspern-Essling (21–22 May) which led to the brilliant planning that got his army from Lobau Island to the Marchfeld. He himself also celebrated three earlier and smaller actions that preceded Wagram in the 1809 campaign: 'The battle of Abensberg [20 April], the Landshut manoeuvres [21 April] and the battle of Eckmühl [21–22 April] were my most brilliant and most skillful actions.' He realized Wagram had changed warfare, as he told Las Cases:

Artillery this day created the true destiny of armies and people. We punched with cannon as if we were punching with fists, and in a battle, as in a siege, the art consists in bringing to bear enormous firepower on a single point. Once the troops have engaged whoever has the ability suddenly to deliver unexpected artillery without it being perceived is sure to carry the day.

Napoleon's genius for improvisation decided the battle. Lenin was fond of quoting Napoleon's maxim on war: *'On s'engage et puis on voit'* ['We engage, and then we see']. Wagram and the Bolshevik seizure of power are examples.

Austria sued for peace. The treaty of Schönbrunn was signed on 14 October 1809. Austria was compelled to cede to Bavaria, one of Napoleon's allies, the provinces of Salzburg and Inn-Viertel. It was also forced to deliver significant territory in Italy, as well as all of Croatia and Dalmatia south of the Sava River. Her Polish territory was divided between Russia and the Napoleonic Duchy of Warsaw. Napoleon and the Tsar had not yet fallen out. Austria lost three million of her 16 million subjects, was saddled with a huge indemnity, and forced to limit her army to 150,000. Wagram marked the physical limits of Napoleonic warfare. There would be great triumphs in 1810 and 1811 – Valencia and Andalusia fell to the French and Sir Arthur Wellesley was driven back to Portugal – but there would not be another victory on the scale of Wagram.

*****

Napoleon, more than anyone else of the day, embodied the dreams, expressed the energy, articulated the passions of the revolutionary generation. But if he dreamed with the men of his generation he brought to those dreams the concreteness of political reality. So entwined were revolutionary idealism, his own radical past, and his ambition that even the transformation of his power into an imperial crown and the adoption of dynastic politics did not stop him spreading the Revolution, continuing its work. In the midst of the German campaign he was locked in struggle with the Papacy. Pius VII, who had unwillingly lent his blessing and presence to Napoleon's coronation and had earlier and also reluctantly signed a Concordat with revolutionary France, was forcibly taken from Rome by General Miollis. Napoleon, not unlike Henry II denying that he had ordered the murder of Thomas à Becket, insisted he ordered the Pope be left tranquilly in Rome. Pius had been a problem for Napoleon since at least 1805 when the Emperor unilaterally extended the Corcordat to Italy. The Pope refused to cooperate. He dragged his feet and encouraged everyone to do so. All this was nothing compared to what happened after 1808 when the French occupied the Papal States. General Miollis, Napoleon's 'satrap' in Rome, complained he was 'paralyzed ... by a passive resistance we found difficult to defeat ...' The Pope's passive counterattack, despite the fact that his lieutenants were under house arrest, stunned Miollis. Even the laity were obedient, immune to threats and exile.

The Pope's arrest brought Napoleon no concessions, and made him a martyr. Pius was finally returned to Rome on 24 May 1814, as the empire collapsed. Napoleon, the great judge of men, had seriously misjudged Pius's character. Men fundamentally motivated by ideology or faith (or both) were an enigma to Napoleon. Deviousness, duplicity, self-interest, vanity, vainglory never escaped him. Such men were susceptible to charm, cajolery, threats, and rewards. Sincere faith was another matter. Even a man as familiar and greedy as his uncle, Cardinal Fesch, was a puzzle. 'A mediocre and limited man, but a sincere believer,' is Marcel Dunan's assessment. He was, Dunan continues, 'an imperious and maladroit diplomat but a conscientious priest'. Pius was much more intelligent, much less worldly, and more profoundly religious than Fesch. The Pope's passive resistance made any reconciliation, let alone collaboration, impossible.

Napoleon and Pius VII clashed irreconcilably. The Emperor's religious views were no secret, and were in perfect harmony with those of the French Revolution. He never restored the Church's confiscated lands nor their monopolies on education and marriage. He reserved for the state the appointment of major Church officials and made no efforts to re-establish the cloistered life in France. He surrounded himself with men whose religious views reflected his own or were often more extreme. Joseph Fouché, then still Napoleon's chief of police, had been a passionate dechristianizer. The Emperor seems to have preferred the company of Deists, atheists, skeptics, indeed all shades of unbelief. Napoleon himself died excommunicated and uttered no regrets. It is telling that among his last acts as Emperor was to continue the secularizing work of the Revolution. He perpetrated 'the War against God' in Italy in 1814 even as he was fighting desperately in Northern France and then Belgium to preserve his throne. The radical, anticlerical spirit of Napoleon was turned loose on the former Papal possessions in Italy. They floundered before a new and different opponent. 'The French did not understand what they were dismantling,' says Michael Broers, 'because they were confronted by an administrative structure where not only was there no division between Church and state, but where the Church was the state'. The Papal Curia was the civil service of the Papal States, the College of Cardinals was the council of state. The arrest of obstructionist cardinals and the application of administrative fiat only stiffened local resistance. This meant the French had no collaborators, and the Napoleonic system of annexation could not survive without them. He faced the same problem in Spain where the guerrillas success-fully cut off the supply of collaborators, especially in rural Spain, where priests often joined the insurrection.

The incident that triggered the open conflict, 'the War against God' that had percolated quietly for years, was Napoleon's demand that Pius annul the marriage of Jerome Bonaparte to Elisabeth Patterson, an American Protestant. The request came at the same time that Napoleon occupied Ancona and introduced the Civil Code there, which secularized marriage and legalized divorce. The scandalized Pope dug in his heels and refused the annulment. Cardinal Fesch, on behalf of his nephew, provided a theological justification for annulment, which Pius rejected. The next year he refused to recognize Napoleon's oldest brother, Joseph, as the king of Naples, and he loudly protested the French encroachment on the Papal States as well as the military occupation of Rome. The Pope's protest came on 21 January 1809. The symbolism that this was the anniversary of the execution of Louis XVI in 1793 could not have been lost on either man:

> 'Try to make the Pope listen to reason, make him reasonable,' [Napoleon instructed Louis de Barral, the Archbishop of Tours] 'Otherwise he can only lose. Tell him that this is no longer the time of Pope Gregory, and that I am not a patient man. Remind him of the example of Henry VIII, without his cruelty; and I have more power than he had. Remind him that whatever intervention I decide on I have 600,000 Frenchmen under arms, maybe even a million. They will march in step with me, for me, and like me. The peasants, the workmen, only know me, they give me blind obedience.'

Pius was unmoved by threats, arguments, pleas, or boasts. He refused to negotiate with Napoleon so long as he was a prisoner.

Spain and the Pope were not Napoleon's only worries after Wagram. The governance of his enormous empire was vexing. Edward Gibbon, reflecting in the *Decline and Fall of the Roman Empire* after he had completed the history of the Western Empire (chapter 38), argued that barring another massive barbarian incursion, most likely driven by religious fanaticism, Europe would remain at peace. No single state would be able to dominate its neighbors by *force majeure*. It was an optimistic 18th-century version of the doomsday strategy that became popular again in our day as a way of stilling fears about nuclear war. European civilization had reached a level of martial technology and material progress that was approximately uniform. No state could hope to overwhelm the others without itself being brought to the brink of extinction. Napoleon's empire proved Gibbon mistaken, as have the massive wars of the 20th century. He had successfully conquered all the continental kingdoms. His empire stretched from the Iberian Peninsula to the borders of European Russia, from the boot of Italy to the North Sea and the Baltic. One would have to return to the European empire of Augustus Caesar to find an equally extensive frontier and territory.

A geographical sketch of the empire in 1809 is misleading. It was far less stable than colored territory on a map proclaimed. Spain had so far proved indigestible, and so it would remain although Napoleon sent some of his best marshals and troops there. The economic war against England depended on Napoleon's ability to secure the empire's endless border against English goods. In addition Napoleon's policies ruined the economies of a number of commercial cities and regions. The German Hanseatic towns fell into a steep decline. They never fully recovered their pre-Napoleonic splendor, but were again flourishing by the 1820s. Bordeaux had to readjust her economy to conform to the Continental System that forbade her to export to England, and never regained her pre-Napoleonic predominance, although the claret trade quickly rebounded. Holland, whose economy was based on shipping, suffered seriously from the blockade. Then there were the Bonapartes. They were a big, talented, egotistical, ambitious, and scrappy family. When the second son became the master of the European world the spoils were unbelievable and irresistible. Family feuds were not merely scandalous; they were significant historical events. 'You would have thought,' Napoleon said describing the vehemence of family fighting, 'I had finagled them out of their rightful inheritance from our father, the late king!' It was one of the rare instances of Napoleonic irony. In the halcyon days of the Consulate and the early Empire Napoleon had no difficulties satisfying the greed and ambition of his family: but their needs expanded with the Empire. Gifts were lavished upon them, and then entire kingdoms.

In November 1806 Napoleon issued the first of the Berlin Decrees, the opening salvo in the economic war he declared against England. Since the Battle of Trafalgar (21 October 1805), Napoleon had been unable to blockade England. The Berlin Decrees were an embargo on European trade unenforced by a French navy. Continental markets and European ships were denied to England but the cost proved prohibitive. Holland was crippled, and Louis, who along with his crown acquired an obligation to provide significant troop quotas for his brother, made the mistake, in Napoleon's eyes, of empathizing with the Dutch. 'What do you want me to say to you?' Napoleon scolded from Schönbrunn:

> You are no king and don't know how to be one. Such things would never have happened in Schimmelpenninck's day and those of the Dutch Republic, which was able to support 40,000 troops ... All your embarrassments and disturbances come from your bad administration, which is the result of your never listening to my advice.

'In mounting the throne of Holland,' he lectured Louis in another letter, 'you forgot that you are French and have even contorted all the faculties of reason and tormented your conscience in order to persuade yourself that you are Dutch.' Louis snapped back with equal vehemence. There was no sense of verbal decorum or respect in the intimacy of the family circle: 'Why don't you stop the skin from sweating!' was his challenge to the man who cut off Holland's life's blood. 'Everyone knows,' the Emperor fumed, 'that without me you are nothing!' In March 1810 Napoleon forced his brother to cede all Dutch territory south of the Rhine. Louis fled to Bohemia on 2 July 1810. On 9 July Napoleon united the Kingdom of Holland with France.

Napoleon's first model for governing his increasingly vast empire was a satellite system coupled to the direct annexation of some territories (the *départements réunis* in Italy). He put his family on all the thrones where he had removed the ruling dynasty or created new kingdoms. Austria and Prussia kept their monarchs while a few allies, notably the Duke (soon King) of Saxony had their status raised and their kingdoms enlarged as a reward for loyalty. He installed his family in the satellite kingdoms. Dynastic politics provided the transition from the Republic he seized to the Empire he would conquer and proclaim. The kings he had created were to behave as he expected his prefects to behave in France. They were instruments of his policies, conduits for his will. The first responsibility of all was to support and sustain the insatiable French war machine. Napoleon's correspondence is filled with sharp letters to his siblings about their obligations and shortcomings as rulers. His hectoring never stopped. Their ingratitude was unforgivable, their independence intolerable. His solution was to take over the Empire himself, which he began doing in 1810. He never finished the work. Joseph remained in Spain until deposed in 1813, but was permanently hamstrung by his brother's instruction that his marshals alone had control of the war; and Napoleon stripped him of all Spain north of the Ebro in 1811. Jerome in Westphalia remained in place but the Emperor's badgering intensified. Murat and Caroline in Naples were a thorn in Napoleon's side, ever scheming to blunt the Emperor's interference. Only Eugène de Beauharnais remained reliable and obedient, but he was only a Bonaparte by adoption.

Napoleon envied the old kings their legitimacy, but he missed the mark. He was too self-absorbed to see beyond his personal plight. As a *parvenu* he failed to appreciate that kings as individuals did not have a license to govern badly, squander the state's patrimony, lose wars and yet survive, which he imagined was among their privileges. He lived in an age when kings sat precariously on their thrones, and he as an agent of the Revolution was one of the chief reasons. War and revolution swept them away. What endured was not this or that king but the institution of monarchy: 'the king is dead, long live the king' was a truism and not a paradox or a formulaic chant. It is one of the reasons the French Revolution insisted on trying Louis XVI. Kings had been assassinated and the monarchy lived on, a verity the revolutionary regicides wanted to end. They were not completely successful, although no one except the most die-hard royalists believed the Bourbons would soon return, if at all. Monarchies had had a long head start. By the time of the French Revolution centuries of assimilation, practice, habit, and ideology had accumulated. The Revolution had only a few years in trying to replace blood inheritance with the will of the people. The difficulty for Napoleon was that he embarked on dynastic politics and yet he wanted to have the advantage of the new revolutionary ideology to sustain him. In a speech on 27 December 1804 he spoke of 'this throne upon which Providence and the will of the Nation had caused me to mount', a phrase the editor of his *Correspondance* signals is in Napoleon's hand. His relationship to the Revolution and its heritage was never straightforward. He lived in a shifting ideological period and was himself responsible for diluting, confusing, and making imprecise both royalist and revolutionary verities. Revolutionary legitimacy was neither reliable nor consistent. From 1792 there had been a steady attack on the popular will, and democratic institutions had eroded, to be replaced by increasingly undemocratic governments. Napoleon soon eliminated institutions for expressing the will of the people. His consolidation of power continued the inclinations of the Revolution but it made him extremely vulnerable. Neither the French – witness Malet's abortive rebellion in 1812 which ignored the heritage of Napoleon's infant son – nor any of the European monarchies accepted Napoleon as legitimate. They yielded, necessarily, to the Grande Armée. When he fell his son did not, could not, succeed him. The wealth accumulated by the Bonapartes, including their princely titles, remained. The dynasts could tolerate personal fortunes, especially when the Bonaparte descendants stayed out of politics. The next Bonaparte to sit on a throne, Louis Napoleon, did so through a bloody *coup d'état*, not by quiet succession.

The structural flaws in Napoleon's Empire trumped the greed and jealousies of his wayward, independent, recalcitrant siblings, his struggles with the Papacy, the endless Spanish war, and the failure of his dynastic politics to provide political stability. He bought domestic peace and relative tranquility at home with foreign conquest. He bought everything with the same coin. Whether it was his enemies who incessantly forced him to fight a perpetual war with the *ancien régime*, as he self-servingly maintained, or his insatiable ambition, which his foes maintained, or the ideological militancy of the French Revolution, does not much matter. He had built a state and empire by conquest. Without the Grande Armée it fell to pieces. Sooner or later the vast fabric he had woven would unravel. Even his powers of improvisation, on and off the battlefield, were inadequate. His brilliant manipulation of the new political culture was ultimately insufficient to save his throne. But in 1809, sitting victorious in Schönbrunn, everything appeared magnificent and manageable.

Entr'acte
Napoleon and the Political Culture of the French Revolution

No one better understood the new political culture created by the French Revolution than Napoleon. He knew that public opinion now ruled and he knew as well that he lacked the talents hitherto used to sway and shape that opinion. He was no orator, he instinctively distrusted democratic politics, and he could not tolerate freedom of the press or assembly. His task and his achievement was to find ways outside parliamentary and democratic politics to command obedience and move and manipulate men while retaining the appearance of a government that derived its authority from the people. His ritualized consultation of the Senate, his careful cultivation of public opinion through censorship, and his use of the army as a kind of idealized republic where authority prevailed but individual merit was celebrated and rewarded, were not wholly cynical. He retained throughout his years of power a predilection for the institutions and habits of the Revolution. Napoleon's political originality was to have forged together the machinery of democratic government and the hierarchical authoritarianism of a military government. The weld was not made with precision but it held for 16 years, reinforced by several inventions of his own.

Among his first acts upon taking command of the Italian army in 1796 was to acquire two newspapers, one in Italian one in French. He duplicated the deed soon after his *coup d'état*, quickly transforming the *Moniteur Universal*, the newspaper of record during the Revolution, into an official organ of the new government. Number 97 of the *Moniteur*, the first issue of the newly reformed paper, was published on 7 nivôse, an VIII (28 December 1799), within weeks of 18 Brumaire. More original than using the newspapers of the Revolution were the Bulletins he wrote and published, sometimes daily, while on campaign. '*Mentir comme un bulletin*', to lie like a Bulletin, was a witticism of the day; but they were a brilliant invention, as original as anything he did militarily or politically.

In a regime based on glory and increasingly focused on the hero who delivered France from the doldrums of perpetual war and corrupt and insecure politics, Napoleon's dispatches from the front were electrifying before they became contemptible. He had created a new genre of propaganda. The word itself, so suspect in our post-Orwellian world, was originally borrowed by the French (in 1689) from the Catholic Church where it connoted an institution for the propagation of the faith. It was special pleading to be sure but was not seen as deliberately mendacious, except of course by non-Catholics. By the time of the French Revolution the word had taken on its modern meaning: influencing public opinion without much concern for the truth. Very soon the new politics spawned a new *métier*: a *propagandiste* was one who made propaganda. Napoleon did not himself use the word but he was a master. Between 1805 and the frantic battle for France in 1814, he wrote hundreds of Bulletins. They were military in appearance, rhetoric, and purpose; but they were addressed to the home front. Cast as official reports, Napoleon dictated most of the Bulletins himself. Those occasionally written by subordinates he approved. The only exceptions were the Bulletins of the Army of Italy in 1805. These were the work of Marshal Masséna. The Bulletins were admirably suited to Napoleon's style: brisk, clear, vividly detailed, and unencumbered by any literary baggage or mannerisms. They march energetically across the page. He himself cultivated what he called a 'natural style' and scolded his brothers, especially Joseph and Lucien, for excess verbiage, ornate phrasing, and the tropes of style. The art of writing, he insisted, was to include only what is useful. Chateaubriand irritated him long before he went into opposition, as did the journalist Sébastien Mercier. The former, he told Bertrand on St Helena, 'proves nothing. He repeats only what is said in school'. Mercier was worse; 'he says nothing concrete. It is all phrases'. 'The great art of governing,' he lectured Joseph, 'is that one must not appear a man of letters or a writer.' Every edict, he continued, going after his brother's thirst for literary effect, 'should have the character of those to whom it is addressed', not the language of philosophy.

Caesar's *Commentaries* are closest in spirit to the Bulletins, which are less polished and completely circumstantial, made for the moment and not written at leisure as a kind of history. Napoleon borrowed freely from Caesar. He too sought to celebrate his military deeds for civilians, made himself the hero in his own accounts. With Caesar he spoke of himself in the third person as if reporting the deeds of another. None of the generals who served royal masters in the period from Caesar to Napoleon, could or did publish a personal account of their campaigns. The court chroniclers were expected to take care of such matters. Napoleon could not or would not depend upon others to sing his praises. He had no Homer, nor even a Joinville to celebrate his deeds, upon which his authority rested. He needed to keep his name and his doings constantly before the public. 'In Paris,' he told Bourrienne, 'they remember nothing. If I do not do anything for a time I am lost. Someone else's renown will replace mine. If I am not seen ... at the theater they no longer think of me.' When in Paris, where he did not spend the bulk of his time, he attended nearly 700 musical and theatrical performances.

From the first imperial campaign, in 1805, Napoleon had mastered the tone, the style, and the content of the Bulletin. None left his hands without celebrating his deeds of word and action, his ability to inspire and lead men, his presentation of self as the controlling intelligence in his battles. In the Bulletins he appears not just as the ruler of the French, but as a fatherly figure, moderate and magnanimous, concerned for the wellbeing of his soldier-children, wanting peace and shedding tears over the fallen. These same qualities would be rendered in the paintings of the age. 'The Emperor's words were like flame,' proclaims the Fifth Bulletin. 'Listening to him, the soldier forgot his fatigues and his privations and was impatient for the hour of combat to arrive.' He shared the hardships of his troops: 'The day was dreadful: the troops were up to their knees in mud. The Emperor had not taken off his boots for eight days.' At Etchingen he came upon some Austrian prisoners whose colonel 'was astonished to see the Emperor of the French soaking wet, covered with mud and more fatigued than the most humble drummer boy of the army'. 'Your master,' Napoleon reports himself saying to the surprised colonel, 'forced me to remember that I was a soldier; I hope that he will realize that the throne and imperial crimson has not made me forget my first profession.' There is no corroborating account of this simple eloquence.

The Bulletins achieved immediacy and concreteness by recording individual deeds of courage and sacrifice. 'The French think of nothing but glory,' reads the Ninth Bulletin:

> Brard, a soldier of the 76th, was going to have his thigh amputated; death had laid hold of him. As the surgeon was preparing to perform the operation, he stopped him: 'I know that I shall not survive, but it doesn't matter. One man less will not prevent the 76th from marching against the enemy, in three ranks with the bayonet in front.'

Death on the battlefield had become mannered, theatrical, moving. The usual complaint about the Bulletins, then as now, is that they exaggerate the enemy dead and wounded while undercounting French casualties. All the aspects of the Bulletins are contrived and exaggerated. This is how Napoleon wants his subjects to see war, and the military theater he presents is as creative as his statistics. 'I regret the loss of my hand,' a quartermaster tells Murat as the cavalry leader rode past, 'because it can no longer serve our brave Emperor.' Napoleon's soldiers are always brave, self-sacrificing, utterly devoted to him, and possessed of a mysterious yet passionate attachment to the symbols of their profession. 'The French soldier,' another Bulletin declares, 'has a feeling for his colors that borders on tenderness. They are the object of his affections, like a present from the hands of a mistress.'

These first Bulletins sounded a theme that would run through all Napoleon's utterances: he fought not by choice but because he had no choice. It was the perfidy of the English, although other states also shared in the opprobrium, that forced French armies into the field. So apparent were English machinations that all saw them. 'The Emperor of Germany [he habitually and inaccurately made the Austrian Emperor the Emperor of Germany],' the day after Austerlitz,

> did not conceal on his own part, or that of the Emperor of Russia, all the contempt that the conduct of England had inspired. 'They are the merchants,' he repeated, 'who put the Continent to fire to secure for themselves the commerce of the world.'

In the Bulletins even his enemies share Napoleon's opinions:

> The English are the perpetual objects of the curses of all the subjects of the Emperor of Germany and of the most universal hatred. Is it not finally time that princes should listen to the voice of their people, and that they should keep themselves from the fatal influence of the English oligarchy?

Despite the posturing and theatrical deaths, there is some, even a great deal of, truth in the Bulletins. Soldiers, civilians, and historians might grouse about their accuracy and reliability, but the Bulletins sing the praises of an army remarkably devoted to its commander-in-chief, an army he inspired with his words, his example of sharing their fatigue and food, and his uncanny memory for individual soldiers over many campaigns and years. Those singled out of an inspection parade never forgot the experience. Napoleon was for them the kind and caring father he painted for the home front. His armies were motivated by glory and individual feats of bravery, from the Marshalate to the foot soldier. When witnessed by the Emperor, which was every soldier's quest, individual courage resulted in instant battlefield promotion and decoration. With their mundane details, seeming truth-telling about setbacks, carefully nuanced to fall short of catastrophe, and matter-of-factness the Bulletins seemed addressed to each reader. The impact of the Bulletins only wore thin as the sheen of glory and constant victory faded, as the body counts mounted and the wars never ended. The Bulletins from Russia, with bland assertions of Napoleon's continuing health and a contrived catalogue of his losses, now entered the realm of Orwellian doublespeak.

The problem of supplying verbal propaganda was that Napoleon, almost alone, was the major wholesaler. He was singularly unsuccessful in finding writers, poets, and historians of outstanding ability to sing his praises, to celebrate his deeds and destiny. It was not until after his death that Las Cases published the *Mémorial de Sainte-Hélène* (1822), which began Napoleon's mythic life and instantly became the gospel of the Napoleonic legend. The great writers and important thinkers of his day – particularly Chateaubriand, Mme de Staël, and Benjamin Constant – hated him. Few men have had so sharp an appreciation of history, and none have been more anxious or more successful than Napoleon in seeing that his place in the important doings of mankind was prominent. On St Helena he enjoyed reading the great poetic dramatists of the 17th century, but at the height of his fame Napoleon's library in the Tuileries and on campaign was nearly exclusively history books. On the convoy to Egypt he reserved for his own use most of the history books. In 1807 Barbier, his personal librarian, catalogued some 50,000 volumes held in the imperial residences. History was Napoleon's preferred reading. He was omnivorous: universal history, ancient and modern history, military history, diplomatic history, the history of religion, of the popes, of the Greeks and Romans, histories of the various European states, the emperors, the kings of France, and the Revolution. The least represented category was the history of his own times.

The great histories of Napoleon and his age would be the memoirs he inspired. Jean Tulard counted more than 1500 in French alone, and he missed a number of them. This massive literature would be published throughout the 19th century. The public was so hungry for recollections of Napoleon that the publishers employed *teinturiers*, literally dyers of cloth or leather, metaphorically the artisans who fed the appetite for memoirs. They were literary hacks – even the young Balzac worked at the trade for a time – who fabricated, eked out, or edited manuscripts, fragments of manuscripts, and miscellaneous papers produced by those who had served Napoleon. Very few of the memoirs or recollections of the age escaped tampering. Some are more compromised than others, but together they present a remarkably full portrait, not least because Napoleon had no control over what the memorialists wrote.

What he did influence to his purposes was the art of the day. It is here, as in the Bulletins, that we see Napoleon as he wanted to be seen. He was exceptionally lucky in his painters. He was born into an age and a tradition enriched by artists of genius. He inherited Jacques-Louis David (1748–1825), the greatest revolutionary artist and the most influential painter of his age. David's colossal ego, his artistic genius, and his *atelier* dominated painting so thoroughly that scarcely any artist could hope to succeed without his backing and blessing. He was relatively old when he won the coveted Prix de Rome in 1774 after three failed attempts which had led him to contemplate suicide. His extraordinary career was launched upon his return to France in 1781 when his *Belisarius Begging for Alms* was shown. The stunning event came a few years later in the Salon of 1785 when his *Oath of the Horatii* was shown. The rough morality of the painting – the three Horatii brothers swear before their father that they will fight for their city's freedom, in which two brothers die and the survivor avenges their deaths – was seen as a summons to patriotic virtue. In 1789, already famous and untainted by any attachment to or commissions from the court, he threw himself into the Revolution and became a passionate Jacobin and *robespierriste*. If the *Oath of the Horatii* celebrated Roman republican virtue, his most famous painting of the Revolution, *Marat's Death*, is in an entirely new register. The verbally bloodthirsty revolutionary journalist was stabbed in his bath by Charlotte Corday who thought him a monster. David's painting is the most famous canvas of the French Revolution. The single figure of the dead Marat in his bath, his head wrapped in a turban, his outstretched arm still holding the quill with which he had been writing denunciations, is a portrait of revolutionary martyrdom. The artist would go on to design the pageants of the Revolution, and serve on the Committee of General Security, which shared with the Committee of Public Safety the Jacobin dictatorship of the Revolution in 1793–94. He was jailed after Robespierre's fall, escaped execution, and never repented of his revolutionary years. His *Sabine Women*, shown at the Salon of 1799, symbolically depicted an end to the Terror and the Jacobin era. David returned to the Roman Republic for inspiration. The huge

Figure 6 *Napoleon Crossing the Great Saint Bernard Pass* (1801–5), by Jacques-Louis David. Perhaps the most famous image made of Napoleon was originally commissioned by the king of Spain and remained in Madrid until Joseph brought it back to France in 1812 and eventually took it to America during his exile. This version now hangs at Malmaison. Napoleon requested three additional versions and David made a fourth which he kept in his atelier. Virtually everything about the painting is legendary, an artistic not a historical rendering. Napoleon crossed the St Bernard on a mule, for example. As the portrait of the young hero the painting is unsurpassed. The names of Hannibal and Charlemagne, under the steed's hooves, puts the young Napoleon in a long line of conquerors, linking his deeds to the first French invasion of Italy and ultimately to classical antiquity.

painting is a message of reconciliation. Hersilia separates her husband, Romulus, from her brother Tatius to stop the fighting. For contemporaries David had painted a modern not an antique scene, whose meaning was obvious: Napoleon, the new hero, would separate the warring parties. David's new hero abandoned his republicanism soon after but the artist was little troubled by Napoleon distancing himself from his Jacobin past. He easily made the transition from celebrating republican rectitude to celebrating Napoleonic conquests.

For an artist whose imagination roamed so freely and creatively in the stories and myths of antiquity, David craved an anchor in the mundane present. Robespierre and then the martyrs of the Revolution, Michel Lepellitier and Joseph Bara, riveted his personal and artistic attention. The former, a Jacobin friend of the artist, was killed by a royalist fanatic for having voted the king's death. The latter, a mere child of 13, was hacked to death for refusing to give up two horses to counterrevolutionaries. The themes were heroism and civic sacrifice, transferred from antiquity to the Revolution. Just as he gave the Jacobins a martyr-hero with *Marat*, he gave the Consulate a hero: *The First Consul Crossing the Alps* (1801), arguably the most familiar image of the age. Napoleon hated to pose and David had to make do by dressing his eldest son as Bonaparte and having his pupil Gérard climb up a ladder so the painter could calculate the angles of vision correctly. The iconography is a masterpiece of David's genius. The young conqueror is presented repeating the marches of Hannibal and Charlemagne whose names, along with his own, are carved beneath the hooves of the steed. His Napoleon is mounted on a fabulous white charger, his cloak flowing about him, his gaze fixed on the future. The sky is a leaden gray, there are a few soldiers in the background, but there is nothing to distract the viewer from the heroic young Napoleon, who loved the painting. He ordered several versions, including one for Malmaison which was later moved with him to St Cloud, and another for the Invalides. The image was engraved and widely distributed, and soon was woven into a tapestry at the Gobelins *atelier*. David had originally wanted to depict his hero, sword in hand, in the thick of battle. 'No,' Napoleon is reported to have said. 'It is not with the sword that battles are won. I want to be painted filled with assurance on a fiery charger.'

In painting as in his Bulletins Napoleon was more interested in what ought to be than in what was. He had crossed the Alps on a mule. The later historical painter, Paul Delaroche, a student of Baron Gros, accurately and scrupulously reconstructed the scene in 1848. Charles Thévenin, a contemporary observer, realistically painted Napoleon's army as it snaked its way up to the St Bernard pass without heroism. The truth was easily overshadowed by David's vision. The hero rode into history on horseback. David also created that other image so dear to Napoleon: a man devoted to the common good, a tireless worker on behalf of the people. His portrait of Napoleon in his study in 1812 is the quintessence of the hero as ruler. The subject is dressed as a colonel of the Guards' Horse Grenadiers, his uniform of choice when in Paris. His right hand is in his vest, a convention that has called forth much unnecessary speculation. All the luxury of imperial design is carefully depicted: the carved and gilded chair in the Egyptian style, covered with the Napoleonic bees, a dress sword laid across it, a beautiful clock, desk, and armoire, bookstand, papers artfully strewn about, and the candles about to gutter on his desk. The Emperor is working long into the night. He now wears, as he has since returning from Egypt, his hair in the Roman style, à la Titus as it was then called. But it is the nobility of his expression, the calm and dignity of a hero, whether in battle or at his desk, that is captivating.

David became officially Napoleon's preferred painter; the best paid and most honored. His canvases commanded extravagant sums that were begrudgingly paid by Napoleon. David was given a studio in the Louvre, close to the Emperor, and was commissioned to paint the great moments in Napoleon's life. The *Sacre*, Napoleon's coronation as Emperor, presented a number of problems aside from including more than a hundred participants in the canvas: the grandees of the new empire, Pope Pius VII, called from Rome to sanctify the crowning as had Pope Leo III for Charlemagne a thousand years earlier, the wives of the grandees wrangling Josephine's massive cape and train, and the artist himself, sketching the scene. David's genius fixed on Napoleon crowning Josephine Empress rather than the Pope crowning the Emperor. Power and legitimacy emanated from Napoleon. The Pope was only a passive witness. This enormous painting was first shown in the Salon of 1808. Napoleon's mother had not been present at the *Sacre* but he insisted David paint her in. The entire Bonaparte clan was to be included. The archbishop of Paris, whom David did not much like, has his face bisected by the enormous crucifix he is holding. The painting was intended to function as a record of the *Sacre*, but history needed enhancement. David stayed with the themes and the technique of his first work: grandeur, civic responsibility, heroic deeds, and statuesque figures, brilliantly clothed, as they were not in his pre-revolutionary work. For battles and action it was David's pupil, Antoine Gros (1771–1835) who transformed history painting from an increasingly academic exercise to an art of contemporary history.

Gros was not a witness to the action of his first famous painting, *Napoleon at Arcole*, during the first Italian campaign. He was chosen by Josephine in Genoa as she traveled to meet her husband. The artist was making a modest living painting miniatures. Because her husband hated posing, Josephine came up with an ingenious idea. She held Napoleon resting in her lap and he held the tricolor revolutionary flag. Gros sketched rapidly and Napoleon's aide-de-camp, Lavallette, testified that the painter 'achieved an amazing likeness of Bonaparte as he was at the time'. But if he captured Napoleon's head he garbled history. Gros has Napoleon holding the tricolor in his left hand and a naked sword in his right – the last time he would be depicted armed and fighting – rallying the troops across the bridge to the village of Arcole. The artist, perhaps in collaboration with the general, made the fighting mythic. Gros's portrait is of a hero worthy to stand beside David's Napoleon on horseback. Nothing in Gros's canvas diverts the eye from Napoleon, gaunt, intense, his hair long and flowing, leading his men to victory. The painting was warmly received at the Salon of 1801. David had already given painters, so many of them his students, a way to paint monumentality, to infuse a canvas with the virtues of self-sacrifice, duty, courage, and dedication, along with a technique for celebrating glory and creating a modern hero to stand with the greatest of antiquity. Gros now gave them history painting that did not invoke antiquity. David adapted himself to changing times, Gros was born into them. He endowed the Bonapartist present with all the grandeur of antiquity, without any of the conventions. Painting contemporary life, whether landscapes or portraits, genre scenes or battles, the doings of the court or portraits of bourgeois patrons, all were thought lesser undertakings than recreating the mythic or legendary past. Painters had to make a living, but if they were truly serious they would choose subjects from classical antiquity. In France it is Gros who first broke with these aesthetic conventions. Under his brush Napoleon became as important as, or more important than, the heroes of antiquity. His deeds were equal to, or surpassed, those of the ancients. *Bonaparte at Arcole* was the first in what would soon become a significant series of paintings of Napoleon's *res gestae*. The next important Gros painting was *Bonaparte Visiting the Plague House in Jaffa*, shown at the Salon of 1804. Based on a true incident, which Gros again did not witness, it celebrates his hero's courage and greatness in another register from the battle scenes. The conceptualization is brilliant. It fixed Gros's reputation. The painting became enormously popular.

The battle of Eylau, the subject of Gros's next painting, was fought on 8 February 1807 in a snowstorm, the bloody harbinger of battles to come. It presents a palpable shift of sensibility which parallels that of Napoleon's career. At the end of a gruesome day slugging it out in the snow the Russians withdrew and the French, now in possession of the field, claimed victory. Eylau has an uncanny resemblance to the battle of Borodino in 1812. More than 20,000 French soldiers, a third of his army, were killed or wounded at Eylau, along with six generals. *Napoleon Visiting the Battlefield of Eylau the Morning after the Battle* was shown at the Salon of 1808 and further enhanced Gros's reputation. The Emperor, with outstretched arm indicating the slaughter, gazes vaguely into the distance, his eyes not meeting those of the viewer. It was the first Napoleonic painting to insist on the horrors of war. The carnage, not the victory, is Gros's subject. This is the stuff of war unvarnished by glory or heroism. Napoleon is not the heroic conqueror at Eylau, he is the deeply human commander lamenting the loss of his soldiers. What Gros at his best did, as Eugène Delacroix recognized in his homage to his colleague, was to raise

> modern subjects up to the ideal; he knew how to paint the dress, manners, and passions of his time without falling into pettiness or triviality, the usual pitfalls of this type of subject.

But he was not always at his best. He would paint a number of superb portraits of Napoleonic grandees but his other battle paintings were without the divine spark that created *Arcole, Jaffa,* and *Eylau*. With Napoleon's fall he lost his way entirely. He returned to the mythological history painting he had so successfully left behind. His final works are technically superb and insipid. His *Hercules and Diomede* was badly received in the Salon of 1835 as a relic of a past and now outmoded taste. Gros, covered with honors bestowed by the Bourbons, became depressed and isolated from the art and artists of his time. Uninspired, bereft of the hero who had been his muse, he put on 'the uniform Napoleon had given him forty years before in Italy, walked to the river and drowned himself'.

For a man with little artistic taste Napoleon understood the power of art, especially in a new state. He had no interest in the techniques of art. His appreciation stopped at contrived mimesis. In battle painting he especially appreciated the work of lesser artists: Siméon Fort, Charles Thévenin, Louis-François Lejeune, Hippolyte Lecomte, Louis-Albert-Ghislain Bacler d'Albe, men whose names are known only to the specialist. They made pictures of his battles that he could understand on a narrative level. Bacler d'Albe, himself a soldier, accurately although too neatly placed the various contingents of Napoleon's army in his canvases and turned out paintings that illustrated the maps and plans of battle his commander-in-chief had pored over. Although Napoleon's taste in painting was more pedestrian than it was in literature, he had the good sense to realize his shortcomings, and take instruction from men of genius, whose work he learned to appreciate. Painting, for Napoleon, wrapped a ruler in the mantle of reverence, legitimacy, and the symbols of power. The kings had always had court painters and so would he. Part of the impetus for his looting of the art of Italy was to surround himself with acknowledged masterpieces. Painting additionally was the means of publicizing his image. He was depicted as the embodiment of the state, of authority, of legitimacy. He wanted pictures to illustrate the stories he told about himself.

He inherited the Salon system unique to France, and transformed it into an active instrument of government, a means of shaping public opinion. In the 18th century the Salon, essentially a juried art show run by the state, was a public forum of taste. The event was biennial and an invitation to hang a picture in the Salon was fundamental to artistic recognition and the commissions it brought. David's reputation was made here, as were those of all artists. The Directory revived the Salons and held them more frequently than had the monarchy. Under the Consulate they were held yearly until settling back into the biennial rhythm after 1802. The institution was ideal for Napoleon's needs. Even without formally invoking censorship the Salon channeled artistic work in directions that were flattering to Napoleon. Censorship was unnecessary. The government could reject any canvas submitted, and the knowledge that this barrier existed, coupled to the enormous expense and time involved in producing historical paintings, always large and sometimes huge canvasses, guaranteed that no painter would risk entering a politically objectionable work. The state regularly bought exhibited paintings, putting the Napoleonic *imprimatur* on an artist's work and making him fashionable to the parvenu military society of the new state. Napoleon, the master of public gesture, attended the Salon and signaled his approbation for specific paintings and artists. He stood silent for minutes before David's *Sacre* before pronouncing it a masterpiece. There were numerous battle scenes at every Salon. In 1806 18 pictures of the Austerlitz campaign were submitted. The fashionable portrait painters who participated in the Salon – Gérard, Prud'hon, Gros, Lefèvre – were much in demand and made a good living. Indeed all the arts flourished under Napoleon, whose taste for luxury resurrected the furniture-makers, the weavers at Gobelins, the porcelain painters at Sèvres, and the silk weavers in Lyon, all of whom had lost their patrons and their livings during the Revolution.

Napoleon found in Dominique-Vivant Denon the ideal commissar of art. Twenty years older than his patron, Denon, an accomplished engraver, had served Louis XV as curator of the royal medals collection and was appointed secretary to the Russian embassy in 1774. Upon his return he made the pilgrimage to Ferney to be received by the most famous man in Europe, Voltaire. In 1777, under a *nom de plume*, he wrote a pornographic novel (*Point de lendemain*). He successfully navigated the Revolution despite a potentially dangerous past as a courtier, thanks to the protection of Jacques-Louis David. Then, like so many others, he fell under Bonaparte's spell. He accompanied him to Egypt, which became a life-altering experience. He was attached to General Desaix's army when it was sent in pursuit of Murad Bey after the Battle of the Pyramids. He saw more of Egypt than did any of the other *savants* on the expedition, sketched everything he saw, and wrote one of the best and most successful travel books of the age. His dedication to Napoleon is a set piece of courtly compliment:

> To combine the luster of your name with the splendor of the monuments of Egypt is to associate the glorious annals or our own time with the history of the heroic age; and to reanimate the dust of Sesostris and Mendes, who, like you, were conquerors, like you benefactors.

His verbal descriptions of men dropping in their tracks and dying of thirst are harrowing. So is his account of the aftermath of the Battle of Aboukir Bay when Napoleon's fleet was destroyed:

> The shore, to the extent of four leagues, was covered with wrecks that enabled us to form an estimate of the loss we had sustained at the Battle of Aboukir. To procure a few nails, or a few iron hoops, the wandering Arabs were busy on the beach burning the masts, gun carriages and boats that had been constructed, at such vast expense, in our ports. Even their wrecks were a treasure in a country where so few of these objects were to be found. The robbers fled at our approach. Nothing was left but the bodies of the wretched victims, drifted on to the sand, by which they were half covered and exhibiting a spectacle as sublime as it was terrifying.

The aesthetic judgment, 'sublime' and 'terrifying', is not usually associated with the grisly flotsam and jetsam of naval disaster. Denon was an urbane man of taste, an observer with rare descriptive powers who moved easily among artists as well as men of state. He deeply influenced Napoleonic art and attached it to the new state. He provided the iconography and conventions for all the painters who sought inclusion in the Salon, he sent sketches and proposals to the Sèvres pottery works and to the Gobelins *atelier*. He made the model for the column in the Place Vendôme, he oversaw national *concours*, beginning with the Battle of Eylau, to get the artists to see events with a uniform eye. He amassed the greatest art collection of the age for the new Napoleon museum in the Louvre. He himself became a serious art collector, and most importantly he tactfully employed the smooth skills of diplomacy to handle all the artists and artisans with whom he dealt on Napoleon's behalf. Denon was in addition an enthusiastic champion of Egyptian art and broadened the aesthetic sensibilities of Europe by popularizing his enthusiasm. He was dumb-struck when he first saw the ruins of Dendra. 'What power! What riches! What abundance!' he gushed:

> What superfluity of means must a government possess that could erect such an edifice and find within itself artists capable of conceiving and executing the design, of decorating and enriching it with everything that speaks to the eye and the understanding! Never did the labor of man show me the human race in such a splendid light.

From their ruins 'the Egyptians appeared to me to be giants!' Ancient Egyptian civilization could not have had a better promoter. On 19 November 1802 (28 brumaire, an XI) Napoleon suppressed the old museum administration and dismissed its functionaries. In their place he created a 'director general of the central museum of arts'. Denon was named to the new post, with an annual salary of 12,000 francs. He held the position until October 1815, when he submitted his resignation to the restored Bourbon king. The Denon Pavilion of the present-day Louvre houses the great collection of French painting, including all the Napoleonic paintings discussed above, and the museum itself is entered from I. M. Pei's huge glass pyramid. Both museum and modern monument are a fitting tribute to the man who assembled the core collections of the new French state. The splendid pyramid reminds visitors of the importance of Egypt in Denon's life and that of the museum.

Chief among his functions was to assemble, classify, and ultimately display the booty in the Musée Napoléon. The spoils of 1796 that Napoleon had sent back from Italy, including the three most famous ancient statues in the world – the Laocoön, the Belvedere Apollo, and the Venus di Milo – formed the heart of the collection. Much was to be added. As Napoleon's artistic proconsul Denon followed the armies, and in Europe as in Egypt his taste broadened. Soon after Austerlitz he wrote Napoleon arguing 'there ought to exist in France a trophy to the victories in Germany as there already is for those of Italy. If Your Majesty will permit me,' he continued, 'I will indicate to him some objects in different genres that ought to be included in the treaties.' There followed a long list of paintings. Hesse-Cassel should provide 'at least forty [paintings], such as those of Albrecht Dürer, Holbein, and others'. Sculpture and coins were also sequestered, along with medals and decorations, 'which contain a number of portraits that cannot be found elsewhere'. Denon's plundering was intellectually more sophisticated than that previously sanctioned by Napoleon: his confiscations were purposeful and rational. As he amassed and catalogued the art treasures assembled in Paris his interests became increasingly historical. The Louvre is still arranged by schools of art and chronologically.

Napoleon's artistic imperialism was never completely realized. With his defeat the bulk of the purloined art was returned to its original owners, amid a complexity of claims and disputes that resound to this day. After Waterloo Denon returned to engraving for his living. He quietly died in 1825 leaving a significant private museum of pictures, medals, bronzes, drawings, antiquities, and curiosities. He was not a rich man but he was a careful and assiduous collector and had more opportunities than most to buy pictures without having to pay market prices. He loved Watteau, a fitting favorite for a man of elegance, refined taste, and a profound appreciation of exquisite craftsmanship. He owned his *Gilles*. He had a van Ruysdael, a Parmigianino, and 56 Italian primitives. He had 81 Flemish paintings and 53 French paintings, and a large collection of drawings and medals. All this was sold at auction in 1826.

When the Empress Eugénie, the wife of Napoleon III, came to see Charles Garnier's plans and models for the new opera house, opened in 1875, she asked him what was the style of the sumptuous building, the most expensive structure of the day. It is Empire style, answered the quick-witted architect. The style of neither the first nor the second Empire is easy to define. There are some general characteristics for the former: monumentality, an emphasis on decorative detail, expensive materials, and deliberate resonances with Roman and sometimes Greek antiquity, which perpetuated the aesthetic preferences of the Revolution, to which were added Pharaonic Egypt. Napoleon built a preponderance of military monuments but all his architecture was inspired by antiquity. The Bourse and the Madeleine are Greek temples. The column in the Place Vendôme is an imitation of Trajan's column in Rome, and his triumphal arches are based on Roman models. The huge, unbuilt palace he intended for his son was inspired by the baths of Caracalla. He made Paris an open-air military museum, which has endured to this day, long after French arms were worthy of public celebration or defined the state. To oversee this work Napoleon created a second commissar for art, Pierre-François-Léonard Fontaine (1762–1853). He was Denon's counterpart in architecture and design as well as his competitor for Napoleon's attention and artistic turf. Fontaine too owed his career to David, who introduced him to Napoleon in December 1799 a few weeks after the *coup d'état*. Napoleon treated his new architects – Fontaine's partner, Charles Percier, was with him – to 'his views of the embellishments he envisioned for Paris' and asked whether the antique statues taken from Italy should be displayed under the dome of the church of St Louis at Les Invalides, the space that now holds Napoleon's tomb.

The First Consul's immediate needs were for a residence fit to receive his guests and collaborators. Fontaine and Percier were employed. Malmaison needed massive renovations, structural changes, and complete redecoration. The most important of Fontaine's gifts was interpreting Napoleon's and Josephine's ideas: the former grandiose, the latter more intimate but very expensive, and both ever-changing. Almost as significant was getting along with a difficult, penurious, and curiously indecisive Napoleon. Fontaine's *Journal*, a superb record of all his dealings with Napoleon, is punctuated with clashes with his employer and the sense of dread that accompanied all the projects that needed Napoleon's approval. Fontaine worked quickly and made lovely watercolors of his proposals. His best work is not architectural; it was Percier who designed buildings. Fontaine had a flair for monuments and fountains. His genius lay in what we would today call renovation, interior decorating, and public ornament. His knowledge of ancient Rome was intimate and exact, just what Napoleon needed and wanted to memorialize his own deeds. Napoleon's passion for monuments was 'almost equal to his passion for war'. He had become convinced in Egypt that monuments would endure and proclaim their builder's glory for millennia, perhaps for eternity.

Josephine proved an architect's dream and nightmare. She spared no expense: 'Madame,' wrote Fontaine in his *Journal*, 'considered Malmaison as her own property.' She wanted 'all the riches that art could produce' assembled there. Fontaine and Percier had laid out a French classical garden, which was Napoleon's preference. 'She wanted everything à l'anglaise', meandering paths rather than the *barbarisme* of the rectilinear. Percier and Fontaine worked steadily at Malmaison for almost two-and-a-half years; Napoleon complained of the expense. The public buildings in Paris were far more important to Napoleon than his country house. Even before he proclaimed himself Emperor, when he was only the crown prince of the French Revolution, he insisted on surroundings that celebrated his glory. Painting was to depict his deeds, architecture to set them in stone. In Egypt he had dreamed of making Paris 'the most beautiful city that can be imagined'. Paris, he told Fontaine, 'lacks buildings. It is necessary to remedy this. It is ridiculous that [the kings] sought to limit the size of this great city. Its population could easily be doubled.' Napoleon was as ignorant of architecture as he was of painting. Fontaine, over the years, with diplomatic skills equal to those of Denon, instructed his master. The Musée Napoléon planned for the Louvre needed a grand staircase. Napoleon's Italian victories should be properly and symbolically celebrated by a triumphal arch at the entrance to the Tuileries, where the First Consul would reside. The German victories would be marked by a victory column. The Place Vendôme and the new column were connected to Napoleon's new street, the rue de Rivoli, and the great Paris palace, the Louvre-Tuileries. An enormously ambitious building program followed: the grand triumphal arch at the Étoile, a fountain in the shape of an elephant for the empty Place de la Bastille, where the dreaded prison had been razed, a number of other fountains, a canal system, bridges across the Seine, a Bourse and a temple of peace (the Madeleine), several covered markets, an abattoir, a domed central grain market, the complete rehabilitation of the chateaux of St Cloud and Rambouillet, and eventually an entire new official city on the Champ de Mars, where the Eiffel Tower now stands. Across the river at Chaillot he envisioned a huge palace, the largest in Christendom, for his son, the King of Rome. These last two projects were never realized, and the elephant fountain, built only in a plaster facsimile, disintegrated. Only Fontaine's drawings survive.

Of all the palaces of the kings the Tuileries was the least congenial and comfortable, yet its choice as the seat of the new government was inspired. The king of the Revolution would have a palace in the center of the capital that was more identified with the Revolution than with the Bourbon kings. It had been Louis XVI's virtual prison and the site of the 10 August 1792 attack that toppled the monarchy. The palace complex was not only the largest in France, it was the most prestigious secular site in Paris. Following Louis XIV's abandonment of the city for Versailles in 1682 the Tuileries lay unoccupied until Louis XVI was forcibly brought back from Versailles (6 October 1789), a prisoner of the Revolution. The elected assemblies of the Revolution, once they had followed the king from Versailles to Paris, met in the Manège, Louis XV's riding stable across the gardens from the Tuileries, until a new meeting hall was built in the Louvre. The Tuileries, rich with revolutionary history, was the perfect home for the heir of the Revolution. When Napoleon moved into the Tuileries in 1800 the courtyard and the grounds were filled with squatters, the walls of the rooms where the Convention Assembly had met were painted with revolutionary slogans, and the apartments had been uninhabited for years. Fontaine demolished all the houses on the grounds as well as some stables, and scraped the barnacles of 'small shops, boutiques, and bizarre buildings in the worst taste' from the Tuileries. Napoleon had the 'Trees of Liberty', planted by patriots during the Revolution, uprooted. There were to be no reminders of the mobs of the Revolution. The meeting room of the Convention Assembly, along with its slogans, was torn down. Fontaine looked down his nose at the archeological evidence of the Revolution. It was 'a monstrous mélange of grandeur, audacity, ignorance, and puerile precautions that is difficult to imagine.' He lamented that some artillery holes remained on the façade, with the words 'August 10, 1792'. The Manège too, where the king's trial took place, was razed, as were all the buildings along the Terrace of the Feuillants, opening the view to the Place Vendôme and the new column celebrating the victory at Austerlitz.

Each year Napoleon fixed the budget for work on the Tuileries and each year it was exceeded. He demanded luxury. He had his apartments 'furnished in lilac-blue and yellow silk, fringed with gold and white; the walls were hung with great paintings; there were Sèvres vases on the tables; his wife was bedecked in the jewels of Marie-Antoinette'. Prince Metternich, then the Austrian ambassador in Paris, commented on 'the prodigious expense' of refurbishment, and Talleyrand spoke of 'the absurd luxury of the court'. The imperial court spent 16 million francs on the civil list. Nothing was thought too good for the new dynasty that used magnificence and ostentation to make up for its lack of ancestry and age. The Revolution had a king.

The rue de Rivoli, the one major street Napoleon created, displays the many aspects of the Empire style, as well as Napoleon's inability to realize what he had imagined. It was the first significant east–west thoroughfare cut in Paris, designed to be at once strategic and aesthetic, but it was not carried to the Place de la Bastille as originally planned until Baron Haussmann did so in the 1860s. Percier produced a plan of uniform, large, imposing, and austere buildings, built with the best cut stone and a massive arcade. Artisans and workers 'who used hammers' in their trade were forbidden to live here. There were to be no food sellers and no commerce that used an oven. The arcades could carry no signs or markings of any kind. To encourage those capable of buying these expensive apartments a new decree (1811) gave the owners a thirty-year exemption from property taxes.

Napoleon was monarch of France for only 15 years. Before him there had been a Bourbon on the throne for 180 years. Yet the new king of the Revolution changed Paris more than had all his predecessors. Paris, not Versailles, was his home. The militant revolution is everywhere enshrined in stone, some of it useful, some of it merely decorative, and some of it both. Napoleon's mania for monument building made his capital a martial city, but these testaments of his glory were reifications of the triumphant Revolution. We too easily forget just how popular Napoleon was for the first years of his reign. Things do not begin to sour until the economic crisis of 1810–11, soon followed by the catastrophic Russian campaign. By that time the monuments to his and France's greatness were built or well under way. Of projects begun, only the arc de Triomphe at the Étoile was not finished in his lifetime. The Restoration turned its back on Napoleonic glory. The July Monarchy completed the great arch. He did not reign long enough to realize the Plan des Artistes, a vast urbanization project drawn up after Thermidor, but he set Paris down this path. It is an utterly unpredictable consequence of another revolution, that of 1848, from which Napoleon's nephew seized power in 1851, that we owe the perpetuation of Napoleon's vision of Paris. Even without Napoleon III Napoleonic Paris would have remained impressive. Napoleon was right: monuments do tell the story and long outlive their creator.

VIII
Catastrophe and Decline

If Napoleon's dynastic politics was to endure he needed an heir. He determined to anchor his government and his dynasty with a marriage, the time-honored practice of monarchs. It was a sharp break with the Revolution. Despite this the Napoleonic monarchy, redolent with familiar historical harmonies, was not a return to the *ancien régime*. The Revolution had a king, but he was the incarnation of the militant Revolution, his fellow monarchs saw their thrones threatened by a Jacobin who disdained them and whose reforms challenged their power, authority, and presumptions. Now, paradoxically, he sought the conventional mechanism for preserving his work and maintaining his family in power.

He saw only two possible alliances: Austria or Russia. Depending on the choice a complex series of consequences would unfold. He first toyed with the idea of a marriage with one of Tsar Alexander's two sisters. The Grand Duchess Catherine was charming and witty, but had been married to a German prince in 1808. The Grand Duchess Anna was only 14. The diplomatic drawbacks of a Russian marriage were several but Napoleon was never deterred by the subtleties or ramifications of a choice that intrigued him. A Russian marriage would cause a diplomatic revolution. Russia would become a part of Western Europe, Poland would cease to be a buffer holding Russia at bay. Napoleon would have to abandon his vague promises to establish a Polish state under French protection. Austria and Germany would have Russia at their doorstep, a fear that had for half a century frightened the German states and dictated much of their foreign policy. On the other hand Napoleon thought a Russian marriage would assure the success of the Continental System in Eastern Europe and the Baltic states, where it

163

leaked contraband to the point of hemorrhage. His influence would stretch unchecked into Asia itself.

When Napoleon asked for the hand of the Tsar's younger sister Alexander temporized, pleading his mother's skittishness about the match. Tsar Paul, before his assassination, had given his consort, now the Grand Duchess Catherine, absolute power to choose husbands for his daughters. She loathed Napoleon, but it was impolitic to say so. Instead she dithered, pleading that having lost one daughter to marriage the remaining child could not marry until she was 18. Napoleon had no time to lose on such scruples, whether real or feigned. He had simultaneously been negotiating with Metternich, which infuriated the Tsar. He now turned to Austria and the house of Habsburg, the most prestigious in Europe. The Corsican parvenu was tempted at the prospect of marrying a Habsburg. He joked with Bertrand that before the marriage Prince Metternich had 'wanted to publish a document that established that my ancestors had reigned at Treviso' (in the Veneto). 'I told M de Metternich that this would be ridiculous.' He had no illusions about his family's past glories. 'I am what I am,' he said. Metternich, trying to reestablish himself after having urged the disastrous 1809 war, needed the French marriage. It would keep the Russians at bay, pry apart the Franco-Russian alliance, and rescue Austria from reduction to a second-rate power. The treaty of Vienna that so offended Russia looked very good to Austria. It meant the end of any French rapprochement with Russia. Rupture would become inevitable, which was precisely Metternich's hope. It is for Dominic Lieven, the historian of the Russian campaign, the beginning of the war that ultimately destroyed Napoleon: 'It was no coincidence that in early March 1810 the new minister of war, Mikhail Barclay de Tolly, drafted his first memorandum on measures for the defense of Russia's western border from French attack.'

Napoleon officially asked for the hand of Marie-Louise on 6 January 1810. It was granted the next day. Austrian *amour-propre* was publicly soothed by presenting the match as the spoils of the victor. There was scarcely a murmur in Europe, but France was another matter. Austria had been an enemy for decades. Marie-Antoinette, the great-aunt of Napoleon's new empress, had been publicly insulted in the 1780s; *l'Autrichienne*, as she was contemptuously called, was derided as a foreigner, the very incarnation of court frivolity and scandal, and a woman who meddled in politics, the business of men. She was vilified in scurrilous pamphlets. She was reviled anew at the beginning of the Revolution, and the slanders of an earlier decade were recycled. The same venom was spewed when she was put on trial in October 1793. Her young son then testified in open court against his mother, accusing her of sexual corruption and introducing him to depravity. Even Napoleon, who habitually found little in his own conduct to criticize, realized he had made a political mistake in marrying another Austrian princess. 'One never knows what one should do,' he uncharacteristically confessed to Bertrand. 'The most promising events turn contrary. So it was with my marriage with Marie-Louise, which appeared to have anchored my entire system and which ruined me.' He had offended everyone and his Hapsburg marriage brought no legitimacy. The Austrians saw it as nothing but expediency, as did everyone else, including his old comrades. Expedience was betrayal of the Revolution.

The break with Russia came soon enough. On the last day of 1810, in the midst of a crippling economic crisis throughout the empire, Alexander issued a *ukaz* heavily taxing French goods and *de facto* taking Russia out of the Continental System. This was a declaration of economic war and became the immediate cause of a shooting war. Napoleon insisted that all his wars had been forced upon him by his many enemies. His own provocations and bullying were never mentioned. In fact the restoration of a Polish kingdom under Saxon domination, which blatantly violated the convention between Napoleon's ambassador, Armand de Caulaincourt, and the Tsar's minister, M. P. Rumianstsev, was the French declaration of war, far more serious than his matrimonial diplomacy. Napoleon's handling of the Polish question was cynical, even for him:

> All I want out of Poland [he told Narbonne] is a disciplined force to furnish a battlefield. That's the whole question: how to excite the spirit of national liberation in Poland, without re-exciting the fiber of liberalism? And where would I find a king for Poland? I haven't got one in my own family, and it would be dangerous to take one from somewhere else.

Napoleon was politically and socially niggardly toward the Duchy of Warsaw. He was not in a giving mood. He granted the Poles, who served him loyally, a far smaller kingdom than they desired, and left the landlords their vast authority, carefully avoiding any significant social dislocation. He abolished serfdom in the Duchy of Warsaw but the land upon which the free peasants now lived and worked remained the property of the *seigneur* who had the right to evict his tenants. Some, but not all, of the most obnoxious feudal obligations and dues persisted, including forced labor, the hated *corvée*. In the long and painful history of the Polish peasantry 'the Napoleonic period constituted an episode of minor importance' although it 'accelerated the pauperization of the peasantry'. The Poles were deeply disappointed. Napoleon correctly calculated that even the little he granted was more than they could expect from anyone else, and was vastly preferable to Russian occupation and control. During the Russian campaign he used his Polish troops for some of the toughest fighting, as he had earlier in Spain.

Much more serious for the Empire was the economic crisis. The budget deficits from 1811 on were due to war: military expenditure rose from 40 per cent of the budget in 1806 to 58 per cent in 1813. Napoleon depended on extraordinary exactions to pursue his ambitious policies and plug the holes created by his enormous military expenditures. His axiom that war should pay for itself meant that he inflicted huge indemnities on those he conquered in addition to the vast and violent depredations of his troops during the fighting and subsequent occupation. The forced contributions of Prussia and Austria were the first such transfusions into the *Trésor de l'armée*, created in 1805. There would be many more. In 1810 he created the *Domaine extraordinaire*, reserved for his own use, to receive lands and income from his vassal states. Even these huge extractions were not enough. Napoleon insisted on a fixed metallic currency and refused to borrow. He well remembered the collapse of the *assignats* in the Revolution and the drastic measures taken by the Directory to stop the runaway inflation by disavowing their bonds. In the entire Napoleonic period there was no devaluation, no monetary crisis. 'For the first time in France money of account coincided with the money actually in circulation: the intrinsic value of money was equal to its nominal value.' But his campaigns had a serious deflationary impact on the French economy. Because he enjoyed no major victories after Wagram the imperial fisc spent far more than it took in. The only proposal Napoleon offered was the possibility of a great victory that would restore his own and the state's fortunes.

The Empire could have weathered economic crisis had it been confined to one, or even two sectors. It was the concatenation that proved overwhelming. The agricultural crisis of 1802-03 returned in 1812–14. An industrial crisis (1810–11) struck at the same time, along with what the economic historian Jean Bouvier calls a crisis of the 'First Empire' type, characterized by deflation brought on by the costs of war and a monetary crisis brought on by a lack of confidence. Together the three created a general crisis. The agricultural crisis of June 1811 to September 1812 was familiar in an economy not much changed since the Revolution. It was caused by bad harvests. Expensive bread meant market riots which could easily infect the larger society. Those of 1789, the *locus classicus* of revolutionary rioting, had toppled the Bastille and fueled the Women's March on Versailles. Bread riots had been transmuted into political uprising. In 1811–12 the price of bread rocketed. The traditional round loaf disappeared from the markets by early morning, even for those who could afford it. Napoleon behaved as had the revolutionaries and the kings before him: he called out the soldiers and imposed price controls. He reintroduced the hated *maximum,* the economic legislation of the Terror which fixed the prices of food staples and froze wages. Only the word *maximum* was avoided. The imperial decree of 8 May 1812, just before the invasion of Russia, imposed a tax that determined the maximum price for a hectoliter (a hundred liters) of flour in the *département* of the Seine and surrounding regions. Paris at least would be fed.

Silk weaving in Lyon collapsed at the same time. Cotton weaving in Paris similarly suffered. An army of weavers in both cities were out on the streets, victims of the Continental System coupled to the fallout from the agricultural crisis. The manufacturing crisis of the Empire followed the cyclical movement of salaries characteristic of the 18th century. Napoleon's massive reforms in the Consulate and the first years of the Empire were not economic. He had been lucky: there was only one year of agriculture failure (1802–03) and the Consulate easily weathered the storm. Then, with the Berlin Decrees (1806), he directly interfered in the unreformed economy. Buoyed up by the stunning success of the Grande Armée at Austerlitz he imposed an embargo on British goods. The Continental System and blockade, his most important economic policy, was proving enormously complicated, its desired results elusive. Some economies sheltered behind protection from British competition. Others suffered spasms of contraction. Then came the Spanish war, which not only drained money and men but, ironically since it was instigated by Napoleon's need to staunch the flow of British goods into Europe, opened the Iberian peninsula to massive amounts of contraband. François Crouzet, the historian of the Blockade, argues that had Napoleon not invaded Spain and thus stimulated the British boom of 1809–10, the economic consequences of the Blockade would have been desperate for England, who acutely felt the pinch by 1812.

It is notoriously difficult to assess the impact of economic warfare. The Continental System, even after 1810, cannot be compared with the complete economic warfare of the First or Second World War, which inflicted profound hardships on Germany and contributed to her defeat. It is equally difficult to ascribe the crises in specific industries to the blockade. Dutch industry and trade were in decline before the French Revolution. The Continental System accelerated the process. The same was true of the Hanseatic cities whose conservative oligarchs clung to their power and wealth by desperately defending an archaic economy. Napoleon saw the situation through the dual distorting lens of short-sightedness and his habit of commanding obedience. The war exacerbated everything. The ineluctable logic of his war with England took another turn. Napoleon became obsessed with Russia. He was determined to destroy England and needed complete hegemony over the Continent. Before returning to Spain he was determined to punish Alexander for withdrawing from the Continental System, teach him a lesson about treating the conqueror of Europe as an upstart, unworthy to marry a Romanov, and incorporate Russia in his 'system'. The future of the Empire would be decided in Russia. It was his greatest gamble.

Napoleon began preparing for the campaign of his life. So too did Alexander. Napoleon attended to every detail. His correspondence demonstrates once again his utter familiarity with every brigade, regiment, and battalion. He knew where each was stationed, who commanded, how many reinforcements each needed to be brought up to fighting strength, what armaments each had or required, and how soon each would be ready to move east. No detail escaped his scrutiny. Even the lettering on military badges received his attention. He pored over the available maps, which soon proved inadequate and inaccurate, and assembled a huge bridging train to move his army across the numerous rivers. 'One can expect nothing of the country,' he told General Davout, 'and we shall have to carry everything with us.' The nature of the coming campaign, the sheer size of the enterprise, meant that fundamental principles of Napoleonic warfare had to be abandoned or compromised. Not only was the invading force the largest Napoleon or anyone else had assembled, the country in which they would be operating more vast and devoid of good roads than any he had hitherto conquered, but his unprecedented army had to be supplied by its own devices in this huge and hostile landscape. It required 850 carts to carry a day's food and forage for an army of 120,000 men and 40,000 horses. These numbers had to be more than tripled for Napoleon's invading army. The horses and drivers of the supply train had also to be fed. 'In a vicious circle very familiar to pre-modern generals the army's supply train could end up by eating all the food it was attempting to deliver,' Lieven points out. Napoleon improvised a supply system relying on flotillas of river boats as well as wagon convoys to move from Danzig and Königsberg.

He designed special carts, drawn by two or four oxen, to carry flour to the front, where the beasts, having done their work, would be slaughtered and eaten. The system soon broke down. His army marched hungry to Moscow. Things were infinitely worse during the retreat.

Part of the reason for the breakdown, according to Caulaincourt, the Master of the Horse who was charged with transportation, is that Napoleon consulted no one when making his preparations. All the army's transport equipment was built for metalled roads:

> The first sand we came across overwhelmed the horses; for the loads, instead of being cut down in proportion to the weight of the vehicle and the distance to be covered, had been increased in the notion that the daily consumption would sufficiently lessen them.

Napoleon resisted consultation throughout the campaign and made a series of fatal mistakes his subordinates tried to correct. Caulaincourt, who had spent several winters in Russia when he was ambassador, took sacks of coal along, which he kept under lock and key. He used them to fire the forges to make ice shoes for the imperial horses, a need Napoleon had not foreseen. 'During the retreat,' he wrote,

> horses fell and lay by the roadside chiefly because they were not properly shod to keep their footing on ice, and once down, and vainly having attempted to rise, they ended by lying where they fell, and were cut up for food before they were even dead.

His descriptions of men sliding down hills on the ice and being crushed to death by their horses sliding after them is one of many unforgettable horrors of the retreat.

A metaphor of how overburdened was the army is Napoleon's own equipment, an ostentatious display of his growing love of luxury. He had never before gone to war as a potentate. His household on the march to Moscow had 150 saddle horses, 500 additional horses and mules, 50 carriages, including a specially built vehicle from which he ran the campaign and the Empire, and a mobile hospital. Liveried servants, mounted on mules, carried multiple sets of silver flatware bearing the imperial coat of arms. He had chefs, valets, and a staff of servants, as well as a dozen secretaries, who also had servants. He brought ministers along, for the Empire would be governed from his tent, which had two drawing rooms, a study, and a bedroom. There were seven additional tents for his staff and retinue, and a number of tents that were never set up, equipment that was never unpacked. He had, while in the field, a guard of 100 cavalry officers, plus two infantry battalions and *gendarmes d'élite*. There were 100 postilions stationed along the road to supervise the movement of mail between Paris and headquarters. So reliable was this service that dispatches arrived every afternoon around two o'clock. Because he dined at irregular hours his staff had to be prepared at a moment's notice to serve a hot meal. He and his guests ate on gold dinner service, often on tables set outside the imperial tents, with sterling silver flatware, and massive silver serving pieces. His dinners on the Russian campaign resembled those of the Tuileries. He drank his favorite wine, Chambertin, throughout the invasion and the retreat. Not since Mirabeau's lavish entertainments in the first years of the Revolution had a revolutionary leader so indulged himself. Not since the wars of the *ancien régime* had a commander taken the field so encumbered with comfort.

Napoleon was a sultan going to receive tribute and homage from an over-mighty subject. His original plans, obsessively detailed, were perfectly in character. He sought a decisive battle early on, followed by an imposed peace. He knew the Russian campaign would be longer than any earlier adventure, although he did not plan for an extended war of several years as did Alexander. It is what he would do after the victory, after he had executed his carefully planned withdrawal, that was left unprepared. Leaving aside everything that went wrong, Napoleon's plans for conquering Russia are at best half-baked. As always he relied heavily on improvisation. He threatened freeing the serfs, a reasonable act for a former Jacobin. This would break the back of Russian feudalism and undermine the landlords. But he never seriously meant the threat. Everywhere he attacked the *ancien régime* he was careful not to cause social disruption. Unleashing the serfs would have been disastrous for the French as well as the Russians. There was no Bonaparte brother to put on the Russian throne. Even had there been, by 1812 Napoleon was disillusioned with his siblings as kings. A satellite kingdom was out of the question. Perhaps he thought to make Alexander a vassal king. But the Tsar, who had spurned a marriage alliance with Napoleon, was not the King of Saxony, willing to do the Emperor's bidding. Russia was no German principality to be bullied or bought off. Russia could hardly be annexed. Napoleon lacked the army or the administration even to consider such a solution. What would he have done with Russia had he won the single decisive battle he envisioned?

The timing of the invasion was fixed by the harvest. It was impossible to haul enough fodder for the horses. They would be fed on hay and oats cut in Russia. Cavalrymen were issued with a sickle. The crop would not be ready until the end of June at the earliest. Napoleon began assembling his massive army in the winter of 1812 but could not invade until the summer. This left him with a very short campaign season: less than four months. He needed a quick and decisive victory. He got neither.

Alexander too had prepared. He created a Ministry of the Armed Forces and lavished money on it. Military spending rose more than three-fold. The army soon consumed about 50 per cent of the budget. He extended the draft. The total number of men under arms at the beginning of 1812 was 590,000, and in March he added an additional 65–70,000. By September he had 904,000 men. Count Rambuteau reports an interview he had with Alexander. 'My dear Count,' said the Tsar,

> I am convinced that Napoleon is the greatest general in Europe, that his armies are the most battle-hardened, his lieutenants the bravest and the most experienced; but space is a barrier. If, after a few defeats, I retreat, sweeping along the population, if I leave it to time, to the wilderness, to the climate to defend me, I may yet have the last word over the most formidable army of modern time.

To the Prussian king Frederick William III he was even more explicit. In May 1811, more than a year before the French invasion, he wrote:

> We have to adopt the strategy which is most likely to succeed. It seems to me that this strategy has to be one of carefully avoiding big battles and organizing very long operational lines which will sustain a retreat which will end in fortified camps, where nature and engineering works will strengthen the forces which we use to match up to the enemy's skill. The system is the one which has brought victory to Wellington in wearing down the French armies, and it is the one which I have resolved to follow.

Everyone knew Russia's vastness. The defeat of the German knights, drawn deep into Russia by Alexander Nevsky in the 13th century, was a part of national mythology. More recently (1709) Peter the Great had crushed Charles XII at Poltava in Ukraine. But it is only in retrospect, when the Russian armies refused to give Napoleon the big battle he craved, and retreat verged on rout, that the Tsar's insouciance appears prophetic. At the time he, his generals, and his staff were paralyzed as the Russian armies fled Napoleon, drawing him ever deeper into the Russian heartland. Unable to stop the French, Russia ceded vast stretches of territory, including major cities. The Tsar's advisers and generals underestimated the size of the Grande Armée. The highest Russian guess was 350,000 invaders, which would have made a confrontation feasible. Once the Grande Armée crossed the Niemen River none of the generals – not Barclay, nor Bagration, nor Toll, nor Bennigsen – was willing to face Napoleon.

Napoleon's was a mongrel army. French was not the dominant language of the soldiers. His plan, writes David Chandler, 'is both ingenious and inspiring, proving that Napoleon's planning capabilities were still undimmed'. But there were serious flaws. The 'problems of time and distance were to prove too great for the capacity of a single mortal, even when that man was Napoleon'. 'The aim of all my moves,' he wrote Marshal Davout in May, 'will be to concentrate 400,000 men at a single point.' This proved impossible. Napoleon's strategic schemes broke down incessantly, his subordinates misunderstood or bungled their tasks. He himself displayed an uncharacteristic lack of energy and drive. He spent more time in his splendid tent than among his troops. He was not at the top of his game, and everyone noticed. The Grande Armée crossed the Niemen on 24 June. Napoleon entered Vitebsk a month later (28 July). He had not fought a single major battle but his army had been reduced by a third. This terrible attrition was attributable to the ferocious heat, killing thirst, short food supplies, the endless sandy tracts that proved a graveyard for horses, massive desertions, and dysentery that carried off countless soldiers and left a foul swath of diarrhea marking the army's march through Russia. Napoleon paused in Vitebsk before pushing on to Smolensk on 13 August. Clausewitz, by then in Russian service, thought Napoleon's decision to attack the city was the greatest error of the campaign. Smolensk was strategically unimportant, and the partial destruction of the city stiffened Russian resolve. There was no decisive battle offered, but the many stubborn encounters – Davout, Ney, and Gouvion St-Cyr all won isolated victories, and St-Cyr earned his marshal's baton – gave Napoleon the city, with its extensive stores. The cost was high: casualties that he could not replace, lost days he could not regain. He left Smolensk on 25 August and a new obsession, Moscow, filled his imagination. What had begun as a short campaign with a quick, decisive battle, had become something quite different.

On the 29th the Tsar replaced Barclay de Tolly, the original architect of the Russian strategy, with Kutuzov. It was a fateful appointment. Mikhail Hilarionovich Golenischev-Kutusov (1745–1813) was the son of a military engineer. Originally commissioned as an artillery officer under Tsarina Catherine, he later transferred to the light infantry. He fought with distinction in Poland (1764–69) and Ukraine, and then in the Crimea (1770–74). It was here he lost his right eye. He was appointed to the command of the main Russian army during the wars of the Third Coalition, but arrived too late to fight at Ulm. He did, however, lead a classic rear-guard action against the pursuing French and saved his army. He was pressured by the Tsar and the Austrian Emperor, neither of whom knew anything about war, into an ill-advised intervention at Austerlitz, which he opposed. He was rehabilitated soon afterwards and given the command of forces in the Russo-Turkish war (1811–12). He cut off the main Ottoman army and forced surrender. 'In so doing he made one of his greatest contributions to the 1812 campaign before it had begun.' His victory freed the army of the Danube to be deployed against Napoleon. By autumn they posed 'a huge threat to Napoleon's communications and his retreating army.'

Alexander had himself thought of taking command of his retreating army, by then a wretched force of about 120,000 men, but was dissuaded by his advisers who remembered his earlier military ineptitude in Germany. He succumbed to court pressure and appointed the general whose advice he had rejected at Austerlitz. Kutusov was 67, suffered from gout, and was so obese he could not mount his horse without help. He drank excessively, was an old *roué*, and lazy to the point of somnolence. But he was a respected and inspiring field commander, though well beyond his prime. He was given the command when time was on his side and he played this advantage, which dove-tailed perfectly, brilliantly, with his character and inclinations. Napoleon underestimated his foe as he did all those he fought. He considered Kutuzov intelligent, but reminded Caulaincourt of his failure at Austerlitz. Now with 'an enfeebled and demoralized army he would certainly not prevent the French from reaching Moscow'.

It has become fashionable to think of Kutusov, following Tolstoy's portrait in *War and Peace*, as a man of the people, a son of the Russian soil, the embodiment of peasant wisdom, religiosity, and long-suffering endurance, of Mother Russia herself. Soviet historiography, driven by Stalin's need to glorify his own role as a war leader, made Kutuzov, stripped of his piety, a greater general than Napoleon. In fact he was a cultivated courtier, a man of refined tastes who issued his orders in impeccable French. In addition to the accumulated experience of 52 years as a soldier, he had a gift for getting his peasant troops to fight beyond what any general could reasonably expect and military theorists

Figure 7 Mikhail Kutuzov. Engraving of an anonymous portrait of Napoleon's nemesis. Kutuzov, his *embonpoint* already obese, which rendered him unable to mount a horse unaided, is depicted without his eye patch. His sightless right eye – he lost it in the Crimea in 1774 – is clearly visible.

thought impossible. The sheer tenacity of the Russians at Borodino stunned Napoleon and made him pay excessively, in irreplaceable men and horses, for his dubious victory.

There had been a passionate war council in Smolensk before Napoleon set out for Moscow. The consensus was either to stay in Smolensk and await the next campaign season, or to turn back. Napoleon's old comrades in arms still retained the familiarity of their youthful wars and bivouacs. 'Never was a sovereign,' wrote Caulaincourt, 'surrounded by more capable men, men who were honest before all else and not mere courtiers … wherever the Emperor cared to probe he was sure to find, if he wanted it, a sterling and even disagreeable truth rather than mere flattery.' No doubt he got an earful from his cronies. As soon as he was again in the midst of his soldiers, inspired by martial bustle, 'the wise thoughts he had entertained at Smolensk yielded to the enticements of Glory'.

It was not, however, an emotional decision to march on to Moscow, now only two weeks away. Caulaincourt's reservations notwithstanding, all Napoleon's decisions were rational. He could not remain away from France for a year nor could he sit idly in Smolensk with an undefeated Russian army roaming freely. It was unimaginable that capturing Moscow would not give him the same triumphs he had enjoyed when he took Vienna or Berlin. Retreat from an unfinished campaign would be politically dangerous, perhaps fatal. The vultures in Europe who were now his reluctant allies watched for any sign of weakness.

Caulaincourt saw his master daily and often rode with him. He was shocked by Napoleon's mood swings. The Emperor would speak dispassionately and accurately about the campaign, and 'the next instant' he was again 'obsessed ... by his old illusions and returned to his gigantic projects':

> The most insignificant skirmish, the arrival of reinforcements, the appearance of some ammunition wagons, a report from the king of Naples, a few cries of '*Vive l'Empereur!*' at a parade, and above all the letters from Vilna [where his foreign ministry had set up office], were enough to turn his head once more.

Napoleon's obsession with reaching Moscow became a refrain. 'We must be in Moscow within the month ... In war, luck is half of everything,' he told his secretary, Baron Fain. 'Peace' and 'Moscow' were always uttered together. 'Why wait here for eight months,' he asked Fain in Smolensk, 'when twenty days' march are enough for us to reach our goal?' 'Peace and Moscow' would finish his creation of the European system. 'The cause of the century' would be won, 'the Revolution [would] be accomplished'. A far different end to the Revolution than that declared in 1799:

> My glory will be in the success and in my equity [he imagined]. Back in France, in the bosom of the fatherland, great, strong and magnificent, tranquil and glorious, I shall associate my son with me as Emperor. My dictatorship will be over.

Napoleon attached the Revolution to his glory just as it teetered in the balance. The Revolution would save his dynasty once he had completed the work of spreading it throughout Europe. He now imagined the recreation of the first settlement of the Revolution in 1791 as a constitutional monarchy to be ruled by his son. Not unlike Robespierre, who envisioned the Terror as a necessary road to a Republic of Virtue, Napoleon saw the Russian war as the necessary road to constitutional monarchy.

'Peace lies in Moscow,' he reiterated to Caulaincourt:

> When the great nobles of Russia see us masters of the capital, they will think twice about fighting on. If I liberated the serfs it would smash all those great fortunes. The battle will open the eyes of my brother Alexander, and the capture of Moscow will open the eyes of his nobles.

Napoleon's monologues on the march from Smolensk to Moscow are so passionate, angry, and fantastic it is no wonder his advisers and staff were bewildered and worried. The man of acute political judgments, the cynical realist, the penetrating appraiser of character, had become a devotee of 'his star', a man waiting for fortune to smile upon his desperate endeavors. He attributed blindness and feebleness to his foes, while his own illusions grew unchecked by reason or reality. The Tsar was a weak and indecisive prince, a mediocre military leader, and a foolish womanizer, all of which earned Napoleon's contempt. But at the core of his character was the conviction that God had chosen him to rule, which engendered a tenacious fatalism. His was a character Napoleon could not understand any more than he could understand the personal courage and defiance of Pope Pius VII. Neither man made sense to Napoleon: he misread and underestimated both. Alexander had put his fate and that of his country in the hands of God, whose agents, Kutusov and Rostopchin, the governor of Moscow, made decisions the Tsar could not have imagined or condoned. He refused, despite the ruin of his country, to negotiate with the invader. Napoleon was dumbfounded.

Alexander's character eluded and frustrated his contemporaries and has had the same impact on historians. Lieven provides a shrewd appraisal:

> An excellent actor, who operated behind a screen of charm and flattery, he remained secretive, opaque, distrustful and elusive. To many observers ... he appeared to be a mass of contradictions. On the one hand he was a champion of enlightened and liberal principles, but on the other he did very little to ameliorate the authoritarian system of government he inherited, or the world of serf and master on which it rested. He sounded like his grandmother, Catherine II, when he spoke of liberal reforms, but acted like his father, Paul I, in his

obsessive concern for the correct drill and appearance of his soldiers on the parade ground. In foreign affairs he put forward high-minded schemes for international peace and order, while simultaneously pursuing a policy of realpolitik. All this has persuaded some critics that he was simply confused and hypocritical.

Eighty-two days after the Grande Armée crossed the Niemen, marched more than 825 miles, fought one important battle and a number of minor ones, Napoleon was to have the battle he sought. His army was now reduced to perhaps 130,000 men. The Old Guard was the only unit still completely intact. Kutusov chose to stand at the crossroads village of Borodino, 75 miles west of Moscow. The decision, even more than the battle itself, reveals Kutusov's shrewdness, perhaps his greatness. His choice of battlefield was perfectly suited to his needs. He would fight a battle of attrition, the kind of battle that handicapped Napoleon. Borodino was cramped and left little room for maneuver. 'It would, in the most literal sense cramp Napoleon's own genius.' The price to be paid in casualties would be enormously high. It would be the logical conclusion to the Russian defensive campaign. Kutuzov's army was in tatters, incapable of taking the offensive, but still with enough fight to prevent Napoleon from doing so. More than anything he needed to save what he could, force Napoleon to pay dearly for his probable victory, regroup and rebuild. Kutusov's great, and determining, advantage over his opponent was that he could reconstitute his battered army if only he had a little time. He needed to get Napoleon off his tail. He needed a distraction. Zamoyski says, overdramatically, that Kutusov's resolve to sacrifice Moscow to save his army and ultimately Russia was 'the only brilliant decision he made during the whole campaign'. It was what was needed. 'Moscow is the sponge which will suck him in,' Kutusov explained to Colonel Friedrich von Toll. So it proved. Napoleon, accustomed to dictating peace to the vanquished in their own capital and palace, could not resist the lure of doing so in the Kremlin. In his ardor to possess Moscow he forgot what he knew: St Petersburg was the administrative capital which held all the institutions of state. The loss of Moscow did not weaken the state's ability to function. He found it unthinkable that the Tsar would sacrifice the old capital, despite the fact that he had already sacrificed the holy city of Smolensk. Once Napoleon had Moscow Alexander and all Russia would be his. It was a fatal miscalculation.

The French began the battle. At 6 a.m. approximately 102 guns opened fire from their right flank. The range proved too great for effective shooting. They stopped firing and moved the guns forward. Napoleon had failed to learn the extent and strength of the Russian left flank, his main attack thrust proved too weak, and from his command post, just east of the redoubt near Shivardino, he could see neither the villages of Borodino nor Orano on his own extreme left flank, where some of the most important fighting took place. He was also suffering from a severe cold, dysuria that made urination extremely painful, and a throbbing migraine. Once Kutusov had placed his troops, densely spread out evenly along his front, he put his trust in the legendary stubbornness of the Russian soldier to defend a prepared position. The Great Redoubt, where he had concentrated his field guns, and the three flèches – only two could be seen by the French until they attacked – proved the key to the battle. His small reserves and his cavalry were too close to the front and unsheltered. They came under artillery fire from the start. So did Napoleon's cavalry. For almost nine hours Murat's massed cavalry sat immobile on their mounts awaiting the order to charge. They suffered constant and murderous bombardment, while the artillery and infantry slugged it out, capturing and recapturing the flèches and finally the Great Redoubt:

> for strong, healthy well-mounted men a cavalry battle is nothing compared with what Napoleon made his cavalry put up with at Borodino. To hold out inactively under fire must be one of the most unpleasant things cavalry can be called upon to do. There can scarcely have been a man whose neighbour didn't crash to earth with his horse or die from terrible wounds, screaming for help.

Kutusov behaved with insouciance. He was some three miles behind the front, where he received and reacted to staff officers who galloped up carrying a unit commander's request or suggestion. With a wave of his hand Kutuzov would say 'C'est bon, faites-le!' He would sometimes turn to Toll and ask his opinion: 'Karl, whatever you say I will do.' Clausewitz, whose history of the Russian campaign profoundly influenced all subsequent accounts, said the old general contributed nothing to the fighting: 'He appeared destitute of inward activity, of any clear view of surrounding occurrences, of any liveliness of perception, or independence of action.' General Bonamy confirms this appraisal. Bleeding and helpless, he was taken to Kutusov's headquarters where the general was lunching and chatting with his staff officers. He called for a surgeon and then went back to his small talk. Napoleon too was strangely detached. He seemed often only a spectator. He remained deaf to the requests, and soon the demands, of his commanders to use the Imperial Guard. Around 11 a.m. there was a lull in the fighting. Murat sent one of his ADCs (Colonel Morelli) to Napoleon. From the Shevardino redoubt he heard voices also calling for the Guard. 'And what if there's another battle tomorrow,' Napoleon asked Morelli, 'what shall I fight with?' Murat later made a second request, and this time sent his chief-of-staff, Belliard. 'Before I commit my reserves,' he told Belliard, 'I must be able to see more clearly on my chessboard.' Marshal Ney also asked for the guard. His disappointment was not polite: 'If he's tired, why doesn't he retire to the Tuileries and leave the fighting to the real generals.' 'I'm not going to have my Guard destroyed' was Napoleon's response. 'When you're eight hundred leagues from France you don't wreck your last reserve.'

Soon after Napoleon's last refusal to engage his Guard, the battle turned. After a murderous and stupendous effort the Great Redoubt was captured. By 6:30 the guns fired only sporadically. 'A kind of stunned stupor seems to have fallen on both armies.' The battle was over. The Guard had not fired a shot. In the early morning hours of 8 September, as Napoleon was about to make his tour of the battlefield, Kutuzov led his battered army away in good order. He had lost between 45,000 and 50,000 men against perhaps 35,000 French casualties. Bagration's Second Army had been nearly destroyed. He could fight no more.

The Count de Ségur, who wrote a classic and critical account of the Russian campaign, rode out with Napoleon on the 8th to survey the killing fields:

> It was impossible, [he writes] no matter how careful one was, always to walk one's horse on the ground. The Emperor, I saw, was still ill, and the only animated gesture I saw him make was of irritation. One of our horses, striking one of these victims, had drawn a groan from him ... Upon one of us remarking that the dying man was a Russian, the emperor retorted: 'There are no enemies after a victory!' and immediately had Roustam pick the man up and give him a drink from his own brandy flask which the Mameluke always carried on him.

Borodino now held the record for the greatest massacre in military history. Artillery did much of the killing. The statistics are in doubt, but one source says the French fired off 91,000 rounds and the infantry and cavalry discharged 1,400,000 musket-shots, which 'averages out at a hundred cannon shots and 2300 rounds of musketry per minute'. The slaughter of officers was unprecedented: 33 generals of brigade,

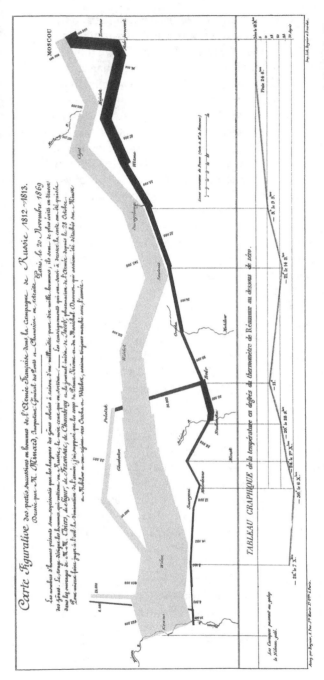

Figure 8 Charles-Joseph Minard (1869), *Figurative map of the losses of the French Army in the Russian campaign of 1812–13*. The lighter-colored broad top band represents the march to Moscow of Napoleon's army. Minard's figures were drawn from the histories and memoirs of Thiers, Ségur, Fezensac, Cambray, and the unpublished journal of M. Jacob, a pharmacist in the army. From their calculation he estimated 422,000 men crossed the Niemen River and approximately 100,000 reached Moscow. The black lower band represents Napoleon's retreat. By the time the remains of the army again crossed the Niemen approximately 10,000 men remained. The *Tableau graphique* at the bottom of the map gives the temperatures below zero during the retreat in Réaumur degrees. The disastrous crossing of the Berezina River is represented by the thick band between Botr and the river, where the retreating army and camp followers is cut nearly in half. Minard's ingenious map plots six variables: the size of the army, its location in two dimensions, the route followed by the army, the temperature on various dates during the retreat. Although there are no universally agreed figures Minard's map clearly shows acceptable magnitudes and the fact that Napoleon lost the bulk of his army marching *to* Moscow. What remained was destroyed in the retreat, once the winter had set in.

14 of division, along with 37 colonels, 37 staff officers, and 86 ADCs. The Gates of Moscow were open. Murat was the first to ride in from the west on 14 September, just after the Russian rear guard rode out on the east. Napoleon waited for two hours at the gates for an official surrender of the city. When he received the news that the city was deserted his normally impassive face, 'showed instantly and unmistakably the mark of his bitter disappointment'. There were already fires burning in the city. During the night of the 15th–16th they raged out of control. The fire was so intense 'it was impossible to stand more than a moment in one spot: the fur on the grenadiers' caps was singed'. Only the northern district near the Kremlin was saved, when the wind shifted to the west. Of the great mansions in the suburbs many survived, but the house of Moscow's governor, Rostopchin, had been razed. The notice he had posted was brought to Napoleon:

> For eight years I have improved this land, and I have lived happily here in the bosom of my family ... I am setting fire to my mansion rather than let it be sullied by your presence. Frenchmen! – in Moscow I have abandoned to you my two residences, with furniture worth half-a-million roubles. Here you will find only ashes.

The weather was splendid. Napoleon joked with Caulaincourt that the dreaded Russian winter was a fiction. He took up residence in the Kremlin, where Mme de Staël had visited just before he arrived:

> This citadel, from which the emperors of Russia defended themselves against the Tartars, is surrounded by a high wall whose cornice is denticulated and which more recalls a Turkish minaret that a fortress resembling most of those of the West ... Seeing Moscow one is reminded of Rome ...

She cannot refrain from adding: 'It was left to the same man to profane both.' Napoleon had a splendid view of the Moscova River, and from the fortress of the Tsars he governed his Empire. His troops looted the destroyed city. The retreat of the Grande Armée is marked by miles of abandoned booty as winter took hold and the soldiers discarded everything that was not needed for survival. Moscow was untenable. Caulaincourt and Berthier had both advised Napoleon before he entered the city that he should quit it in 48 hours and return to Vitebsk for the winter. Once more they were ignored. 'Out of vanity,' wrote Stendhal, who was present at the Russian campaign, 'and to erase the disasters in Spain, he wanted to take Moscow. This imprudent act would not have had any consequences if he had only stayed twenty days in the Kremlin; but his political genius, always inferior [to his military genius], dominated him and caused him to lose his army.' He sent message after message to Alexander offering to parlay. He waited in vain. On 13 October, the first snow fell. On the 19th Napoleon began his withdrawal. He ordered Marshal Mortier to blow up the Kremlin before leaving, and specifically to torch the town houses of Rostopchin and Count Razumovsky (a diplomat he personally disliked, and the patron of Beethoven's three great opus 59 string quartets). On the morning of the 23rd the army units who last departed Moscow could hear the dull thuds of the exploding charges. 'This ancient citadel, which dates from the foundation of the monarchy, this first palace of the Tsars, no longer exists!' declared the 26th Bulletin. It was one of the few Napoleonic acts of vengeful, wanton destruction, a temper tantrum equal to his anger and frustration. He succeeded only in damaging the Kremlin.

The march from Moscow was Napoleon's first retreat. 'We must be ready in advance to destroy everything so as to leave no trophies for the enemy,' he told Caulaincourt. 'I would rather eat with my fingers for the rest of the campaign than leave the Russians with a fork with my crest on it.' He contributed to the trail of discarded loot. The cross of Ivan Veliki, torn from the Kremlin church, which he had intended to mount on the dome of the Invalides, was jettisoned. The Cossacks retrieved it from the lake. On 23 November, following the Battle of Borisov, Napoleon ordered all official papers burned. Daru had been calling for the destruction of all this documentation for some time. Also included in the holocaust were all the reports and projected decrees of several ministries, and 27 additional portfolios that had piled up, unattended to by Napoleon as he fled.

Accounts of the retreat differ greatly, depending on the memoirist. It is not only a question of the writer's temperament. The vanguard and the rearguard were seldom less than 20 miles apart, and often as many as 60 miles. Depending on where one was, units marched through varying weather on the same day, fought different skirmishes with the Cossacks, found food more or less scarce, the ice more or less polished by the endless march of men and horses, the snow more or less rutted, the frozen bodies of men and horses more or less numerous. Those who record an orderly retreat until Smolensk – all are agreed that discipline collapsed completely at Smolensk – and those who record chaos from the outset may both be correct. Kutusov's army had blocked the southern route and the Grande Armée was compelled to return over the same road it had taken to Moscow, the countryside already stripped of food and fodder. 'With every step I take,' Napoleon told Caulaincourt,

> I shall find reinforcements ... while Kutuzov, who will likewise be worn out with marching, will be getting further away from his reserves. He will be left in a countryside which we have exhausted. Ahead of us there are supplies in store. The Russians will starve to death back here.

The winter of 1812, despite Napoleon's pronouncements and the repetition of historians, came relatively late and was less severe than many, until December, which even by Russian standards was exceptionally cold. The temperature fell to minus 35 degrees at night, and averaged minus 13 during the day. The grim morning ritual around innumerable dead campfires was to strip the corpses of those who had frozen to death in the night, taking anything warm, anything that could be eaten. The bodies were not buried: there was neither time nor inclination, and little strength to hack through the ice. There is evidence of cannibalism. Rank collapsed. By the time the French reached Smolensk (9 November) the army had become a rabble. The first troops into the town went on a rampage. The stores of the city were ransacked and the supplies that might have fed many, perhaps all, were wasted, squandered, gorged. Napoleon, in one of his diatribes, this one directed at the military *intendant* Amésée Pastoret, blamed everyone but himself:

> And they accuse me of ambition, as though it was my ambition that brought me here! This war is only a matter of politics. What have I got to gain from a climate like this, from coming to a wretched country like this one? The whole of it is not worth the meanest little piece of France. These Germans with all their philosophy don't understand a thing.

When they reached the Berezina River there were Russian troops on the west bank and Kutusov, who had dogged their steps all the way, was closing fast. The crossing, the last great action of the campaign, would be a triumph of Napoleon's *genié* corps, who built a bridge in the sub-zero temperatures that would save much of what remained of the Grande Armée. The horde of camp followers was left behind to be slaughtered by the advancing Russian army. The bridge was just over 300 feet long, about 15 feet wide, and rested on 23 trestles. 'As a work of craft,' wrote Captain Brandt who had worked on it, 'this bridge was certainly very deficient.' But

> when one considers in what conditions it was established, when one thinks that it salvaged the honour of France from the most terrible shipwreck, that each of the lives sacrificed in the building of it meant life and liberty to thousands, then one has to recognize that the construction of this bridge was the most admirable work of this war, perhaps of any war.

Between 27 and 29 November Napoleon moved his army across the Berezina, fighting Russian troops both fore and aft. The place to be on the bridge, according to Jakob Walter, a Westphalian foot soldier, was in the center of the crossing crowd, safe from the snipers. The butchery was terrible. The estimates range from 2000 stragglers killed (Gourgaud) to 20,000 (Labaume). Zamoyski, weighing all the statistics, concludes 'that during the three days the French lost up to 25,000 (including as many as 10,000 non-combatant stragglers) on both banks, of which between a third and a half were killed in action. Russian losses, all inflicted in the fighting, were around 15,000'.

Napoleon left what remained of his army in Smorgonie (now in Belarus) on 5 December. He appointed Murat commander-in-chief and fled in a closed sledge with Caulaincourt. About 120,000 soldiers of the Grande Armée crossed the Niemen on 13 December. An estimated 30,000 lightly wounded or sick may have come out earlier, and as many as 50,000 deserters had escaped in the first weeks of the campaign. The Russians took about 100,000 prisoners. The guess is that only 20,000 of these eventually returned to Europe, after 1814. Napoleon confessed 'I should have died at the Kremlin':

> Then I would have had the greatest glory, the greatest reputation that ever existed. I would have been in all the great capitals of Europe, I would have vanquished the most civilized peoples. Caesar could not have come up to my garter.

But that was years later. By the time of the Russian invasion Napoleon's army was a mongrel amalgam of troops from his empire. He entrusted his flanks to the Austrians, and they opted not to throw themselves into the breach. The Prussians, similarly compelled to join the vast expedition, betrayed their conqueror. The Cossacks, thus left unchecked, were free to harass the retreating army almost at will, and destroy the stores

Napoleon had so carefully assembled for his withdrawal. The Russian campaign had stretched the envelope of Napoleonic warfare until it tore apart. The limits had been reached at Wagram. In Russia the swollen Grande Armée collapsed under its own weight.

*****

The Russian campaign cries out for an epic historian. In an earlier age it would have been grist for an epic poet. The numbers of soldiers involved, the distances traveled, the battles fought, the cast of characters, the confrontation between Revolutionary France and *ancien régime* Russia, the range of human emotions, sacrifice, and heroism, human behavior at its best and worst, the destruction of an ancient city, the unmasking of a modern hero, and the concentration of all this in time and space makes the six months between June 1812 and December of that year incomparable. Tolstoy was just such a writer: poet, historian, and mythmaker. He came slowly to his subject. His early works, largely autobiographical, gave way in the 1850s to a projected novel on the Decembrists, the conspirators against tsarist autocracy who struck soon after Alexander I's death. They were caught, tried, exiled, or executed. He wrote a few chapters of the novel but was displeased with the results. His interest in the Decembrists led him back in time, as must any historical subject, to the French invasion and the great war. At the outset he wrestled with how to begin, how to handle an enormous cast of characters, how to create fictional heroes for such a saga, how to write a novel in which fiction and historical fact are intertwined, and how to knit a philosophical and political work into a novel of manners. His papers contain the fascinating groping of a great writer toward a masterpiece. Tolstoy wrote 15 separate beginnings to *War and Peace* before he hit upon the drawing room scene in St Petersburg, in 1805, as the prelude to the Russian defeat at Austerlitz. The war of 1812 would surpass Alexander Nevsky's feats and the Great Northern War against Charles XII of Sweden. It would later be invoked by Stalin when the Nazis invaded Russia in 1941. It was he, and not any tsar, who erected the patriotic monument at Borodino.

Tolstoy's view of the French invasion is fundamentally Hegelian, although cast in paradoxes. All the historical actors, he writes, were driven by their own needs, character, and vanity. They had not the slightest inkling of the stupendous results of their petty intrigues:

They were moved by fear or vanity [he writes in Book III, Part 2], they rejoiced or were indignant, they argued and supposed that they knew what they were doing and did it of their own free will, whereas they were all the involuntary tools of history, working out a process concealed from them but intelligible to us. Such is the inevitable lot of men of action, and the higher they stand in the social hierarchy the less free they are.

It is the base, writes Isaiah Berlin, 'which consists of those ordinary men and women whose lives are the actual stuff of history' that matters. Tolstoy's passion was to penetrate to first causes, 'to understand how and why things happen as they do and not otherwise'. He found the usual explanations of why Napoleon invaded Russia to be worthless, irrelevant, and pompous. He mocks the presumption that the will of a single man, even, or especially, if that man be Napoleon, can move the huge wheels of history. His Napoleon is brash, loud, volatile, vain, aggressive, and a bully. He is both the incarnation of the French Revolution and its destroyer, the instrument of the fateful clash between the Revolution and Russia. He is the Revolution on horseback, denied genius and sardonically stripped of the ability to change history. He was lured into Russia by

a most complex interplay of intrigues, aims, and wishes, among those who took part in the war and had no perception whatever of the inevitable, or of the one way of saving Russia. Everything came about fortuitously.

At Borodino Napoleon is a man in a fog. From his command post he received riders all of whose reports were false. It was impossible in the heat of battle to know what was happening at any given moment in any particular part of the battlefield, let alone to know how the battle was going. Those who carried reports to Napoleon had not seen the action for themselves. They were told what to report to the Emperor by their superiors, who also had not seen what was going on. This information, already second and third hand, was even more worthless by the time the rider reached Napoleon. The fighting had continued as he rode and everything had changed. Napoleon, on the basis of such information, sent out his orders, 'which had either been executed before he gave them or could not be and were not executed'.

The elaborate hypotheses and theories of the military historians designed to explain the complexities of battle are without merit. No more than those doing the fighting do they understand what is happening. The causes of victory in battle are, for Tolstoy, self-evident and simple: he 'who is stronger, who is angrier, who is more conveniently situated' will win: 'It all comes down to this: to have the greatest unity, the greatest number of men and to respond most swiftly to any chance events which may arise ...' The conventional comparison of war to a chess match [Book III, Part 2, chapter 7] has no relevance:

> A good chess player who has lost a game is genuinely convinced that his failure resulted from a false move on his part, and tries to see the mistake he made at the beginning of the game, forgetting that at each state of play there were similar blunders, so that no single move was perfect ... How much more complex is the game of war, which must be played within certain limits and time and where it is a question not of one manipulating inanimate objects but of something resulting from the innumerable *collisions* of diverse wills.

The foil to this falsification of war is Kutusov, one of the heroes of *War and Peace*. When Tolstoy first wrote about Kutusov at the Battle of Austerlitz, in some of the early drafts of *War and Peace*, he dismissed him as 'a crafty and faithless voluptuary'. In the course of writing his novel Kutusov, not Alexander, emerged as the protagonist of Napoleon, a Russian Hector for a French Achilles. Tolstoy transformed Kutusov, Isaiah Berlin argues, 'from the sly, elderly, feeble voluptuary, the corrupt and somewhat sycophantic courtier ... which was based on authentic sources, into the unforgettable symbol of the Russian people in all its simplicity and intuitive wisdom'. Kutusov knew it was impossible for one man to direct hundreds of thousands 'struggling with death', just as he knew that battles were not decided by commanders, 'but by that intangible force called the spirit of the army'. He too issued commands based, as were Napoleon's, on useless intelligence. Kutusov's orders are not important for what he said, which was vague and at best inapplicable. 'The sense of his words' is what mattered, because they engendered 'a feeling that lay in the commander-in-chief's soul as in that of every Russian' [Book III, part 2, chapter 35].

Tolstoy's Napoleon is an unattractive, even repellent, character, but he is not unhistorical. He emphasized Napoleon's egotism, his brutality, his temper tantrums, he did not invent them. Kutusov is free of the constraints of historical evidence. His passivity in battle, his detachment from the fighting, his huge bulk and appetites, his vague orders, his fatalism, are all interpreted by Tolstoy as the manifestation of a profound connection to a mysterious force that is best called Russianness. The French Revolution, with its rational schemes for social and human improvement, its rejection of the Christian myth of fallen man, its faith in the capacity of politics to set the world right, has, in Tolstoy's great novel, crashed hopelessly against the historical spirituality of the Russian people.

Borodino was Napoleon's true Waterloo. In 1812 his defeat in Russia was seen as a catastrophe, but few realized it was the beginning of the end. He had not lost a battle in Russia, the Old Guard was still intact, he had few difficulties raising new armies, the current allied coalition, as all its predecessors, could easily fall apart. Few, aside from the choleric General Blücher, were willing to face Napoleon in the field. The Emperor still terrified those who contemplated revolt or disobedience. Tolstoy knew, as we know, that Napoleon never recovered from the disaster. After Russia, so long as the Allies held together, it was only a matter of time before he fell. He never again had an adequate cavalry or commanded an army of veterans. Never again would he command a marshalate to match that which marched to Moscow. He had lost 175,000 horses in Russia. Assuming he could even find anywhere near that number, it took three years to train cavalry horses. The Polish and north-east German stud farms were lost to him and the Austrians refused to sell. The Allies now smelled blood. His fabled military infallibility had been shaken by the Russians. Their infantry had proved more durable, their cavalry had outperformed Murat's, their discipline under fire was unparalleled, and their morale was undiminished. The Russian army was now in Europe. The Napoleonic mystique was fading. He may not have lost a battle in Russia, but he had lost the greatest army ever assembled. The true cost of the Russian campaign could be everywhere seen. *War and Peace* is the epic and the myth of Napoleon's greatest and most disastrous campaign.

Entr'acte
Napoleon Explains the Revolution

Precisely at 10 p.m. on 5 December 1812 Napoleon and Armand de Caulaincourt, his Master of Horse, mounted a coach together in the village of Smorgoni, about 50 miles as the crow flies from Vilnius (today the capital of Lithuania), and set off for Paris, nearly 1100 miles away. He abandoned what remained of the Grandé Armée to the command of Marshal Murat. He had to get back to Paris before news of the military catastrophe in Russia reached his capital. Napoleon and Caulaincourt were accompanied by a small escort which included the Emperor's valet, a Polish officer to interpret, the Duke of Fioul and the Count of Lobau, Baron Fain (the Emperor's private secretary), two bodyguards and his Mameluke Roustam. Napoleon's flight from his retreating and disintegrating army had been kept secret until 7:30 that night, when the Marshals were told. Napoleon and Caulaincourt would share the coach, later a closed sledge, and then another coach for the next 13 days. The Emperor filled the time with talk; Caulaincourt faithfully recorded his words. Every evening, sometime between five and nine, they stopped at a relay, usually a post station, to rest for the night. Napoleon washed his eyes and stretched out for a nap while his dinner was being prepared. Caulaincourt used the time 'hastily to note our conversations, at least the things that appeared of interest to me'. He recorded selectively, sometimes amalgamating different conversations on the same subject. His principle was to preserve 'what is most remarkable in these conversations on each subject'. Despite his editorial intrusions what Caulaincourt preserved accords with the later St Helena dictations on the same subjects to different amanuenses. In Caulaincourt's close company the Emperor first explored not just the Russian campaign but the French Revolution and the meaning of his career, in his customary stream-of-consciousness soliloquies.

General Kutusov and the Russian army are given no credit for Napoleon's defeat. The commander who sacrificed Moscow to beat him has his generalship dismissed as 'the height of ineptitude. It is the winter that killed us. We were the victims of the climate. The good weather [in Moscow] deceived me. If I had left fifteen days earlier my army would be at Vitebsk'. Blaming the disaster on the weather removed human agency, especially his own. His many mistakes through the long campaign were reduced to a single fault: not departing Moscow a few weeks earlier. This would remain his explanation of the Russian debacle. Hitler did not get to Russia soon enough: Napoleon stayed too long. The only other mistake Napoleon admitted was failing to finish the Spanish war before launching the Russian expedition. 'As for the Spanish war,' he lectured, reducing it to a mere annoyance, 'it had become nothing more than a guerrilla war. The day when the English will be driven from the peninsula, there will be nothing but *chouannerie* [the guerrilla war in the west of France that broke out in 1793 and was finally extinguished by Napoleon]' which would be stamped out 'in a few months'. For the rest he presents himself as a man misunderstood, the victim of the selfishness of his enemies. He wants only to set the record straight, for Caulaincourt's benefit and for posterity, a task he would resume and complete on St Helena.

Caulaincourt was a devoted Bonapartist, spent more intimate time with his hero than perhaps any other man before his master's imprisonment on St Helena, and was no sycophant. He was capable of seeing some of the great man's flaws, his misanthropy for example:

> [Napoleon] passed in review almost all the men who had positions at Court, even the insignificant. The way he spoke of a number of them convinced me more than ever that his opinions show he had little esteem for the human race. This explains, it seems to me, the indifference that he often showed to the real faults of several individuals about whom he complained, with good reason, and to whom he did nothing more than distance himself from them for a short time, without a word of reprimand.

For the most part Caulaincourt presents Napoleon's words without much comment. 'I am not ambitious,' the Emperor declared. 'I am too old for sleep deprivation, fatigue, war. I love my bed and repose more than anyone, but I have to finish my work. In this world there are only two alternatives: command or obey.' The behavior of the monarchs was unreasonable. They respected only power. 'I have been forced ... to maintain huge armies.' Those who were conquered and ruled by France enjoyed the

Figure 9 *Tsar Alexander I*, by François Gérard. Although Gérard was the most sought-after portraitist of the day, Alexander did not sit for him. This portrait was made from public observations of the Tsar in Paris in 1814. Despite these constraints Gérard's portrait is a good likeness of Alexander in his glory. The uniform belies the reality that his military exploits as commander were disastrous.

benefits of an administration that was 'dedicated, liberal, adapted to the ideas of the century and calculated to meet the real needs of the people .... I could have treated them as a conquered country,' he boasted, but 'I administered them as a French department.' The new departments proved selfish and short-sighted. They hated the economic sacrifices asked of them and failed to realize they were part 'of a superior order [the Empire] to whose interest France herself had to yield'. As for the wars,

> it is England that pushed me, forced me to do what I did. If she had not broken the treaty of Amiens, if she had made peace after Austerlitz, after Tilsit, I would have remained tranquilly at home ...

> I would have concerned myself only with internal prosperity ... I am not a Don Quixote who needs to go in quest of adventures. I am a reasonable man who does only what he considers useful.

His stormy struggle with the Pope is another subject needing clarification. He might, he told Caulaincourt, disagree 'politically' with the Pontiff but 'religiously I venerate him. I respect his character'. Then he wanders into reverie: 'I have great plans. A year of peace and their realization will astonish ...' As for the Revolution, his views were unsystematic but vigorous. Those who intrigued against the Revolution from abroad, the *émigrés* and the king's brothers, 'are more responsible for the king's death than the Convention'. The deputies who voted to send Louis to the guillotine did so 'through weakness, under the knife of the Jacobins of Paris'. For a man who disliked and distrusted the people Napoleon found 'guts in the men of the people', a quality completely lacking in the faubourg Saint-Germain, his generic term for the *salonnières* who opposed him and lived in this elegant Paris neighborhood. 'They want to regain the influence that they believe belongs to them. Their politics are simple and selfish: the kings should govern for them and the people should obey. That is all the great nobles will allow the monarch if the good times return.' He alone could save the French from their would-be masters, whether old nobles or new ideologues. As First Consul and Emperor,

> I have been the king of the people. I have governed for them, in their interest, without letting myself be distracted by the interests of particular groups. In France they know this. The French people love me. I say the people, which is to say the nation ...

'I closed the anarchic chasm [of the Revolution] and created order out of the chaos,' Napoleon later told Las Cases on St Helena, summing up his work:

> I saved the Revolution from drunkenness, ennobled the people, and stabilized the kings. I stirred [the nation's] zeal, rewarded merit, and defined the limits of glory. These are no mean accomplishments!

'My despotism?,' he asked rhetorically. My work 'demonstrated that a dictatorship was absolutely necessary':

> Will they accuse me of having curtailed liberty? Yet license, anarchy, the great disorders [of the Revolution] remained at our doorstep. Will

they accuse me of having loved war? But the truth is I was always attacked. Will they accuse me of having aspired to a universal monarchy? But they can see that this was rather the fortuitous consequence of circumstances. It was our enemies themselves who led me there, step by step. Finally, what about my ambition? Ah, without doubt, this they will find and in abundance ... To establish, at last to consecrate the empire of reason and the full exercise, the complete enjoyment of all human capacities!

He paused in silent reflection. 'Mon cher,' he continued 'in a handful of words there is my whole story.'

There were tremendous events in the first year of the Revolution, all expressions of principles derived from the will of the people. Some were yearnings: for liberty, equality, fraternity, and a representative government. Some were specific responses to the injustices of the *ancien régime*: the need for a constitution, equality before the law, the abolition of privilege and arbitrary arrest, the right to open trial, the sanctity of property unencumbered by feudal obligations, and religious toleration. Much of this was expressed in the *Declaration of the Rights of Man*. A decade after their declaration the rights of man could not be cast aside. The Consulate and Napoleon were bound by historical verities. The new constitution of 1799 did not include a Declaration of Rights but the rights themselves were largely preserved. Nor was his first constitution a cynical rhetorical exercise. The rights proclaimed in 1789 were, in the course of the first year or so of the Revolution, won through struggle and bloodshed. In 1789 the Bastille was taken and the women marched to Versailles forcibly to fetch the king to Paris, the two key acts in the Paris revolution. The medieval political division of the kingdom into Estates was superseded by the proclamation of a National Assembly (17 June), the fundamental legitimacy guaranteed by a constitution was sworn in the Versailles Tennis Court (20 June), the *Declaration of the Rights of Man and Citizen* was proclaimed (26 August), and feudalism as an economic system was destroyed (4 August) in response to a massive peasant uprising. Church property was nationalized and the *assignats*, France's new paper money, were issued, their value assured by the vast Church real estate now owned by the state. But there was no constitution until September 1791. The powers of the king remained undefined, nobility had not yet been proscribed, although its privileges had been. None of the statements of principle in the *Declaration of the Rights of Man and Citizen* had been fixed in law. There was no new legal system to replace that of the *ancien régime* as it collapsed, the role of the Church, stripped of its worldly wealth, was undecided, the king's brothers had fled the kingdom, as had any number of the nobility, and proclaimed themselves the true France in exile. The king himself was a virtual prisoner in the Tuileries after the Women's March, and the new revolutionary government of Paris, the Commune, which replaced the royal appointees, had no legal standing beyond its own declaration of authority. The *ancien régime* was defunct, the king had come to Paris and offered his submission (17 July), and the only authority for everything that had happened and would happen was the Revolution, already an enormous, ill-defined, and irresistible force in whose name every shade of opinion spoke, celebrated, or threatened. There was much talk about the people and their rights, about the sovereignty of the nation, about liberty, equality, and fraternity, which would dominate revolutionary discourse until Napoleon's fall. Long before he seized power, indeed from its beginning, the Revolution was a giant, masterless and problematic.

Much that was created in 1789 Napoleon would undo, but the fundamental revolutionary changes enumerated above remained, were codified, and eventually exported. Much that was settled was superseded by new needs, more urgent crises. But feudal property and obligations never returned, nor did the three estates and their privileges; and the Church never recovered its property. The Consulate took a different tack from the men of 1789. Napoleon's declaration that the 'principles of 1789' were realized with the Consulate was charged with emotional appeal. Just what he meant, the question of his relationship to the Revolution, would dog Napoleon's life and work. Inherent in his personal dialectic was the pull of opposites. He had to rule constitutionally but his authoritarian bias led him to minimize the role of the people, eventually condemning them to silence and passivity. The only legitimization for the Consulate and then the Empire was to link himself to the Revolution, to appear as its savior, to insist its principles found realization in himself. He was destined, he believed and asserted, to rule France as the embodiment of 1789. On St Helena he was at great pains to present himself as the heir of the French Revolution, but just what he had inherited was open to interpretation. Napoleon could point to no single moment in the Revolution as the genesis of his career, let alone of his authority and legitimacy. During the Consulate he summoned 1789 to assuage any fears that there would be another purge, or worse a renewed Terror. He promised 1789 but his rule more resembled the nearly two years of Jacobin dominance (1792–94), without the social radicalism. He insisted upon his revolutionary genealogy, but spoke little about it. Once privilege and primogeniture were eliminated by the Revolution, which core reforms Napoleon quickly confirmed and reaffirmed in every subsequent constitution, the conventional *imprimatur* of legitimacy through inheritance vanished. It was to be replaced by the will of the people.

The instrument of discovery and expression of the popular will would be elections, which continued through the Revolution, in an eccentric, often hypocritical, form. Relatively unimportant in national politics and almost non-existent for Napoleon, voting for local assemblies remained significant. The Estates-General had been elected by universal manhood suffrage. The Legislative Assembly that succeeded it was chosen by a severely limited electorate, the 'active' citizens defined by how much tax they paid. The Convention Assembly which followed was again chosen by millions of electors, but once they had spoken, their deputies, at least those who escaped the purge in June 1793, remained in power as a rump parliament until 1795, with no constitutional authority. No elections were held to replace representatives who had been purged, retired, resigned, or died. The various assemblies of the Thermidorian period that followed the fall of Robespierre and the end of the Jacobin dictatorship were notoriously selected by ever smaller electorates who voted for a nominated slate proposed by the political elite. Napoleon's *coup d'état* emasculated these assemblies but retained elections. He argued that his immense authority derived from the Directory, whose authority in turn came from elections. The claim was not so much bogus as it was disingenuous. His right to rule was 18 Brumaire, a parliamentary and military *coup d'état*. This truth accorded ill with revolutionary ideals and Napoleon's need of legitimacy.

By the time of the Empire Napoleon had ceased trying to legitimate his original seizure of power. It was the imperial crown that now needed sanction. There was no revolutionary precedent so he invented one. Unbeknownst to himself or anyone else Napoleon, in his need to attach his imperial crown to the Revolution and thus historical legitimacy, had stumbled upon one of Mirabeau's most original political ideas. The first of the great parliamentary tribunes, a role he created, Honoré Gabriel Mirabeau (1749–1791), cast out by the nobility into which he was born, became the most brilliant member of the Constituent Assembly in the Revolution. He was an advocate of constitutional monarchy, but in a new form. In exchange for the court settling his enormous debts Mirabeau laid out his ideas in a series of 50 substantial letters – they fill three volumes, and were published only in 1851 – to his friend, Count La Marck, who carried them to the court. Begun in

1789, these fascinating letters are a brilliant running commentary on the politics of the Revolution linked to Mirabeau's original political thinking. Despite his penchant for deviousness, his addiction to overly clever plots and maneuvers, Mirabeau was much more than an adept parliamentary strategist and riveting orator. He had profound political ideas. If the monarchy was to be saved, he argued, it needed a new basis that went beyond constitutional definition. Divine Right and blood inheritance were defunct. The privileged nobility was stupid, self-serving, and despised. The Constituent Assembly, like all democratic deliberative bodies, was unpredictable and prone to demagogy (including his own). The monarchy, he argued, must be based henceforth on popular support, a brilliant hybrid of democracy and a strong executive, guaranteed by a constitution. The will of the people would be embodied not in a republic, but in the Bourbon monarchy recreated on new, revolutionary principles.

The scheme never had a chance, nor is there any evidence that the king read Mirabeau's letters. Louis XVI believed in Divine Right as he believed in God. The king in Mirabeau's proposals would continue to embody the will of the people, but no longer because he was chosen by God. There would be no mysterious semi-divine embodiment. Louis would become the people's king. Once the Revolution abandoned absolute monarchy, not least because only die-hard monarchists believed the king incarnated the will of the nation, the idea of embodiment passed to the elected representatives. The arguments made in public debate in the assemblies and clubs of the Revolution were not about democracy but about who best represented the will of the people, who best embodied it, articulated the people's longings, confronted their anxieties. Embodiment could not be determined by the vote of the majority. In the Revolution it was most often declared. Robespierre's insistence that he *was* the people is the most celebrated instance. Mirabeau's idea, ignored by the monarchy, would be realized by Napoleon: a new revolutionary king.

Napoleon's *sacre* in Notre Dame (2 December 1804), in the presence of the Pope and all the pomp he could command, was designed to represent, advertise, and proclaim his legitimacy. 'I did not usurp the crown,' he later told Montholon. 'I found it in the gutter. The people put it on my head ... I became the king of the people as the Bourbons were the kings of the nobles ...' His selection by the people was reaffirmed during the Hundred Days during which he made no attempt to gain the support of any royalists. Popular enthusiasm and adherence legitimated his return to power. He was elected by acclamation.

Yet all his assertions of legitimacy notwithstanding, Napoleon knew he remained a revolutionary usurper to the monarchs of Europe and to all those who refused to rally to him. He mentioned it often and was envious of the luxury of the kings he defeated to govern badly, lose wars, and bankrupt their kingdoms without being dethroned. He, the great deposer of crowned heads and reigning houses, was mistaken about the immunity of kings. In Naples, Spain, Holland, and the German lands he swept princes from their thrones, created new kingdoms, and replaced the deposed with his brothers and marshals. He suppressed countless principalities in Germany and Italy, ignoring their traditional and historical rights, privileges, and treaties. Legitimacy saved none of these rulers. The Revolution had made monarchs fungible.

Because he had no personal legitimacy his historical appeal was to the Revolution, a perfectly correct attribution, reinforced by his personal belief in many of its ideals. The problematic was that for Europe's kings the Revolution was precisely what did not bestow legitimacy. It was criminal, satanic, or sinful, or all of these. Napoleon never ceased to be the Revolution incarnate for the kings. As Prince Metternich, here the voice of the *ancien régime*, never tired of arguing, Napoleon was a revolutionary. The traditional rules, customs, habits, and conventions that governed states domestically and internationally meant nothing to him. Napoleon's own appraisal was that the Revolution had conferred power and he maintained it so long as he kept winning battles.

Napoleon never had anything bad to say about the Revolution. He owed the Revolution everything. His judgments, although favorable, are often unexpected, even original. He was a shrewd student of the Revolution, whose politics and ideals he embraced, albeit idiosyncratically and as they suited his immediate needs. For a man so socially conservative, so unwilling to liberate the oppressed wherever he conquered, so anxious to rest his rule on the collaboration of old elites, so committed to a social order that excluded popular participation, so intolerant of ideologues and dissent, and so hostile to democracy, he was unexpectedly drawn to the radicals of the Revolution. He had a kind of revolutionary romanticism. Jean-Paul Marat, a font of indignation and the demand for violent expedients, whose newspaper, *l'Ami du Peuple*, specialized in denunciations and calls for the murder of thousands, is admired by Napoleon. He 'was not without merit,' he told Bertrand. 'Before the Revolution he wrote works that Voltaire spoke about.' Marat, not unlike Napoleon, did not seek to persuade. He dealt in opinions that were 'firm, doubtless often horrible, expressed head-on'. 'He said to the Girondins "you are scoundrels". He called for 80,000 heads to roll.' Napoleon approved: 'that was necessary to affirm the Republic.' There were men more violent than Marat, or at least more likely to act out their anathemas. Chaumette and Hébert, Vincent, Chabot, and Bazire, all firebrands of the Paris popular movement, are mentioned by Napoleon. These men he despised. They were terrorists with no redeeming qualities who achieved prominence by committing or inciting crimes. When these ultra-revolutionaries went to the guillotine Napoleon had no regrets. Their deaths represented 'a veritable revolution' of ideas, a salutary condemnation of violence and anarchy. With the important exception of Joseph Fouché, closely tied to the violent *Hébertistes*, Napoleon avoided the more radical and extreme revolutionaries, few of whom rallied to him.

The *septembriseurs*, the collective neologism coined for those who judged and hacked to death about half the prison population in the first week of September 1792, were not condemned out of hand by Napoleon. 'I would not consider all the *septembriseurs* nothing but brigands,' he told Bertrand. There were extenuating conditions. He had a curious sympathy for the popular justice of the Revolution. Those exonerated by the *ad hoc* popular tribunals set up in the street were joyfully embraced by the murderous mob and 'carried in trumph', a kind of affirmation of popular justice. 'False ideas of liberty and patriotism' led the *septembriseurs* to bloody deeds, but their exaltation signaled sincerity. 'We condemn the St Bartholemew Massacres,' Napoleon lectured Bertrand, 'but were the Guise and all those who ordered or carried out the murders brigands?' They were in the grip of religious fanaticism which Napoleon treats without the horror he reserves for revolutionary, secular terrorists. It is a subtle, perhaps incomprehensible distinction. 'One cannot judge men in revolution as one would judge them in a state of peace,' said Napoleon, echoing the ideas of Saint-Just and Robespierre on revolutionary justice. 'In a revolution they are at war. There is no personal freedom in revolution.' Perhaps he had his own career in mind. 'It is the heat of battle that produces different effects,' he told Bertrand. He told General Gourgaud that the September Massacres 'had a useful impact on the morale of the invaders.' It was not the work of a frenzied, drunken, paid mob, but a species of military action. The invaders had never seen an entire population rise up against them.

Robespierre is no terrorist for Napoleon, but a man of principle sacrificed by the terrorists to save their own heads. From August to January 1793–94, he tells Bertrand, the municipality of Marseilles was governed 'by qualified men who were all federalists'. The representatives of the Convention left them in power because they 'rendered the greatest services during the siege of Toulon'. When Napoleon recaptured the city from the British, Fréron and Barras, two extreme Jacobins sent by the Convention Assembly to handle the crisis, turned on their Marseilles allies and killed them all. 'These are the men who ... went after Robespierre!' Napoleon makes a distinction among terrorists. Robespierre caused many to perish, 'but there is an enormous difference between ordering a crime from afar and carrying it out, covering one's hands in blood'. The sensibility of our times is diametrical. Hannah Arendt and Hugh Trevor-Roper found the desk murderers of the Holocaust infinitely more vile than those who did the killing.

Napoleon's attachment to Robespierre goes back to the siege of Toulon when Maximilien's brother, Augustin, as a representative *en mission*, discovered the young artillery captain and saw to it that he was instantly promoted. Napoleon entered the French Revolution as a *robespierriste*. He never met Maximilien: 'I regret not having known him,' he told Bertrand. When the brothers were purged he privately expressed regret in a letter, realizing he could well have gone to the guillotine as part of the *queue* of Robespierre, many score of whom were arrested, convicted, and killed in the days following 9 Thermidor. The elder Robespierre was destroyed 'for having wanted to stop the Revolution'. '[Robespierre] wanted, by sacrificing [Tallien, Billaud Varennes, and Collot d'Hérbois] to make himself popular ... and to put an end to so much bloodshed. These revolutionaries, seeing where he was headed, resolved to sacrifice him.' The Incorruptible laid out his determination to destroy the terrorists in 'a very admirable speech' on the eve of his death in which he unmasked the Paris Commune as riddled with extremists whose careers depended on perpetual terror, and he attacked the (unnamed) extremists. 'Cambacérès has often spoken to me about it. I wanted to have the speech printed as an historic document and regret never having done so.'

Robespierre was 'no ordinary man'. He was vastly superior to those around him. His speech on the Supreme Being proves it. So too does his public celebration of the revolutionary martyrdom of the children Viala and Bara, which 'inculcated enthusiasm in all the thirteen-year-olds. It was a great political stroke'. Robespierre's civic religion was a subject close to Napoleon's heart and politics: finding a way to restore religion to France without reestablishing the old Catholic Church with its superstitions, worldly pretensions, and reactionary politics often dictated from Rome. Napoleon's Concordat proved far more durable than Robespierre's Supreme Being and revolutionary festivals, but the affinity between the two rationalist revolutionary leaders is striking. Had Robespierre not become its sacrificial lamb, a phrase Napoleon uses a few times, 'he would have been the most extraordinary man' of the Revolution.

Discussing Robespierre, Napoleon has nothing to say about ideology, which was the instrument of The Incorruptible's long hold over his contemporaries. Napoleon is interested in the political leader not the Jacobin ideologue, in the practicalities of governing a revolution, not utopian visions. Robespierre's major fault was sacrificing Danton, another revolutionary Napoleon admired. The Emperor liked to quote Danton's famous call to arms in September 1792: 'De l'audace, puis de l'audace et encore de l'audace!' ['Audacity, more audacity, and even more audacity']. Together Robespierre and Danton had 'made the Commune tremble. They marched in the same line, they should never have separated'. Danton's personal acquisitiveness, the millions he pocketed while *en mission* in Belgium, 'altered his character'. Even so Robespierre should not have destroyed him. The friends of Danton, and there were many, never forgave the betrayal.

For Napoleon the terrorists and the Girondins bear the blame for turning the Revolution bloody. Nothing was more shameful than the conduct of the Girondins, whose ideology of spreading the Revolution by arms he embraced, enlarged, and made fundamental to his own revolutionary views and program. Their political maneuverings – duplicitous, hypocritical, and self-serving – were another matter. The Girondins wanted to save the king but they did not dare say so. 'They voted for his death and for the appeal to the people in order to avoid it', trying to have it both ways. The appeal, introduced by the Girondins, was an elaborate parliamentary strategy to put off the vote on Louis's fate for months. Girondin politics were confused, naïve, and dangerous. 'They had talent. Nevertheless it is probable that they could not have saved France as the [Jacobin] Mountain did.' The whole of his judgment of the Girondins is focused on their inept political maneuvering, not their ideas. When he read the memoirs of Mme Roland, who hosted and contributed to so many strategy sessions of the Girondins at her house, his distaste for what he thought hypocritical and stupid politics fused with his loathing of women meddling therein. He found nothing but trivia and treacle about her friends, her husband, and her own family in her *Mémoires*. He had no patience for her heartfelt sentiments, her feeble facsimile of Rousseau. 'Jean-Jacques Rousseau would have been able to make these details interesting, but one would need his pen for that.' Her self-absorption he found intolerable. 'It is doubtless useful to learn that her father was a merchant. Good. Then it is essential to turn to events.'

Napoleon was always uneasy about the killing of kings and emperors. He found regicide too close for comfort. Louis XVI's execution was no exception. The king's trial and death changed the character of the Revolution. 'The Constituent Assembly made a huge mistake by not deposing the king after the Flight to Varennes [June 1791].' It was left to the Convention to solve the problem of the king. They did so, for Napoleon, in the worst possible way: sending Louis to the guillotine. 'The *conventionnels* were [now] lost if they did not succeed.' The Terror was implicit in the king's death. Sieyès, who had voted for death, once told Napoleon that Louis XVI was a tyrant and deserved to die: 'M. l'abbé [Napoleon snapped], if he had been a tyrant I would not be here and you would still be saying Mass.' On the contrary it is Louis's weakness that brought about the Revolution. He was languid, pusillanimous, and surrounded by spineless advisers. What he should have done was 'to summon the Parlement to the Grande Chambre and have them condemn the Duke d'Orléans and Mirabeau. That would have been the end of the Revolution'. Had Louis failed to act in 1789 he still could have prevented the overthrow of the monarchy on 10 August 1792 had he been willing to fight. 'With 1800 body guards and a battery of cannon he could have taken the attackers [of the Tuileries] in the flank, charged them, and that would have been the end.' This is what Napoleon would have done, what he did when he cannonaded the mob on 13 Vendémiaire and later murdered the Duke d'Enghien. His purge of the Jacobins after the failed bombing attempt in the rue Nicaise (24 December 1800) is but another example of ruthlessness. Swift, unrelenting retribution and punishment, what Robespierre called 'revolutionary justice', was always Napoleon's preference. It worked. Rhetoric or reconciliation did not. 'It is the death of Louis XVI,' he explained to Montholon with cruel irony, 'that saved the Revolution, because the judges of the king were too compromised to hesitate. They said to themselves "Vanquish or die!".'

The Terror, the most vexing revolutionary phenomenon, he thought inevitable: 'How do you tell those who have a fortune and public place: "Go, give up your fortune and your position", without intimidating them and rendering them powerless?' Driven to desperation they turned on the Revolution. He dates the reign of Terror from the night of 4 August 1789 when the fiscal privileges of the nobility were abolished. From that point on it was the people's revolution.

They were willing to preserve with their blood what they had acquired. 'Until that time a significant part of the rural population believed that without the king and the *dîme* collected by the clergy there could not be a good harvest.' Now they realized the new order was preferable. It was only a matter of time before the inexorable logic of the Revolution turned violent. The formal institution of the Terror came a few years later. 'Do you believe that the men who led France in 1793 chose the Terror for pleasure?' he asked Montholon. 'Absolutely not. Robespierre hated bloodshed as much as I. He was constrained by events and, I repeat, by conviction. He did it out of humanity, to stop the massacres, to control the resentments of the people. He created the revolutionary tribunals as a surgeon saves lives by amputating limbs.'

Napoleon's views on the Revolution, as with all his views, emanate from circumstances, his needs, and his convictions. There are for him no standards of judgment outside his psyche, his experiences, his understanding. He is uninterested in philosophical abstractions or first principles. He judged the Revolution according to his likes and dislikes as well as how closely this or that historical actor approximated his own thoughts or behavior. He found the Jacobins far more interesting, more admirable in their obsessions, sincerity, and toughness than the irresponsible Girondins, let alone the horde of trimmers and sycophants. They were hard men, but that is what the Revolution called for. His judgments of the Revolution are in harmony with Jacobin sensibilities and values (with the important exception of their myth of the people). It was France that replaced *le peuple* in his thought. Napoleon's revolutionary pantheon is filled with Jacobins. Weakness, pusillanimity, dithering, these are the venal sins of politics for Napoleon. In the Jacobins he admired their determination, even their fanaticism, as well as their devotion to strong central government guided by a single will. Alongside his Jacobinism is a quirky affection for a disparate group of men, none of whom are much like himself. He would have disciplined, even jailed, most of these. He respected the king's devotion to duty, while deploring his lack of vitality and character. Charles-François Dumouriez, the first and for Napoleon the only great general of the early years of the French Revolution, is another flawed but admired character. 'He won the first victories of the Revolution with troops that had never faced enemy fire. He was loved by them. All that shows a man of the first order.' He later delivered an even more fulsome eulogy of Dumouriez to Bertrand, prophesying he would enjoy 'a gigantic reputation'. The ultimate compliment followed: 'He will be the first after me. He saved

France.' In Napoleon's personal *galerie des batailles* no modern general stands higher than Dumouriez. He says not a word about Dumouriez's betrayal of France and the Revolution; the General deserted his troops and fled in April 1793 when his army refused to follow him into a *coup d'état*. When his services, offered to Germany and Russia, were rejected, he spent the rest of his life in England, advising them about shore defenses to thwart a French amphibious attack, ironically commanded by Napoleon. He later counseled English preparations for an invasion of France.

Equally unexpected is Napoleon's praise of Filippo Buonarroti, Gracchus Babeuf's comrade in clandestine activities after Robespierre's fall. Buonarroti did not share Babeuf's end on the guillotine but he did share his communist ideology and faith in conspiratorial politics. He wrote the classic account of the Conspiracy of the Equals, Babeuf's underground plot, and he was one of the godfathers of conspiratorial revolutionary struggle, much admired by the Bolsheviks. 'He was a man full of *esprit*, a fanatic of liberty but sincere, pure, a terrorist yet a good and simple man. He never changed character ...' He was 'a friend of the common good, a leveler. Too bad':

> I regret never having attached him to myself. I set him free [from prison]. I don't believe that Buonarotti ever thanked me nor ever addressed a word to me ... Buonarroti was a leveler, so alien to my system that it is possible I never paid any attention to him. He could, nevertheless, have been useful to me in organizing the Italian kingdom. He would have been a great professor. He was a man of extraordinary talents. A descendant of Michelangelo, an Italian poet worthy of Ariosto, writing French better than me, drawing like David, playing the piano like Paisiello.

Napoleon is interested in men more than ideas. He looks upon Robespierre, Dumouriez, and Buonarotti as not only intriguing men, but men he understands, and, most important, men he could have used. His judgments are never abstract or disinterested.

Napoleon's political acuity, his close identity with the Revolution and its leaders, and his broad human empathy are surprising in a man usually considered only a gifted and ruthless warlord consumed by ambition. In fact he was a convinced revolutionary, although of a moderate sort, and he had a keen political intelligence. He knew his way through the thickets of the Revolution although he himself had barely trod those tortuous paths in his rise to power. From the anguished security of St Helena he looked back over his revolutionary career and found his instincts excellent even if his judgments seem to us sometimes contradictory. His lifelong wrestling with the Revolution, trying to find the right holds, good leverage, some vulnerable opening, began with the upheaval itself. The Revolution is central to his thought, his career, his very self. The Revolution made him, marked him indelibly.

IX

Napoleon Brought to Bay

As early as 1809 Denis Decrès, Napoleon's Minister of the Navy, had told Marshal Marmont: 'Do you want me to tell you the truth? The Emperor is crazy, completely mad, and we will lose everything, everything that we are, ass over head. It will all end in a monstrous catastrophe.' By the end of 1812 this was no longer private prophesy, but public grumbling, however circumspect and muted. Napoleon still had enormous resources do draw upon. His imperium stretched from the Pyrenees to the Vistula. He had, he assumed, but to issue the orders and decrees and a new army would materialize. And so it did. Conscription, painstakingly established and enforced throughout the Empire and the German Confederation, continued to work smoothly. His desires, his needs, his will, his genius would recreate the Grande Armée. The Allies were divided and skittish. Keeping the sixth coalition poised for the kill, defining goals, placating personalities, securing a common purpose, proved enormously difficult. After 25 years of revolutionary upheaval the European states realized that only unconditional surrender was acceptable to all the powers, and only their cooperation could bring it about. Yet unity remained fragile. If the sixth coalition held together Napoleon was doomed. It was a very big 'if'. England and Austria were willing to negotiate separately with Napoleon as late as March 1814 at the Congress of Châtillon, their allies were not.

In the end it all came down to time, which the Allies now controlled. Napoleon would not be given the leisure to build a new army. His cavalry and their horses left in Russia would not be reconstituted. Even Napoleon could not transcend the physical losses of the Russian catastrophe. He would fight on without the ability to set cavalry screens or pickets, disrupt the enemy line with skirmishes, turn their flank, deliver the hammer blows that broke a battered foe. Nor could he pursue the remnants of a broken army to destruction. His reconnaissance suffered, his communications were dangerously compromised, his couriers rode unprotected and at risk. He was able to find the men,

Figure 10 *Chateaubriand* (1808), by Anne Louis Girodet. Painted in Paris soon after Chateaubriand's return from the Holy Land and his recovery from serious illness, the portrait was exhibited in the salon of 1810 discretely titled *Man Meditating on the Ruins of Rome*, for the writer had already gone into opposition. The Coliseum is in the background on the left. On the right are the hills of Rome. In his *Mémoires d'outre-tombe* Chateaubriand, who recognized the brilliance of the portrait, writes that 'Girodet put the final touches to my portrait. He made it black, as I then was; but he filled it with genius'. Napoleon said the portrait was of a man who '... had the look of a conspirator who came down the chimney'. The portrait, as its subject, became an icon of the Romantic sensibility. Chateaubriand willed the painting to St Malo, his natal town.

but the political cost, for the first time in his career, was prohibitive, the available recruits increasingly mediocre. If the Allies pressed him his recruits would be even more incompletely trained. Raising men now meant imposing an increasing blood tax on the Empire, and more importantly on France. War horses were even more difficult to replace. Eugène de Beauharnais met Napoleon's new demands as did Jerome in Westphalia, although his state was brought to the brink of open rebellion and collapse by the new impositions. Maximilian of Bavaria, long loyal, was sacrificed to the Emperor's needs. So too would be the king of Saxony. The others, who had acquiesced in Napoleon's overlordship because they had no choice or judged resistance futile, now considered their loyalties flexible. They conducted some sharp bargaining with Metternich who had to agree to let them keep what they had gotten from Napoleon and to stay out of their domestic affairs. The German princes and lesser rulers ran true to form, resisting any sacrifice for the common good, which they saw as the aggrandizement of Austria (or Prussia) at their expense. Their self-serving was hardly admirable, but they were not mistaken. France, long shielded from the demands he imposed on others, now felt the full weight of Napoleon's desperation, which only intensified after his defeat at Leipzig. All the domestic gains and privileges of the last ten years were jeopardized. The propertied classes, upon whom his rule at home ultimately rested, found it harder to keep their sons out of the insatiable conscription, replacements were hard to find and their price had increased. The reality of perpetual adventurism and the possibility of defeat became palpable. Their only political weapon was sullen civil disobedience, manifested as passivity or lethargy. They wielded it.

Once Napoleon had the men, scraped from the bottom of the barrel or prematurely taken from future draft pools, he had to equip and train them. He lacked the matériel for the former and the time for the latter. He was forced not only to face superior numbers, for the first time since the Italian Campaign, but better troops. He had set himself the target of providing five field guns for every thousand men, a target he never reached. At Leipzig, where he had 600 guns, he could count on only three cannon for a thousand men. The Allies had more than 900 pieces of artillery. The odds were even worse in the Battle for France. He improvised brilliantly, and some of the old effervescence, agility, and dash that had befuddled the Austrians in Italy was reawakened. But even Napoleon at his best could not sustain the magic. He checked the Allies over and over but sheer numbers and firepower eventually won out, aided, in Charles Esdaile's words, by his 'pride and overconfidence'.

The German campaign launched in 1813 was seen by the Allies and Napoleon alike as a showdown. Napoleon's strategy had not changed since he assumed the Italian command in 1796: take the offensive, split the enemy, fight the divided armies separately, force and win a decisive battle from each, and impose a treaty. All of these goals proved impossible. Before Leipzig the Allies were unaware of how hopelessly stretched were French resources. Napoleon had had to strip his security forces bare to reinforce the Grande Armée. Any loses he suffered could not be replaced. It was a continuation of the Russian campaign: any victory short of a crushing, definitive blow only postponed the denouement. He prepared for a battle that would reestablish or lose his empire. He evacuated East Prussia and the Grand Duchy of Warsaw, but could not incorporate these troops into his army. He used some 50,000 of them to garrison the region's fortresses. Although they pinned down substantial numbers of the enemy, these were troops desperately needed elsewhere. Napoleon could not, would not, acknowledge that his empire was shrinking. The garrisons would, he imagined, provide the bases from which he would reassert his hegemony over Central Europe. He fought short-handed at Lützen, Bautzen, Dresden, and Leipzig. On 2 May he defeated the Allies at Lützen. On 20 May and 21 May he won again, at Bautzen. Neither victory was decisive. His comrade Duroc was killed, he suffered enormous losses, and again the enemy executed a successful retreat. Then he made the first of a series of mistakes. He agreed to an armistice (signed at Pläswitz, lasting from early June until 10 August). This was the turning point in the campaign. The armistice 'saved us and condemned him,' said one Russian general. It gave the Allies, who had significant resources, time to mobilize. On 12 August Austria declared war on France. On 26–27 August, at Dresden, Napoleon enjoyed his last victory on German soil before all his gains of the past decade were wiped out at Leipzig. It was one of the last times Napoleon might have made peace on favorable terms. He could have preserved his dynasty and kept for France significant territory. He spurned the offer. 'I might even consider giving Russia a piece of the Duchy of Warsaw,' he ranted at Metternich, 'but I will not give you anything, because you have not beaten me; and I will give nothing to Prussia, because she has betrayed me.' He calmed down slightly and candidly continued:

> Your sovereigns, born on the throne, can afford to let themselves be beaten twenty times and still return to their capitals; I cannot, because I am a *parvenu* soldier. My authority will not survive the day when I have ceased to be strong and therefore, to be feared.

His obsession with a definitive battle that would determine the outcome of the war and his future took over. He chose to gamble, as he always had. All or nothing.

Before the wars of the French Revolution only a handful of battles had involved more than 100,000 combatants. Wagram, the largest of the gunpowder age up to that point (1809) involved 300,000 soldiers. Four years later Leipzig had more than 500,000 combatants, who suffered 150,000 casualties, an unheard-of toll. It was, next to Borodino, the most severe battle of the Revolutionary and Napoleonic Wars. The fighting began on 16 October with an inconclusive clash between Napoleon and the army of Bohemia, and Marshal Marmont's loss to Blücher just north of Leipzig. Had Napoleon withdrawn on the 17th he would have kept an army of around 160,000 intact. Instead he took up a defensive position around Leipzig. The next day the 177,000-strong Grande Armée faced more than 300,000 Allies. The French broke under the onslaught and as they retreated along a causeway it was accidentally blown up. About 30,000 French troops were killed or captured. These losses, added to the 38,000 already suffered, not to mention all those who had earlier been lost in the campaign, constituted a blow from which even Napoleon could not rebound. When the victorious Allies entered Leipzig on 19 October all of Germany east of the Rhine had been liberated. 'I have just returned from the battlefield on which the cause of the world has been won,' Metternich wrote jubilantly to his wife. 'The shame in which he [Napoleon] covered us,' wrote Baron vom Stein to his wife, 'has been washed away by torrents of French blood.' It was Napoleon's first total defeat.

The Allies pursued him into France for a winter campaign, driven by the urgency of Prussian revenge, the belief of the Allies that only Napoleon's definitive defeat could insure peace, and by Tsar Alexander's *idée fixe*. Napoleon had victoriously entered Moscow: the Tsar was determined to ride triumphant into Paris at the head of his guard, drums beating, flags aflutter. Having shown the world his glory he would then display his magnanimity. The campaign, which would end in Napoleon's abdication on 13 April, is interesting militarily and psychologically. It 'shows perhaps more clearly than any other Napoleon both at his best and at his worst,' writes Ralph Ashby. He was outnumbered and outgunned, the weather was filthy, he had his back to the wall as never before, comrades who had fought with him from the beginning of his fabulous career were dead or had gone over to the Allies. He was not outgeneraled, but the odds were too great, even for a gambler of genius; 1814 was the rebirth of the Bonaparte of 1796. Fat, still licking the wounds inflicted at Leipzig, he journeyed imaginatively into his own past.

Much about 1814 looks, quickly glanced, like 1796. His army was rag-tag, inadequately equipped, and heavily outnumbered. He was facing two substantial *ancien régime* armies – Field Marshal Blücher's Army of Silesia and Field Marshal Schwarzenberg's Army of Bohemia – who would be irresistible should they successfully join forces. He had no cavalry to speak of and his losses could not be replaced. Memory, even for someone as clear-sighted as Napoleon, now proved a distorting lens. The similarities between 1796 and 1814 are largely superficial. The Army of Italy he had inherited was not only a veteran force with a lot of fighting under its belt, it was also heavily Jacobin in sentiment. Bonaparte himself was at the time far closer to his recently shed Jacobinism than he was in 1814, although his imaginative revival of the past stirred up the long-dying embers of his revolutionary heritage and enthusiasm. He fought with immense personal courage, was often in the thick of danger – on one occasion General Gourgaud saved his master from the Cossacks – and transferred some of his élan to his mostly raw troops. Blücher and Schwartzenberg were not the old men he had fought in Italy. The former was 72 in 1814, but was as aggressive as Napoleon, as his sobriquet 'General Vorwärts' testifies. The latter was younger than Napoleon, and although beset by caution as a commander he had come to maturity in the midst of vast military reform. Henry Houssaye's witty characterization is less true than clever:

> Prince Schwarzenberg was no miser when it came to issuing orders and counter orders. He sometimes issued three different ones on the same day and would change the last of these the following day. He always believed that the best path to follow was the one he had not taken.

Both had fought Napoleon before. More importantly Prussia and Austria had been fighting him since Italy. They had learned much from the experience. Their armies were reformed, they knew how to deal with Napoleon's brilliance, and they had the self-confidence of having just beaten him soundly at Leipzig. These changes he dismissed, forgot, or ignored. Because he was outnumbered he hoped to substitute inspiration, leadership by example, and his incomparable tactical skills, energy, and agility for the troops he did not have. His dealings with

Marshal Augereau, whose army was at Lyons, is revealing. He wanted Augereau to strike northwards at the rear areas of the Allied armies and ordered the Army of Lyons to begin operations. Nothing happened. He wrote directly to Augereau reminding him of the glory days of 1793 and 1796:

> Be the first among the bullets ... When Frenchmen see your *panache* at the advanced posts and they see you expose yourself to the first musket shots, you can make them do whatever you will!

Augereau was 57 at the time, 12 years older than Napoleon. He was worn out physically and mentally from all the fighting, and would die two years later. He answered Napoleon's call, but without enthusiasm.

'Why,' wailed General Belliard, 'can't the Emperor be everywhere!' The lament was not ironic. The old magic seemed irresistible. After Napoleon beat them at Brienne, where he had gone to school, the Allies agreed to negotiate. By the time the Congress of Châtillon convened in the first week of February Napoleon had been defeated at La Rothière: the first time he was defeated in person on French soil. The Allies took off the table any settlement that included France retaining her 'natural frontiers'. The diplomatic war would see-saw with the shooting war. In February the Allies suffered five defeats in three weeks and appeared more willing to let Napoleon keep more of France. But the Emperor was determined to fight on and get even better terms. Here was the other dimension of his nostalgic return to being the young Bonaparte. None of his brilliant victories in 1814 were final. It was in the nature of things that Napoleon could not deliver a definitive defeat in France, let alone drive the enemy out. In the first Italian campaign Bonaparte was within 75 miles of Vienna when the Austrians threw in the towel. Such victories were gone forever. In France he twice turned away from an army he had beaten but not destroyed.

The Allies recovered quickly. Napoleon's inflated optimism prevented him from believing this possible and accurately evaluating the enemy's strength. He had boasted, 'I have 50,000 men and myself, that makes 150,000 men'. A dangerous conceit. Blücher's battered Army of Silesia was soon reinforced. The depletions of 10–14 February were wiped out and the Field Marshal resumed his advance on Paris along the line of the Marne River. When he crossed the Marne to escape Napoleon's pursuit, cutting the bridges behind him, the French, without a bridging train, were stranded. Napoleon railed against General Clarke for not providing the necessary equipment with which, he absurdly insisted, he could already have destroyed both Schwartzenberg and Blücher. The idea that sheer courage could overcome all odds, another manifestation of Napoleon's myopic optimism, should have been dispelled by the Battle of Craonne on 7 March, which was, despite the relatively small forces engaged, an exceptionally bloody encounter. Napoleon suffered heavy losses among his high-ranking officers. They were irreplaceable and fundamental for an army of new recruits pursuing a strategy of 'leading by personal example'. Between 7 and 10 March he had lost nearly 12,000 men. Many of the killed and wounded had been Young Guard conscripts and volunteers, while Marmont's conscripts accounted for the largest part of those taken captive.

Then there was the interception of Napoleon's letters. He had not enough troops to spare to escort his couriers. His dispatches often were captured. The batch taken on 24 March told the Allies Paris was unstable, there was Royalist activity in the capital, and the city's defenses were weak. When Tsar Alexander saw the dispatches he insisted the Allied armies march immediately on Paris. The Tsar was convinced the French had had enough and would not resist. But the same psychology that had afflicted Napoleon since the Russian campaign kept him from being reasonable. He prepared to defend Paris, street by street if necessary. He gave his brother Joseph precise orders. 'If the enemy advances on Paris with such force that all resistance becomes impossible ... Do not leave my son behind, and remember that I would rather know that he is in the Seine than in the hands of the enemies of France.' Sacrificing his son, were it not infected with his own *amour propre*, was a subject David might have painted. Parisians who saw the imperial family and government depart had a more sombre reaction:

> What we saw passing [wrote the wife of Marshal Oudinot, who was among the escapees ... was the Empire, the Empire ... with all its pomp and splendor, the ministers ... the entire council of state, the archives, the crown diamonds, the administrations.

As Pons de l'Hérault tartly observed, 'the regency did not know how to organize anything, even flight'. Having sent his family and the government to safety Napoleon expected Paris to fight on. 'If the enemy reaches Paris,' he wrote, 'the Empire is no more.' So it proved. Marshal Marmont, charged with the troops guarding Paris, saw the fruitlessness of a fight and agreed to an armistice. This has passed into Bonapartist historiography as his betrayal. The other marshals pressured a reluctant Napoleon to abdicate unconditionally.

The restoration of the Bourbons, in the person of Louis XVIII, was an understandable though surprising compromise. Napoleon's proposal that his son, then three years old, rule under a regency, was spurned by all as a veil for his father's continued rule. A republic was seen by the Allies as even worse: a return to Jacobin rule and the Terror. The name of Louis-Philippe, first-cousin of the Bourbons, was bruited, but had little support. He had fought with the Revolution, his father had voted for the king's death (and been guillotined in the Terror). These reminders of the year II were unwelcome, even frightening. The Tsar disliked the Bourbons and toyed with the idea of putting Marshal Bernadotte, who had even less support than did Louis-Philippe, on the throne. His distaste for the Bourbons was reinforced some months later when Louis XVIII entered the Tsar's dining room and sat in the only armchair. Alexander had to take an armless chair. The snub, reminiscent of the etiquette of Versailles, perhaps reminded Alexander, as the restored king intended, that he belonged to a cadet branch of the house of Holstein while his guest was descended from St Louis and Louis XIV. The Bourbons had retained the art of polite ridicule despite the Revolution and Napoleon. The Allies had few alternatives. Pressured by the insistence of Lord Castlereagh and Metternich, they agreed to restore the Bourbons. France was to be de-fanged but remain an integral part of a new Europe based on a balance of power which would assure peace. Alexander – who now enjoyed his finest hour, dispensing magnanimity with considerable charm – insisted on a constitution, which Louis XVIII grudgingly issued, calling it a Charter. Its preamble proclaimed that the historical and constitutional checks on his authority were given voluntarily by the king's grace.

The surviving Bourbon brothers, Louis and Charles, the counts of Provence and Artois, had been absent from France since 1789. The Duke of Wellington said they were as unknown to France as if their family had never reigned. Chateaubriand, never so prosaic, thought Louis XVIII and the future Charles X as unfamiliar 'as the children of the Chinese emperor'. Except in the south of France where the fall of Napoleon occasioned a few tumultuous but not bloody riots, the change of regime passed calmly, under the approving eye of the authorities. Louis XVIII's younger brother, whom Lady Holland described as 'a man of slender abilities and violent passions; before the Revolution he was weak and volatile; now he is weak and revengeful', entered Paris to general acclaim on a perfect day (12 April), riding a white horse bearing a red saddle decorated with fleurs-de-lis. When he emerged from Notre-Dame Marshal Ney, who had gone over to the Restoration, remarked to Baron Vitrolles, 'Can you believe such enthusiasm?' The problems inherent in a Bourbon restoration would come soon enough.

The peace terms, negotiated by Talleyrand and modified by Alexander, were lenient. Article 2 of the preliminaries to peace, signed on 25 April, stated that the Allies would remove their troops from any French territory they held in order to return France to her frontiers of 1 January 1792, pushed to 1 November by the treaty signed on 30 May 1814. Napoleon was sent to the isle of Elba, along with a miniscule army drawn from his Imperial Guard, a single frigate, a sizeable household, and an annual income of two million francs to be paid by the restored Bourbons. The rest of the Bonaparte family was equally well provided for. Many of France's colonies were restored and she had to promise to abolish the slave trade within five years. There was no indemnity, no army of occupation, and no move to retrieve all the looted art. Then the Allies assembled in Vienna to negotiate a general peace and to guarantee there would not be another French Revolution.

X
Ending the Revolution

At 6 a.m. on 7 March 1815, during the Lenten term when there were no balls at the Congress of Vienna, Metternich was awakened by his valet. He handed his master a dispatch marked 'urgent', from the Imperial and Royal Consulate at Genoa. The prince laid it unopened on his night-stand and went back to sleep. Only at 7:30 a.m., by his own account, did he open the envelope:

> The English commissioner Campbell has just sailed into the harbor to enquire whether there has been any sighting of Napoleon, given that he has disappeared from the Island of Elba. The answer being negative, the English frigate put to sea without delay.

Napoleon had escaped. By 10 a.m. the plenipotentiaries of the other four major powers were meeting. A few hours later Wellington received some additional details from the British minister at Florence. Napoleon had only about a thousand men with him, not much of a threat; but no one knew where he was headed. The best guess was that he would land in Italy to link up with Marshal (now king) Murat in Naples. News that he had landed on the south coast of France reached Vienna on 10 March. His march to Paris began what would become known as the Hundred Days, the most extraordinary adventure of his extraordinary career. Napoleon's abdication and the return of the Bourbons lulled France and the Allies into complacency. The end of the wars that had consumed an entire generation made Napoleon's return to power unimaginable, until it happened so easily. On Wednesday 1 March at 1 p.m., the *Inconstant* entered the Gulf of Juan. By 3 p.m. Napoleon and his followers had disembarked. The news was not known in Paris until Sunday 5 March. The slowness of communications was important for Napoleon's success.

Not until 7 March, at the town of Laffrey, did he encounter any troops. 'Soldiers of the 5th battalion of the line,' he shouted at them on foot, his chest exposed as he held open his redingote, 'recognize me! If there is one among you who would kill his general, his emperor, let him fire. Here I am.' The soldiers went over to him, *en masse*. His march to Paris was an uninterrupted triumph. On 18 March Napoleon encountered Marshal Ney, who had promised to bring him back 'in a cage', in Auxerre, the town of the Emperor's first posting. The two embraced: Ney and his soldiers joined Napoleon. The act would cost him his life. Napoleon reached Paris on 20 March and entered the Tuileries in glory at 8:30 p.m. Louis XVIII had earlier fled.

Napoleon's resumption of power was seamless. On Tuesday 21 March he greeted the entire imperial court, headed by the former queens of Spain and Holland, and the wives of the marshals. Benjamin Constant had thundered in the *Journal des Débats* against the new Attila, as he called him: 'I will not play the miserable traitor, going from one power to another, to veil infamy with sophistry.' Two weeks later he accepted a position from Napoleon and set to work on a new constitution. Mme de Staël never forgave her former lover. Constant's and Ney's apostasy was imitated by many, despite the oaths they had sworn to the restored Bourbons. Those who retained their scruples retired into private life. Those whose ambition or hatred trumped their scruples conspired against him. In this latter group was Talleyrand, who saw all his deft diplomacy go up in smoke when Napoleon returned, and Fouché, who during the three weeks after Waterloo played the greatest political role of his devious career, 'with clairvoyance, cold-bloodedness, and machiavellian invention that presents one of the most stunning performances of our history ... but not one of the most edifying'. But this is to get ahead of our story.

Napoleon had only one option: to prepare for the coming battle with the Allies. He returned to the emotional universe of the 1814 campaign and embraced once more his revolutionary youth, a cynical strategy yet paradoxically sincere. The Revolution and its ideals were never far from his thought. He invoked the nation in danger, his rhetoric redolent of the patriotic summer of 1792 when an ill-prepared revolutionary government, with a wretchedly equipped army, confronted an officer corps whose loyalty was untested and suspect, and a duplicitous court united to destroy the Revolution. Only the Revolution could provide the passion, the vocabulary, the patriotism Napoleon now needed. He even courted the old Jacobins whose deep hatred of the clergy and the nobility, long dormant in political discourse, was awakened. *La patrie en danger* brought the Emperor back to his origins and the nation to its heroic revolutionary past.

Napoleon had never abandoned the militant Revolution nor his devotion to much of its work that had shaped him, moved him, and made his fabulous career possible. He was still its disciple, even acolyte. The Hundred Days rekindled his youthful revolutionary ardor, dreams, and energy. The brilliant military end-game he had played in 1814, under the same inspiration, would be resumed, this time with an ideological edge earlier lacking. But even Napoleon, armed with a new constitution, filled with promises of reform, posing once more as the Revolution on horseback, could not work miracles. A vast number of Frenchmen reasonably stood aside. A few of his old comrades remained in retirement. He cobbled together one of his least impressive armies and prepared for the fight of his life.

Among all his battles Waterloo, because it was the last, occupies a special place. It was far from one of his best. Waterloo was fraught with catastrophic mistakes. It was so badly conducted by both sides that the carnage was terrible. But it could have been won, and Napoleon himself set the style for the perennial imaginary re-fighting of Waterloo. On St Helena he returned compulsively to the battle. He regretted having decided to pierce the center of Wellington's army, dividing the Allies rather than employing an oblique attack, *la manoeuvre sur les derrières*, that he had successfully used in half his battles. This is one of the few faults he admitted, along with the minor mistake of deciding to sleep the night before the battle at Fleurus (site of an important Revolutionary victory) rather than march on. Marshal Ney, who joined him nearby, thus missed his chance to occupy Quatre-Bas – which became one of the most contested and bloody epicenters of the battle – without a fight. Had the French seized Quatre-Bas they would have cut communication between the British and Prussian armies and the battle of Waterloo would have been fought 24 hours earlier. The Prussians would not have figured in the fighting. This kind of hypothesizing is, of course, endless.

To Gourgaud Napoleon lamented his fallen or absent comrades: 'If I had had Bessières at Waterloo my Guard would have decided the victory.' Those he commanded on 18 June 1815 were not the men of 1792:

> The generals were afraid of everything. I should probably have delayed a month to instill more consistency in the army. I needed a commander of the Guard. If I had had Bessières or Lannes there I would not have been beaten.

Lannes died at Wagram, Bessières at Lützen. He lamented to Montholon the absence of Murat to lead the Guard and told Montholon he lost

> because Soult made bad choices for his general staff, not one of whom knew how to carry my orders. If those sent in pursuit of Grouchy had not behaved like fools, if my orders had been carried to Guyot in the middle of rifle fire, he would not have engaged the cavalry of my Guard.

Modern students are more willing to fix a good deal of the blame on Napoleon himself. Uncharacteristically the Emperor left much of the tactical conduct of the battle to his subordinates: generals Ney, d'Erlon, and Reille. They were experienced in the difficulties of fighting Wellington, but they 'nonetheless repeated all the old errors and devised some new ones,' writes Rory Muir. David Chandler is even more pointed. d'Erlon's handling of his corps was 'slipshod', his staff work 'defective', and Ney was guilty of 'sheer pigheadedness', all of which was seconded by 'a certain lapse of energy and clear-sightedness on the part of the Emperor'. Grouchy was equally pigheaded, insisting Napoleon's orders be interpreted with complete literalness. He heard the guns at Waterloo yet kept going toward Corbaix, following orders. Had he marched a bit to the left he would have caught the Prussians. Instead Bülow's army eluded the French and arrived on the battlefield in time to assure Napoleon's defeat.

All these desired hypotheses obscure the reality: even had Waterloo been won it was only a matter of time before the Allies would have definitively destroyed Napoleon. He had exhausted his resources, everyone wanted peace; the initiative as well as the access to men and matériel lay with the Allies. Nicolas-François Mollien, Napoleon's director of the treasury, saw clearly that the French economy had already lost the war. 'England fought a modern war,' he wrote in his *Mémoires*, 'Napoleon fought an old-fashioned one. The age and circumstances made anachronism fatal.' England's best weapon was her finances. Public credit and her monetary system were the solutions of the future. 'Before he lost on the field of battle', Pierre Branda sums up, 'he was beaten by [English] money.' The Allies had finally become in reality what the French Revolution had only imagined and feared: a single will, the enemy of the Revolution, the *ancien régime* militant.

*****

The French Revolution introduced a new theorem into domestic and international politics: revolution begat war, and war revolution. The linkage would endure through the 20th century. For the kings, princes, and plenipotentiaries who gathered in Vienna it was clear the settlement they assembled to negotiate would have to prevent revolution by banishing or at least limiting warfare. There had been European-wide wars settled by treaty. Westphalia (1648) ended the Thirty Years' War, Utrecht (1713) ended Louis XIV's wars. Neither treaty successfully diminished let alone ended war, although continent-wide conflagrations were temporarily stopped, at least until the Seven Years' War, through exhaustion rather than reasonableness or cooperation. Before 1789 wars were an incessant plague, but they were largely limited to armies driven by cabinets and dynasties, and confined to those bits of real estate and their innocent populations through which the armies marched and fought. None of these wars, and the 18th century was almost constantly beset by war, shook the social foundations of any of the states involved. Now all was changed. France was permanently transformed by war and revolution, and all the European states felt the aftershocks. Prussia had had to emancipate her serfs and open the officer corps to all classes of society, at least in theory. In Spain, Sicily, and Sweden political revolution was spawned by the wars of the French Revolution. There were huge popular revolts in Valencia (1801) and Lombardy (1809). Even England was rocked by wide-scale naval mutinies and labor unrest that panicked the government. Everywhere Napoleon's armies occupied states were reformed and secularized, Church property was confiscated, feudalism was curtailed if not quashed, civil liberties were extended to Jews, and the Napoleonic Code was imposed.

For Metternich, born only three years after Napoleon, the French Revolution 'was an assertion of will and of power'. It was antithetical to this cool, rational, timid, virtuoso diplomat whose ideas and temperament were formed by the *ancien régime*. For him the 'essence of existence was proportion, its expression was law, and its mechanism an equilibrium'. The Austrian minister and his allies feared and distrusted Napoleon not because he was a treacherous ally (as Spain had discovered in 1808) or because he violated the treaties he himself had dictated (as he did when he invaded Russia). Napoleon's willful disregard for the conventions of international politics were not considered dirty tricks by the European states who had thrice partitioned Poland. Napoleon was feared and distrusted because he embodied the French Revolution, which held in contempt not only the conventions of international politics but virtually all the verities of the *ancien régime*. The armed exportation of *liberté, égalité, fraternité*, in their Napoleonic incarnation, permanently changed Europe. Tocqueville thought one had to go back to the Protestant Reformation to find a similar upheaval derived ultimately from universal ideas that easily transgressed borders and overturned social hierarchies. Napoleon's revolution, mounted on horseback, carried the French Revolution everywhere on the Continent. His fall not only promised the princes that they would keep their thrones, but gave them the opportunity to write an insurance policy for themselves and their world.

Many, perhaps most, of the Allies recognized a new kind of peace was needed if they were to remain in power. The principals (Tsar Alexander, Lord Castlereagh, Prince Metternich, and Frederick William of Prussia) could think only in traditional political terms: a return to a European balance of power. This conviction was clouded by the irresistible territorial spoils. The Allies' greed, shared by all except England, was insatiable. Their immediate response to the world turned upside down and the dangers created by the Revolution was a massive land grab, thenceforth to be maintained by a balance of power reinforced by repression. This would, so it was hoped, deter the great powers from war and their subject states from revolution. Domestic police and security forces grew exponentially. Fear of revolution, years before Karl Marx and Friedrich Engels invoked the specter of Communism, haunted Europe. Fine words were spoken about legitimacy as the principle of the Congress of Vienna to replace 'anarchy', the code word for Revolution. The problem at Vienna, as Castlereagh mournfully noted, was territorial greed on an unimagined scale: 'It unfortunately happens that never at any former period was so much spoil thrown loose for the world to scramble for.' Friedrich von Gentz, a Prussian who attached himself to Metternich and became the secretary of the Congress of Vienna, was disgusted by the acquisitiveness and hypocrisy of the participants:

> The great phrases about 'reconstructing the social order', about 'lasting peace founded on a just distribution of force', and so on, and so on, were meant to calm people and to give this solemn gathering an air of dignity and grandeur, ... but the real aim of the Congress *was the dividing up between the victors of the spoils stolen from the vanquished.*

Some who had their lands returned when Napoleon's empire collapsed tried to obliterate the revolutionary years. King Victor Emmanuel of Sardinia immediately closed down the University of Turin and decreed a return to the laws as they had been in 1770. Torture, flogging, quartering, and breaking on the wheel were all reinstituted, along with royal arrest warrants, the detested *lettres de cachet* that had been one of the catalysts for the French Revolution. He described everything that had happened since 1798, when he had been chased out by the French, as 'a long dream; and therefore immaterial'. In the Papal Estates as well legitimacy proved vengeful. All the old tribunals were reinstated, along with feudal privileges. Jews were returned to the ghetto, the Inquisition was revived, as were the outlawed Jesuits. Everything French was anathematized and abolished. The sale of Church property was undone, the Code Napoléon was suppressed, the National Guard dissolved, vaccination was forbidden, and street lighting was turned off: the Enlightenment, the philosophy of the French Revolution, was declared defunct. In the German states, whose Jewish population had been the beneficiaries of French occupation, the Congress capitulated to local prejudice by leaving each state to decide on their status, with predictable results.

The other watchword of the Congress, cooperation, was similarly disregarded. Here Austria provides the best example. Spoils gave her the direct rule of the whole of Lombardy-Venetia as well as Illyria, and a preponderating dominion over all the minor southern states. She had become, with the *imprimatur* of the Congress, the guardian of the entire Italian peninsula and the Adriatic Sea. She was, however, dependent upon the other signatories to the treaty to hold her possessions since she could not police all of Italy. The Austrian land-grab was no more arbitrary than those of her allies. Legitimacy was only cynically invoked. With the exception of England who had no desire for continental real estate, any one of the other major powers would have been pleased to have the Veneto, or almost any Italian city, and felt as entitled as was Austria. They saw no advantage in doing Vienna's dirty work. Self-interest and fear regularly swamped principle, whether proclaimed or tacit, during the negotiations at Vienna.

Unexpectedly, national egotism and the self-interest of states sometimes resulted in reasonableness and a thoughtful concern for Europe's future. It was the need for peace, universally felt, that motivated the powers to try and cooperate, to assure each other's security lest their own be challenged. They could devise no mechanism beyond behaving decently, which none of the powers thought likely. The master idea of balance of power came to little more than setting up countervailing powers to hold each state within its new borders and ambitions. When the Tsar presented his idea of a Holy Alliance for assuring international cooperation to Metternich the Austrian could scarcely suppress his snickers. The powers signed on, but shared Metternich's skepticism, and perhaps his amusement. The principle at work was *realpolitik* not altruism. Austria feared Prussia and Russia more than France. She needed, and England desired, a viable France to keep Russia in check. France, although vanquished, had to preserve her territorial integrity from Prussia, whose ambitions hovered on the east bank of the Rhine, which she was poised to cross. England, once the Scheldt River and Antwerp were in friendly hands thus assuring her economic interests, wanted only peace and quiet on the Continent, upon which she now turned her back. All the smaller powers, whose greed and appetites matched those of the great states, lacked the power to satisfy them except from the table scraps thrown by the mighty.

The mood of the imperial Austrian court was festive. The gaiety, the social whirl, the frivolity were intoxicating. The Emperor of the Austro-Hungarian lands hosted the peace talks. The *ancien régime* gave one of its most glittering performances for the occasion, spending millions. The old elites had much to celebrate, and this theater of society and diplomacy, both public and intimate, at times intruded on the hard bargaining. Tsar Alexander's 'incessant and sometimes disreputable flirtations', in Harold Nicolson's fussy phrase, came into competition with Prince Metternich's dalliances and chilled their relations. Through it all the Allies were agreed: Napoleon was 'the Revolution on horseback'. His disruptions were over. The French Revolution was, they hoped, at an end. Poland, Saxony, and France were the central problems at Vienna. The Tsar demanded the Napoleonic Duchy of Warsaw, and considerably more, to form an independent state under his protection. Independence was a mask, protection a euphemism for Russian expansion into Europe. This mish-mash of idealism and *realpolitik* was typical of Alexander's complex personality where irreconcilable urges remained unmediated by reason. His passions demanded immediate attention and satisfaction. He yearned at Vienna to be the mediator of Europe as he had, in 1814, been the mediator of France. He easily forgot that his settlements, often whispered in his ear by Talleyrand, were undone in the Hundred Days. Bound to his mercurial will was Frederick William of Prussia, who had no other champion at the Congress. A weak and vacillating man who freely promised far more than he was able to deliver, often offering the same inducements to several states simultaneously, the Prussian king remained single-minded and stubborn. He wanted to be compensated for the part of Poland he controlled from the 18th-century partitions with land, preferably the entire kingdom of Saxony. Russia would get Poland and the king of Saxony, one of Napoleon's principal German allies, would have his kingdom dismembered. Gaining Saxony would give Prussia dominance in Germany, which Austria opposed. Frederick William and Alexander linked the two huge transfers of property into a cause-and-effect nexus, an international *quid pro quo*. This became the principal headache of Metternich and Castlereagh, aided and abetted by the wittiest of all those gathered at Vienna, Talleyrand.

Charles-Maurice de Talleyrand-Périgord was the wild card at Vienna. The Hundred Days had destroyed all his diplomatic work of 1814 and he, along with vanquished France, had no legal standing at Vienna. Talleyrand saw immediately that the attempt of the great powers, constituted as the Quadruple Alliance, to exclude all the lesser states gave him his opening. He became the spokesman for the excluded, posing as a disinterested representative, the voice of legitimacy and legality. France had no chance to share the spoils. She herself was on the menu of several of the powers: a meal to be devoured, one province at a time. Talleyrand could afford the luxury of dispassionate idealism. Once he gained admittance to the inner circle of diplomacy at Vienna, aided in no small part by his brilliant table presided over by the great chef, Carême, and his equally brilliant salon, presided over by Dorothée, the daughter of one of his mistresses, and enlivened by his wonderful wit, Talleyrand deserted the lists as champion of the lesser states.

France was to be punished for welcoming Napoleon back from exile. All the gains of the militant Revolution were now confiscated. Her new frontiers would be reduced to those of 1 January 1790. She now was forced to give up about two-thirds of the territory acquired between 1790 and 1792. This meant that Savoy, the territory along Lake Geneva, the land around the fortresses of Condé, Philippeville, Mariembourg, Givet and Charlemont, along with Sarrelouis, Landau, and the forts of l'Ecluse and Joux were all taken from her. She lost not only real estate but the defense of her eastern frontier. France was also to pay 600 million francs in war reparations, and another 200 million for the construction of enemy forts on her borders. The Allies would garrison 150,000 men in a number of forts, for whose maintenance France would also pay. The looted art was to be returned. Vivant Denon now had the melancholy task of packing up the treasures he had collected and returning them to the victorious Allies. The film of Napoleon's artistic depredations was run backward. The British were the brunt of popular anger when they dismounted from atop the Carrousel arch the famous bronze horses taken from St Mark's Cathedral in Venice. The soldiers charged with the removal took turns sitting in the chariot, their antics jeered by menacing crowds. The arch itself they left in pitiful condition.

Bas-reliefs and statues lay broken at its base. So threatening was the crowd that Austrian troops were called out to clear the Tuileries courtyard and the surrounding streets. A few days later, when Wellington took his box in the theater, he was booed and forced to leave. He himself had privately possessed Canova's nude statue of Napoleon for his London house. It had originally been intended for the Carrousel arch but was thought indecent by the Emperor. The British government, which had not been looted, demanded none of the art. Alexander, whose looted art was abandoned during the ghastly French retreat in 1812, did not have to line up at the Tuileries to retrieve his treasures. Instead he bought, from Eugène and Hortense de Beauharnais, their mother's private collection.

The Congress of Vienna fixed international politics until 1918. It is often celebrated as a triumph of good sense and cooperation, a new principle in peace-making and the instrument that gave Europe general tranquility for a century. Vienna is far more ambiguous. The great victor was undoubtedly England. Of all the powers only she got everything she wanted and was, with the exception of the Crimea, uninvolved in the 19th-century wars of Europe. Her overseas colonies and domestic labor unrest absorbed all her attention, military, economic, and political. The British triumph at Vienna was the culmination of decades of anti-revolutionary struggle. Castlereagh was a protégé of the Younger Pitt, who until his death in 1806 was a consistent and tenacious foe of the French Revolution. He alone among the leaders of the great powers saw and realistically analyzed the threat and the meaning of the Revolution for the *ancien régime* almost from its beginning. Castlereagh had the luxury of an island with an overseas empire, guarded by the greatest navy in the world, financed by the first modern, capitalist economy. Despite his relative freedom from the revolutionary struggles of the Continent, his hatred of the Revolution was sincere, principled, and drove his foreign policy. He had lived through the humiliations of the American Revolution. He had seen the dangers, the havoc, the bloodshed, albeit from a safe distance, first in America and then in France.

Prussia too emerged victorious from Vienna. She did not get all of Saxony, but she did reach the Rhine and become the dominant state in Germany, amply compensated for the part of Poland she ceded to Russia. Prussian success had been germinating for more than a century. From an unimpressive princedom whose lands were not contiguous and deserving of the sobriquet of Germany's sandbox, Prussia had become the heir apparent of German unification. Her king during Napoleon's day was most unpromising. The quip was that his wife Louise was the only man in the kingdom. Her death, in 1810, left Frederick William shattered. But if he had no heroism and was frequently paralyzed by inaction and indecision, especially after his wife's death, he was a master of mendacity and was driven by an *idée fixe*: to enlarge his kingdom. Prussia's rebound from the ruin of 1806, her indispensable military contributions to Napoleon's defeat at Leipzig and eventually at Waterloo, and her king's unswerving obsession with national aggrandizement were rewarded at Vienna.

Austria and Russia got much of what they wanted, but in the case of the former the price was to become second fiddle in Germany, experience difficulties in holding onto Italy, and the perpetuation of the same sprawling, indefensible, and essentially unmanageable empire she had had when the Congress first assembled in Vienna. Russia remained in Europe and Poland almost at once became a satellite, as all the representatives at Vienna had feared. The balance of power, with the lynchpin of a viable France, worked in keeping Russia from further penetration into Western Europe, but she had unchecked access to Eastern Europe. The Congress of Vienna had successfully thwarted and then diverted Russia's expansion westward.

The most interesting case is France. The Vienna settlement looked very unpromising. She had been beaten in war, invaded and occupied, suffered a punishing peace, and had had imposed upon her a king who had been in voluntary exile from France during the most transformative period of her history and had so recently fled, unlamented by his subjects, at Napoleon's approach. In line for the throne was his brother, a vainglorious and shallow prince filled with vengefulness. Yet Louis XVIII proved himself worthy of the role thrust upon him by a turbulent history. When the Count de Chabrol, the prefect of the Seine, met Louis after he returned to Paris following Waterloo, he provided the name for the period that separated the first from the second Restoration: 'A hundred days have passed,' he publicly harangued the king, 'since the fatal moment when Your Majesty left his capital ...' Louis listened and responded:

I separated myself from my good city of Paris only with the most passionate sorrow. I return with emotion. I have foreseen the evils that menaced her. I desire to pre-empt and efface them.

There is no reason to suppose these remarks were not heartfelt. Unlike his older and younger brothers he had the gift of brief eloquence delivered with dignity. He and his government would take a significant series of false steps and be saddled with an opposition that was unre-lenting and supporters who were uncontrollable, but France rebounded economically in a remarkably short period of time, her intellectual life flourished again after the long Napoleonic winter. A generation of peace was the best medicine.

Everywhere the Allies attacked the French Revolution, except in France itself where virtually all the social, legal, political, cultural, and economic changes wrought by the Revolution, institutionalized by Napoleon, and guaranteed by his army, were maintained. France was not quarantined and dismembered, nor was it made a pariah state. France had a constitution and elected representatives. The former had its limits and constrictions and the latter was circumscribed to a tiny minority, but neither was more restrictive than when Napoleon ruled. The mas-sive confiscations and land transfers carried out by the Revolution, both ecclesiastical and noble, were reaffirmed. Even the revolutionary tradi-tion lived on, albeit in the shadows. The Congress of Vienna was willing to accept all this in France, or felt unable to destroy it, so long as they held sway in their own lands. It had not been Napoleon's conscious intention to perpetuate the Revolution. He had wanted to end it on his own terms, bequeathing to his son a constitutional monarchy and a substantial empire. He had failed. But his failure had taken 16 years to be realized. In all that time he kept France from being isolated, and compelled his enemies to adopt many of his reforms. His government was efficient, enlightened, and secular. It allowed him to mobilize the entire state to attack Europe. Far more successfully than his revolu-tionary predecessors he carried the French Revolution throughout the Continent. He had cleared away much of the *mortmain* of centuries of bad, clumsy, inept government, and he gave the French Revolution a generation-long breather in which to solidify its conquests. His was a very Hegelian triumph, an inadvertent, unintentional triumph for the French Revolution.

Leaving the institutionalization of the Revolution in France intact proved a grave error to the triumphant Allies, however necessary. The Congress had set out to eliminate the possibility of revolution. They had failed. The land grab and the purely political and diplomatic perspec-tive that dominated the Congress and its work did not end the age of revolution. Quite the contrary. New borders, fresh alliances, the revival of the old elites along with the beefed-up machinery of repression and reaction solved none of the social, economic, or political problems that beset post-Napoleonic Europe. The revolutions that broke out in France in 1830 and 1848 reverberated across the Continent. Only England and Russia were spared, and they had their hands full without barricades. Revolution had entered the mainstream of politics, certainly in France. The specter Karl Marx said was haunting Europe was not Communism: it was the French Revolution. No ghosts had been laid at Waterloo or Vienna.

Entr'acte
Reputation

Napoleon wanted to conquer the future and assure his posthumous reputation as passionately as he sought to control everything. His comrades, colleagues, and collaborators proved remarkably useful and mostly malleable. So did the *savants* and the artists he carefully cultivated. German intellectuals were an unexpected gift to his reputation, but he cared little and knew less about what they said. The great francophone writers eluded his grasp. Balzac and Stendhal were Bonapartists but both worked after his death and Stendhal's great novels were ignored for many years. The major British writers, among them Byron, Hazlitt, and Scott, early established Napoleon's Anglophone reputation as the national enemy, a bias that continues to blemish British historiography. In France there was a deluge of memoirs from soldiers, collaborators, and busybodies. Among Napoleon's contemporaries the two most important writers of the age, Mme de Staël and Chateaubriand, were fierce opponents. They established the so-called *legende noire*. Both attacked and debunked Napoleon's revolutionary heritage, one from the Left the other from the Right. For both Napoleon was the great betrayer, the hero corrupted, the savior who proved a false prophet and then a god who failed. Napoleon's own version of himself as the heir of the French Revolution was shaped and perpetuated by Emmanuel Las Cases.

There is no snug fit with a literary *genre* describing these works. All three are both memoirs and self-conscious historical works, a form with roots in antiquity. Mme de Staël and Chateaubriand wrote histories of their own time in which they themselves appear. The template was probably established by Herodotus, and subsequently used by writers as different as Joinville, Clarendon, and Trotsky. Chateaubriand, Mme de Staël, and Napoleon-Las Cases independently found a way of writing the history of their own times and the part they played. *Res gestae* takes precedence over the personal intimacy of autobiography. All three are simultaneously eye-witnesses, sources, and omnipotent voices commenting on their ideas, their feelings, their reactions. In Napoleon-Las Cases the bulk of the work is conversations, a precious record of Napoleon's talk, but his talk burnished by the recorder. Both Chateaubriand and Mme de Staël met Napoleon and record some talk but they see him predominately from a distance. The three works also offer epistemological variations. What each author knows is what he or she has lived, heard, or seen rather than what each has extracted from sources and authorities. The latter are sometimes consulted, but mostly to substantiate or reinforce what they already know. The value of the three works is not in scrupulous or ingenious scholarship, but their knowledge, feelings, and impressions as contemporary historical actors. In this Chateaubriand, Mme de Staël, and Napoleon-Las Cases are closer to their models than to the literary habits and practices of their age.

All three share the same assumption: Napoleon and the French Revolution are inextricably linked, a single gigantic phenomenon. The distinctness of a Napoleonic era, the *Episode napoléonien* in Louis Bergeron's formulation, is absent from all thee works. Napoleon's dictations to Las Cases are obsessed with his inheritance of the Revolution, his filial piety toward his spiritual parent, his perpetuation of its values and continuation of its work. Chateaubriand is the antithesis. For him Napoleon embodied and ruthlessly realized all that was demonic in the Revolution. He had the chance to end the Revolution by becoming the French George Washington, but he spurned the possibility, carrying the upheaval to a kind of logical frenzy: the tyranny of a single man who leveled all society so he would stand above it. For Mme de Staël it is Napoleon's betrayal of the Revolution, by which she means the liberal Revolution that reflected the views of her father, Jacques Necker, which were realized in a constitutional monarchy, that informs her work.

The *Mémorial de Sainte-Hélène* is the most unorthodox book of the three. Napoleon dictated his life and deeds which are filtered through Las Cases's mind. It is impossible to separate out the Emperor's words from Las Cases's own. Las Cases is much more than an amanuensis but where and to what degree he imposed himself on Napoleon's words, skewed his purpose, or led him to a desired expression, subject, or thesis cannot be determined. Las Cases made every effort to capture Napoleon's words verbatim, even inventing a personal shorthand, but when he assembled the *Mémorial* from his notebooks he sometimes rearranged conversations by topic and took other liberties as well. He imbued Napoleon's soliloquies with artistic and literary coherence. He directed Napoleon's discourse into an ideological mold from which the Emperor emerges as the legitimate heir of the French Revolution. At best Las Cases preserves an approximation, a facsimile, of the Emperor's inimitable torrent of words, but the *Mémorial* is much more worked and mannered than the diaries kept by the other St Helena exiles. There is also a posthumous reworking of the text. Las Cases published editions of his remarkable work in 1823, 1824, 1830, 1835, 1840, and 1841–42. The differences between them are significant. He freely moved entire sections to different locations, augmented and deleted passages, and interpolated apocryphal letters, adjusting his book to changing political times, the need to dodge the censors, as well as pursuing his own literary tampering. Jean Tulard cautions against taking literally 'the presentation of the persecutions Napoleon endured on Saint-Helena' or the image Las Cases presents 'of a liberal emperor, the defender of various nationalities'. Nevertheless this is the most influential of all contemporary accounts of Napoleon.

Of the three myth-makers Las Cases is the most unexpected, the least likely to have written a classic and passionately favorable account of Napoleon. By birth, education, experience, habit, and conviction he should have stood with Chateaubriand, another descendant of an old noble house. Both men had fled the Revolution and suffered sharp privations for their birth and beliefs. Both rallied to Napoleon for similar reasons. Las Cases came later to the fold but remained faithful and was long excluded from France for his loyalty. How and why he managed to secure a place on the *Northumberland* for himself and his son to accompany Napoleon into exile remains murky. There are hypotheses, and his desire to write a book about Napoleon is not unimportant. He paid a high price for his attachment, which mitigates purely mercenary motives; and the very existence of the *Mémorial* turns on chance. Las Cases shared Napoleon's exile for only 18 months. His notebooks, filled with the Emperor's dictations and his own commentary, were confiscated when he was banished from St Helena. They were, almost miraculously, preserved intact by Hudson Lowe, and returned after Napoleon died. Ironically the *Mémorial de Sainte-Hélène* is not only a moving account of Napoleon's exile, the most important gospel in the Napoleonic cult, and a literary masterpiece in its own right, but it is the *locus classicus* of the black legend of Hudson Lowe himself.

Las Cases rallied to the Empire only in 1806, after the great German victories. He threw himself into his new career and allegiance, was awarded the legion of honor and became a baron of the Empire, shedding his marquisate of the *ancien régime* and the cross of Saint-Louis he had received at the hands of the Duke d'Angoulême. In 1809 he became one of Napoleon's chamberlains. He fled to England during the first Restoration and rejoined Napoleon during the Hundred Days. He was unwelcome in France after Waterloo. 'Do you know where this will lead you,' asked a surprised Napoleon when Las Cases sought to share his exile. 'I haven't made the calculation,' he responded. Whatever Las Cases's motives it is clear that his attachment, along with his book, rotated on the armature of his fascination with and devotion to Napoleon. A penetrating judge of men, Napoleon saw in Las Cases a providential instrument for his self-presentation to contemporaries and posterity. An *émigré*, a nobleman, and a royalist who had rallied to the Empire, Las Cases could portray Napoleon as he wanted to be seen. None of his generals who followed him into exile and also took dictation had either Las Cases's credentials or his literary abilities. His noble *bona fides* would inoculate his portrait against accusations of military cronyism, revolutionary opportunism, and the spite of restored Europe. He was also a cultivated man with broad tastes to whom the Emperor could talk, no small consideration for Napoleon. He had mastered English when in exile in London and served as Napoleon's interpreter as well as his tutor. Before moving on I cannot resist a delicious anecdote, Napoleon's first letter written in English. It should not be taken as a recommendation for Las Cases's pedagogical skills:

> Count Las Cases. – Since sixt wek, y learn the english and y do not any progress. Sixt week do forty and two day. If might have learn fivty word, for day, y could know it two thousands and two hundred. It is in the dictinary more of foorty thousand; even he could most twenty; bot much of tems. For know it or hundred and twenty week which do more two years. After this you shall agree that the study one tongue is a gret labour who it must do into the young aged. – Longwood this morning, the seven marsh Thursday one thousand eight hundred sixteen after nativity the yors Jésus-Christ. – Count Las Cases, chambellan of the S.M. Longwood; into his palac: very press.

'What will we do in this God-forsaken place,' Napoleon asked Las Cases. 'Sire, we will live in the past ...' 'Eh bien!' said Napoleon, 'we will write our *Mémoires*.' And so they did. Publication of the *Mémorial de Sainte-Hélène* in 1822–23 caused a sensation. The first printing almost immediately disappeared. The cult of Napoleon, whose unsystematic ideology was a *pot-pourri* of opinions, actions, anecdotes, and political *dicta* lumped together to form Bonapartism, a none too precise concoction of nostalgia for a glorious past and visions of a luminous future, was now buttressed with the Emperor's own words, rendered more grandiloquent and less rambling than they came from their creator. The thousands and thousands of words Las Cases shaped into a polished and satisfying narrative acquired added weight and pathos from the misery of life on St Helena, which Las Cases details. He was a talented writer whose seemingly unadorned and artless prose proved the perfect and subtle instrument for presenting his hero seemingly unvarnished. Not only was he completely in accord with Napoleon's over-arching theme of himself as the heir of the French Revolution, but he was discreetly self-effacing. Everyone let Napoleon talk. Las Cases let him talk in print and to the point:

> Napoleon emerged from the crowd to climb to a supreme height, marching at the head of a Revolution that he had completely civilized, which circumstances led him into a struggle to the death against Europe, a struggle in which he succumbed only for having wanted to end it ...

Las Cases was certainly not the first to compare Napoleon's island imprisonment to the fate of Prometheus, but he put that famous image, which pleased the Emperor and resonated in Europe, at the center of his portrait:

> Finally, seventy days after having left England and one hundred ten days after having left Paris, we anchored around mid-day [at St Helena]. The anchor touched the sea bed, and this became the first link of the chain that would nail the modern Prometheus to his rock.

There is much that Las Cases leaves out. His purpose was not to chronicle Napoleon's life nor present it warts and all, but to render it both heroic and tragic. Napoleon dictated a detailed account of his childhood, family, and early life, which, alas, did not find its way into the *Mémorial*. Napoleon's passionate belief that he was not only the legitimate heir of the Revolution, chosen by the people, but the necessary and even providential savior of France, to which he was utterly devoted, is the thesis of the *Mémorial*. He presents himself as a reluctant warrior goaded by the European monarchies into battle. The *Mémorial* enshrines these master themes and adds a powerful indictment of England's treatment of their prisoner in the person of Sir Hudson Lowe, a narrow-minded, snobbish, petty, and punctilious jailer. He is the perfect foil.

Didier Le Gall subjected the *Mémorial* to a close verbal analysis, detailing Las Cases's myth-making. He identifies a series of 'word-concepts' – country, nation, people(s), honor, equality, and liberty – fundamental to Napoleon's thought about himself and France. Le Gall is interested in the context in which these words appear, and he is sensitive to the dialectic between Napoleon and Las Cases. The gaps and ambiguities in Napoleon's political thought become all the more noticeable in Las Cases's efforts to impose coherence. The confusion between establishing his legitimacy democratically first on the sovereignty of the people and then on dynastic heredity, sometimes concomitantly, is apparent in Le Gall's examination of *peuple* and its derivatives in the text.

As for equality, Napoleon favored a democracy whose participants were limited by income and merit, which would be socially expressed in a new aristocracy he defined as a *classe supérieure*. Napoleon's democracy rested on sanctioned inequalities. His envisioned society favored the middle class which he considered the only group capable of commanding, obeying, and accepting the political choices he offered. To the charge of despotism and the comparison with George Washington, invidiously invoked by both Chateaubriand and Mme de Staël among others, Las Cases leads Napoleon to make his case. If he is the heir of the Revolution why did he not become the Washington of the French Revolution? Placed in the same circumstances, Napoleon argues, Washington would have reacted as he himself did. 'For myself,' he told Las Cases, 'I could only be a crowned Washington.' What makes the *Mémorial* so important is not that it presents Napoleon's political thought cogently and provides him ample scope for presenting himself to contemporaries and posterity. What makes the book so compelling is the portrait of Napoleon, built up out of his talk artfully arranged and presented. Many others recorded Napoleon's words. Even his enemies left penetrating portraits of the man and his deeds. Many had access to Napoleon at important moments of his life. A few have written wonderfully of their encounters, but no other book about Napoleon combines all these qualities as successfully as Las Cases's. He collected his materials when Napoleon no longer moved the world. Sycophancy and hatred were less important than they had been when Napoleon was a demi-God. In Las Cases's pages Napoleon is anxious to manipulate posterity. In the hot-house world of the French exiles on St Helena, redolent of a fabulous past now vanished, Napoleon's universe is, perhaps inadvertently, filled with sadness that rises to tragedy.

Marooned with his tiny court on a god-forsaken island Napoleon talked about whatever came into his mind. He had never exercised much editorial discipline. Now he exercised none as he sought to fix his place in history. 'I mounted the throne,' he told Las Cases, forgetting that he was the heir of a violent revolution, 'a virgin to all the crimes of my position ... Are there heads of dynasties who can say as much?' His recurring refrain about how he was not responsible for acts and orders that were his alone was much reiterated:

> Never was a project more important for the interests of civilization [he said speaking of the invasion of England] conceived with more generous intentions ... And what is remarkable is that the obstacles that caused me to fail were not the work of men ... In the Midi it was the sea that thwarted me. In the North it was the Moscow fire and the winter ice that did me in. Water, air, fire, all from nature and only from nature.

His self-celebration of how he saved the Revolution was also much reiterated. 'Nothing will henceforth destroy or erase the great principles of our Revolution,' he declared:

> these great and beautiful verities will remain forever ... we have drowned the first blemishes [*souillures*] in waves of glory ... Generated at the French tribune, cemented with the blood of battles, adorned with the laurels of victory, celebrated with the acclamations of the people, sanctioned by the treaties and alliances of sovereigns, familiar to the ears as the mouths of kings, they will not be undone!

The careful oratorical structure of this paragraph hardly sounds like the unmannered and often rambling rhetoric of Napoleon. Las Cases also had a good eye for the telling anecdote, the small but significant action worthy of a nice turn of phrase. His Hudson Lowe is thoroughly odious, driven by an absurd obsession that Napoleon might escape; his crimes are those of a narrow-minded cheese-parer. He skimped on wine at Longwood and made it increasingly difficult for Napoleon to get water for his bath, one of his few pleasures in captivity. It is this level of detail that nails down the misery of Napoleon's imprisonment: the grandeur of the past and the man-made wretchedness of the present. Lowe's character is brilliantly built up from petty tyrannies and insensitivities. Here as much as anywhere in the *Mémorial* Las Cases reveals himself as an accomplished literary creator. One day Napoleon was evaluating his several companions. Bertrand he considered a part of his destiny. Gourgaud 'is my creation, my child'. Montholon is 'a child of the Revolution and the camps'. 'You, *mon cher,"* he said to Las Cases and then paused, 'well you, *mon cher,* by what devilish chance do you find yourself here?' 'Sire,' Las Cases responded, 'through the goodness of my star, and for the honor of the emigration.' It was a perfect explanation of one of history's great collaborations.

*****

François René, Vicomte de Chateaubriand, was born at Saint-Malo in 1768, the youngest of ten children. He was Napoleon's exact contemporary, a fact that intrigued him throughout his life. The two men, permanently marked by the French Revolution, could not have been more different. Chateaubriand was a noble who could trace his lineage back to Louis IX, the only canonized king of France. Napoleon mocked the sainted king's generalship as a Crusader, although his own Egyptian campaign was hardly more successful. The only nobility he could claim was his father's bogus assertion of a connection with a long-extinct Florentine family, a fiction the son spurned. Chateaubriand's father, a sea captain, later an *armateur* or ship's outfitter, and an occasional investor in the slave trade, was obsessively devoted to restoring the family fortunes. In 1761 he acquired the chateau of Combourg, determined to make it the seat of his once-distinguished family. He chose a career at sea for his youngest son, but the boy rebelled, spent two idle years at Combourg with his sister, and then enlisted in the army as an infantry officer. From 1786 to 1789 he did garrison duty at Cambrai and Dieppe, every bit as bored and lonely as the young Bonaparte, then at his Burgundy garrisons. 'No one,' he later recalled, 'paid any attention to me. I was, like Bonaparte, a skinny second lieutenant, completely unknown.'

Jean-Baptiste, René's older brother, made a good match because of his name. He married a granddaughter of Chrétien Guillaume de Lamoignon de Malesherbes, the most distinguished member of a distinguished legal family. As an old man he returned from the safety of emigration in 1792 to defend Louis XVI at his trial. He was guillotined for his moral courage, along with his daughter and granddaughter. Chateaubriand's brother died on the same scaffold that day. The writer's mother and sister died in revolutionary prisons. Malesherbes had advised Chateaubriand to flee the Revolution and travel to America. The trip changed his life. It made him a writer, and a prophetic one. He arrived in America 'a Cato who everywhere sought the rectitude of the original Roman virtues' and was 'scandalized to find everywhere luxurious carriages, frivolous conversation, unequal fortunes, immoral gambling dens, and the din of ballrooms and theaters. In Philadelphia I could have believed myself in Liverpool or Bristol'. He took refuge in his imagination. He returned from America in 1792, his literary work yet unwritten. 'Revolutions,' he wrote, 'like rivers, grow as they flow. I found [the French Revolution] enormously swollen, overflowing its banks. I had left with Mirabeau and the Constituent Assembly; I returned to Danton and the Legislative Assembly.' After a short stay in Paris as the monarchy was unraveling he and his brother fled to Brussels. René joined the army of the counterrevolution, was wounded in the thigh, and eventually (in May 1793) made his way to London. Here he lived on the edge of starvation and wrote his first political book, the *Essai historique, politique et moral sur les révolutions anciennes et modernes* (*An Historical, Political, and Moral Essay on Modern and Ancient Revolutions*). Steeped in antiquity, both Latin and Greek (which language he did not know), Chateaubriand mined his knowledge of the ancient world and its literature to come to grips with the French Revolution. He began the work in 1794 but the Revolution changed so quickly it outran his pen. He felt as if he was 'writing on a ship during a storm'. Sometimes 'it was necessary to erase at night what I had written during the day'. The *Essai* did not give him serenity. Recurrent nightmares are not banished by literary excursions. 'My mother,' he writes reintroducing the *Essai* to a new audience in 1826,

> after having been thrown, at the age of seventy-two, into prison where she saw some of her children perish, died on a miserable cot ... She charged one of my sisters, with her dying breath, to call me back to the religion in which I had been raised. My sister sent me the last wishes of my mother. When the letter reached me beyond the seas [in England], my sister herself no longer existed. She too died as a result of her imprisonment.

'These two voices from the tomb,' he continues in the elegiac and lachrymose prose of which he was a master, 'struck me. I became a Christian ... I sobbed and I believed.' The great themes of his life were fixed.

Chateaubriand, unexpectedly, was one of the earliest of the noble Napoleonic *rallié*. Ever anxious to seduce the old aristocracy and capture a great writer, Napoleon welcomed Chateaubriand who was fascinated by the man, his power, his genius, and charmed by his ability to flatter convincingly those he needed, wanted, or could use. For Chateaubriand the lure was enhanced by his ambition and craving for a public life. It became a pattern. America had provided enough solitude for a lifetime. Henceforth the writer, the prophet, and the statesman would march hand in hand. In another pattern that marked his life, passionate entanglements with many women, his mistress from some years earlier, Mme de Beaumont, mortally ill, traveled to Rome to die in the arms of her lover (1803). The letter Chateaubriand composed on her death, and distributed in numerous copies to his entourage, 'is one of the treasures of funereal literature'. The public enactment of love, death, and grief were very much *à la mode* for the Romantic sensibility which Chateaubriand did so much to shape. It is another death, the execution of the Duke d'Enghien (21 March 1804), that cut Chateaubriand's tenuous ties to Napoleon. The last of the descendants of Louis de Bourbon, Prince of Condé (1621–1686), the duke had been kidnapped by Napoleon's agents on foreign soil, brought to the chateau of Vincennes, secretly tried by a military court, and shot by firing squad. France and Europe were shocked by the illegality and brutality of the act. Chateaubriand judged it the work 'of his Corsican temperament, an example of cold-blooded violence, of preventive passion against the descendants of Louis XIV, an ever-present specter'. He resigned his position and went into permanent opposition. It was a courageous act, although his letter of resignation avoided mentioning the execution at Vincennes. Napoleon is reported to have said only 'c'est bon' when he read the letter: 'So be it.' His inflection and gestures are not recorded.

Chateaubriand reemerged only in 1814, publishing *De Buonaparte, des Bourbons, et de la nécessité de se rallier à nos princes légitimes pour le bonheur de la France et de celui de l'Europe (Of Bonaparte, the Bourbons, and the Necessity of Rallying to our Legitimate Princes for the Happiness of France and of Europe).* It appeared on 4 April 1814, four days after the victorious Allies entered Paris, while the Cossacks grazed their horses on the Champs-Elysées. This rhetorically impressive collection of invective and calumny is one of the founding documents in the Black Legend of Napoleon. The times were desperate. The end was near. Napoleon retreated toward Paris with the Allies on his heels. Only the reluctance of his marshals to fight to the death in the streets of Paris and the machinations of Fouché and Talleyrand prevented Napoleon from staging a *Götterdammerung* in the capital. Chateaubriand, as attuned to history as he was to the harmony between the state of his soul and that of his contemporaries, set to work on a pamphlet. 'I worked incessantly on my brochure,' he writes, preparing 'a remedy for when the moment of anarchy arrives.' Every night, he dramatically confessed,

'I locked myself in my room, put my manuscript under my pillow, and kept two loaded pistols on my night table. I slept between these two muses.' In the canon of royalist pamphleteering the accusations of *De Buonaparte* – he deliberately used the Italian spelling which Napoleon had rejected nearly two decades earlier – are familiar. Chateaubriand disputes Napoleon's military talents, dissociates the Grande Armée from its leader, a general he considered cruel and mediocre, laden with the unnecessary deaths of hundreds of thousands (whose numbers he exaggerates). Nor was Napoleon's vaunted administration anything more than cold numbers, calculations whose human cost meant nothing to the conqueror: 'how much wheat, wine, or oil a province produces, what is the last *écu* that can be extracted, the last man taken [to the army]'. Children are ripped from their families and

> put in schools where they are taught irreligion, debauchery, contempt for the domestic virtues, and blind obedience to the sovereign, all to the beat of a drum. He wants to turn them into some kind of godless Mamelukes, without family or country.

In Egypt Bonaparte poisoned his own troops and commissioned Baron Gros to paint him showing compassion to plague victims. When Bonaparte was not murdering Egyptians 'he violated in the evening the laws he had made in the morning'.

Chateaubriand's xenophobia is pernicious. Bonaparte is a foreigner, sometimes a Corsican or extravagantly an African; and the pamphlet is filled with nativist rants. Soon after the Revolution men were desperate to return to the authenticity of the past, he writes, 'to find among the French a brow to bear the crown of Louis XVI'. Tragically they chose 'a Corsican' who devoured their heritage. By what right 'does a Corsican ... shed the best and most pure blood of France. Does he want to replace the French family he came to extinguish with his half-African family?' Bonaparte 'had not an ounce of this blood in his veins' which for Chateaubriand explains the excessive barbarity of his wars, the prodigious shedding of French blood. The 'least significant Frenchman would be preferable to Buonaparte ... at least we would be spared the dishonor of obeying a foreigner'. This half-barbaric, alien usurper is 'the child of our Revolution' and closely resembles his parentage. The true France is to be found in her kings, whose blood, like Chateaubriand's own, runs pure through the centuries. Louis XVI's younger brothers are presented as the embodiment of France. Louis XVIII is endowed with 'fixed ideas', and the moderation and good sense 'so necessary for a monarch'. He is also 'a friend of literature, well-educated and eloquent as [have been] several of our kings, [and possessed of] a broad and enlightened intelligence, a firm and philosophic character'. Few would recognize the restored Bourbons from Chateaubriand's appreciation.

This co-mingling of blood, history, habits, and institutions proved a heady and durable concoction. In the *Grand Larousse du xixe siècle*, one of the scholarly monuments of the Third Republic, all these scurrilous accusations are repeated. The *légende noire* has become historical truth, as has French nationalism based on blood. Napoleon is 'a foreigner by race and by his ideas', reads the *Grand Larousse*, 'his regime was a pure imitation of Byzantine caesarism'. Chateaubriand's is the vision of a man enthralled by bloodlines. 'I was born a gentleman,' he writes more thoughtfully some years after the feverish *Du Buonaparte*:

> I have profited from the chance of my birth, I have cherished the love of liberty that belonged principally to the aristocracy whose last hour has sounded. The aristocracy had three successive ages: that of superiority, that of privilege, that of vanity. Leaving behind the first it degenerates into the second, and is extinguished in the last.

Unlike Edmund Burke's historically based conservatism, Chateaubriand's views are anchored in the abstractions of race, xenophobia, and the mysteries of blood. It would prove a tragic example and a worse inheritance.

Chateaubriand wrote vast, sprawling books whose ostensible subjects – Christianity, Christian martyrs, his travels, classical revolutions – provided the context of the dominant subject: himself. His account of Napoleon occupies close to 400 of the 2000 pages that make up his autobiography, *Mémoires d'outre-tombe* (*Memoirs from Beyond the Grave*). He originally began a work, entitled *Mémoires de ma vie*, the year before he resigned from Napoleon's service and retired from public life. In Rome he scribbled a few lines: 'After having wandered in error on this earth, passed the best years of my youth far from my country, and suffered almost everything that a man can suffer, including hunger, I returned to Paris in 1800.' He did not begin systematic composition until 1811. The *Mémoires* were published posthumously, literally justifying its odd title: it was a voice from beyond the grave. The *Mémoires* are obsessed with love, politics, and their author's sensibility. His portrait of Napoleon, more measured, more brilliantly written, and more thoughtful than the hysterical indictment of his 1814 pamphlet, is, with that of Mme de Staël, one of the most searching. The *Mémoires* sometimes use the conceit of a Plutarchian parallel life, himself and Napoleon. His judgments on the events of his tumultuous times and the men and women who made and lived them are well-informed, memorably expressed, and penetrating. 'The tomb,' he writes, 'relieved Mirabeau of his promises and put him beyond the reach of dangers which, in truth, he could not have overcome. His life had revealed his weakness to do good. In death he still had the power to do evil.' His description of Robespierre is equally brilliant:

> At the end of a violent discussion I saw a deputy of ordinary appearance mount the tribune. He was bland and self-contained in appearance, carefully coiffed, correctly dressed, like the manager of a good estate or a village notary fastidious about his person. He delivered a long and boring report which no one listened to. I asked his name. It was Robespierre.

The French Revolution was divided into three great epochs for Chateaubriand, each with a dominant revolutionary figure:

> Mirabeau for the aristocracy. Robespierre for democracy, and Bonaparte for despotism. France has paid dearly for three famous men who could not recognize virtue.

He first met Napoleon face-to-face at a party given by Lucien Bonaparte to celebrate the adoption of the Concordat with the Papacy. 'I was in the gallery,' he writes, 'when Napoleon entered. He made an agreeable impression on me. I had never before seen him except at a distance':

> His smile was caressing and beautiful. His eyes were admirable, especially by the way they were placed in his face and set off by his eye-brows. There was then no charlatanism in his gaze, nothing theatrical or affected.

He goes on to remark that Napoleon had read his *Génie du christianisme* and had a 'prodigious imagination that animated his calculating politics'. He concluded 'all these men who have lived great lives are made up of two natures, because they must be capable of action and inspiration. The latter imagines, the former does'. Virtually all the other contemporary portraits of Napoleon, and there are many score, fix upon the contrast between his unimpressive stature and the grandeur of his deeds. Chateaubriand seeks the essence of the man behind a few physical characteristics, with no mention of his slight frame. The great fabulist was not one of Napoleon's intimates. His insights are derived from a powerful mind and a poet's and novelist's imagination rather than close observation. His account proceeds biographically and chronologically, beginning in Corsica and ending in St Helena. From his earliest acts, Bonaparte, 'although a revolutionary, showed himself an enemy of the people'. He succeeded in the Revolution because he was unhindered by the constraints imposed by innocence. 'The Revolution was kind to those who had shared her crimes.' Some of Bonaparte's power, he falsely charges, 'came from having mixed in the Terror'. Napoleon had nothing to do with the Terror nor did he share in the crimes of the Revolution, unless serving in the army counts.

Terrorist or not, Chateaubriand's Napoleon had unexpected gifts not often found in military men. On a number of occasions he singles out a Bonaparte letter for praise as memorably written. 'What vivacity! What diversity of genius!' he writes of a letter sent to Lazare Carnot, then minister of war, from Italy in 1796: 'With the intelligence of heroes are mixed pell-mell, in a triumphal profusion, the paintings of Michelangelo, [and] biting raillery against a rival.' That same day Bonaparte wrote to the Directory informing them 'of the suspension of hostilities granted to the Duke of Parma and sending Correggio's *Saint-Jerome*' to Paris. Juxtaposition, a literary device Chateaubriand himself brilliantly played with, is what struck him. In Bonaparte's correspondence 'we see the course of a needle [*navette*] through the series of revolutions descended from ours.' At the same time he scolded Bonaparte for his undisciplined mind. In his traveling library 'one finds *Ossian*, [Goethe's] *The Sorrows of Young Werther*, [Rousseau's] *New Heloise*, and the *Old Testament*: an indication of the chaos in Napoleon's head'. He indiscriminately mixes hard facts with romantic sentiment, philosophic systems with chimeras, serious historical studies with the phantoms of imagination, wisdom with folly. The Empire is the reflection 'of these incoherent creations of the century ... an immense illusion ... Like the disordered night thoughts that gave it life'. A curious objection from a writer whose work shares many of the same qualities.

'The patricians began the Revolution, the plebeians ended it' is Chateaubriand's celebrated epigram. Napoleon's role was to insure the plebeian triumph. He was 'the proletarian king'. When he ascended the throne 'he had the people sit with him' while 'he humiliated the kings and the nobles in his antechambers':

He leveled the ranks of society, not by debasing them but by elevating them. Lowering the upper classes would have better appealed to the jealousy of the plebeians. Raising the level flattered their pride. The vanity of the French was inflated by the superiority that Bonaparte gave them over the rest of Europe. Another cause of Napoleon's popularity came from the suffering of his last days. After his death, to the degree that they learned what he had suffered on St Helena, they began to feel sympathy.

His personal triumph was blighted by his immorality. 'So long as he attacked the anarchy [at home] and the enemies of France, he was victorious. He found himself despoiled of his vigor as soon as he followed corrupt paths'. 'Two acts, both evil, began and then led to his fall: the death of the duc d'Enghien and the war in Spain.' In France Napoleon

> transformed himself into a king of the old race who attributed everything to himself, who spoke only of himself, who believed he could gratify or punish by saying merely that he was satisfied or displeased. Many centuries of royal rule and a long series of tombs at Saint Denis would not excuse such arrogance.

Because he brutally violated the natural order of things Chateaubriand's Napoleon is a species of monster, sometimes described as a wild, wounded beast, sometimes as a hysterical child. His famous temper tantrums – 'I will go to St Petersberg, I will cast that city in the Neva River' – he likens to the roar of a wounded lion. When Napoleon crossed the Dnieper, leaving his army behind, he burned the papers 'he had brought along to write his life in the long, tedious winter days, had Moscow remained unburned and permitted him to establish himself there'. In a fit of pique, 'he threw the enormous cross of St John' into the lake'.

Unlike other men, Napoleon had no pity. From his lips there came no sympathy for the sorrows of France: 'Bonaparte levied on us suffering like a tribute that was due him.' 'It was in blood that Bonaparte was accustomed to wash the linen of the French.' He was 'the greatest genius of action who ever existed' but he cannot be judged 'by the rules that apply to the greatest geniuses, because he had no magnanimity'. He had an amoral and protean suppleness. Like Satan he could fit his unparalleled self into 'a confined space'. He had the means of transforming himself, 'changing at will habits and costumes, as perfect in comic as in tragic [roles], this actor knew how to appear perfectly natural in the tunic of a slave as in the robes of a king, in the role of Attila or that of Caesar ...' His egotism was 'ferocious'. He surrounded himself with the most shameful and disgraced men. Joseph Fouché, his chief of police, was a blowhard, a maker of 'hollow phrases' filled with philosophical nonsense who spoke 'of the most frightful disasters with lightness and indifference, like some genius above such sordid things'. Talleyrand distanced himself from violence and corruption. He was a man deprived of energy. This married priest 'was so dishonorable he could not be a great criminal'. He never troubled himself over the 'difficulties that flowed from good or evil, because he could not see them. He lacked a moral sense'. His most quoted characterization of the two is sometimes, incorrectly, attributed to Napoleon:

> The door opened at once and vice supported on the arm of crime silently entered. M. de Talleyrand walked supported by M. Fouché. The infernal vision slowly passed before me, entered the king's study and disappeared. Fouché came to swear fealty and homage to his Lord. The regicide, on his knees, put his hands that had caused Louis XVI's head to fall into the hands of the martyred king's brother. The apostate bishop provided a guarantee of the oath.

Only a great writer could be so eloquently venomous.

Chateaubriand's losses, both personal and cultural, could never be restored. The ghosts that haunted him were never laid to rest. His portrait of Napoleon is not balanced but it is brilliant: he could write and think as few are capable of doing. His comparison of Napoleon with George Washington is a stunning conceit. It allows him simultaneously to appreciate the historical reality of the Revolution and Napoleon's genius yet envision another outcome. He writes of having visited Washington in Philadelphia, a reality that has been questioned. In another passage he writes only of having seen the great man as he rode past: 'his gaze fell upon me! I felt warmed for the rest of my life.' Unlike Napoleon 'there is virtue in the gaze of [this] great man'. The American retired to his Virginia estate. Bonaparte awaited exile at Malmaison:

> Nothing had changed in the life of [Washington]. He returned to his modest habits, he was not elevated above the happiness of the laborers he had set free. Everything was overthrown in the life of Napoleon.

Every comparison of Napoleon and Washington is invidious. The former fought brutally and 'wanted only to create his own renown'. He was 'in a hurry to enjoy and abuse his glory, like a young fugitive'.

Perched like a bird of prey over the world 'with one hand he cast down kings, with the other he killed the revolutionary giant. But in destroying anarchy he stifled liberty, and ended by losing his own liberty on his last battlefield'. Washington 'wanted what he should have wanted'. He committed no great crimes and 'blended his existence with that of his country'. 'His glory is the patrimony of civilization. His renown was elevated like one of those public sanctuaries from which flow a nourishing and inexhaustible fountain.'

Near the end of his life of Napoleon Chateaubriand paints one of his moving elegiac scenes:

> I found myself in front of a poplar planted at the edge of a field of hops ... I crossed the road and leaned against the trunk of the tree, my face turned toward Brussels. A south wind had risen carrying with some clarity the sound of artillery. The great battle, still without a name, whose sounds I heard echo from the foot of that tree, and where a village clock began sounding the death knell of a soul unknown, was the Battle of Waterloo.

The poet who lived so deeply in his thoughts and reveries of the past, who had been forced by history into the politics of the present, would much have preferred to return to that vanished world of his dreams, fantasies, and fictions. The Revolution and Napoleon had made that impossible. Chateaubriand never forgave them.

*****

That 'crow'. That 'bitch'. That 'miserable woman'. That 'whore'. These were Napoleon's epithets for Mme de Staël. She got under his skin in ways that go far beyond her books, her brilliant salon, her flamboyant life. He pursued her obsessively and his punishments were cruel. Mme de Staël was everything he hated: a blue-stocking, the very incarnation of the liberal ideologues of Saint-Germain he distrusted and loathed, an aggressive woman who meddled in politics, the mistress of many (including a few of his foes), the friend and celebrator of English freedom and German culture, a plain woman who dressed extravagantly and provocatively, the fabulously rich daughter of a foolish father, and a writer whose semi-autobiographical novels attacked his core beliefs about women and the family. On the long list of those who had done him real harm – including Fouché, Talleyrand, Tsar Alexander, Emperor Franz, Metternich, the Duke of Wellington – there are none he so vilified. Mme de Staël, along with

Hudson Lowe, occupies a special place in his malevolence. Her life is inseparable from the two books she wrote about herself and Napoleon whose titles faithfully convey her approach. She worked on *Considérations sur la Révolution française* (*Considerations on the French Revolution*) and *Dix années d'exil* (*Ten Years of Exile*) simultaneously in the last few years of her life, transplanting passages from one to the other. Both were published posthumously, and both were heavily edited by her son who was her literary executor. Napoleon read the *Considérations* and, not surprisingly, despised the work. Together the books comprise a single autobiographical history of Mme de Staël's age and are fundamental texts, along with Chateaubriand's *Mémoires*, in the *légende noir* of Napoleon.

Germaine Necker was born in Paris in 1766 and never lost her love, indeed her addiction, to the city. Her father, Jacques, although Swiss and Calvinist, was twice Louis XVI's Controller General, first in the late 1770s and early 1780s when he published the first and only budget of the French monarchy. The *compte rendu* proclaimed a sizeable surplus when the fisc was hopelessly in debt and obscured the dimensions of the kingdom's bankruptcy. His disgrace (in 1789) set in motion or coincided with the chain of events that culminated in the attack on the Bastille. He was recalled to office and again dismissed (in 1790), this time under pressure from the Constituent Assembly. He strongly opposed their suppression of titles of nobility, a view also held by his daughter. He retired, with his substantial personal fortune, to his estate at Coppet, on Lake Leman in Switzerland, and spent his retirement justifying his ministries, lamenting the fact that his advice went unheeded, and defending his view that the best government was a monarchical republic dominated by a social and intellectual elite. Germaine's mother, Suzanne Curchod, the daughter of a Swiss pastor, was the woman over whom Edward Gibbon 'sighed as a lover' and 'obeyed as a son' when his father forbade their marriage.

Germaine was no beauty. The Baronne d'Oberkirch, who had spent much time at the court of Louis XVI and knew the value of beauty, thought her ugly. But she was brilliant. Her mother had put the child through a course of study so rigorous and relentless, one of her biographers argues, that the daughter came to fear and even hate Suzanne. Her father she adored. History played a nasty trick on Germaine. She had the brains, the wit, the self-confidence, the connections, the money, and the passion for politics to take her place in the world of affairs. She had always associated with the best and most sophisticated company, whether in literature, politics, the arts, or banking. When her father was the crown's first minister her mother presided over one of the

Figure 11   Portrait of Mme de Staël as Corinne (1807–8), by Elizabeth Vigée-LeBrun. The artist, herself long in exile from France, painted Mme de Staël as the most famous of her fictional heroines. The canvas is large for Vigée-LeBrun, nearly 5 feet by 4 feet, presents Corinne/de Staël as a bard strumming a lyre, a familiar symbol of the poet and a reference to the vogue for the (forged) *Ossian* poems, an enthusiasm Napoleon shared. The subject has a look of exaltation, creative rather than religious in this case. On the hilltop in the background is the Temple of the Sybil at Tivoli, striking another symbolic chord: the prophetic quality of de Staël's work. Both symbols were dear to the early Romantics.

most important *salons* in Europe, the last such in France before the Revolution. She moved easily and comfortably among those the world took an interest in, and she could talk and argue with the best of them. But she was a woman. She found the constraints placed upon her intolerable and unbreakable. The best she could hope for was to impinge upon events through the career of a man, or the indirect and dubious influence of her scintillating conversation and her books. She married the baron of Staël-Holstein, the Swedish ambassador to the French court. He may have had a hand in the assassination of his king, Gustav III, but he made few conjugal demands on his bride. She bore him a child, retained his name and title, and lived her own life apart from the accommodating baron. Her lovers included some of the most brilliant and influential men of the day: Talleyrand, Benjamin Constant, and the count of Narbonne to name a few. She briefly helped make Narbonne a minister of the crown just as the monarchy itself was going under. She would later attempt the same with Benjamin Constant. She aspired to join Napoleon, as wife or lover, as the arbiter of Europe.

She first set forth her political principles and dialectical skills in *Des Circonstances actuelles qui peuvent terminer la Révolution en France* (*Real Conditions which Could End the Revolution in France*), in 1798, which she did not publish. Her first publication, *De la littérature* (*On Literature*), which appeared in 1800, offered the relative safety of a book not obviously about politics. She was 34 years old and already a formidable intellectual, although her major works were yet to come. She had recently met the hero of the day, the young Napoleon, just returned from his Italian triumphs. For one of the few times in her life Germaine stood with the majority on 6 December 1797 to welcome the victorious Bonaparte home. Talleyrand reports that Napoleon paid little attention to her. Four days later the Directors hosted a solemn reception in the courtyard of the Luxembourg Palace. They were dressed in togas, Napoleon in a simple uniform. Talleyrand, in his welcoming speech, praised the general's 'insatiable love of Fatherland and humanity' along with his contempt for pomp and his love of the poetry of *Ossian*. Bonaparte at first felt ill at ease in her company, and would soon camouflage his ineptitude with women of the world with the bonhomie of male vulgarity. Germaine, always impetuous, set out to charm Bonaparte, as she had already charmed his brothers Joseph and Lucien. She described her first impressions of him years later when early infatuation had worn off:

> He then at least looked less disagreeable than he now is. He was thin and pale and one could believe that his own ambition devoured

him, while after some years, he seemed puffed up from the evils he caused. But he was always short and ignoble, his gaiety was vulgar, his politeness *gauche* ... and his manner was to be gross and rude, above all to women.

Despite her shaky first encounter Germaine later welcomed the hero home from Egypt. 'This man,' she wrote her friend Henri Meister, 'is worth more than an army', which he had just left behind. She welcomed the *coup d'état* of 18 Brumaire, shedding no tears for the end of the Directory. Years later things looked different. 'If it had been a question of seeing Jacobinism reestablished in France,' she explained, 'or supporting Bonaparte, not then knowing that his reign would cost almost ten million men [an invented and exaggerated figure], I would have done as France did, which did not love him but preferred him [to the other possibilities].' All her statistics are bloated, whether for effect or out of ignorance, and she never spent any sustained time in Napoleon's presence. She was not at St Cloud when he drove the senators out. She viewed the whole of his career from a distance and depended on the testimony or gossip of friends for details both intimate and social. Only years later did she record reaction to the *coup d'état*: I 'felt in that moment difficulty breathing, which soon became, I believe, the affliction of all those who lived under Bonaparte's authority.' The shrewdest observers of Napoleon studied him from the outside.

Mme de Staël remained infatuated until she suffered a severe rebuke, a narcissistic injury from which she never recovered. The most celebrated anecdote of the inauguration of their bitter enmity dates from the winter of 1801 at General Berthier's. It would be the last time she and Bonaparte came face to face. Germaine had been tongue-tied when they first met. This time she prepared in advance, anticipating the questions the hero might ask. Bonaparte, with his brother Lucien, passed through the throng. He stopped before Mme de Staël and stared at her décolletage. Along with her large often feathered turbans, her cleavage was always prominent. 'No doubt,' said Bonaparte, 'you have nursed your children yourself?' Here was a remark she had not anticipated. 'You see,' said Bonaparte turning to Lucien, 'she doesn't even want to say yes or no.' Blunt, vulgar, misogynist, dismissive. Not a word about her books, her ideas, her self. The war between the two was not just a clash of personalities. They held diametrical ideas, not least about the Revolution. Once Napoleon's insult had driven Germaine into opposition their very real political differences came to the fore. It was a completely lopsided contest. The master of the greatest European empire was bullying a single woman.

Then there was the matter of two million francs her father had loaned the Royal treasury in 1778 to buy bread for the poor during one of the periodic harvest crises. Almost a decade later he tried to recover his money with interest. For years he had received 100,000 francs a year in interest and was content to let the capital pay its dividend. In 1793 the Convention suspended payment of dividends and nationalized the debt. The Directory was uninterested in returning Necker's millions. With Bonaparte and the reestablishment of social order Necker and his daughter became again optimistic and renewed their request. Mme de Staël's correspondence with Bonapartist officials, and she knew them all, is filled with requests for the two million expressed in all the registers of politeness, insistence, cajolery, or need. She even sent her son, Auguste, to negotiate reimbursement with Napoleon himself. He received the boy and treated him to a tirade:

> Your grandfather was an ideologist, a madman, a senile maniac [he barked at Auguste]. [He was] a stubborn old man who on his death-bed kept twaddling about the government of nations ... It was he who overthrew the monarchy and led Louis XVI to the scaffold ... Yes, I am telling you, even Robespierre, Marat, Danton have done less harm to France than Monsieur Necker. It's he who made the Revolution.

The millions became an obsession. Germaine's daughter became betrothed to the Broglie family, a match she passionately desired, but they would not budge on the dowry. Marriage into a great noble house was ever the stuff of hard bourgeois bargaining. Germaine desperately needed money. In 1814 she wrote the Bonapartists and the Royalists simultaneously arguing her case and pledging her allegiance to each, unsure of who would ultimately sit on the throne. Louis XVIII finally restored the money, with interest. He was not discouraged by the shameless flattery Mme de Staël poured upon him.

Chateaubriand's *Mémoires d'outre-tombe* is suffused with longing for a vanished past and the melancholy and unutterable sadness that the murder of his family in the Terror etched into his soul. The French Revolution and Napoleon mark the end of the only life he thought worth living. All this is expressed with superb literary art. Mme de Staël's posthumous books about Napoleon are filled with anger at her personal hardships caused by exile, the nagging and unresolved business of her father's money, and a long catalogue of Napoleon's cruelties and caprices. Her style is that of a great talker rather than a great writer.

Jacques Norvins, an *émigré* who would rally to Napoleon and eventually become one of his earliest and best historians – his account of the disastrous expedition to St Domingue (Haiti) is superb – knew Mme de Staël in Coppet. She later would save his life by having his *émigré* status expunged so he could return to France. He remembered her presiding over 'a kind of open-air Olympus where, under her auspices, some deities of French civilization, dethroned and pursued by new Titans, found an asylum, and where, as did those of ancient Greece, they consoled themselves for the loss of their grandeur in the enjoyment of humane society'. What he remembered 50 years later, in feeling and not detail, were the conversations in her salon: brilliant, improvisational, often sublime, and always scintillating. Nothing is so ephemeral as conversation. Her writing, for Norvins, presented only an approximation of her verbal fireworks. 'Writing for her was a kind of diminution' of her talk which depended on 'a harmony' between heaven and earth. When she wrote, he continues, she translated her conversation. Stendhal, who had never heard Mme de Staël talk but disliked her for her opinions, discerned the conversational origin of her writing. 'Mme de Staël's book,' he told a friend, 'is only written conversation, a contradictory and childish work, ... on its knees before the greatest evil of society itself, the nobility.' The oral basis of her prose may account for the lack of tight, sustained argument, the disorderly arrangement of her materials, and the interspersed *bon mots* that have an improvisatory flavor, happy phrases struck off in inspired conversation.

Considérations is filled with a close record of her emotional responses to her long struggle with Napoleon. Though it is not a conventional history of the French Revolution and Napoleon, she makes few factual errors. The erudite Jacques Godechot, who edited the book, gives her high marks for accuracy. He notes that she did look at some sources and authorities, but precious few. The *Considérations* and the *Dix années* are more works of sensibility than scholarship, observation rather than analysis, memory rather than study, argument rather than narrative. Recollections and encounters are woven together and it is Mme de Staël's personality that holds the books together. The liberal Mme de Staël and the royalist Chateaubriand are often in complete accord. Her Napoleon is a monster of egotism. 'Bonaparte is not merely a man, but a system.' As a man he had no humanity. Everything was calculated for his immediate benefit. 'Whenever he saw some advantage in cruelty he indulged it ... although his nature was not sanguinary.' He shed blood as easily as well-off men spend money when it is needed. If his ambition was checked he did not hesitate for a moment to 'sacrifice others to himself'. She cites his behavior in Egypt for proof. He was a 'genius of storms' and truly alive 'only in agitation'. He only 'breathed freely in a volcanic atmosphere'. He was not a religious man. His only faith was 'in the cult of himself'. His natural inclination was toward despotism and 'he would have loved the *ancien régime* of France more than anyone, if he could have persuaded everyone that he was descended from Saint Louis'. Even his military genius, grudgingly accepted by almost all his enemies, was tainted for Mme de Staël, as it was for Chateaubriand. 'He risked everything to gain everything, counting on the mistakes of his enemies whom he despised; and he was ready to sacrifice his partisans, whom he cared little for, if he did not gain a victory.' He was interested only in 'the considerations of the moment, and looked at things only in terms of their immediate usefulness'. She adds, in a fine metaphor, 'he wanted to hold the whole world as a *rente viagère*' [a life tenure that disappeared at death].

Mme de Staël's psychological portrait of Napoleon paints him bigger than life. His egotism was pure, preventing him from feeling pity or concern for others. Neither religion nor morality could 'deflect him for an instant from his goal'. He was, in the first of a series of fine phrases, 'the great bachelor of the world'. He was 'first in the art of personal calculation, last in the realm of feelings'. An accomplished 'chess player whose opponent was humanity, which he strove to check-mate'. He was a rude bully: 'I believe,' she writes, 'that France never had a head of government who said so many unpleasant things to those who surrounded him.' Not unlike Mm de Staël, he loved to hear himself talk, but his talk was not a search for truth, a display of wit, let alone a manifestation of civilization. It was a 'cyclone' of political dissimulation. Despite the torrent of words 'one could not repeat any single utterance of his that had grace or true grandeur'. He was mendacious and manipulative. Had the Revolution not given him a social and political blank slate upon which to write his lies he could never have triumphed. He could not bear the talk of others. Every three months the armchair he sat in during meetings of the *Conseil d'état* had to be reupholstered, because impatient during meetings 'he hacked at it with a small knife'.

In no man, for Germaine, had so much grandeur been combined with so much cynicism. Tocqueville remarked that Napoleon was as great as a man can be who lacks the least shred of virtue. At times her hatred of the man compromised her good sense and left her writing absurdities. Unlike Caesar 'general Bonaparte only faced adversaries whose names are not worth mentioning'. As the master of '80 million men, unencumbered by any opposition, [he] was incapable of founding a single state institution' or securing his own power. He was so upset upon learning of the death of Tsar Paul I, Alexander's father, that for the first (and perhaps only?) time in his life the words 'Oh my God' escaped his lips. Bonaparte was made by the Revolution, but for Mme de Staël it is 'the violent and debased Revolution' that formed him, 'certainly not that which the leading classes of society had desired and imagined'. Like Chateaubriand in his more violent moments, Napoleon is not so much the Revolution incarnate as the embodiment of its crimes.

Napoleon met Jacques Necker only once, in 1800, on his way to Italy. His daughter's account of the interview differs from the First Consul's. Napoleon was polite enough, even respectful, in Mme de Staël's telling, for her father commanded respect. Necker, for his part, she reported, later praised Napoleon in print as 'the necessary man' who saved France from anarchy. On St Helena Napoleon told Las Cases he found Necker 'a stupid college regent, pompous and shallow'. He told Montholon 'M. Necker ... was incapable of saving the throne. I talked with him when I passed through Geneva. He was a competent first secretary of the treasury, nothing more'. He found the entire first third of her *Considérations*, devoted to Necker, unreadable. 'She stands in adoration before her father. He is a man without faults, who only did marvelous things!' In fact, Napoleon offers his own overblown and false analysis, the same one he had delivered to Mme de Staël's son: 'he caused the Revolution by [supporting] the double representation of the Third Estate, although he could not have wished it.' Chateaubriand was more generous but agreed about Necker's limitations. He was

> a capable paymaster, but an economist without answers. A noble writer but pompous. An honest man but without the highest virtue, this banker was one of those old personages who appear before the proscenium and disappear when the curtain goes up, after having provided a prologue for the audience ... his vanity kept him from admitting that his true claim on posterity would be the glory of his daughter.

Necker's French Revolution, which he foolishly thought his few acts and superficial understanding could direct, was inherited and embraced by Mme de Staël. She distrusted the masses and paid them little or no attention, loathed the Jacobins, and believed, with her father, that the Revolution had gone hopelessly awry when men of her class lost control, early in the Constituent Assembly. Necker's opposition to abolishing titles of nobility, in 1790, is a convenient *point de départ*, a symbolic and real moment when the initiative passed from the hands of the moderate, reforming monarchists, of whom Necker was one, definitively into the hands of the radical orators of the Third Estate. They systematically dismantled the social, political, and economic structures and distinctions of the *ancien régime* and thus betrayed the Revolution. Napoleon became the inevitable despot who emerged from a revolution based on force, brutality, and terror.

She believed that society was best managed and freedom achieved when the rich, the well-born, and the able, to echo John Adams, governed under the rule of law. Not unlike Napoleon she confined equality to the law and showed little interest in social justice. It was Napoleon, she curiously believed, who carried the Revolution's obsession with equality to its perverse conclusion. 'You want equality,' she imagines him saying. 'I will do even better. I will give you inequality tipped in your favor. The de la Trémoiles, the Montmorencys, and their ilk, will be legally simple bourgeois in the state, while all the titles of the *ancien régime* ... will be attached to the most vulgar names, so long as they please the emperor.' Although she believed enlightenment was spread by education and many, perhaps all, were capable of it, this would take time. Until the day the people became enlightened and able to govern themselves in a republic under the guidance of superior men and women, she and her friends would govern in the interest of all. Although she distrusted the masses and remained enthralled by the values and wealth of her class, she was a passionate advocate for individual freedom, not least because as a woman she had so little. Had she not been the heiress of a great fortune she would have been far more miserable than she was. Mary Wollstonecraft, who had no personal fortune and struggled always, twice attempted suicide; Mme de Staël wrote a pamphlet on suicide in which she considered the special problems confronting women.

More than her political writings, however, it is in her fiction, now little read, where her pleas for freedom – individual, sexual, and social – are best heard. *Délphine*, her first novel, is both autobiographical and a *roman à clef*. It is also a passionate brief for freedom, and concludes with an appeal to a future France. Bonaparte himself wrote an anonymous diatribe against the novel in the *Journal des Débats*. He denounced its principles as 'completely false, antisocial, and very dangerous', encouraged others to do the same, and savaged its author. He forbade its sale at the Frankfurt book fair and warned Germaine's friends that if she came to Paris 'I will be obliged to have the *gendarmerie* accompany her to the border'.

Napoleon, Mme de Staël argued, might have saved France and the Revolution had he not been an egotistical monster. He could have limited his kingdom to its natural borders, the Rhine and the Alps, and created within these borders a 'free constitution the example [of which] would gradually have affected the entire continent'. The ideals of the Revolution would have corroded the obfuscation, ignorance, and superstition of the *ancien régime*. 'One would no longer have heard it said that liberty can only thrive in England because she is an island.' Instead Napoleon chose personal glory, violently completed the work of the Revolution that had been betrayed by demagogues, created a despotism, and ruined France. His constitution established a monarchy, she says, quoting the Younger Pitt, 'which lacked only legitimacy and limits'. Nothing short of Napoleon's defeat, which meant the defeat of France, could end his reign. She boldly and dangerously hoped for his defeat, beginning in 1800 with the battle of Marengo.

Napoleon continued to fulminate against her, even as she lay dying. In his tirades we see him at his worst, his most vulgar, petty, and cruel. 'She said,' he ranted to Bertrand, 'that the empress Josephine was an imbecile unworthy to be my wife; that it was only she, Mme de Staël, who belonged with me. She was crazy about me.' The two women were 'antipodes'. 'One was a woman from her toes to her head; the other was nothing but a cunt.' She was 'very dangerous because she gathered together in her salon all the extremists ... she united them all against me ... It is she,' he rambled obsessively, 'who began the corruption of [General] Bernadotte.' He banned her from living within forty leagues (120 miles) of Paris because of *Délphine*. To supervise the printing of *De l'Allemagne* (*On Germany*), her most influential book and the earliest exploration of the uniqueness of German culture in its classical age, she moved (1810) to the magnificent château of Chaumont-sur-Loire, in the department of the Loir-et-Cher, whose prefect was lenient and humane. She submitted the manuscript to the censor, Portalis, an intelligent and decent man. He asked for a number of changes, all of which she made. As soon as Napoleon got wind of all this he instructed his chief of police, Savary, to confiscate the work and expel its author. He had the proofs seized and destroyed, and demanded the original copy as well. She managed to save only two copies.

Out of spite he forbade her son, Auguste, to enroll in the École Polytechnique, and when he learned that Necker's millions were needed to pay her daughter's dowry, he adamantly refused yet again to release the money. 'I have merited, I hope, this exile for myself,' she wrote. 'But Bonaparte, who took the trouble to learn how further to wound me, wanted to disturb the intimacy of our domestic life, by blaming my father for my exile.' For Germaine exile from Paris was banishment from the life she loved and needed. Paris was the center of the civilized world in which she had grown up:

> One can voluntarily pass one's life outside one's country, but when one is constrained to do so, one imagines ceaselessly that the objects of one's affections might be ill without being permitted to be with them, without perhaps ever seeing them again.

'In Europe-France' there was no escape from Napoleon's despotism. Only England offered a haven, and England was France's enemy. The victory at Waterloo devastated Mme de Staël, who lamented the humiliation of France, although not Napoleon's ruin.

It is the image and the reality of Mme de Staël, her family, and her entourage, wandering across Europe, that remains a perpetual rebuke to Napoleon's long vendetta. She even traveled to Russia where the great Pushkin much admired her observations on his country, reaching Moscow just ahead of Napoleon's armies. Despite her many friends, her large fortune, and her fame, she was only a single woman, relentlessly pursued by the most powerful man of the age. It is that contrast that sets in high relief the courage that sustained Mme de Staël. When Napoleon returned from Elba he seduced Benjamin Constant into becoming a minister. He also sought Germaine's blessing and offered blandishments, including her father's two million. She was by then weary, although only 50, and the chance to live in Paris before she died was compelling. But she kept her integrity to the end. She spurned Napoleon.

XI
The End of the End Game

It took the *Northumberland* 71 days to sail from Plymouth to the island of St Helena. The officers of the 78-gun warship were instructed to keep their hats on in Napoleon's presence and address him only as 'General'. His assigned cabin measured nine by twelve feet, and even for a man who took little pleasure at table he thought the food fit only for a British warship. His comrades in exile, excluding his household staff, were an inharmonious quartet. Henri-Gatien, Count Bertrand was a general and marshal in the *génie*. Napoleon, exaggerating, called him 'the best engineer since Vauban'. He was taciturn, efficient, deeply loyal despite the vexations of sharing Napoleon's exile, and one of the two comrades who stayed until his master's death. The other was Charles, Count Montholon, a general descended from an old noble family. He was more distinguished for his supple diplomatic skills and elegant manners of speech and comportment than the rougher virtues of the garrison, the bivouac, or the battlefield. He too was profoundly loyal to Napoleon, his attachment sometimes described as 'filial'. His loyalty was later transferred to Napoleon's nephew. Montholon was implicated in the ill-conceived attempted *coup d'état* at Boulogne in 1840 and went to prison with Louis Napoleon. The other two, General Gaspar Gourgaud and Emmanuel, Count Las Cases, proved the most interesting.

Gourgaud, 33 when he sailed on the *Northumberland*, was the youngest of the four. His social origins were common. He was the son of a court musician and one of the nurses for the Duke de Berry. His life is a testament to Napoleon's policy of careers open to talent. His gift for mathematics earned him a place at the École Polytechnique and he was subsequently commissioned an artillery officer (in 1801). He rose quickly with the fortunes of the Grande Armée. He fought in most of the great battles and obsessively recounted how, as a captain on the Russian campaign, he had saved Napoleon's life. He discovered a cache of powder in the Kremlin that could easily had exploded in the Moscow fire and killed the Emperor and his staff. He was, despite his rank, instantly made a baron of the Empire. At the battle of Brienne (29 January 1814) he more directly saved Napoleon's life by killing a Cossack about to spear the Emperor. Las Cases we have already met. These are Napoleon's Four Evangelists. Bertrand's plain, blunt account is the most complete diary, although 1820 is almost a complete blank, of his and Napoleon's doings as well as the mundane life of the tiny French community. It was inaccessible until 1950 when Paul Fleuriot de Langle, after years of painstaking decipherment, published the first of three volumes as Bertrand's *Cahiers de Sainte-Hélène*. He completed the project in 1959. For reasons unknown Bertrand had kept his notes in a shorthand so deliberately idiosyncratic it was cryptographic. He is without literary gifts, guile, or pretensions. Honest, duty-bound even to the detriment of his marriage, he usually wrote down each night what he heard and saw during the day, while the words were fresh in his memory. His prose (and gaze) is clear, his account is the most comprehensive of the four, and his honesty and diligence as a chronicler unimpeachable.

Montholon wrote long after he had left St Helena (1846) and after he had read Las Cases, from which he drew extensively, in a manner we would today consider plagiarism. In addition it is at least circumstantially convincing that his wife Albine, whom he separated from as soon as he returned to France after Napoleon's death, was the Emperor's mistress. Montholon is thought the least reliable of the Evangelists. He wrote years after the events from scanty notes. He is imprecise and often unreliable about details and chronology. There is some suspicion that when he was imprisoned in the fortress of Ham with Louis Napoleon, Alexander Dumas *père* had a hand, perhaps a heavy hand, in preparing Montholon's notes for publication. But his *Récits de la captivité de l'Empereur Napoléon à Sainte-Hélène* has some information not elsewhere available, which some think reinforces skepticism about his *Récits*. Despite all the reservations about Montholon's reliability, it is perfectly possible that the conversations with Napoleon he reports did take place for they ring true. Montholon had ready and daily access to the Emperor, and was with him when he died. There is a hypothesis based only on circumstance and conjecture that Montholon, working for *Monsieur* (the future Charles X), poisoned Napoleon with arsenic. The cause(s) of Napoleon's death have been debated since 1821. This is discussed in an appendix (pp. 296–7).

Gourgaud's *Journal de Sainte-Hélène* is convincing, spontaneous, and lively but it covers only a few years. He is the most neurotic of the Evangelists. The general felt constantly slighted, unappreciated, and unloved by Napoleon. He was consumed with jealousy. He detested both Las Cases and Montholon, as he frequently told the Emperor. 'The latecomers are the most loved,' he lamented. He himself had seen 'Lannes, Bessières and Duroc' die. 'They were the true servants, the disciples of His Majesty' yet Napoleon 'regretted them less than Las Cases' who early returned to the mainland. Gourgaud was always resentful, lonely, and often morose. His journal, unlike any of the others, is punctuated by incessant and revealing complaints about the miseries of St Helena, the filthy weather, the poisonous relationships in Napoleon's entourage, worries about his future, and his almost unrelieved *ennui*. These complaints are important aspects of his *Journal* and make it compelling.

The weather was hideous at Longwood. The wind howled incessantly, destroying trees and vegetation and driving everyone indoors. The wallpaper peeled off the perpetually damp walls, and the rats scampered through the rooms and could be heard scratching behind the walls. They were regularly hunted by Napoleon's domestics. One of the hypotheses advanced for poisoning is that the rats were killed with arsenic. Gourgaud records all these details. He writes without literary affectation or self-consciousness, his chronology is sure and precise, he has a good eye for physical details as well as the psychology of the French who accompanied Napoleon, and he nicely captures his master's personality, never editing the vulgar language, as did Las Cases, or fudging the hurtful impact of the many rebukes he suffered from Napoleon. When Gourgaud left St Helena in March 1818 his departure removed a painful presence. He unburdened himself to Bertrand:

> I am three times, four times, ten times happier since Gourgaud has left [said Napoleon]. What fatigue! ... He told Ali that he would kill Las Cases, if he saw him. He was jealous ... It was his character. In truth that would have made me love hypocrisy. We all have faults, but hide them. We wear *culottes* to cover our behinds. We have base souls but do not reveal them to the whole world. [Gourgaud's behavior] is sincerity pushed so far it becomes a bad quality.

*****

On 15 October 1815 the *Northumberland* anchored off St Helena, which lies 1988 statute miles from Cape Town, 1553 from the west coast of

Africa, and 2174 from the coast of Brazil. The nearest land, Ascension Island, is 1087 miles to the north-east. St Helena is about six miles wide and ten-and-a-half miles long. When Napoleon first saw it he told Gourgaud, 'This is not a happy place to live. I should have stayed in Egypt. I would now be emperor of the entire Orient'. Lost empire would become a chronic lament. Chateaubriand, who saw St Helena only in his imagination, had the perfect description: 'A catafalque of rock.' The atmosphere of the place, to a latter day visitor, was 'threatening, gloomy'. The black cliffs, nearly a thousand feet high, fall sheer into the ocean. 'It gives the impression of a ravaged fortress.' The volcanic island was one of the few uninhabited places in the world when it was discovered by the Portuguese in 1502. Once England gained possession (1659) she continued to use the island as had the Portuguese, as a way-station from the Far East. The Duke of Wellington had stopped briefly on St Helena on his way home from India and later proposed it for Napoleon's prison. England could not have found a more secure or bleak penitentiary. There is only a single suitable anchorage, on the north side of the island; it is here that Jamestown, the only city, is sited. No ship can approach undetected, let alone anchor and land. At the time of Napoleon's arrival the place had a bit more than 5000 extremely diverse inhabitants: a small number of Europeans in a population of Africans, some of them slaves, Chinese, Malays, various Asians, and Madagascarians. To secure their prisoner the British poured troops onto the island until Napoleon and his entourage could hardly take a step without running into a sentry. Each of the victorious Allies sent an observer to watch over the prisoner. Their only duty was 'to assure themselves of his presence'. None ever saw Napoleon face to face, although one viewed him dead. Claude-Henri de Montchenu, the French commissioner, had been chosen by Talleyrand. 'It is my only revenge, but it is terrible,' he told a friend. 'What torture for a man like Napoleon to be obliged to live with an ignorant and pedantic chatterbox. I know him; he cannot endure such boredom; he will become ill, and die as by a slow fire.' Napoleon never encountered Montchenu.

The Cabinet in London was haunted by the possibility of Napoleon's rescue or escape. Hudson Lowe was their zealous and hysterical agent. He followed orders from Lords Bathurst and Liverpool with 'a humiliating compound of meanness and panic,' writes Lord Rosebery. Lowe's inaugural visit to Longwood was on 16 April 1816. 'He is hideous,' was Napoleon's first impression. 'He has a face fit for the gibbet. But let us not be hasty. Character, after all, may transcend what is sinister in this face.' Las Cases describes him as of 'medium height, thin, bony, dry, with red hair and a complexion marked by blotches, with an oblique gaze that avoided eye-contact and rarely looked at you directly, with blond eyebrows, both narrow and prominent.' Subsequent meetings, there were only six in all and none in the last four years of Napoleon's imprisonment, confirmed his first impressions. Lowe's job of jailer made any relationship with the prisoner difficult, but the man himself was the kind of soldier Napoleon's despised. 'M. Lowe is nothing but a scribe like so many we have seen on general staffs, who has done nothing in his life but write worthless reports and tally accounts,' he told Admiral Sir Thomas Reade. Lowe's faults 'come from his life. He has never commanded any troops except foreign deserters (Piedmontese, Corsicans, Sicilians), all renegade traitors to their country, the dregs, the scum of Europe. If he had commanded men, English troops ... he would have some feeling for those he ought to honor.' The greatest captain of the age knew well how to humiliate such a soldier.

The war of the powerless against the petty was uninterrupted by armistice, truce or treaty. One of Hudson Lowe's first acts, which he thought a gesture of polite kindness, was to invite Napoleon to dinner: 'Should the arrangements of General Bonaparte admit it, Sir Hudson and Lady Lowe would feel gratified in the honor of his company to meet the countess at dinner on Monday next at six o'clock.' There was no response. Lowe summoned Bertrand and asked if he had delivered the invitation:

> *Bertrand*: I gave your letter to the Emperor. He has begun to read English. He read it himself and told me he had no response to make ...
> *Lowe*: But it is not as governor that I wrote. It was an invitation to dinner.
> *Bertrand*: I told His Majesty that you asked for a response and I prayed him to tell me what I should reply. 'Write,' he told me, 'that I have no response.'
> *Lowe*: But this is singular! Did he clearly understand that this was an invitation to dinner? That the Countess Loudon [the wife of the governor of India] had arrived? That I invited him as an occasion to meet her? Did he understand all this?
> *Bertrand*: I think so.
> *Lowe*: This is completely extraordinary. At least one should respond. This is not correct. It is an astonishing way to act.

Less than a year earlier Napoleon had been the master of Europe, access to him governed by an elaborate and strictly hierarchical etiquette, applied to kings and commoners alike. Now the man who scrupulously refused to call Napoleon 'emperor' for his government had forbade it – he would neither deliver mail addressed to nor receive notes from the 'Emperor' Napoleon – was shocked that his invitation 'to meet the countess' went unanswered. Lowe treated his prisoner as the equivalent of a British general in disgrace, permanently without a command. The invitation was in his eyes 'an amiable condescension'. Even after Napoleon's death Hudson Lowe maintained his scruples. The Emperor's followers wanted the simple inscription 'Napoleon', with the date and place of his birth and death, engraved on the coffin plate. Lowe refused unless 'Bonaparte' was added. The plate was left blank.

Hudson Lowe ordered that Napoleon be viewed by himself or his sentries twice a day. Napoleon barred the door to the governor, threatened to shoot him if he forced entry, and closed the shutters at Longwood against British spies. The area where Napoleon was accustomed to ride was gradually circumscribed, and he was forbidden to ride without a British escort. He would occasionally take a few turns in his calèche, also with a British escort, but eventually ceased even this. He took no exercise for years, in protest against Lowe's restrictions. The governor sent a long list of food items England would no longer pay for. The expenses of Napoleon's imprisonment were to be shaved. General Montholon, in charge of the Emperor's cellar, complained that the wine sent to Longwood 'was what the lowest class in [French] society drank'. Hudson Lowe was indignant. It might not be what Napoleon was accustomed to drink but the British government provided 'the best it could get'. To publicize the cheese-paring of the British government Napoleon had a significant part of his table silver broken up and ostentatiously sold by weight in Jamestown so he could pay for his own upkeep.

At Longwood the etiquette of Napoleon's now pathetic court was strictly maintained. It kept mundane misery at bay, sustained the fading illusion of greatness, and provided an antidote to Hudson Lowe's surveillance. Life centered on the Emperor. Napoleon filled his days with reading, long soaks in a very hot tub, sometimes nightly public readings from the French classics, chess – he who visualized battlefields as a chessboard was a mediocre player – solving mathematical puzzles with Gourgaud, dictating his life and battles in the morning and less formally talking about himself until he retired for the night. His only deeds were hiding from and infuriating Hudson Lowe. His life had become one of words. His comrades listened and recorded what he said. He was never without an audience and the torrent of words uttered on St Helena were dutifully recorded by this entourage. He knew he spoke always on the record and undoubtedly for posterity. From the time he crowned himself Emperor in 1804 Napoleon had virtually stopped writing. He dictated, making no attempt to accommodate his amanuenses who had trouble keeping up but were too intimidated to ask the great man to slow down or repeat. Almost his entire household, at one time or another, was designated to record their master's utterances. What they produced was a good and invaluable approximation of what he said. All those who listened and transcribed had Napoleon's voice in their inner ear, he often repeated his stories, and there was little else to do on St Helena. His words were twice filtered: his own memory and the tricks it could play, especially when personal glory and the need for myth conflicted with truth, and the written version, more or less influenced by the note-taker and the time that passed between Napoleon's talk and when it was recorded. Las Cases did more editing of Napoleon's dictations than the others, but often there are two or three, and occasionally four, accounts of his utterances which substantially agree.

Taking dictation from Napoleon was no easy exercise. Las Cases complained at length. He had to invent 'a kind of hieroglyphic writing' to keep up with the torrent of words. His ideal, often unrealized, was to capture 'as close as possible ... literally all the Emperor's expressions'. Once Napoleon had started talking he could not be interrupted: 'He paid no attention and continued on to the end.' Las Cases soon gave up interrupting for clarification, afraid he would lose too much while making the request. Napoleon talked in three distinct but related registers. The official recounting of his life and deeds regularly scheduled for the mornings, was somewhat formal, and the outcome was intended for publication. He assigned Gourgaud, Montholon, and Bertrand to record specific battles and campaigns. He began with the Egyptian campaign but the entire series was never completed. Digressions were common. The desultory airing of his opinions on everything, his table talk, was made in less purposeful sessions, most often in the evening when the court gathered. His soliloquies are best characterized as rants delivered as a species of stream of consciousness. He said whatever came into his mind. These verbal rambles, often marred by internal inconsistencies, taken together form a copious collection of his self-presentation as an embodiment of the Revolution, the passionate champion of equality, the man of tireless devotion to duty, and the selfless agent of glory for France and her citizens who was goaded into fighting by his enemies. His interlocutors tried to channel the powerful verbal flow by asking specific questions, but once Napoleon started talking the only control on the process was his own will. The soldiers, Bertrand, Gourgaud, and Montholon, had the manners and the habits of the bivouac. They wanted to hear Napoleon's opinions on his own and enemy generals, his battles and thoughts about war, and recollections of his (and their) glory days. Las Cases, alone among the Evangelists, led Napoleon to tell the story of his life more or less chronologically. Napoleon read and edited his dictations to Las Cases as well as those of his campaigns as soon as a fair copy was made, usually the following day.

The passionate reader of history was dissatisfied with what others had written. On St Helena Napoleon become his own historian. His views on history are original if often predictable. 'Reason,' he told Bertrand, 'is the criterion and eloquence of history', a sound 18th-century opinion, although his tastes often ran against the Enlightenment grain. He had read the master texts of the age as a young man, but he makes only occasional, and usually disapproving, mention of Rousseau, who had enthralled him in his youth, or Voltaire, whose *Charles XII* he read on the Russian campaign. Diderot's dialogues are not mentioned and *l'Encyclopédie*, the most famous work of the Enlightenment, is also absent. Montesquieu's essay on the grandeur and decadence of the Romans is not mentioned nor is his masterpiece, *l'Esprit des lois*. The materialist philosophers are not mentioned nor are the historians Mably or Raynal. Hume and Gibbon are mentioned in passing. Among the ancients Napoleon has very little to say about the books that formed or inspired the minds of his contemporaries. Plutarch, so important to the revolutionaries and to his own youthful longings, is neither discussed nor appraised. He had early lost interest in the moral dimension of history and Livy's epic sweep held little interest. Caesar was a favorite and the *Campagnes d'Egypte et de la Syrie*, the first dictated and the most polished of his military accounts, is profoundly indebted to his predecessor's *Commentaries*. There is no overt indication that he appreciated or maybe even read the ancient Greek historians – Herodotus, Thucydides, and Xenophon are not mentioned – although Alexander's career is often invoked. His rants on St Helena are confined to Tacitus especially, and Suetonius occasionally. He considered both men debasers and polluters of historical truth.

Suetonius was nothing but a 'libelist'. His *Twelve Caesars* is filled with 'inconceivable things'. 'It is a libel identical,' he tellingly says, 'to those they write against me.' The story of the emperor Caligula making his horse consul is dismissed as nothing but a joke-threat made by the emperor when angry with the Senate. 'It is inconceivable that Claudius attended the second marriage of [his notorious ex-wife] Messalina, or that Nero had wanted to burn down his capital ... What pleasure could a sovereign find in such a crime?' Suetonius writes that Tiberius went to Capri 'to commit with children acts of libertinage that I do not believe. Not only because I do not understand how one can find any pleasure in such acts ... but because all the libertines [I know about] in Paris, Rome, or Constantinople do not practice such pleasures.' Tacitus is worse. He is nothing but a colorist, 'a painter and not a historian'. Napoleon says nothing of the fear that gripped the Julio-Claudians, although nine of the 12 emperors were murdered, a fact he knew. Nor does he show any interest in the corruption (and depravity) engendered by absolute power.

The *métier* of history demands that one instruct, make the facts and their causes known, and explain them. 'Men do not act without reasons, whether good or bad. Tacitus explains nothing'. He had made the same arguments to Goethe and Wieland at Erfurt. It is not surprising that he detested the senatorial writers and their anti-imperial, salacious rumor-mongering. He was made uneasy by the assassinations that the senatorial writers tacitly approved (no pun intended). There was, moreover, no grandiosity, no glory in Tacitus and Suetonius; only the grossly exaggerated sordid deeds of repellent rulers and their horrible families. It was not how he wanted himself memorialized. In addition the ancient historians 'loved the marvelous'. When the historian encounters unrealistic events or details Napoleon thought he 'ought to make them disappear'.

Of the historians of his own day, with whom he shared a number of philosophical assumptions, he found David Hume 'too compressed, he doesn't describe the situation of things; one cannot form an opinion about anything from him'. He conceded Hume was 'a philosophic writer' who 'probably wrote well' but the reader was forced to adopt the historian's view of events. Every action, he continued 'ought to have three parts: an exposition, a body, a *dénouement*. Without all three life is lacking'. History should be structured like a French tragedy. He could himself tell the story of 18 Brumaire 'in seven lines' but 'one would not understand the event, one would not know the state of mind [of the participants], the obstacles [involved], or the means'. The only section of Hume's *History of England* Napoleon specifically mentions is the reign of Henry VIII. He thought the English king a monster. 'There is nothing to equal him in ancient history ... I would not believe it if such things were said in an ancient history': but there can be no doubt about Henry's cruelty or Hume's accuracy describing it. 'To chop off Anne Boleyn's head and then marry another wife the next day is an atrocity without parallel ... What an atrocious folly!'

For a man who lived by the sword he was more kind-hearted than they, a reflection of the softening views of the Enlightenment. His relationship with his two wives, whom he remembered affectionately on St Helena, would not have inclined him to Henry VIII. He was a misogynist but not a brute.

Writing from Schönbrunn in 1809 he ordered 'a Gibbon, in duodecimo' for his personal library. He later told Bertrand he was disappointed in *The Decline and Fall of the Roman Empire*. He found Gibbon's account of the reign of Julian the Apostate, a champion of Paganism and one of the historian's heroes, inadequate. He says nothing about the notorious anti-Christianity chapters (XV and XVI), although he shared many of Gibbon's views on religion. Tacitus had offered him no reflections: Gibbon had too many. He 'ought to be abridged to two volumes because [most of his work] is only reflections.' Voltaire 'deformed history by presenting for the veneration of posterity Marshal Soubise and the duc de Richelieu. They are the shame of France':

> The duc de Richelieu was covered with vice. He was a libertine, a thief, and having done nothing [Voltaire] attributed to him the victory of Fontenoy. Every man deserves justice. The victory of Fontenoy was due to Louis XV who remained on the field of battle. If he had crossed the Escaut, as Marshal de Saxe wanted, the battle would have been lost.

Voltaire was the most contemptible kind of military historian: 'He sought only to mention the names of the *seigneurs* and their regiments and made no effort to know the principal movements [of a battle].' So much for the great philosophical historians of the Enlightenment.

Napoleon became his own historian out of necessity. He had panegyrists aplenty but easily saw through their flattery and falsification. The history he imagined, craved, and dictated only he himself could write. It turned out not much different from the hagiography he despised. His history was not about sordid details, the mundane failings of great men, private vices or marital discord. Nor was it about mundane politics, whether of court or parliament. It was about 'intrepid heroes, severe legislators, generous peace-makers, charitable victors, an emperor who is noble, the father of his troops, a loving husband, an excellent administrator, an indefatigable worker, a prudent builder, the friend of science, letters, and the arts'. In a word Napoleon himself, the great man of his century, the hero of the French Revolution. The plastic and dramatic arts proved better able to depict what was important to Napoleon.

Napoleon's painters created images rich in significance, imbued with myth and legend. History has constraints. If the hero did not cross the Alps on a white charger he should not be depicted as having done so. Those who had literary and historical genius, especially Chateaubriand and Mme de Staël, were his enemies. So too were the great military historians of the age, Jomini and Clausewitz. Napoleon had no one of sufficient talent to write his history, which he thought should resemble and emulate the Bulletins he dictated while on campaign: filled with facts and figures, glorious deeds and heroism. The historical truth is of secondary importance. The Revolution had no time to write its own history. Oratory, the most practical of the literary arts, was the history of the day: rhetorical, devoted to persuasion, deliberately imitative of antique models, and self-consciously striving for renown, it nevertheless did not address personal reputation. Napoleon had no oratorical genius and he had no intention of leaving his remembrance to his enemies. He had seen how Robespierre, or Marat, or Danton fared after their deaths. He was determined to avoid their posthumous fate.

Napoleon's literary judgments resemble his judgments of historians. Both spring from his egotistical needs. He loved the French classics, especially the dramatic poets of the 17th century. Many an evening at Longwood was passed with Napoleon himself or one of his court declaiming Corneille or Racine. A good tragedy was not some drama 'fit only for chambermaids'. A noble tragedy was the school of great men. It was the duty of sovereigns to encourage these plays and present them. He explained to Las Cases:

Tragedy heats the soul, elevates the heart, can and should create heroes. Considered in this way France owes to Corneille some credit for its fine deeds. *Messieurs*, if he were alive I would make him a prince.

He knew many of the tirades of Corneille and Racine by heart. He has not a bad word to say about either tragedian. The combination of poetry, elevated passions, and psychological profundity he found deeply moving. That the heroes and heroines were noble, as were their passions, appealed to the parvenu Emperor. Whatever Corsican ideas about honor, women, or family he carried throughout his life, Napoleon's love of French literature was, although an acquired passion, unalloyed. The Duke of Wellington is reported to have said Shakespeare was the only history he read. For Napoleon Corneille and Racine occupied his private pantheon. Voltaire's tragedies did not. When the exiles read *Mahomet* it became 'the subject of the most passionate criticism' of both character and the poetry:

> Voltaire [said the Emperor] has here betrayed history and the human heart. He prostituted the great character of Mahomet by the basest intrigues. He caused a great man, who changed the face of the earth, to act like the most vile criminal, fit only for the gibbet. He travestied the noble character of Omar in the same way ...

Gourgaud remembers the scene a bit differently than Las Cases, but Napoleon's scorn remains in his dismissal of the play as 'in bad taste' and good only 'for chambermaids and shop girls'. Voltaire turned 'the great Omar into a Figaro. He believed that the great affairs of the world were a matter of intrigue'. When they read *Œdipe*, however, Napoleon was fulsome in his praise. It had 'the most beautiful scene in our theater' yet was marred by the ridiculous loves of Philoctète. He attributed these particular scenes to 'the mores of the age and the great actresses of the day who imposed the law'. Las Cases remarks: 'This eulogy of Voltaire struck us. It was as new for us as it was rare coming from the Emperor's mouth.'

Napoleon used his Evangelists brilliantly, as he used all men who served him. At the height of his glory he needed no assistance, no conduits for his presentation of self. With his Bulletins and articles for the *Moniteur* he nurtured the public persona he had created. In the plastic arts he was extremely fortunate that painters of genius were devotees. Napoleon had 'no original taste' but his choice of style was constant. He embraced 'the formal universe of the new classicism', that had been the aesthetic of the Revolution. Lucien Bonaparte told David 'my brother is interested only in paintings in which he appears'. Hardly a substantial aesthetic principle, but fundamental to the cult of personality he created and encouraged. To assure a steady stream of pictures whose meaning (and aesthetic) pleased Napoleon Vivant Denon intervened to 'suggest' symbolism or iconography, and even subject matter. He sponsored *concours* where the painters competed for imperial favor. His monument-makers, his sculptors, his architects also did the Emperor's bidding, instructing his untutored taste and translating grandeur, glory, and Roman models into modern celebrations. On St Helena, with only words to command, he was consumed with writing his own history.

Nowhere is the problematic of writing history as Napoleon desired clearer than in his account of the Battle of Waterloo. He was uninterested in the past for its own sake, unconcerned to provide a balanced account, and unable to take responsibility for any but the most minor mistakes. He held his opponents in contempt and turned a blind eye to mundane details. Glory, courage, devotion, purposeful sacrifice, was the stuff of Napoleonic history. He wanted history that approximated the concerns and even the moral and psychological elevation of classical French tragedy. On the first anniversary of Waterloo Napoleon was overwhelmed with sadness. 'An incomprehensible day,' he sighed. 'The concatenation of unbelievable, fatal events! ... Grouchy! ... Ney! ... d'Erlon! ... Has there ever been so much calamity! ... Poor France! ...' He covered his eyes with his hand. 'Yet everything that could have been done was! ... it all collapsed when everything had succeeded!':

> A singular campaign [he went on]. In less than a week I three times saw an assured triumph for France slip from my hands ... Had it not been for the desertion of a traitor I would have annihilated the enemy at the beginning of the campaign. I would have destroyed them at Ligny if my left wing had done its duty. I would still have triumphed at Waterloo if my right wing had not been lacking.

Napoleon's two obsessions in his presentation of self on St Helena were the French Revolution and the Battle of Waterloo. It was not a large battle by the standards of late Napoleonic warfare, nor an innovative one. The French were vastly outnumbered, as they had been ever since the Russian campaign. The Battle of Ligny (16 June) is sometimes misleadingly detached from Waterloo. It is the beginning of the struggle. Napoleon attacked the Prussians and drove them from the field. He did not crush them. They retired in good order with their army intact. This force would decisively return to Waterloo. Napoleon sent Marshall Grouchy and 30,000 men in pursuit of the fleeing Prussians, setting in motion what would become one of the fatal pivots of the battle. With the remaining 74,000 men and 266 guns he prepared to attack the English center. Drouet d'Erlon was responsible for the attack. Success depended on holding Wellington's right and left wings in check while the bulk of the French army dismembered the center. Napoleon characteristically underestimated his opponent. Had he spent more time in Spain, or listened to his generals who had, he might have learned to appreciate Wellington's immense defensive skill. It was not, Napoleon insisted, distinguished generalship that won Waterloo, it was *la force des choses*. He likened Wellington's victory at Waterloo to

General Dumouriez's at Valmy, when a rag-tag army of raw recruits beat the Austrians because the French did not dare leave the field lest their army be totally destroyed. Retreat was more dangerous than holding their position. Wellington found himself in the same predicament at Waterloo. 'His glory is completely negative, his mistakes enormous.' He did nothing to earn the victory: 'Had he been able to begin his retreat, he would have been lost.'

Wellington had taken up a formidable defensive position, with his infantry just over the crest of the pompously named Mont Saint-Jean, which was little more than a hill, out of the reach of French cannon. To get at the English the French would have to cross an area that offered no natural shelter, then climb up Mont Saint-Jean completely exposed to English fire. A number of farms stood between the French and the English positions and offered Wellington strong defensive outposts for his left wing, which he proposed to re-enforce with the Prussian troops when they arrived. On his right was the chateau of Hougoumont. Jerome Bonaparte, no seasoned commander, was ordered to attack. He needlessly sacrificed men and failed to take Hougoumont. Another pivotal mistake.

Early in the battle Napoleon had foreseen the eventual arrival of von Bülow's forces and so committed his entire Young Guard Division, plus some Old Guard battalions, to the village of Placenoit on his right flank to hold them off. These were troops he could not spare. Late in the battle, when the French launched their final attacks and Ziethen's Prussians arrived on the battlefield, the French were woefully over-stretched and overcommitted. The kind of elasticity Napoleon had always counted on toward the end of his battles was unavailable at Waterloo. Just as he was preparing to attack the English center, after the filthy wet weather had delayed the start of the battle, he learned that von Bülow's corps had arrived on the battlefield. He immediately sent a letter to Grouchy who was pursuing them: 'do not lose a moment to maneuver towards us, join us, and destroy Bülow whom you will take unawares'. Grouchy heard the cannon from Waterloo but refused to march to the gunfire. He was determined to carry out the letter of his orders to find and destroy Bülow's army. At the battle of Jena a general rule had been laid down: 'To march to the cannon fire is the duty in any army column for all the corps who form a part of that column.' This Grouchy disregarded. He assumed, as did Napoleon, that the Prussians who arrived at Waterloo were not the main force. When Grouchy finally reached Wavre, his destination, all he found was a decoy force.

By 3 p.m. it was clear that Napoleon's main attack had failed. It cost him 5,000 men. At 3:30 he launched the famous cavalry charge, whose immense shock rocked Wellington's forces. Some of his infantry squares were broken, but the squares, not all of which were British troops, were three lines deep and many more held. Here was born the tradition that the Battle of Waterloo was won on the playing fields of Eton where the British officer class, who stood without assault weapons amid their troops on Mont Saint-Jean, had been schooled to command and rule. A second desperate cavalry charge was launched by Marshal Ney around 5:30. It too, without sufficient infantry, failed. By 5 p.m. all the French attacks had been repulsed. Then von Bülow counter-attacked. Napoleon checked the attack but at this moment the Prussian corps Ziethen arrived. Napoleon had only the Imperial Guard in reserve. Now they were used, failed, and destroyed. By 9 p.m., following Wellington's counter-attack, the English troops were exhausted. Blücher, driven by his enraged hatred of Napoleon who had first humiliated him in 1806, launched the pursuit the British could not. The beaten French panicked. They were mercilessly cut down as they ran. The battle was lost. Even had Grouchy suddenly appeared there was no hope. Napoleon fled.

The shifting fortunes of the battle, the numerous mistakes made by the French, and the final rout that destroyed Napoleon have given Waterloo its dramatic and tragic stature and created a plausible, counter-factual climate. Napoleon himself is the source of many of these imagined alternatives. Napoleon had a long, lugubrious list of fallen and absent comrades, the men who had managed the matchless triumphs of the Grande Armée. Napoleonic warfare, especially the premium he placed on individual heroism, levied a heavy blood tax on general officers. Yet even if his dead marshals could be raised they would have commanded inferior troops. 'The men of 1815,' he told Gourgaud, 'were not the same as those of 1792 ... I would perhaps have been better off to delay [the battle] for a month in order to instill more consistency in the army.' The heroism of the Revolution was as much on his mind as his dead comrades. He lamented the patriotic exultation of the citizen-soldiers who fought at Valmy and gave the Revolution its first victory. As the reasons for Waterloo accumulated he blamed Soult's general staff and indicted the inexperience of his own. Ney's attack on Haye-Sainte was only partial and his decision to redirect the guns to protect his troops prevented his advance. He regretted not sending General Pajol, rather than Grouchy, in pursuit of Blücher. A few months later he tells Gourgaud that had he had 'four

24-pounders I would have been the master of all!' Changing gears he rambled in another direction:

> Great events have petty causes. I lost the Battle of Waterloo through the fault of an ordnance officer who carried to Guyot the order to engage the horse grenadiers. Had this not happened I would have had them in reserve and I would have reestablished the battle with them.

He made a similar lament to Montholon. The pattern of exculpation is clear and familiar. For all his talk of fortune or his star, Napoleon was a rational fanatic. He pored over maps and spent countless hours planning a campaign. Nothing was left to chance, very little was delegated to others. He was uninterested in theory. On the battlefield he reserved for himself the task of fixing, thanks to his prodigious *coup d'oeil*, anything that had been overlooked, any developments that had somehow escaped his catalogue of contingencies when planning. He was supremely self-confident in his abilities and convinced that he could will the execution of his desires. If something went awry during the fighting the fault had to lie in the failure to execute his orders. His unbroken string of victories, beginning with the siege of Toulon in 1793 when he was 24, made him seem, to himself and for a long time to contemporaries, invincible. There had been personal mistakes aplenty but he had gotten away with them. The Grande Armée, when he himself commanded it, continued unbeaten. It was his marshals who were defeated or stalemated. Even in the catastrophic Russian campaign Napoleon was not defeated in battle.

Victory came so early to Napoleon and lasted for so many years that he believed he was invulnerable, the god of battles. By the time of Waterloo he had abandoned all self-criticism. His strengths – the willingness to gamble, to stake all on a single battle, to inspire his troops, to be impetuous, always on the offensive, his faith in his will-power and his capacity to plan a campaign and lead an army better than anyone he might face – were now untempered by the reality of his desperate plight. He was outnumbered, outgunned, his troops were mediocre, inadequately trained, and ill-equipped. He had no cavalry to speak of, his old comrades were dead or absent, the enemy was determined and capable, his own resources were nearing exhaustion, his personal popularity had all but vanished. France and his marshals had had their fill of war. Even if he won Waterloo the next battle or the one after that would destroy him. Where was the historian who could tell this story? Only a Napoleonic Bulletin could burnish his achievements.

Contemporaries are always too close to events to see much beyond their personal responses. Intellectual and emotional distance takes time. Napoleon used his Evangelists to preserve his words and perpetuate his deeds. They received the dictations for his most elaborate and extensive Bulletins, the history of his career dictated on St Helena. Napoleon brilliantly imposed his view of himself and events on the future. Even the debunkers, Tolstoy first among them, have only dented the colossus. This was his most enduring victory.

XII
Death and Rebirth

The year 1821 began, as had every new year on St Helena, with the exiles coming to pay their respects to the Emperor and receive his blessing. Napoleon received his valet, Louis-Joseph-Narcisse Marchand, in bed. 'So,' he said, 'what do you have to give me for the new year?' 'Sire,' said the faithful servant, 'the hope to see Your Majesty soon up and about and leaving this climate that undermines his health.' 'That, my son,' responded Napoleon, 'will not be long in coming. My end approaches. I haven't far to go.' Marchand countered that this was not the sense of his wish. 'So it will be,' said Napoleon, 'it is what heaven wants.' The new year was the prelude to his death agony, which began on 17 March when he took to his bed which he did not leave until he died on 5 May. He dressed only rarely, his legs would not hold him, and he was carried from one to another of the two camp beds in his room, and very occasionally to a chair. He could not bear to have a light in the room, and tolerated only a single candle in an adjoining alcove. His feet were constantly cold and regularly wrapped in hot towels, his fevers were treated with swaddling in flannel regularly changed by whoever was watching over him. Montholon reports that one night he changed the swaddling seven times; 'each time the flannel and linen were soaking, including the madras cloth he tied around his head.' He could not keep any food down, even bouillon.

Montholon and Bertrand helped Marchand keep a bedside vigil. All three made notes of Napoleon's final months, days, and eventually hours. Bertrand, ever forthright and bluntly honest, asked his commander for a few minutes of confession on 30 April. 'Eh bien, speak,' said Napoleon. 'I have kept notes of your conversations as Your Majesty seemed to wish,' Bertrand said. 'I have kept a journal throughout these five or six years. These notes of your conversations on events, men, the works you have read, on the nation, on a great variety of subjects, are of great interest to posterity.' 'Ah!' was all Napoleon said before he closed his eyes without responding. Taken together these notes, variously worked up and published many years later – Bertrand's journal, alone of the Evangelists, was published more or less as originally recorded, unsullied by editorial tampering – provide a detailed record of Napoleon's end. The Emperor long knew he was dying. He had months to prepare. With the same precision and attention to detail he displayed planning a campaign he set his affairs in order, prepared his will. He told Bertrand he wanted his correspondence with the European monarchs published. 'It is a monument for history.' His brother Joseph could have the letters printed in America, assuming they survived in the French archives and could be recovered, which he thought would be a matter of chance: 'there are perhaps some at the Archives staunchly opposed to this.' Changing registers, he detailed, in three distinct categories, everything that belonged to his private fortune and could be willed. The chateau at Rambouillet had been furnished with items that belonged to him when he was a general of the Republic, as had his apartment on the rue Chantereine and la Malmaison. These furnishings he considered private property, although he carefully avoided mentioning that personal as well as public plunder was habitual during the Italian campaign. Once he became First Consul and moved into the Tuileries and Saint-Cloud, he insisted, he had bought with his own money most of the furnishings and 'had as much right to dispose of [them] as had any other public functionary'. The third class of property he claimed for himself was '500,000 to 600,000 francs of diamonds [in the collections of the Crown] that he had bought with his own funds'. The keeper of the jewels, he asserted, could testify to this fact. Hudson Lowe, ever pedantic and punctilious, refused to consider Napoleon's will valid since it had not been made according to English law. The will, along with all the possessions of the French community, were to be put under seal and sent to England where the government would decide these weighty matters.

Preparing his will triggered memories and reflections: his fondness and sexual passion for Josephine, his wish that Marie-Louise not remarry, the fate of his son and his natural children. He reminisced salaciously about Josephine's genitals. He provided for his children. His natural son, Léon, was left 150,000 francs to be invested by his tutor for the eventual purchase of a small plot of land in the Berry. He asked the Grand Marshal to see this was done. Marie-Louise, he lamented, would be married off to 'some petty archduke among her cousins'. He begged her to look after the education of his son whom the Bourbons would probably make a cardinal. 'The most important thing for him is that he never become a priest' and that he 'always glory in being born French'.

He told Bertrand he was 'happy to have no religion'. Although 'it is a great consolation, I have no imaginary fears, and do not fear the future'. He accepted the last rites of the Church, out of habit, respect, and physical weakness rather than belief. On 1 May, when Bertrand was away for an hour-and-a-half, the Corsican priest Vignali, who had been sent to St Helena by Madame Mère and Cardinal Fesch, consecrated a makeshift altar in Napoleon's room and gave him extreme unction. It is unclear if the Emperor was conscious at the time for there were no witnesses. Napoleon died an excommunicant and made no attempt to reconcile himself with the Church. His last utterances, as he died, were about France, his son, and the army. Vignali, perfectly aware of the importance of the drama of death for a Catholic and perhaps especially anxious to save this extraordinary soul, was always near in Napoleon's last days. Bertrand made sure that Vignali was available should the Emperor call, but wanted to prevent 'the libellists and the enemies of the Emperor from getting any ammunition to claim that he died like a Capucian and always wanted to have a priest with him'.

His doctors, in his final illness, were a different matter. Napoleon had always scorned the medicine of his day and remained a skeptical and reluctant patient at his end, only allowing treatment at the pleading of his companions or when he was too weak to resist. 'I do not fear death,' he told Marchand. 'I will do nothing to hasten the moment, but I will not grasp at straws to live.' He had the misfortune in his final days to be attended to by Francesco Antommarchi, a young Corsican doctor, also sent by his mother and uncle, whom he considered especially ignorant. Napoleon refused all Antommarchi's treatments until he became too feeble to assert himself. He unleashed one of the last of his famous and feared tirades about Antommarchi. 'Let him waste his time with his whores,' he ranted to Bertrand, and then catalogued the sex acts he should engage in with them. 'Spare me this man. He is an animal, ignorant, stupid, without honor.' He asked for the English doctor Arnott.

Archibald Arnott was the surgeon of the 20th Infantry corps. He had fought in Spain and at Walcheren, and came to St Helena with his regiment in 1819. At an early consultation Napoleon delivered his set-piece diatribe against the British government, which Marchand recorded:

It is your ministers who have chosen this horrible rock that consumes the lives of Europeans in a few years ... they have forbidden me to receive any news of my wife or my son. For a residence they have given me the least inhabitable place on the island, most exposed to the murderous tropical climate. They have forced me to stay confined within four walls, breathing foul air, me who rode across Europe on horseback ... I am being slowly assassinated, bit by bit, with premeditation, and the infamous Hudson Lowe is the executor of the commands of your ministers ... I bequeath the opprobrium of my death to the reigning house of England.

Napoleon and his entourage were sure Dr Arnott reported to Hudson Lowe, but they so distrusted Antommarchi that for the Emperor's peace of mind they admitted a spy into Longwood. Napoleon's father had died at 38 of stomach cancer. Napoleon described his own abdominal pain, which he located near the liver, as resembling that of a knife twisted in the guts. He was convinced he had his father's fatal illness and there was nothing the doctors could do. 'My father had a tumor of the duodenum,' he told Bertrand. He believed his own was hereditary and asked, 'Can it be healed once it has formed?' The question was rhetorical. Dr Arnott's appraisal was cautious: he would do what he could. Antommarchi was less reserved. He tried all the conventional treatments of the day. He gave his patient pills to relax the stomach, opium for the pain, various other concoctions, and at the end a massive dose of calomel, a purgative, which probably brought on the crisis that killed the already weakened patient.

In the final week of his life Napoleon's entourage keep a perpetual vigil. Bertrand (and occasionally his wife), Montholon, and Marchand (who slept each night in his master's room) were the principals. As Napoleon faded they often just sat with him. There was no conversation. It was heartbreaking for these loyal men. Napoleon had once dictated to four secretaries simultaneously: now he suffered stretches of dementia, asking the same questions again and again. The master of the world, this terrible man whose word had moved states, now asked for 'a spoon for his coffee ... obeyed like an infant ... had the docility of a child. Voilà the great Napoleon, miserable and humble,' lamented Bertrand. He hallucinated: 'I saw my good Josephine,' he told Montholon, 'but she did not want to embrace me. She vanished as soon as I tried to take her in my arms. She was not changed. Always the same, always completely devoted to me. She said to me that we were going to see each other again and never part. She assured me ... Did you see her?'

He died at 5:50 in the late afternoon on 5 May. Bertrand, Montholon, and Marchand were at his side. Their descriptions agree, their reactions are unique. 'At the moment of the crisis [writes Bertrand], a slight movement of his pupils, a regular movement of his mouth and chin, like the controlled movement of a pendulum.' Montholon was less circumstantial:

> He remained immobile until 5:49 p.m., when he breathed his last. He lay always on his back, his right hand draped over the side of the bed, his gaze fixed, appearing absorbed in some profound meditation, without the appearance of any suffering. His lips were lightly contracted, the whole of his face expressed a kind of sweetness.

Marchand, the valet, was the most poetic:

> At 5:50 p.m. the cannon marking the end of the day could be heard. The sun disappeared into waves of light. This was the very moment when the great man who had dominated the world by his genius, was enveloped in his immortal glory. Dr Antommarchi became more anxious. The hand that had guided victories, whose pulse he took, was cold. Dr Arnott, his eyes on his watch, counted the intervals of each breath: fifteen seconds, then thirty seconds, then a minute. We waited in vain for another. The Emperor was no more.

The next day at 2:30 p.m. an autopsy was performed. Seventeen witnesses were present, including Bertrand, Montholon, Vignali, Marchand, Ali, and Pierron from Napoleon's entourage, three British officers and seven doctors (Arnott among them), and Antommarchi, who conducted the procedure. There was no definitive cause of death and modern doctors, reviewing the autopsy report, have wrestled with its imprecision. Antommarchi and his colleagues found a small bladder that had caused Napoleon to urinate frequently. There was a problem with his heart that slowed blood circulation, and a misshapen left kidney. None of this was fatal. It was the area around the stomach that caused Napoleon's last agonies and proved most affected. The doctors found tumors, some of them ulcerated, in the pylorus, that part of the duodenum closest to the stomach. One had pierced the stomach and Antommarchi was able to put his little finger through the wound. A perforated ulcer would doubtless have caused an infection in his peritoneal cavity that could well have killed Napoleon. The perforation would most commonly have been caused by an ulcer although it could also have been caused by a stomach cancer. In this same area the stomach adhered to the liver, which was somewhat enlarged. This last detail is not in the English version of the autopsy. Dr O'Meara and then Dr Arnott had earlier hypothesized cirrhosis and/or hepatitis when they examined Napoleon. Hudson Lowe refused to credit the diagnosis. He thought it fixed blame for Napoleon's death on the English. There was no diagnosis of cancer as the cause of death.

The next day around 4 p.m. Antommarchi took a death mask. Bertrand, who does not explain why the doctor waited a day before casting the mask, thought Napoleon's face 'completely disfigured'. An hour later they sealed in lead the silver vase with an eagle crest filled with ethyl alcohol that contained Napoleon's heart. At 7 p.m. they placed his body in a coffin that was too narrow for his hat to fit on his head. The most famous hat in history was laid on his knees. They sealed the coffin in tin and then lead. On 9 May a mass for the dead was chanted in the morning. The lead-encased coffin was then placed in a wooden coffin draped in blue velour on which was placed the coat that Napoleon had worn at Marengo, a crucifix, and a cushion of white satin on which reposed his sheathed sword. They bore the coffin to a waiting carriage. Vignali, in his priestly robes, was followed by Bertrand, Antommarchi, and Arnott. Napoleon's body was carried in his calèche draped in black, the rest of the funeral cortège followed. At the gate of Longwood several companies of British soldiers who had guarded Napoleon in captivity lined the route and held back the curious who sought a glimpse of the dead Emperor. The cortège left the main road and followed a smaller road that led to the burial site. Three salvos marked the descent of the coffin from the calèche while the naval and coastal guns boomed intermittently. The coffin was lowered into the tomb which was sealed with a huge rock. The British fixed the rock in place and then covered the entire area with cement. The work was done in less than two hours.

In his careful final preparations Napoleon told Bertrand he wanted to be buried on the banks of the Seine. If this was not possible he preferred one of the islands where the Rhône and Saône meet, at Lyon. If this was not possible he wanted to be buried in Corsica, in the cathedral where his ancestors lay. 'But,' he concluded, 'the English government will have anticipated my death. In case instructions have been given that my body remain in St Helena ... bury me in the shadow of the weeping willows where I sometimes rested on my way to see you at Hutsgate, near the fountain where they fetched my water every day.' None of these requests was honored by Napoleon's captors. On 12 May 1840 during a markedly boring session of the Chamber of Deputies during which appropriation bills for public works were being introduced, Charles de Rémusat, the minister of the interior, requested the necessary funds to bring back Napoleon's remains from St Helena and construct a tomb to receive them at Les Invalides. It was a stunning intervention. None of the deputies knew the July Monarchy had successfully negotiated with the English nor had there been any hint of the project. It made perfect sense given Louis-Philippe's genuine desire to embrace all of France under his umbrella. Versailles had been turned into a national historical museum, Napoleon's statue atop the Vendôme column, removed by the Restoration, had been restored, and the Arc de Triomphe at the Étoile, left unfinished, had been completed. But this was Paris, the July Monarchy was beset by opponents to Right and Left, the Bonapartists were a tiny but not despised faction, France was bored with the bourgeois prudence of the government, the social tensions that would blow up in February and July 1848 were palpable, and controversy had never been a soothing exercise in public discourse for the Parisians.

The first steps went smoothly. The Prince de Joinville, Louis-Philippe's third son, set sail from Toulon on 7 July 1840. The ship and its sacred cargo returned to Cherbourg on 30 November. Here Napoleon's coffin were transferred to a steamboat and carried up the Seine, making several stops en route, arriving in Courbevoie on the morning of 15 December. The funeral cortège proceeded to the capital following the huge specially designed funeral chariot, more than 35 feet tall, covered with allegorical sculpture and drawn by 16 black horses. The cortège passed the Arc de Triomphe, moved down the Champs-Elysées, crossed the Seine before reaching its destination, the Church of Saint Louis in Les Invalides, Louis XIV's greatest Paris building. Napoleon's coffin was placed on a monumental catafalque directly under one of the greatest domes in Paris, built by Jules Hardouin-Mansart between 1679 and 1706 to cap the architecture of Libéral Bruant. The *Guide Bleu* pronounces it 'the most beautiful dome in France'. Here the coffin remained on display for enormous crowds of visitors before being moved to the side chapel dedicated to St Jerome, where it rested for two decades. The problems had begun. It would prove as difficult as it had been in his lifetime to integrate the restless, revolutionary Napoleon, even dead, into society. The original proposal drew immediate criticism and a long list of alternative proposals followed for the next two decades. Every site had its opponents and proponents, all the iconography was found objectionable by some group or other. Consensus, hardly an appropriate description of how French politics proceeded, proved impossible. The debate over Napoleon's tomb became a public referendum on his place in French history and mythology.

Paris is an old city into whose fabric virtually every king and government has embroidered itself. Rémusat and Louis-Philippe had decided upon Les Invalides for Napoleon's final resting place. It was from its inception an army building, a hospital and residence for veterans. The central hall displayed all the flags Napoleon had captured from his enemies in battle. But turning the St Louis chapel into Napoleon's tomb associated him with the most autocratic of French kings, who had proclaimed his divine right to rule, as had his many apologists. For the Bonapartists, children of the Revolution, Divine Right was embarrassing, and associating Napoleon with one of the most bigoted and superstitious French kings was anathema. The pious were horrified that the excommunicated Emperor would lie in a church. Many felt unease about emphasizing Napoleon's conquests and many more were concerned that the monument would stir Bonapartist passions. One of the reasons Les Invalides was chosen was its isolation from the 'dangerous' neighborhoods of Paris. Not only is that part of the seventh arrondissement that holds the great building decidedly wealthy, but Les Invalides itself is splendidly detached from the surrounding urban fabric by a magnificent esplanade.

Napoleon himself, years earlier, had imagined being buried in the basilica of St Denis, the first of the great Gothic cathedrals, about six miles from the center of Paris. He had signed a decree (20 February 1806) consecrating the church, the traditional crypt for the kings of France, heavily vandalized in the Revolution. He ordered it made fit to receive his remains and those of his family and descendants. He commanded four chapels be built: one for himself and his successors and one for each of the three dynasties of kings. The royalists were beside themselves. Napoleon was nothing but a usurper, a parvenu desperate to associate himself with the legitimate kings of France. Any site *but* St Denis was their cry. The July Monarchy too was unhappy with St Denis. They wanted to present Napoleon as a law-giver and a military hero rather than an emperor and founder of a dynasty with which king Louis-Philippe had no connection.

A crypt under the Vendôme Column was proposed. The new monument, built by Napoleon to celebrate the victory at Austerlitz had no relationship with the royal past, although it was built in the middle of one of Louis XIV's great squares after the royal equestrian statue had been smashed and removed by the French Revolution. Burial here would disentangle Napoleon from the historical monarchy. The problem for the Bonapartists was that burial under the Column would present Napoleon only as a military hero, a limitation they found intolerable. He was the

Emperor of France and deserved memorialization as such. Burial in the recently completed Arc de Triomphe presented the same problems as the Vendôme Column. There was, additionally, the insult that burial in either monument to French arms would inflict on the rest of Europe, with whom the July Monarchy was at peace. What about the Panthéon? It offered a historic church long desacralized, with yet another great Paris dome, this one built in the 18th century by Jacques Germain Soufflot. The Panthéon had the added advantage (a severe disadvantage for some) of being the traditional tomb of France's great men. Voltaire and Rousseau were the first to be buried under Soufflot's dome. With the Revolution, however, pantheonization became a precarious honor. Some who were there entombed soon fell out of favor as the Revolution whirled. Great men lost their status with shifting factions and were removed from the Panthéon. Mirabeau, pantheonized in 1791, was removed the following year when evidence of his secret dealings with Louis XVI was discovered. In addition the Panthéon had no specific tradition that evoked Napoleon's many accomplishments, and no ruler of France had ever been buried there. Pantheonizing Napoleon would diminish his greatness, not enhance it, so the Bonapartists thought. Perhaps a wholly new building, devoted exclusively to Napoleon, would avoid all these pitfalls. But where in central Paris could such a tomb be built? The Expiatory Chapel built by the restored Bourbons to honor their executed brother, Louis XVI, was relatively obscure, tucked behind the Elysée Palace on the Right Bank. Napoleon needed something grander. Besides, a new building would deny his memory the association with the legitimate rulers of France, an association he had craved during his lifetime.

In the midst of the intense and inconclusive debates, history intervened. In February 1848 the July Monarchy was overthrown, the Second Republic was established, and Napoleon's nephew, Louis Napoleon, was elected president. Everything changed. The architect Louis Visconti (1791–1853) had been given the original commission to design the tomb and despite the ongoing public debate his plans for Les Invalides had been approved and work had gone forward, albeit in fits and starts. Now it came to a halt. The new republican minister of the interior, Ledru-Rollin, appointed a committee of 13 to study the project. On 29 May they sent their report to the minister. There was some praise of Visconti's work, but not unexpectedly the committee sharply condemned most of it and lambasted the administration and policy of the arts pursued by Louis-Philippe's government. The committee would have welcomed the abandonment of the tomb project. Louis Napoleon had his own views. He was uninterested in excoriating the artistic administrators of the former government, yet the tomb project languished for another 13 years before it was completed. Louis Napoleon did not much like Visconti's plans, but according to the historian of the tomb, Michael Driskel, he made little or no attempt to change them. Nor did he, curiously, make much effort to impose his own will.

Louis Napoleon's ambitions, his utter devotion to his uncle whose grandeur he sought to borrow as a source of his own legitimacy, led him to seek a particular kind of remembrance, missing in Visconti's project. Napoleon III had no military ability. He had actively campaigned for a second Napoleonic Empire by insisting it meant peace, as he told the *Bordelais* in a famous speech. Napoleon's 60 battles would, of course, figure in his tomb, but not be centered. The same fate awaited his least controversial work, his great reforms. Louis Napoleon was not anxious to emphasize his uncle's transformation of the French state. To do so would suggest that Napoleon ruled because he was a good governor, an efficient administrator. Louis Napoleon wanted to legitimate his own empire on different grounds. He had to perform some alchemy to make the French forget his destruction of the Second Republic in a bloody *coup d'état* that inaugurated an authoritarian government. It was a problem in the manipulation of public opinion not unlike that faced by his uncle in the first years of the Consulate. Louis Napoleon's legerdemain could best be accomplished if the Second Empire was clearly the heir of the First, which would be presented as wholly legitimate, the fourth dynasty to rule France, not the reign of some usurping adventurer. Les Invalides smacked too much of Napoleon's military *coup d'état*. Another location was needed. The abbé Suger's, the great Gothic church.

The return to St Denis was never realized. On the afternoon of 2 April 1861, at 2 p.m., Napoleon's body was at last installed in Les Invalides in the gorgeous porphyry sarcophagus designed by Visconti. The ceremony was private, attended only by the imperial family, ministers of state, and the highest ranking generals in the army. Almost precisely 40 years after his death Napoleon had come home to Paris. The tomb brilliantly steers a convoluted course between all the noisy controversies. There is no heroic statue of Napoleon, only a huge red porphyry sarcophagus resting on a base of green Vosges granite, set dramatically below floor level under Hardouin-Mansart's dome. Twelve colossal neo-Hellenic statues representing Napoleon's major victories, some of the last work of Jean-Jacques Pradier, surround the circular space. The outer circle presents, in texts incised in the wall, Napoleon's legal reforms. Jerome and Joseph Bonaparte are buried here as well, as are the remains of Napoleon's son.

Marshals Foch and Lyautey were later interred, as were the remains of the great military architect Vauban and Louis XIV's finest general, Turenne. Napoleon would have appreciated the company over which he dominates. The tomb is among the most visited monuments in Paris, along with the Louvre. At the tomb one hears a Babel of tongues. It has become unfashionable to celebrate conquerors but Visconti's tomb does so with a nice combination of grandeur and symbolism. Napoleon's complex heritage has been deftly but only partially presented. His revolutionary credentials and convictions are quietly passed over.

Epilogue
Napoleon and the Revolutionary Tradition

For no other historical figure are the ironies and paradoxes of unintended consequences so striking. Napoleon was the heir of the French Revolution yet abhorred some of its most profound hopes, notably democracy. He compromised equality by reintroducing hierarchy and hereditary titles, albeit based on service. He so narrowly described liberty that those who saw him as the gravedigger of the Revolution have a case: there was virtually no political life during the Empire except that emanating from Napoleon, no freedom of the press, assembly, or expression, France's literary life has been accurately described as a desert, and an active and intrusive police monitored French citizens. The rule of law was frequently violated by Napoleon himself. Despite such serious incursions much of the work and the spirit of the French Revolution was preserved and survived not only Napoleon's rule but his fall.

None of his imperial arrangements survived Waterloo, but the Revolution he had striven to tame or end endured. The myth of the savior, to borrow Jean Tulard's conceptualization, proved durable in ways Napoleon neither imagined nor desired. What he saved, contrary to his own wishes, was the integrity and the heritage of the French Revolution which burst into actuality almost every generation in the 19th century, shaped the contours of French history in countless ways, and put the Revolution on history's agenda. For all his authoritarian ways, his sacrifice of civil life to the exigencies of the military, and his resurrection of dynastic politics, he was a revolutionary, a child and heir of the French Revolution, and its perpetuator. His reforms of the law, education, administration, and the army, realized and fixed in durable form the longings of his age and the promise of the Revolution. His work was idiosyncratic, profoundly imbued with the needs of the new state, inspired by a military man's insistence on order, centralization, regimentation, and hierarchy. It was much influenced by his fear of popular politics and the *canaille*, and his own need to control everything, while pursuing a foreign policy that was increasingly unpopular and ultimately fatal. He gave the Revolution an authoritarian, military, and bureaucratic twist that was certainly not the intention of the men who approved *The Declaration of the Rights of Man and Citizen* in 1789 or wrote the constitutions of 1791 and 1793; nor of those who considered themselves republicans after Thermidor. Yet it is arguable that everything he did had roots in the Revolution. 'A large part of the traditional historiography of the Revolution,' Thierry Lentz reminds us, 'stops the Revolution at the Brumaire *coup.*' This habit is being broken, but only gradually.

Napoleon did indeed undo some of the work of the radical Revolution and modify much. At the same time he reaffirmed and enforced a good deal that was fundamental, especially the property settlement and all the economic and social consequences thereof, as well as the triumph of equality, now narrowly defined, as it was in 1789, as equal access to distinction based on merit and equality before the law. These values endured his personal undoing. His work honored the spirit, the example, and often the letter of revolutionary change. It would not otherwise have been accomplished. Those who rallied to Napoleon not merely out of convenience, to further their careers or hang onto their property, did so in no small measure because he represented the Revolution and would continue its work. That he had broken with radical Jacobinism was considered by many comforting. One could have the benefits of the Revolution without the Terror. Even in the last years of the Empire *biens nationaux* were for sale. The most fundamental work of the Revolution continued, at home and abroad.

The Revolution would pass into the 19th century largely in the form Napoleon imposed upon it, with the tremendous exception of his military expansionism that vanished at Waterloo. Unexpectedly the complete collapse of his empire did not bring down any of the social, governmental, administrative, educational, or legal structures he had erected in France, which endure, despite modification, to our own day. It is via Napoleon's mediation that the Revolution came to define modern France. The Allies who gathered at Vienna to settle accounts with 'the Corsican ogre' realized that they could not undo what Napoleon had built at home. The Bourbons returned to the throne, but their crown was hedged not by divinity but by the institutions of the Napoleonic, revolutionary state. Equally importantly he exported the French Revolution, although in an imperial and military form.

He embraced the revolutionary Messianism first preached in the spring of 1792 by the Girondins. By putting the Revolution on horseback, which is how monarchical Europe saw him, he staved off a fate that befell subsequent revolutions and would surely have afflicted France: invasion, dismemberment, occupation, quarantine, legally sanctioned counterrevolutionary violence, and severe, perhaps perpetual domestic repression. Dumouriez had saved France from invasion in 1792. Napoleon could not prevent the Allies from occupying the country in 1814, but his years of aggression had given his revolutionary work time to set down deep roots. By the time the Allies won a deciding voice in French destinies, after Waterloo, it was too late to do what many itched to do. The 16 years of Napoleonic rule and conquest had insured that his domestic revolutionary policies would endure.

The subsequent history of revolutions does not follow a script, but there are significant similarities that invite comparison. Suppose Europe had successfully contained revolutionary France after 1794, fixing her boundaries long before they were set by the Peace of Paris in 1814. France would have been condemned to domestic stagnation, the Themidorian government and the Directory, already teetering on the edge of collapse, would have responded to isolation and quarantine not only by *coups d'état* but, arguably, with the reimposition of severe repression, perhaps the Terror, forced on the bottled-up nation, preventing it from carrying the war beyond its borders. The destruction of the Revolution would have been achieved, ironically by a republican government. Instead the wholly unpredictable advent of Napoleon saved the Revolution. A comparison with 20th-century revolutions reinforces the point.

Russia, China, and Cuba, to take only the most famous of the successful revolutions in recent history claiming descent from the French Revolution, were all isolated and quarantined. In each case their economies were perverted. A massive repression administered by authoritarian governments determined to stay in power played on xenophobia, fear, and very real civil war backed by foreign powers to produce a permanent police state. All opposition and dissent was crushed, the revolutionary promise turned nightmarish. There is no reason to suppose the Directors, quarantined and forcibly isolated, would have behaved differently. Instead a particular aspect of the French Revolution triumphed, in the person of Napoleon. His expansion of French hegemony in Europe transformed or destroyed the *ancien régime,* the war against the kings and priests was aggressively continued, and the rest of the Continent, under French leadership, was forcibly reformed and rationalized.

Napoleon did not destroy what he had inherited. He chose from a vastly rich recent past that which suited his dreams, his ambition, his character, and his profound and sure grasp of the political realities of the age. Napoleon's militant revolution proved remarkably successful, if brief. His cynical appraisal of the French as concerned only with equality (interpreted as careers open to talent), and glory, which are not so obviously compatible, proved accurate. He made the Revolution palatable to many, not least because he domesticated it. All the violence and instability of the Revolution was exported. Stability was preserved at home, at least until 1814. The ranks of those who served him are filled with men of ability who rallied to either the Consulate or the Empire. Thierry Lentz is 'struck by the quality of the men who sat on the councils of the Consulate and the Empire'. He signals some of those who 'are still known today to the general public: Portalis, Molé, Mollien, Boulay de la Meurthe, Chaptal, Fourcroy, Pasquier, [and] Daru.' The republican and monarchical faithful remained aloof, actively conspiring or disdainful of politics. But they were not the majority. The Napoleonic Revolution pursued a middle way and readily found collaborators among revolutionaries and *émigrés* alike.

The wars played the major role and not only because Napoleon had to keep winning to stay in power. So long as France was at war he successfully wrapped himself in the national flag, as the Girondin war party of 1792 had done. Even those who hated the Empire and Napoleon had little desire to see France defeated and overrun. Mme de Staël found herself in the untenable position of many opponents: she hated Napoleon but was deeply distressed by his defeat at Waterloo. He wedded to patriotism a good deal of visionary revolutionary zeal, including the promise of a better world that lay, like a mirage, at the end of what became endless war. His own analysis of the need for a few more years, a respite from war, for his plans to come to fruition and his son to inherit his throne is overly optimistic or cynically myopic. If he was to do what he dreamed of doing he needed time, which his wars and the eventual cohesion of the Allies denied him. In the immediate short run he needed time if he was to defend France. He was defeated in 1814 and again in 1815 because he ran out of time. Even the frenzied resurrection of his old energy, improvisatory genius, and military inventiveness could not slow or stop the sand trickling through the hourglass of his final doom. There was not time to train his men, arm them, or get them adequate mounts. In the end it was war, not any failure of his revolutionary ideas or practices, that was his undoing. France did not rise up to cast him out nor demand his reforms be destroyed. Everything that was left undone, even his delusions about what he would soon accomplish, became the text of Las Cases's *Mémorial*, which enjoyed stunning popularity.

Napoleon was unable to stop fighting not because Europe entered into coalition after coalition against him, as he obsessively argued. War was his medium and the chief instrument of his politics. Between 1800 and 1805, it is true, there was relative quiet on the Continent, although his armies occupied parts of Italy, but he was even then actively belligerent toward England and was creating what would become the Grande Armée, a weapon made for conquest not parades. He negotiated nothing during his 16 years of power. He conquered and imposed peace terms. None of his peace treaties held for very long, none of his artificially constructed kingdoms lasted, and none of the European powers was willing to sacrifice itself to the fantastic and frightening promises of a Napoleonic future. Holland and the Hanse cities did not see it as their duty to sacrifice their economic life for some vague greater good. Nor did Bordeaux, Marseilles, or Nantes. Napoleon was a Machiavellian: he believed men were ruled by force and fraud, but he was not treacherous in the manner of Cesare Borgia, let alone monstrous in the manner of Hitler or Stalin. He was unable to see his enemies as his equals, unable to accept their arguments, their interests, their point of view as anything but obstacles to the world he envisioned. He considered the stick far more useful and necessary than the carrot; and he enjoyed wielding it.

He shed vast quantities of the blood of his contemporaries, both those who followed him and those he fought; and he did so without any pangs of conscience. This was war and he was utterly ruthless; no better or worse than any of the contemporary commanders he faced. None of his military foes castigated him for how he fought. He was no more cruel or rapacious, he was just better at what he did. The shudder of horror he felt at the domestic violence of Henry VIII or the sadistic cruelty of Carrier or Tallien during the Terror was genuine. It is the terrorists who besmirched the Revolution, not Robespierre, the lawyer from Arras who envisioned a society of virtue. Those who rallied to Napoleon did so not merely because he was so remarkable a man, but because of the hope he held out. Perhaps these men were deluded, besotted by glory, or riches, or titles – this last 'the child's rattle' Napoleon said governed men. Some were sycophants, but they were not fools. The Revolution lived in Napoleon. However different his Revolution might be from their own understanding of what it was about he remained a revolutionary, and was seen as such. Only he of the surviving revolutionaries had the power to do anything. None of the republican Directors was able to inspire the nation as did Napoleon, or rise above self-interest. None of the surviving Jacobins had a following. None of the monarchists was trusted, nor were the competing generals. The sincere republicans in all the post-Thermidorian governments were mostly ineffectual. Napoleon alone occupied the revolutionary space of the age. The more self-serving of those who rallied to the Consulate or the Empire could persuade themselves that the dreams of the Revolution were hopelessly idealistic and Napoleon offered a means of improving one's material circumstances while serving France. The more idealistic could persuade themselves that life was a very messy and unpredictable business and at least Napoleon was traveling in the right direction. He would not realize many of the dreams of the Revolution, but he would draw a line against retreat and reaction. Some came along for the ride. Some hoped to do some steering. For both groups he was neither Polyphemus nor Don Quixote.

Here and there in his unsystematic and meandering judgments of the Revolution Napoleon spoke of the role of ideas and public opinion. His Enlightenment faith in reason applied to social and political questions was fundamental to his intellectual makeup. But when one governed or commanded it was force and fraud that mattered. He shared Rousseau's disturbing doctrine: men could be 'forced to be free'. Ideas, for Napoleon, were weapons to control the state and those in it. Once the Revolution was over, and he seems to have thought ending it would be his ultimate work, as did all the leaders of the Revolution who preceded him, things would change. 'I can govern as I like,' he once said. 'But my son will have to be a Liberal.' Even if the King of Rome had not been whisked off to Vienna, out of the reach of the French, it is doubtful there would have been a peaceful succession. Napoleon for all his genius was unable to establish his dynasty.

*****

On 30 July 2007, in preparation for scheduled abdominal surgery to stop internal bleeding, Fidel Castro 'temporarily' handed power to his brother Raul. Some days later the transfer was declared permanent. This is an abrupt reminder of the difference between the French Revolution and the subsequent revolutions that have traced their descent, inspiration, or heritage back to this great source. Those who wielded individual power in the French Revolution could not have devolved it so easily and arbitrarily. Robespierre's brief dominance rested on his political and rhetorical gifts, the emergency government of the Committee of Public Safety, and his control of the Jacobin Club, all of which demanded constant monitoring, none of which was transferable. Napoleon's regime was self-consciously civilian. The army was kept well out of France, but without his personal standing among his troops, his ability to accumulate glory for himself and France on the battlefield, it is difficult to imagine him able to govern. It is impossible to imagine an arbitrary and successful transfer of his authority to another. Which of his brothers, we may ask, could have been placed on his throne? He institutionalized his power in familiar dynastic forms, but when he was defeated his dynasty evaporated. Even the rumor of his death in Russia was enough to lead many to bypass his son and convey power via a *coup d'état*. The French Revolution, the grandfather of all the democratic and then socialist revolutions it sired, never became a dictatorship of a single man who could willfully or even 'legally' dispose of the state.

The *genre* of comparative revolutionary studies is still practiced, although with some diminishment over the last couple of generations of historians, political scientists, and sociologists. But if the vogue has crested there remain a number of interesting and intelligent works deposited by the receding tide. These studies fix their attention on the similarities, largely political, in the several revolutions they examine and compare. It is the state, politics, and ideology that matter, with some consideration of social and economic questions. I am not here interested in whether such inquiries are valid or fruitful. It is the general approach of all these studies, stressing similarities and parallels, marginalizing differences, that I question. The contrasts between all the revolutions that trace their lineage back and compare themselves or are compared to 1789 seem far more significant to me than their similarities. The most recent of these comparative studies, Arno Mayer's *Furies*, which examines revolutionary terror in the French and Russian revolutions, makes precisely this point. His big book soon becomes a series of separate historical experiences, parallel only because they pursue the theme of revolutionary violence. He fails to provide a faithful mirror in which the two revolutions are reflected, either theoretically or historically. The two terrors do not look very similar, nor does the lynch violence of the mob.

Fidel Castro's bequest of post-revolutionary Cuba to his brother is very good evidence that his original revolution lost its way. The same can be said of Russia and China. In all three cases after the revolution had overthrown the *ancien régime* an authoritarian government composed of revolutionary heroes took over, perhaps with the sincere intention of being temporary and transitional. First they settled scores with the hated past as a prelude to building a desired future. There was a good deal of self-purging in the ranks of the revolutionary elite as they jockeyed for power, for control of the inevitable succession that would come with the deaths of Lenin, or Mao, or Fidel. All this was done in isolation, as would be virtually all their revolutionary work. Modern revolutions were quarantined by the rest of the world. Cut off from more modern economies, denied economic, educational, and technological intercourse with the outside world, burdened with the destruction of their primitive and inadequate infrastructure and government institutions, as well as their unreformed economies, the children of the French Revolution struggled for survival under the most crippling circumstances. Additionally battered by civil war, under perpetual threat of military intervention from surrounding enemies and from the very real presence of spies and sabotage, they quickly became belligerently deaf to external criticism and international norms. Russia was dismembered at Brest-Litovsk during World War I and then invaded when the war ended. The ensuing civil war, approved, supported, and partly financed by the western democracies, proved more devastating than had the February Revolution or the October Bolshevik *coup*. It destroyed whatever remained of the fragile infrastructure inherited from Old Russia. For decades after 1949 mainland China had no recognized international existence. 'China' was, in international politics, absurdly confined to Taiwan, which was devoted, with the financial assistance of the USA, to the destruction of her huge rival across the straits. When Russia withdrew the only technological support available to the People's Republic of China, the Soviet-made tractors rusted in her fields for lack of expertise and parts. Cuba's monoculture, the heritage of colonial days, was frozen in place by international quarantine, especially that by the USA. Her machines and automobiles broke down and could not be repaired for lack of parts. To survive she had to abandon the pursuit of modernization and continue to grow mostly sugar, her single cash crop, which for many years only the Soviet Union bought.

Autarky also extracted a heavy tribute from the new political order. Stalin says somewhere that modernization is accomplished by cadres, and he was in a position to know. The forcible transformation of primitive economies, resting on historically appropriate social structures, demanded the constant application of state muscle, which was applied by a highly select and ruthless group: the party in a single-party state. Discipline, uniformity, obedience, rectitude, and terror all were imposed forcefully and relentlessly; a powerful secret police provided the necessary fear for bureaucratic dictatorship to function. The Terror in the French Revolution lasted from July 1793 to July 1794 (and was 'the order of the day' only from 10 October 1793), the year of the greatest crisis in the French Revolution. The Terror was popular at its inception and for a time appeared to many a necessary response to the possibility that the Revolution would be destroyed by force. Two civil wars raged, dozens of France's 83 departments were in rebellion or beyond the control of the government in Paris, there were food shortages and spiraling inflation, the National Assembly had been purged and some of those not arrested had fled to the provinces to raise rebellion. Tensions between Paris and the countryside as well as Paris and the national government were growing, there were notorious independent terrorists in the provinces conducting their own bloody justice, army morale and discipline was non-existent in some places, and the new constitution had been shelved. An emergency wartime government headed by the Committee of Public Safety ruled. As the year wore on the specter of military defeat faded and the Committee of Public Safety increasingly ruled by terror. It completely abandoned democracy, attacked enemies to the right and left in what looked like a permanent political purge, dismembered the Paris Commune after destroying its leaders, and lost popular support. The Terror was centralized in Paris and Robespierre provided an intellectual pedigree for terror, linking the Enlightenment to the crimes and excesses of the Revolution. But unlike later revolutions terror never reappeared in France after his fall – a fact Napoleon was proud to invoke. He occasionally tempered his self-congratulatory observation with a reminder that he could have reintroduced the Terror if he had wished – a dubious assertion.

Terror in modern revolutions has not been a temporary phenomenon. The dependence of post-revolutionary governments on terror was, at least in part, forced upon them by a hostile, armed, and belligerent world that compelled centralization and defensiveness for survival. This is a necessary but not a sufficient cause. Permanent terror soon became one of the mainstays of government. It is at best doubtful that the post-revolutionary governments of Russia, China, or Cuba could have survived without terror. I do not want to argue that Russia, or China, or Cuba had no option but to institutionalize terror. They chose terror from the moment of their triumph, and in some cases, as in China when Mao at Yan'an after the Long March began purging the party through self-criticism, even before they seized state power. Internal, arbitrary policing, dreaded prisons, and equally dreaded internal exile, became increasingly prominent in the hot-house revolutionary culture of the new quarantined states. All rivals had to be broken, all criticism quashed, all power concentrated, all decisions unquestioned. Modern revolutions looked inward as their enemies circled the wagons. They saw their survival as completely dependent upon their own efforts, discipline, militancy, and ruthlessness. If democracy anywhere but within the party was ever in their plans, which appears highly doubtful for Lenin, Mao, and Castro, it was early sacrificed in the name of the survival of the revolution and the new state. It soon disappeared from the party as well.

None of these things happened in the French Revolution. Not because the French were more decent or humane than their successors. Not even because they made or desired to make a democratic revolution, as their successors did not, either in word or deed. Not even because they were somehow luckily spared the horrors of invasion, quarantine, isolation, and dismemberment, but not civil war. France was lucky, it is true, in her economic development at the time of the Revolution. With the exception of industrializing England, France was the wealthiest country in Europe. Hers was not a backward economy, let alone a colonial economy that needed massive reform and transformation to compete in the world and defend herself against better-armed, economically more powerful neighbors. Once the constraints and privileges of feudalism in its twilight had been removed, on 4 August 1789, the peasantry tilled the soil with renewed energy, agricultural production improved. The peasantry, who were 75 per cent of the population, largely removed themselves from active political participation during the first years of the Revolution following the massive *jacquerie* of 1789. They later returned as a significant factor during the civil wars that began in 1793; but for a few crucial years the French Revolution was spared peasant unrest. France was able to feed herself throughout the Revolution despite the few desperate crop failures she suffered. Monarchical Europe first attacked the Revolution in 1792 and the desire to at least quarantine if not dismember France remained until Napoleon's fall. It was seriously discussed at the Congress of Vienna.

What saved France and the French Revolution from the fate of modern revolutions was Napoleon. The Revolutionary Wars, begun in 1792, lasted, with occasional short stretches of peace or relative quiet, until 1815. France originally sought preemptively to defend herself against invasion. The war was preached not only as defensive but as a crusade against monarchical Europe. The Girondin orators, especially Brissot, Vergniaud, and Gaudet, argued that the war would save France, spread the Revolution, convey power into the hands of the patriots, and expose and discredit the court as counterrevolutionary. Preempting foreign invasion was the immediate reason for mobilizing the nation, but this was not what captured the imagination of contemporaries. The revolutionary wars had a strong messianic component which continued until Napoleon's defeat. Long after French aggression could be described as defensive, which happened in mid-1794 when it became and remained expansionist, the creation of the Grande Nation in Napoleon's formulation, revolutionary messianism still strongly resonated. Those who were the recipients of the French Revolution at bayonet point, including Napoleon's foreign collaborators, soon lost any enthusiasm they once had for revolutionary messianism, which translated as forceful liberation and exploitation at the hands of French soldiers and administrators. Some kept their revolutionary faith, but French occupation increasingly could not be choked down. A few intellectuals, Hegel and Heinrich Heine among them, never lost their conviction that only a strong dose of the French Revolution could save Germany or Italy from the benighted tyranny of the princes or the papacy. Everyone else was happy to see the French armies depart. In a frenzy of reaction the elites of the *ancien régime* got rid of what the occupier had imposed, including some very good laws and much-needed reforms. Only French efficiency in collecting taxes was perpetuated by the restored kings, princes, and the Pope.

The revolutions in Russia, China, and Cuba so besmirched the promise of a new society, so completely and brutally destroyed any and all opposition, that there was no reassertion of the revolutionary tradition let alone the possibility of renewed revolutionary action. Stalin's proclamation of 'Socialism in one Country', more than dubious as a theory of revolutionary socialism, was the expression of Soviet Russia's isolation, precarious existence, and national chauvinism. It became a pretext for a foreign policy that subjected all non-Soviet Communist parties to Russian dominance and manipulation. France escaped all this. Revolutionary China's renewal of imperialism, now directed toward Tibet and eventually Taiwan, follows a similar pattern. Only tiny Cuba was successfully bottled up. France, on the other hand, experienced the revival of her revolutionary heritage, which had not been destroyed by Napoleon. In 1830, 1848, and 1871 she became the vanguard of European radicalism and revolution for a century in social turmoil. Each revolutionary upheaval invoked the Great French Revolution, self-consciously repeating, imitating, or mythologizing its events and leaders. The names of the newspapers that sprang up resurrected the names of the newspapers of Marat, Hébert, and Desmoulins, the radical journalists of the Revolution. No less a thinker than Alexis de Tocqueville argued that the uprisings of 1830 and 1848 were continuations of 1789,

one great revolution whose work remained unfinished in his lifetime
(he died in 1859). He wrote his friend Kergorlay that the Empire might
be the key to understanding the French Revolution:

> For a long time, I have had the thought ... of choosing, from the
> long stretch of time which extends from 1789 to the present and
> which I continue to call the French Revolution, the ten years of the
> Empire ... The more I think about it, the more I believe that this
> period would be a very apt choice. In itself it is not only great, but
> singular, even unique ... What is more, it sheds a bright light on the
> period that preceded it and on the one that follows.

One of the reasons great men have attracted so much attention from historians is their mysterious capacity to embody and express their times:
none more than Napoleon. The habit of speaking of the age of this or
that king, thinker, or historical manifestation fits Napoleon better than
most to which it is applied. He *is* the great man of the Revolution, the
link connecting the past to the future. Chateaubriand and Mme de Staël
have given us penetrating psychological portraits. David and Gros made
images that have lodged permanently in our mind's eye. The St Helena
Evangelists and Caulaincourt have preserved his talk; his letters and
Bulletins have preserved his written utterances. The many hundreds of
contemporaries who observed him and were enthralled, fascinated, or
repelled by his personality have left a vast record of his behavior, his
quirks, his physical presence. Of all those who sought to explain him to
themselves and to posterity no one, I think, has come closer to the truth
than Hegel. 'The World Spirit on horseback', despite its philosophical
jargon, is as good an explanation of Napoleon's importance as we have.
We have come full circle, back to an encounter in Jena in 1806, when
Hegel first saw Napoleon, and in a moment of intuition grasped the
logos of the French Revolution.

Appendix

Some Remarks about Arsenic Poisoning

A word about the case for arsenic poisoning, originally made more than 40 years ago, is in order.

The evidence for arsenic poisoning comes principally from the autopsy performed on Napoleon, the modern assays of the amount of arsenic in his hair, and the *Mémoires* of Louis Marchand, the Emperor's first *valet de chamber*. The most detailed hypothesis is the work of Dr Sten Forshufvud, a Swedish dentist and Napoleon buff. The hair analysis upon which Forshufvud relies was done by Hamilton Smith, a senior lecturer in forensic medicine at the University of Glasgow. Their findings have been popularized by Ben Weider, another Napoleon buff with the advantage of a private fortune used to popularize his obsession. The doctors on St Helena involved in the autopsy did not agree on the cause of death. Some favored complications of chronic hepatitis, some favored a tumor where the stomach joins the duodenum, some favored stomach perforations caused by ulcers. At a conference of the participating and attending doctors called by Hudson Lowe a plausible but not medically proved compromise was struck: Napoleon died of the same cancer that had killed his father. This nicely removed any nefarious hypotheses of responsibility from Napoleon's English jailers. Modern analyses of the autopsy reports stumble on the disharmony between medical terminology in the early 19th century and our own usage. 'Tumor' and 'ulcer' were, for example, interchangeably used when speaking of cancer. Besides, there could be no medical confirmation of the diagnosis of cancer. Only a histological examination, which is what is used today, could determine diseased cells. Such a test had not been discovered in 1821.

The large amounts of arsenic found in Napoleon's hair is the central evidence for poisoning, and there is no question it is present. What is now clear is that the poison could not have been administered orally and carried in the blood. Dr Pascal Kintz proved recently that the arsenic in Napoleon's hair was mineral not organic and was in the medulla of the hair. It could not have been ingested from an organic source. Lentz and Macé have convincingly eliminated arsenic contagion from the environment at Longwood: the dyes in the wallpaper, some of the medicines he took, the coal regularly burned in his rooms, or the powder traditionally used for hair were not the source. In addition there is no possible control experiment. We have no tests of the hair of any of the other inhabitants of Longwood for comparison. Recently Italian researchers at the National Institute of Nuclear Physics in Milan tested not only strands of Napoleon's hair from four periods of his life but samples from his son and his first wife, Josephine. They found that the high levels of arsenic in Napoleon's hair did not alter from his childhood to his death, and that his son and wife had similarly high levels. They concluded that high levels of arsenic were not uncommon. Obviously the arsenic found in hair samples taken long before Napoleon's exile to St Helena remove any possibility of murder by poison administered on the island.

The contemporary literary evidence also presents problems. Marchand's *Mémoires* were written long after Napoleon's final illness, from fragmentary notes, and not published until 1952 and 1955. Although he saw Napoleon several times a day and was with him throughout his final illness, Marchand's testimony, which does not argue for arsenic poisoning, has to be used with care. Those not enamored by the hypothesis of poisoning do not find Marchand a compelling witness for the prosecution. Without corroborating evidence Marchand's testimony is not enough to convict. The case against Montholon as the poisoner is completely circumstantial. It rests only on his proximity to Napoleon, his control of the wine cellar, the assumption of revenge for his wife's betrayal, and his sometimes troubled life involving separation from his wife, imprisonment, and an interrupted military career. A few of these observations are true, their meaning as possible motive is nothing but conjecture and wildly out of character. Since there is no *prima facie* case for or against deliberate arsenic poisoning all the assumptions about Montholon's motives do not, cannot, prove he poisoned the Emperor.

The persistence of theories and hypotheses about how Napoleon died and whether the remains returned from St Helena in 1840 are indeed his and not those of his servant, Cipriani, who died a few years before his master – a proposal equally anchored in conjecture, invention, and logic redolent of *Alice in Wonderland* – need not detain us longer. Historical reconstruction and writing is constrained by the evidence. When there is none we should not confect it or resort to conspiracy theories that cannot be substantiated. The causes of Napoleon's death, given the evidence we have, both scientific and historical, cannot be known definitively. The argument that it is Cipriani's remains that lie in Les Invalides and not those of his master are sufficiently far-fetched and unsupported by evidence to vitiate any calls to exhume Napoleon's tomb. Even if we could prove deliberate arsenic poisoning and the substitution of one corpse for another it would not change the story of his fabulous life and deeds, nor how we interpret them.

Notes

No one who has worked on Napoleon will be unfamiliar with the sources and authorities. I have tried to make my scholarly *bona fides* as unobtrusive as possible, not endlessly repeating what is obvious and well known. For Napoleon, as for almost no other historical figure, we have a precious mother lode: his talk and his letters. I have used his words often and it would have been tedious and unnecessary to provide chapter and verse for every utterance. Rather than giving the page of every quotation from Napoleon's letters and orders or the most celebrated of those who recorded his talk the notes for each chapter identify the source, although usually not the precise location of the quotations, pay homage to those whose work I have leaned upon, and list books that support each chapter. Almost all sources and authorities are identified only by name. Complete references to all the works mentioned in the notes are in the bibliography. All the translations are mine unless otherwise indicated.

Preface

Burns, *Dreyfus, A Family Affair, 1789–1945,* did the figuring. For all the details about Napoleon see Lentz, *Nouvelle histoire du Premier Empire,* III, p. 10.

Prologue   Napoleon and the French Revolution

This chapter rests upon everything I have read about the Revolution over the years. Most immediately I have leaned on the fine work of Sydenham, *The First French Republic,* Tulard, *Les Thermidoriens,* and François Furet's ideas about Thermidor in *La Révolution* and the *Dictionnaire critique* as well as Lentz, *Nouvelle histoire du Premier Empire,* and Lyons, *Napoleon Bonaparte and the Legacy of the French Revolution.* For the constitutions of France, *Les Constitutions de France depuis 1789* is a convenient collection.

I   Becoming a Revolutionary

Carrington, *Napoleon and His Parents,* is the best book on his Corsican years. For an introduction to historical Corsica see Wilson, *Feuding, Conflict, and Banditry in Nineteenth-century Corsica.* For Napoleon's doings on Corsica once the Revolution began, Masson, *Napoléon dans son jeunesse,* remains reliable and detailed. Rousseau, *Du Contract social,* book 2, chapter 10 is the source of this celebrated quotation. The subsequent quotations from Rousseau are, respectively, pp. 6, 7, 17, 19, 24. The Boswell quotations are from *An Account of Corsica,* pp. 161, 227, 167, 211.

Many have commented on Napoleon's unsure grasp of French structure and spelling. Here are a few of the howlers highlighted by Lentz, III, 509: *mon pays de nécense* (for *naissance*); *amnistie* for *armistice, session* for *section.* He was, perhaps as a result of his own difficulties with French, tolerant of the shortcomings of others. 'Let these brave men keep their Alsacian dialect,' he said. 'They always wield their sabers in French.'

II First Revolutionary Steps

For Napoleon's early career in France I follow Sydenham, *First French Republic*, who is very good on politics, and Tulard, *Les Thermidorians*, the best recent book on the subject. For all economic matters the great authority is now Branda, *Le Prix de la gloire, Napoléon et l'argent*.

The quotations from Toulon are from Markham, *Napoleon*, p. 12. Michelet is quoted from Tulard, *Les Thermidorians*, pp. 7–8. The quotation from Sydenham is on p. 187. La Reveillière-Lépeaux is quoted from the same source, p. 42.

III Italy and Empire

The essential works are Broers, *The Napoleonic Empire in Italy*, and *The Politics of Religion in Napoleonic Italy*, along with Woolf, *Napoleon's Integration of Europe*. Blanning, *The French Revolutionary Wars, 1787–1802*, is good on the Italian campaign, and Chandler, *The Campaigns of Napoleon*, remains classic. Branda, *Le Prix de la gloire*, is indispensible. Mainardi, 'Assuring the Empire of the Future', has best analyzed the meaning of Napoleon's art plundering.

Clausewitz is quoted from Blanning, p. 147, as is Napoleon's appraisal of himself. His account of Arcole is in *Correspondance*, #1196. Joseph Sulkowski, one of Napoleon's aides-de-camp, tells the story, Reinhard, *Avec Bonaparte en Italie*, pp. 178–9. The numbers are from Treue, *Art Plunder*, pp. 149–50. Boissy d'Anglas is quoted from Lentz, 'Napoléon, les arts, la politique', in *Napoléon et le Louvre*, p. 14.

All the quotations from Melito are from his *Mémoires*, I, 112–13, 163–4.

The comparison of Napoleon to Aemilius Paulus is from Mainardi, p. 158, as are the subsequent passages. The words of the Goncourt brothers are quoted from Chatelain, *Dominique Vivant Denon et le Louvre de Napoléon*, p. 166. The remarks on Italy after Napoleon are from Broers, *Europe Under Napoleon, 1799–1818*, pp. 286–7.

IV Egypt

The essential works are Cole's splendid book, *Napoleon's Egypt* (whose account of the Battle of Aboukir Bay I follow closely) and Laurens, *L'Expédition d'Egypte, 1798–1801*, both by distinguished orientalists. Denon's *Voyage dans la Basse et la Haute Egypte pendant les campagnes du Général Bonaparte* as memoir is one of the best of the age. There is a selection translated into English with commentary in Russell, *The Discovery of Egypt*. Napoleon's own account, *Campagnes d'Egypte et de Syrie*, is the best of his dictated histories of his campaigns. Tulard, *Thermidorians*, and Branda, *Le Prix de la gloire*, remain fundamental.

On French myopia about Egypt, Al-Jabarti, *Napoleon in Egypt*, pp. 32, 28. On French ignorance of Egyptian wealth, see Branda, p. 172. Denon's enthusiastic remarks are quoted from Russell, p. 144 (his translations). Napoleon's letter of despair is #2635. Denon's account of the battle of Aboukir Bay is in Russell, p. 53. Napoleon's version is *Correspondance*, #2870 and #2850. The tribute to Brueys is in *Campagnes*, p. 133. Al-Jabarti's account of the Cairo uprising is quoted from Laurens, pp. 213–14. Napoleon's attitude about how to govern Turks is quoted from Cole, *Napoleon's Egypt*, p. 105. Napoleon himself recounts his words to General Menou in *Campagnes*, p. 284.

V   Power

Tulard, *Thermidorians*, and Sydenham, *First French Republic*, are again central, as is Branda, *Le Prix de la gloire*. In addition I often follow Gueniffy, *Le Dix-Huit Brumaire*, for 18 Brumaire and Brown, *Ending the French Revolution*, on the growing influence of the army, the nature of the Directory state in its final years, and repression following Brumaire. Lyons, *Napoleon Bonaparte and the Legacy of the French Revolution*, is invaluable for the details of Napoleon's relationship with the Revolution. His is the most comprehensive study of the subject.

Roederer is quoted from Bainville, *Napoléon*, p. 26. The details of growing army influence are from Brown, pp. 119, 129, 209, and the description of the place of the army after Thermidor relies on the same authority. The quotations about Sièyes are from Gueniffy, pp. 196, 198, as is his judgment of Napoleon (p. 253). Lucien's harangue to the troops is quoted from Bainville, p. 107. Mme de Staël is quoted from *Dix Années*, p. 74. Thibadeau, *Mémoires de A. C. Thibaudeau*, p. 22 on Brumaire. Napoleon's coronation oath is in Bluche, *Le Bonapartisme*, p. 31. Napoleon on the failures of the Revolution is quoted from Gueniffy, p. 36.

Entr'acte   Revolution and Empire

The fundamental modern book is Davois, *Bibliographie Napoléonienne Française, jusqu'en 1908*. Rambaud, *Naples sous Joseph Bonaparte*, remains a classic account. Both Broers' books, *Europe Under Napoleon, 1799–1818*, and *The Napoleonic Empire in Italy, 1796–1814*, as always with Italy, are indispensable.

This and all the subsequent references to the correspondence between Napoleon and his older brother are from the splendid edition of their correspondence by Haegele, *Napoléon et Joseph*, #240. The report on Naples' wealth is quoted from Davis, p. 147. Marie-Caroline's characterization of Napoleon is quoted from Connelly, *Napoleon's Satellite Kingdoms*, p. 9. The English characterization of the Queen is in Rambaud, p. 37. Napoleon to Miot de Melito is quoted from Davis, p. 137. Haegele, #287 on Napoleon's advice to be brutal. On Saliceti see #897, #879. Napoleon on Roederer is quoted from Miot de Melito, *Mémoires du comte Miot de Melito*, II, p. 274. Napoleon on making his brother king of Naples is from Roederer, *Journal du comte P.-L. Roederer*, p. 249. Miot de Melito's portrait of Joseph is in his *Mémoires*, I, 141. King Ferdinand's manifesto is quoted in Rambaud, p. 37. Colletta is quoted from Davis, p. 2. On the Calabrians and the dirty war see Haegele, #312, #320, #450, #469; #620 contains Joseph's complaints about the difficulties he faced. On Zurlo see Davis, p. 162. General Dumas is quoted in Rambaud, p. 226. On the reforms of Naples I follow Davis and Rambaud. Details on Neapolitan feudalism are in Rambaud, pp. 400–3.

Napoleon's *Correspondance inédite*, #410 on the salt tax. His celebration of the Code is in his general *Correspondance*, #10314. The epistolary discussion of the Code is in Haegele, #398, #823. His badgering advice to Joseph is in letters #283, 286, 287, 484, 289, 303. Joseph's responses are #655, #340, #666. Napoleon's objection to Joseph's choice of advisers, #717, #773. On war, #265, #453, #464, #501, #271, #686, #410, #370.

VI   The Weapons of Revolution

The classic authority is Morvan, *Le Soldat imperial (1800–1814)*. Horne, *How Far from Austerlitz?*, is filled with interesting detail. So too is Elting, *Swords around a Throne*. He is aggressively partisan, and his gaze falls seldom on the soldiers themselves. Forrest's books, *The Soldiers of the French Revolution*, and *Napoleon's Men*, are fundamental for the lives of the soldiers, so often neglected in favor of the general staff. As always Branda, *Le Prix de la gloire*, is invaluable. There is a very good portrait of Portalis by Langlois in the indispensible *Dictionnaire Napoléon*, the first book to consult on all matters pertaining to Napoleon. The first volume of Beaucour's edition of *Lettres, decisions et actes de Napoléon à Pont-de-Briques* is of fundamental importance for the making of the Grande Armée.

In everything having to do with money and finance I follow Branda. On all matters relating to training the Grande Armée I follow Morvan. All the quotations from Portalis are from his *Discours préliminaire*. In the Code itself, Livre premier, titre premier, chapitre III is devoted to 'acts of marriage' and Titre VI concerns divorce. Talleyrand, in *Mémoires: L'époque Napoléonienne*, relates the anecdote about Cobenzl, pp. 55–6. He also quotes the passage from *Iphégenie*, p. 169. His description of Erfurt is on p. 162.

Entr'acte   A Sighting in Jena

Hegel's *Letters* are translated in a good scholarly edition by Clark Butler and Christiane Seiler. All the citations are from this work. Pinkard, *Hegel: A Biography*, is the best recent life. On Germany in the 19th century, Holborn, *A History of Modern Germany, 1648–1840*, although old, remains a superb guide.

Heine's description is also oft-quoted. It first appears in H. Brandenberg, ed., *Das Denkmal. Heinrich Heine: Denkwürdigkeiten, Briefe* (Munich, 1912), pp. 29–30. The well-known passage is in Hegel's *Letters*, p. 114, to his friend Friedrich Emmanuel Niethammer. Heine's description is also oft-quoted. Subsequent citations from the *Letters* are pp. 580, 632, 196, 141, 29, 605, 312, 123, 307. The philosophical quotations are from *The Philosophy of History*.

VII   Napoleon at Zenith

Chandler, *The Campaigns of Napoleon*, is indispensable. For the siege of Vienna, Stoye, *The Siege of Vienna*, is the best recent study. On the city, Musulin, *Vienna in the Age of Metternich from Napoleon to Revolution 1805–1848*, is reliable and readable. Rothenberg, *The Emperor's Last Victory*, complements Arnold on Wagram. The first volume of Lentz's remarkable *Nouvelle histoire du Premier*

Empire: Napoléon et la conquête de l'Europe is, as are all four volumes, the best and most comprehensive survey of the period, incorporating all the most recent scholarship. For Haydn's last days the undisputed authority is Landon, *Haydn*. For Beethoven, Thayer, *Thayer's Life of Beethoven*, is the classic authority and Solomon, *Beethoven*, is the best modern biography. On Spain, Lynch, *Bourbon Spain, 1700–1808*, is superb. Esdaile, *The Peninsular War*, although hostile to Napoleon, is the best modern account.

Neither Pasquier nor Mollien was an eye-witness to the imperial tantrum. The former heard it from Denis Decrès, the minister of marine, who was present at the memorable Council meeting. Where Mollien got his celebrated details is unknown. All the details about preparations for the siege of Vienna are from Arnold and Musulin. See Musulin, pp. 85ff, for the political aftermath of the battle. Details of the battle and its statistics are from Arnold and Rothenberg. On Napoleon's demeanor see, respectively, pp. 146 and 267–8. What the battlefield sounded and smelled like is reported by Marbot, *Mémoires du Général Baron de Marbot*, II, 266–7. General Miollis is quoted in Broers, *Napoleonic Empire*, p. 53 and see pp. 101–16 for an account of Miollis's work in Rome. Dunan's assessment of Cardinal Fesch is in *Dictionnaire Napoléon*, I, 798. Letters to Louis Bonaparte are in *Lettres inédites*, see #527 and #555.

Entr'acte   Napoleon and the Political Culture of the French Revolution

Jourdan, *Napoléon, héros, imperator, mécène*, is the best book on the subject and I follow her arguments. Holtman's work, *Napoleonic Propaganda*, is still useful. There has been much good and sophisticated work on Napoleon's artists, particularly O'Brien, *After the Revolution*, on Baron Gros and Wilson-Smith, *Napoleon and His Artists*, who deals with the entire phenomenon. Chatelain, *Dominique Vivant Denon et le Louvre de Napoléon*, is a good introduction to Denon whose *Correspondance administrative* (more than 4000 letters) can be read online at www.napoleonica.org/denon/index.html. I quote the Bulletins from Markham, *Imperial Glory*.

Napoleon to Bourrienne is quoted from Jourdan, p. 73. The quotations of the Bulletins are Markham (his translations), pp. 15, 16, 19, 21, 43, 56 and 38. I follow O'Brien's view of Gros. Delacroix is quoted from O'Brien, p. 237. Gros's death is presented in the words of Wilson-Smith, p. 164. The quotations from Denon are from Russell, *The Discovery of Egypt*, pp. 256, 53, 144. The petition of the artists to the Directory is quoted from Chatelain, pp. 74–5; for the catalogue of European paintings collected by Denon see p. 169. The catalogue of Denon's private collection is in Wilson-Smith, p. 274. Chateaubriand, *Mémoires d'outre-tombe*, I, p. 1004 on Napoleon.

VIII   Catastrophe and Decline

The best book by far is Lieven's *Russia against Napoleon*. Written in the grand manner and resting on admirable scholarship, most notably in the Russian archives that are seldom used in accounts of the campaign, he has changed how we view the catastrophe. His history is the scholarly parallel of Tolstoy's

War and Peace and will remain the standard and essential work for years to come. Zamoyski's *Moscow 1812* is a good narrative and, with Lieven, distinguished by the use of sources in several Slavic languages. Austin's *1812* is a fascinating narrative that seamlessly weaves together the sources, almost all western European, with his own words, to create a facsimile of an eye-witness account. Caulaincourt, *With Napoleon in Russia*, especially Volume 2, is indispensable. The introduction and notes by Jean Hanoteau are a model of their kind. The manuscript is one of the few that was untampered with until this careful 20th-century scholarly edition. The English translation of Volume 2, *With Napoleon in Russia*, makes this wonderful memoir accessible to Anglophones. Berlin's celebrated essay on Tolstoy's *War and Peace* is brilliant. Feuer, in *Tolstoy and the Genesis of War and Peace*, lays out the difficulties Tolstoy experienced composing the greatest of novels about the Russian Campaign and how the figure of Kutuzov was shaped to his purposes. For the controversial Russian commander see the biography by Nabokov and Lastours, *Koutouzov: Le Vainqueur de Napoléon*. As always Branda, *Le Prix de la gloire*, is the authority on economic matters, with the addition of Soboul, *La Civilisation et la France napoléonienne*.

The great question of the meaning and significance of war is first posed in its modern form by Clausewitz, *On War*. There are far too many books on the subject to list here. John Keegan's first book, *The Face of Battle* – which includes an interesting chapter on Waterloo – introduced the stench, the look, and the sound of war on the battlefield into military writing and shifted the focus of the conversation from the commanders to the men. Rory Muir carries this kind of analysis to the Napoleonic wars in his *Tactics and the Experience of Battle in the Age of Napoleon*. Bell's ambitious and sharply intelligent book, *The First Total War*, is the most thought-provoking new study.

Napoleon on his marriage to Marie-Louise is from Bertrand, *Cahiers de Sainte-Hélène, 1816–1821*, I, 302. I have translated *culbuté* as ruined. The details of Napoleonic luxury and ostentation are in Austin *1812: The March on Moscow*, I, pp. 151–2. Alexander is quoted from Zamoyski, *Rites of Peace*, pp. 128–9 and Lieven, p. 93. The quotations from Caulaincourt about Napoleon's mood and the Smolensk conference are I, 90, 70, 82–3 and 69. Napoleon's vision of what the capture of Moscow would mean is from Austin, I, 157–8. The murderous exposure of Napoleon's cavalry is quoted in Austin, I, p. 296. The figures of battle casualties and ammunition spent are from Lieven, Zamoyski, and Austin. As all such figures of the age they are only approximations. Ségur is quoted from Austin, I, 315. Details of the fire are from Caulaincourt, who was there. On remaining in Moscow see Stendhal, *Napoléon*, p. 147. Captain Brandt's celebration of the Berezina bridge is from Zamoyski, p. 466. On the composition of *War and Peace* I follow Feuer.

Entr'acte Napoleon Explains the Revolution

The sources are Caulaincourt, *With Napoleon in Russia*, vol. 2, Las Cases, *Le Mémorial de Sainte-Hélène*, Gourgaud, *Journal de Sainte-Hélène*, Montholon, *Récits de la captivité de l'Empereur Napoléon à Sainte-Hélène*, and Bertrand, *Cahiers de Sainte-Hélène, 1816–1821*.

IX   Napoleon Brought to Bay

Bertier de Sauvigny's classic, *La Restauration*, has not been surpassed. The story of Napoleon's defense of France can be followed in Houssaye's fervently partisan *1814*. The best modern account is Ashby who combines careful scholarship with more balance than most have achieved. I follow his account of the French campaign closely. Chandler, *The Campaigns of Napoleon*, remains essential and Esdaile's recent *Napoleon's Wars* equally so. For all diplomatic matters Schroeder's magisterial history, *The Transformation of European Politics, 1763–1848*, is fundamental, despite his dislike of Napoleon.

Decrès is quoted from Bertier de Sauvigny, p. 13. The figures on Napoleon's losses and the mistakes at Leipzig are from Esdaile, pp. 513–16. See Houssaye, *1814. Quatre-vingt-treizième édition*, p. 303 on Schwartzenberg. Napoleon's boast about his value in battle is quoted from Houssaye, p. 117. He doubles the figure that Metternich, among others, had applied to his skills and presence on the battlefield. Napoleon on saving his son is quoted from Bertier de Sauvigny, pp. 35–6. Lady Holland's appraisal of Charles X is quoted from Nicholson, *The Congress of Vienna, a Study in Allied Unity, 1812–1822*, p. 74.

X   Ending the Revolution

For an unmatched account with all the recent scholarship, Lentz, *Nouvelle histoire du Premier Empire*, Volume IV, is indispensible. Mackenzie, *The Escape from Elba*, tells the story of Napoleon's escape from Elba. As always I lean upon Chandler, *The Campaigns of Napoleon*, and to a lesser degree Esdaile, *Napoleon's Wars*. Zamoyski's *Rites of Peace*, is filled with anecdotes. Kissinger, *A World Restored*, is thought-provoking and Nicholson, *The Congress of Vienna, a Study in Allied Unity, 1812–1822*, although dated, is the work of a professional diplomat. Schroeder, *The Transformation of European Politics, 1763–1848*, remains in a class by itself. Branda, *Le Prix de la gloire*, as always, is a sure-footed guide to finances. Alexander, *Bonapartism and Revolutionary Tradition in France*, is a good place to study Napoleon's invocation of the fatherland in danger and his appeal to Jacobinism.

There are several accounts of Napoleon's challenge to troops sent to arrest him. I quote from Tulard and Garros, *Itinéraire de Napoléon*, p. 463. The harsh but true judgment on Fouché is by Bertier de Sauvigny, *La Restauration*, p. 109. I follow Esdaile, pp. 533–4 on the transformation of politics by war and the need of the Congress of Vienna to devise some way of putting the revolutionary genii back into the bottle. The characterization of Metternich is from Kissinger, p. 10. Von Gentz is quoted from Zamoyski, *Rites of Peace*, p. 397. Louis XVIII is quoted from Bertier de Sauvigny, p. 114.

Entr'acte   Reputation

All the quotations from Las Cases are from the Pléiade edition, as they are throughout this book. The editor, Gérard Walter, uses the 1830–2 edition, the third version that appeared in Las Cases' lifetime. The changes and variations in the several texts are significant and notorious: entire passages have been suppressed, others have been augmented, the initials of individuals have been replaced by their names, a couple of apocryphal letters are included, and so on. Walter prints all the variants at the end of each of his two volumes. The edition by Marcel Dunan has exceptionally good and erudite notes. The most penetrating treatment of Las Cases' great work is Robert Morrissey, *Napoléon et l'héritage de la gloire*, Chapter V. All the quotations from Chateaubriand are to the Pléiade edition. Jean-Paul Clément's edition has excellent notes. Herold, *Mistress to an Age*, although dated is impressively erudite. Guillemin, *Madame de Staël et Napoléon*, is more recent. Le Gall, *Napoléon et le Mémorial de Sainte-Hélène, Analyse d'un Discours*, is a recent analysis of Las Cases's discourse. See p. 93 for his explanation of the author's method. The best recent treatment of Napoleon's reputation is Hazareesingh, *The Legend of Napoleon*. For Napoleon on the people, see Le Gall pp. 173, 190, and for the middle class, p. 228.

Germaine's letter to Meister is quoted from Guillemin, p. 28. Napoleon's insult of Mme de Staël is quoted from Herold, pp. 227–8, as is Napoleon's tirade to her son (pp. 357–8). See Norvins on Mme de Staël's conversion, II, 100, 108. Stendhal's comment is from his *Correspondance* (Pléaide, 1962), p. 941.

XI   The End of the End Game

Kauffmann, *La Chambre noire de Longwood* (available in an English translation, *The Black Room at Longwood*) is the most recent and most fascinating book on Napoleon's captivity. It not only tells the story exceedingly well but is also an inquiry into the nature and psychology of captivity. Lord Rosebery's *Napoleon, the Final Phase*, is a classic that retains its authority and is beautifully written. Tulard's edition of selections from the Evangelists (*Napoléon à Sainte-Hélène*) provides a chronology of Napoleon's exile, a *dramatis personae* of the French colony, and a good bibliography.

The 'ravaged fortress' is Kauffmann's description, p. 6. Talleyrand is quoted from Rosebery, p. 152. The subjects Napoleon preferred in history writing is quoted from Jourdan, *Napoléon, Héros, Imperator, Mécène*, p. 293. The characterization of Napoleon's artistic taste is from Chastel, *L'Art français*, p. 168.

XII   Death and Rebirth

Montholon, *Récits de la captivité de l'Empereur Napoléon à Sainte-Hélène*, and Bertrand, *Cahiers de Sainte-Hélène, 1816–1821*, along with Marchand, *Mémoires de Marchand*, are indispensable. I discuss the question of Napoleon's poisoning in an Appendix. There is a good summary of Napoleon's death in Martineau, *La Vie quotidienne à Sainte-Hélène au temps de Napoléon*, including an analysis of the autopsy report. For Napoleon's Paris tomb I follow Driskel, *As Befits a Legend: Building a Tomb for Napoleon, 1840–1861*. Peter Brooks's novel, *The Emperor's Body*, is a fine telling of the story of the return of Napoleon's remains, accompanied by the kind of rich detail only a novelist can provide.

Epilogue   Napoleon and the Revolutionary Tradition

There are so many books on the theory and practice of revolution that I cannot list more than a few. Among those who have sought to find common themes, practices, or patterns in revolutions I would mention Brinton, *The Anatomy of Revolution*, Moore, *Social Origins of Dictatorship and Democracy*, Skocpol, *States and Social Revolution*, and Trotsky, *History of the Russian Revolution*.

Thierry Lentz on historiographical habits is in *Nouvelle histoire du Premier Empire*, III, p. 31; on the talent Napoleon attracted, III, p. 64. Napoleon on his son's reign is quoted from Rosebery, *Napoleon, the Final Phase*, p. 28. Tocqueville is quoted from Jardin, *Tocqueville: A Biography*, p. 485.

Appendix   Some Remarks about Arsenic Poisoning

The best survey of the several hypotheses and the evidence of arsenic poisoning is Lentz and Macé, *La Mort de Napoléon*. The first presentation of Forshufvud's and Weider's hypothesis was in 1978. Weider and Hapgood later (1982) published a more dramatic account of the hypothesis in *The Murder of Napoleon*. Martineau has a careful analysis of the autopsy and is available in an English translation as *Napoleon's St Helena*. The evidence that the arsenic found in Napoleon's hair could not have been ingested is in Lentz and Macé, p. 124. For the most recent analysis of Napoleon's hair see *The New York Times*, 10 June 2008, in the Science section for an account of the work, published in the Italian Journal *Il nuovo saggitore*. There is a good summary of the literature and the case for poisoning in Macé, 'Empoisonnement' de Napoléon' in *Dictionnaire Napoléon*, vol. 1, pp. 720–24.

A Select Bibliography

Lettres de Napoléon à Joséphine et Lettres de Joséphine à Napoléon (Paris: Le Livre Club du Libraire, 1959).

Lettres inédites de Napoléon Ier (an VIII–1815), 2 vols, ed. Léon Lecestre (Paris: Plon, 1897).

General Wilson's Journal, 1812–1814 (London: Kimber, 1964).

Code Napoléon, edition originale et seule officielle (Paris: l'Imprimerie impériale, 1808).

Correspondance entre le comte de Mirabeau et le comte de la Marck, 2 vols (Brussels: Auguste Pagny, 1851).

Napoléon, images et histoire: Peintures du château de Versailles (1789–1815) (Paris: Editions de la Réunion des musées nationaux, 2001).

Abeille, M. J., *Notes et piecès officielles relatives aux événements de Marseille et de Toulon en 1793*, (1815, n.p.).

Agulhon, Maurice, Vovelle, Michel and Constant, E., *Histoire de Toulon* (Toulouse, 1980).

Alexander, R. S., *Bonapartism and Revolutionary Tradition in France: The Fédérés of 1815* (Cambridge: Cambridge University Press, 1991).

Alison, Archibald, *History of Europe* (Edinburgh: William Blackwood and Sons, 1838).

Al-Jabarti, *Napoleon in Egypt: Al-Jabarti's Chronicle of the French Occupation, 1798* (Princeton: Markus Wiener, 1997).

Arnold, James, R., *Napoleon Conquers Austria: The 1809 Campaign for Vienna* (New York: Praeger, 1995).

Austin, Paul Britten, *1812: The Great Retreat* (London: Greenhill Books, 1990).

——, *1812: The March on Moscow* (London: Greenhill Books, 1993).

——, *1812: Napoleon in Moscow* (London: Greenhill Books, 1995).

——, *1815: The Return of Napoleon* (London: Greenhill Books, 2002).

Bainville, Jacques, *Napoléon* (Paris: Editions Balland, 1931).

Balzac, Honoré de, *Le Médecin de campagne* (Paris: Pocket Classiques, 1994).

Barbé-Marbois, François, *Journal d'un déporté non jugé* (Paris, 1834).

Barker, Thomas M., *Double Eagle and Crescent: Vienna's Second Turkish Siege and Its Historical Setting* (Albany: State University of New York Press, 1967).

Beck, Lewis White, 'The Reformation, the Revolution and the Restoration in Hegel's Political Philosophy', *The Journal for the History of Philosophy*, 14 (1976): 51–61.

Bell, David A., *The First Total War. Napoleon's Europe and the Birth of Warfare as We Know It* (Boston: Houghton Mifflin, 2007).

Bergeron, Louis, *France under Napoleon*, trans. R. R. Palmer (Princeton: Princeton University Press, 1981).

Bergeron, Louis and Chaussinand-Nogaret, Guy, *Les Masses de granit, cent mille notables du Premier Empire* (Paris: Editions de l'Ecole des hautes-études en sciences sociales, n.d.).

Bertaud, Jean-Paul, Forrest, Alan and Jourdan, Annie, *Napoléon, le monde et les Anglais: Guerre des mots et des images* (Paris: Editions Autrement, 2004).

Bertholet, Denis, *Les Français par eux-mêmes 1815–1885* (Paris: Olivier Orban, 1991).

Bertier de Sauvigny, G. de, *La Restauration* (Paris: Champs-Flammarion, 1974).

Bertrand, Général, *Cahiers de Sainte-Hélène, 1816–1821*, 3 vols (Paris: Editions Albin Michel, 1950–1959).

Biver, Marie-Louise, *Le Paris de Napoléon* (Paris: Librairie Plon, 1963).

——, *Pierre Fontaine, premier architecte de l'empereur* (Paris: Editions d'histoire et d'art, Librairie Plon, 1964).

Blackburn, Julia, *The Emperor's Last Island* (New York: Vintage, 1993).

Blanning, T. C. W., *The French Revolutionary Wars, 1787–1802* (London: Arnold, 1996).

Bluche, Frédéric, *Le Bonapartisme, aux origins de la droite authoritaire (1800–1850)* (Paris: Nouvelles editions latines, 1980).

Bonaparte, Louis-Napoléon, *Des Idées Napoléoniennes* (Paris: Paulin, 1839).

Bordes, Philippe, *Le Serment du Jeu de Paume* (Paris, 1983).

Boswell, James, *An Account of Corsica, the Journal of a Tour to That Island and Memoirs of Pascal Paoli* (Oxford: Oxford University Press, 2006).

Bourrienne, Louis-Antoine Fauvelet de, *Mémoires de M. de Bourrienne sur Napoléon*, Edition nouvelle, refondue et annotée par Désiré Lacroix, 5 vols (Paris: Garnier, 1899–1900).

Boyer, Ferdinand, 'Les Responsabilités de Napoléon dans le transfert des œuvres de l'étranger', *Revue d'histoire moderne et contemporaine*, 1964: 241–62.

——, *Le Monde des arte en Italie et la France de la Révolution et de l'Empire* (Turin: Società editrice internazionale, 1969).

Branda, Pierre, *Le Prix de la gloire, Napoléon et l'argent* (Paris: Fayard, 2007).

Brinton, Crane, *The Anatomy of Revolution*, revised edition (New York: Prentice Hall, 1952).

Broers, Michael, *Europe Under Napoleon, 1799–1818* (London: Arnold, 1996).

——, *The Politics of Religion in Napoleonic Italy: The War against God, 1801–1814* (London: Routledge, 2002).

——, *The Napoleonic Empire in Italy, 1796–1814* (Basingstoke: Palgrave Macmillan, 2005).

Brooks, Peter, *The Emperor's Body* (New York: W.W. Norton, 2011).

Brown, Howard, *Ending the French Revolution: Violence, Justice, and Repression* (Charlottesville: Virginia University Press, 2006).

Burns, Michael, *Dreyfus, A Family Affair, 1789–1945* (New York: HarperCollins, 1991).

Burton, J. K., *Napoleon and Clio. Historical Writing, Teaching and Thinking during the First Empire* (Chapel Hill: University of North Carolina Press, 1979).

Cantarel-Besson, Yveline, Constans, Claire and Foucart, Bruno, *Napoléon: Images et histoire (Peintures du Château de Versailles, 1789–1815)* (Paris: Réunion des Musées nationaux, 2001).

Carrington, Dorothy, *Napoleon and His Parents: On the Threshold of History* (New York: Dutton, 1990).

Caulaincourt, Armand de, Duke of Vicenza, *With Napoleon in Russia: The Memoirs of General de Caulaincourt, Duke of Vicenza*, trans. George Libaire (New York: William Morrow and Company, 1935).

——, Caulaincourt, Général Armand de, duc de Vicence, *Mémoires du Général de Caulaincourt, Duc de Vicence, Grand Ecuyer de l'empereur*, 3 vols (Paris: Librairie Plon, 1933).

Chandler, David G., *The Campaigns of Napoleon* (New York: Macmillan, 1966).

Chaptal, Jean-Antoine, *Mes souvenirs sur Napoléon* (Paris: Plon, 1893).

Chastel, André, *L'Art français. Le temps de l'éloquence, 1775–1825* (Paris: Flammarion, 2000).

Chateaubriand, François René de, *Mémoires d'outre-tombe. Edition nouvelle établie d'après l'édition originale . . .* par Maurice Levaillant and Georges Moulinier, 2 vols (Paris: Gallimard, 1997).

——, *Mémoires d'outre-tombe*, ed. Jean-Paul Clément, 2 vols (Paris: Gallimard, 1997).

——, *Mémoires d'outre-tombe*, 2 vols (Paris: Gallimard [Pléiade], 1947).

——, *Grands écrits politiques*, 2 vols (Paris: Imprimerie nationale, 1993).

——, 'Essai sur les Révolutions anciennes', *Œuvres Complètes*, vol. 1–2 (Furne: Charles Gosselin, 1837, 12 vols).

Chatelain, Jean, *Dominique Vivant Denon et le Louvre de Napoléon* (Paris: Libraire Académique Perrin, 1999).

Clausewitz, Carl von, *On War*, ed. and trans. Michael Howard and Peter Paret (Princeton: Princeton University Press, 1976).

——, *The Campaign of 1812 in Russia* (New York: Da Capo, 1995).

Cole, Juan, *Napoleon's Egypt: Invading the Middle East* (New York: Palgrave, 2007).

Collins, Irene, *Napoleon and His Parliaments 1800–1815* (London and New York: St Martin's Press, 1979).

Connelly, Owen, *Napoleon's Satellite Kingdoms* (New York: The Free Press, 1969).

——, *Blundering to Glory: Napoleon's Military Campaigns* (Wilmington: Scholarly Resources, 1999).

Constant, Benjamin, *De l'esprit de conquête et de l'usurpation dans leurs rapports avec la civilization européenne* (Paris: Imprimerie nationale, 1992).

Cottin, Paul, *Toulon et les Anglais en 1793* (Paris: Ollendorff, 1898).

Crouzet, François, *L'Economie britannique et le blocus continental* (Paris: Economica, 1987).

——, *Les Sources de la richesse de l'angleterre vue par les Français du xviième siècle* in Crouzet, *De la supériorité de l'Angleterre sur la France* (Paris: Perrin 1985): 105–19.

Cuoco, Vincenzo, *Essai historique sur la Révolution de Naples*, texte établi par Antonino de Francesco, intro., trad. et notes de Alain Pons, préf. de Michel Vovelle, Bibliotheque Italienne, bilingue ed. (Paris: les Belles lettres, 2004).

Davois, Gustave, *Bibliographie Napoléonienne Française, jusqu'en 1908* (Paris: l'Edition Bibliographique, 1909).

de la Barre de Nanteuil, H., *Le comte Daru ou l'administration militaire sous la Révolution et l'Empire* (Paris: J. Peyronnet & Cie., 1966).

Delestre, Jean-Baptiste, *Gros: sa vie et ses ouvrages* (Paris, 1867).

Denon, Dominique Vivant, *Voyage dans la Basse et la Haute Egypte pendant les campagnes du Général Bonaparte* (Paris: Gallimard, 2001).

——, *Journeys in Upper and Lower Egypt*, 1803.

Descotes, M., *La Légende de Napoléon et les écrivains français du xixème siècle* (Paris: Lettres modernes, Minard, 1967).

Dhombres, Nicole et Jean, *Naissance d'un nouveau pouvoir: sciences et savants en France, 1793–1824* (Paris: Editions Payot, 1989).

Driskel, Michael Paul, *As Befits a Legend: Building a Tomb for Napoleon, 1840–1861* (Kent: Kent State University Press, 1993).

Duport, Anne-Marie and Vovelle, Michel, *Terreur et Révolution, Nimes en l'an II 1793–1794* (Paris: J. Touzot, 1987).

Dwyer, Philip G. (ed.), *Napoleon and Europe* (London: Longmans, 2001).

——, *Napoleon* (New Haven: Yale University Press, 2007).

Dwyer, Philip G. and Forrest, Alan (eds), *Napoleon and His Empire, Europe, 1804–1814* (Basingstoke: Palgrave Macmillan, 2007).

Elting, John R., *Swords around a Throne: Napoleon's Grande Armée* (New York: The Free Press, 1988).

Englund, Steven, *Napoleon, A Political Life* (Cambridge, MA: Harvard University Press, 2004).

Epstein, Robert M., *Napoleon's Last Victory and the Emergence of Modern War* (Lawrence: University Press of Kansas, 1994).

Esdaile, Charles, *The Peninsular War* (Basingstoke: Palgrave Macmillan, 2003).

——, *Fighting Napoleon: Guerrillas, Bandits and Adventurers in Spain, 1808–1814* (New Haven: Yale University Press, 2004).

—— (ed.), *Popular Resistance in the French Wars: Patriots, Partisans and Land Pirates* (Basingstoke: Palgrave Macmillan, 2005).

——, *Napoleon's Wars: An International History, 1803–1815* (New York: Viking, 2007).

Fain, P., *Mémoires de Baron Fain* (Paris: Librairie Plon, 1909).

Feuer, Kathryn B., *Tolstoy and the Genesis of* War and Peace, ed. by Robin Feuer Miller and Donna Tussing (Ithaca: Cornell University Press, 1996).

Fierro, Alfred (ed.) *Les Français vus par eux-mêmes: Le Consulat et l'Empire* (Paris: Robert Laffont, 1998).

Fleischman, Théodore, *Napoléon et la musique* (Paris: Brepols, 1965).

Fleischmann, Hector, *Napoléon par Balzac: Récits et épisodes du Premier Empire tirés de la Comédie Humaine* (Paris: Librairie universelle, 1913).

Fleury, M. and Gille, B., *Dictionnaire Biographique du Conseil Municipal de Paris et du Conseil Général de la Seine* (Paris: Imprimerie municipale, 1972).

Fontaine, Pierre François Léonard, *Journal, 1799–1853*, 2 vols (Paris: Ecole nationale supérieure des Beaux-Arts, 1987).

Forrest, Alan, *The Soldiers of the French Revolution* (Durham, NC: Duke University Press, 1990).

——, *Napoleon's Men: The Soldiers of the Revolution and Empire* (Hambledon and London: Continuum, 2002).

Forshufvud, Sten and Weider, Ben, *Assassination at St Helena: The Poisoning of Napoleon Bonaparte* (Vancouver: Mitchell Press, 1978).

Fouché, Joseph, *Mémoires de Joseph Fouché, duc d'Otrante* (Paris: Imprimerie Nationale, 1993).

Furet, François, *La Révolution, de Turgot à Jules Ferry, 1770–1880* (Paris: Hachette, 1989).

Furet, François and Ozouf, Mona, *Dictionnaire critique de la Révolution française* (Paris: Flammarion, 1988).

Ganière, Paul, *Napoléon à Sainte-Hélène*, 3 vols (Paris: Librairie académique Perrin, 1957).

Gassier, Pierre and Wilson, Juliet, *The Life and Complete Work of Francisco Goya*, ed. by François Lachenal (New York: William Morrow, 1971).

Gautier, Paul, *Mme de Staël et Napoléon* (Paris: Plon, 1933).

Geyl, Pieter, *Napoleon For and Against*, trans. Olive Renier (New Haven: Yale University Press, 1949).

Godechot, Jacques, *Les Institutions de la France sous la Révolution et l'Empire* (Paris: Presses Universitaire de France, 1968).

——, 'La Revolution française et les juifs (1789–1799)', in Bernhard Blumenkranz and Albert Soboul (eds), *Les Juifs et la Revolution française* (Toulouse: Privat 1989).

Goines, Donald, and Vovelle, Olivier, *Vendeurs de mort,* trans. Olivier Vovelle, Série Noire (Paris: Gallimard, 1994).

Gorer, Geoffrey, et al., *Ni pleurs ni couronnes, précédé de pornographie de la morte* trans. Hélène Allouch (Paris: Epel, 1995).

Gourgaud, Général Baron, *Journal de Sainte-Hélène,* 2 vols (Paris: Flammarion, 1947).

Goya, Francisco, *The Disasters of War* (New York: Dover Publications, 1967).

Gueniffey, Patrice, *Le Dix-Huit Brumaire: L'épilogue de la Révolution française* (Paris: Gallimard, 2008).

Guerrini, Maurice, *Napoléon et Paris* (Paris: Librairie P. Téqui, 1967).

Guillemin, Henri, *Madame de Staël et Napoléon* (Paris: Editions de Seuil, 1987).

Gusdorf, Georges, *La Conscience Révolutionnaire: Les Idéologues* (Paris: Payot, 1978).

Hazareesingh, Sudhir, *The Legend of Napoleon* (London: Granta Books, 2004).

Heckscher, Eli, *The Continental System: An Economic Interpretation* (Gloucester, MA: P. Smith, 1964).

Hegel, Georg Wilhelm Friedrich, *The Philosophy of History,* trans. James Sebree (New York: Dover, 1956).

——, *Hegel: The Letters,* ed. and trans. Clark Butler and Christiane Seiler (Bloomington: Indiana University Press, 1984).

Herold, J. Christopher, *Mistress to an Age: A Life of Madame de Staël* (Indianapolis: Bobbs-Merrill, 1958).

Himelfarb, Hélène, *'Versailles, Fonctions et Légendes': Les Lieux de Mémoire,* ed. Pierre Nora (Paris: Gallimard).

Holborn, Hajo, *A History of Modern Germany, 1648–1840* (New York: Knopf, 1964).

Holtman, Robert B., *Napoleonic Propaganda* (New York: Greenwood Press, 1969).

Horne, Alistair, *How Far from Austerlitz? Napoleon 1805–1815* (New York: St Martin's Press, 1996).

Houssaye, Henry, *1814. Quatre-vingt-treizième édition* (Paris: Librairie Académique Perrin, 1937).

Howard, Michael, *Clausewitz* (Oxford: Oxford University Press, 1983).

Howarth, David, *Trafalgar: The Nelson Touch* (London: Collins, 1969).

Hughes, Robert, *Goya* (New York: Alfred A. Knopf, 2003).

Jardin, André, *Tocqueville: A Biography,* trans. Lydia Davis and Robert Hemenway (New York: Farrar, Straus, and Giroux, 1988).

Johns, Christopher, *Antonio Canova and the Politics of Patronage in Revolutionary and Napoleonic Europe* (Berkeley: University of California Press, 1998).

Jourdan, Annie, *Napoléon, Héros, Imperator, Mécène* (Paris: Aubier, 1998).

——, *L'Empire de Napoléon* (Paris: Flammarion, 2000).

——, *Mythes et légendes de Napoléon* (Toulouse: Privat, 2004).

——, (ed.) *Louis Bonaparte, roi de Hollande* (Paris: Nouveau Monde, 2010).

Jourquin, Jacques, 'La Chevauchée Fantastique', *Historia,* 1984.

Kauffmann, Jean-Paul, *La Chambre noire de Longwood: Le Voyage à Sainte-Hélène* (Paris: La Table Ronde, 1997).

——, *The Black Room at Longwood: Napoleon's Exile on Saint Helena*, trans. Patricia Clancy (New York: Four Walls Eight Windows, 1999).

Keegan, John, *The Face of Battle* (New York: Viking Press, 1976).

Kissinger, Henry, *A World Restored: Metternich, Castlereagh and the Problems of Peace, 1812–1822* (London: Weidenfeld and Nicolson, 1957).

Knapton, Ernest John, *Empress Josephine* (Cambridge, MA: Harvard University Press, 1964).

Künzi, Frédéric, *Bicentenaire du Passage des Alpes par Bonaparte, 1800–2000* (Martigny: Fondation Pierre Gianadda, 2000).

Landon, H. C. Robbins, in association with Henry Raynor, *Haydn* (New York: Praeger, 1972).

Langlois, Claude, 'Religion et politique dans la France napoléonienne', in Centre des Recherches pour l'Etude des Religions, *Christianisme et Pouvoirs Politiques de Napoléon à Adenauer* (Université de Lille: Editions Universitaires, 1973).

——, et al., *Atlas de la Révolution francaise: Religion* (Paris: l'Ecole des hautes études en sciences sociales, 1996).

Las Cases, Emmanuel Comte de, *Le Mémorial de Sainte-Hélène. Première edition intégrale et critique, établie et annotée par Marcel Dunan*, 2 vols (Paris: Flammarion, 1951).

——, *Le Mémorial de Sainte-Hélène. Edition établie par G. Walter*, 2 vols (Paris: Gallimard, 1956).

Laurens, Henry, *L'Expédition d'Egypte, 1798–1801* (Paris: Editions de Seuil, 1997).

Le Gall, Didier, *Napoléon et le Mémorial de Sainte-Hélène, Analyse d'un Discours* (Paris: Editions Kimé, 2003).

Lefebvre, Georges, *Napoléon* (Paris: Presses Universitaires de France, 1969).

Leflon, Jean, *La Crise Révolutionnaire, 1789–1846*, in Augustin Fliche and Victor Martin (eds), *Histoire de l'Eglise*, vol. 20 (Paris: Bloud & Gay, 1949).

Lentz, Thierry, *Nouvelle histoire du Premier Empire*, 4 vols (Paris: Fayard, 2008–10).

—— and Macé, Jacques, *La Mort de Napoléon: mythes, légends, et mystères* (Paris: Perrin, 2009).

Lieven, Dominic, *Russia against Napoleon* (New York: Viking, 2010).

Lynch, John, *Bourbon Spain, 1700–1808* (Oxford: Blackwell, 1989).

Lyons, Martyn, *Napoleon Bonaparte and the Legacy of the French Revolution* (New York: Palgrave, 1994).

Mackenzie, Norman, *The Escape from Elba: The Fall and Flight of Napoleon, 1814–1815* (Oxford: Oxford University Press, 1982).

M[éry], [Joseph], 'Napoléon amateur d'échecs', *Le Palamède*, I, No. 1, 1st ser: 12–13.

Mainardi, Patricia, 'Assuring the Empire of the Future: The 1798 Fête de la liberté', *Art Journal*, Summer 1989.

Marbot, Général Baron de, *Mémoires du Général Baron de Marbot*, 3 vols (Paris: Librairie Plon, 1891).

Marchand, Louis, *Mémoires de Marchand*, 2 vols (Paris: Plon, 1955).

Markham, Felix, *Napoleon* (London: Weidenfeld and Nicolson, 1963).

Markham, J. David (trans.), *Imperial Glory: The Bulletins of Napoleon's Grande Armée, 1805–1814* (London: Greenhill Books, 2003).

Marquiset, Alfred, *Napoléon sténographié au Conseil d'etat* (Paris, 1913).

Marseille, J. Abeille de, *Essai sur nos colonies et le Rétablissement de Saint Domingue*, 2 vols (Paris: Chomel, 1805).

Martineau, Gilbert, *La Vie quotidienne à Sainte-Hélène au temps de Napoléon* (Paris: Hachette, 1966).

Masson, Frédéric, *Napoléon chez lui: la journée de l'Empereur aux Tuileries* (Paris: E. Dentu, 1894).

——, *Napoléon dans sa jeunesse, 1769–1793* (Paris: Librarie Paul Ollendorff, 1908).

——, *L'impératrice Marie-Louise (1809–1815)* (Paris: Librairie Paul Ollendorff, 1911).

——, *Napoléon à Sainte-Hélène* (Paris: Librairie Paul Ollendorff, 1912).

——, *Joséphine Répudiée (1809–1814)* (Paris: Librairie Paul Ollendorff, 1914).

Mayer, Arno, *The Furies: Violence and Terror in the French and Russian Revolutions* (Princeton: Princeton University Press, 2000).

Melito, Miot de, *Mémoires du comte Miot de Melito*, 3 vols (Paris: Calmann-Lévy, 1880).

Molé, Mathieu, *Souvenirs de jeunesse, 1793–1803* (Paris: Mercure de France, 2005).

Moore, Barrington, *Social Origins of Dictatorship and Democracy: Lord and Peasant in the Making of the Modern World* (Boston: Beacon Press, 1966).

Morrissey, Robert, *Napoléon et l'héritage de la gloire* (Paris: Presses Universitaires de France, 2010).

Morvan, Jean, *Le Soldat imperial (1800–1814)*, 2 vols (Paris: Plon, 1904).

Müller, Friedrich von, and Charles-Otto Zieseniss, *Souvenirs des années de guerre, 1806–1813. Présentation et traduction par Charles-Otto Zieseniss* (Paris: Fondation Napoléon, Tallandier, 1992).

Montholon, Charles Jean Tristan, *Récits de la captivité de l'Empereur Napoléon à Sainte-Hélène*, 2 vols (Paris: Paulin, 1847).

Muir, Rory, *Tactics and the Experience of Battle in the Age of Napoleon* (New Haven: Yale University Press, 2000).

Musulin, Stella, *Vienna in the Age of Metternich from Napoleon to Revolution 1805–1848* (London: Faber and Faber, 1975).

Nabokov, Serge and de Lastours, Sophie, *Koutouzov: Le Vainqueur de Napoléon* (Paris: Albin Michel, 1990).

Napoléon [Bonaparte], *Campagnes d'Egypte et de Syrie* (Paris: Imprimérie nationale, 1998).

——, *Correspondance de Napoléon Ier publiée par ordre de l'Empereur Napoléon III*, 32 vols (Paris: Plon and Dumaine, 1858–1870).

——, *Correspondance générale publié par la Fondation Napoléon*, ed. Thierry Lentz et al., 7 vols (Paris: Fayard, 2004–2010).

——, *Lettres, decisions et actes de Napoléon à Pont-de-Briques*, 4 vols, ed. Fernand-Emile Beaucour and Jean-Baptiste Beaucour (Levallois: Société de sauvegarde du chateau imperial de Pont-de-Briques, 1979–2004).

——, *Lettres inédites de Napolèon Ier (an viii – 1815)*, ed. Léon Lecestre, 2 vols (Paris: Librairie Plon, 1897).

——, *Lettres inédites de Napoléon 1er à Marie-Louise, écrites de 1810–1814*, ed. Louis Madelin (Paris: Bibliothèque nationale, 1935).

——, *Lettres d'amour à Joséphine* (Paris: Fayard, 1981).

——, *Lettres au Comte Mollien* (Paris: Editions Charles Gay, 1959).

——, *Napoléon et Joseph, correspondance integral, 1784–1818*, ed. Vincent Haegele (Paris: Tallandier, 2007).

——, *Œuvres littéraires et écrits militaires*, ed. Jean Tulard, 3 vols (Paris: Bibliothèque des Introuvables, 2001).

Nicolin, Günther, *Hegel in Berichten Seinger Zeitgenossen* (Hamburg: Felix Meiner, 1970).

Nicholson, Harold, *The Congress of Vienna, a Study in Allied Unity, 1812–1822* (New York: Harcourt, Brace, 1946).

Norvins, J. de, *Mémorial de J. de Norvins*, 3 vols (Paris: E. Plon, Nourrit et Cie, 1896).

O'Brien, David, *After the Revolution: Antoine-Jean Gros, Painting and Propaganda under Napoleon* (University Park: Pennsylvania State University Press, 2006).

Olivier, D., *L'incendie de Moscou* (Paris, 1964).

Palmer, R. R., *J.-B. Say: An Economist in Troubled Times* (Princeton: Princeton University Press, 1997).

——, *The Age of the Democratic Revolution: A Political History of Europe and America, 1760–1800*, 2 vols (Princeton: Princeton University Press, 1959, 1964).

Parker, Harold T., *Three Napoleonic Battles* (Durham, NC: Duke University Press, 1944).

——, 'Napoleon's Philosophy of Governing Conquered Territories, 1805–1807', *South Atlantic Quarterly*, 51 (1952): 70–84.

——, 'Why Did Napoleon Invade Russia? A Study in Motivation and the Interrelations of Personality and Social Structure', *Journal of Military History*, 54 (1990): 131–46.

Petiteau, Natalie, *Napoléon, de la mythologie à l'histoire* (Paris: Editions du Seuil, 1999).

——, *Lendemains d'empire, Les Soldats de Napoléon dans la France du xixe siècle* (Paris: La Boutique de l'histoire, 2003).

Pinkard, Terry, *Hegel: A Biography* (Cambridge: Cambridge University Press, 2000).

Poniatowski, Michel, *Talleyrand et le Consulat* (Paris, 1986).

Portalis, Jean-Etienne-Marie, *Discours préliminaire au premier projet de Code civil* (Bordeaux: Editions Confluences, 1999).

Rambaud, Jacques, *Naples sous Joseph Bonaparte* (Paris: Librairie Plon, 1911).

Regenbogen, Lucian (ed.), *Napoléon a dit, Aphorismes, citations et opinions* (Paris: Les Belles Lettres, 1998).

Reinhard, Marcel, *Avec Bonaparte en Italie, d'après les letters inédites de son aide de camp Joseph Sulkowski* (Paris: Hachette, 1846).

Ridley, Ronald T., *The Eagle and the Spade: The Archaeology of Rome during the Napoleonic Era, 1809–1814* (Cambridge: Cambridge University Press, 1992).

Roederer, comte P.-L., *Journal du comte P.-L. Rœderer* (Paris: H. Daragon, 1909).

Rosebery, Lord, *Napoleon, the Final Phase* (New York: Harper and Brothers, 1900).

Rothenberg, Gunther, *The Emperor's Last Victory* (London: Weidenfeld and Nicolson, 2004).

Rubel, Maximilien, *Karl Marx devant le Bonapartisme* (Paris-The Hague: Mouton, 1960).

Russell, Terence M., *The Discovery of Egypt: Vivant Denon's Travels with Napoleon's Army* (Stroud: Sutton, 2005).

Scharf, Aaron, *Art and Photography* (Harmondsworth: Penguin, 1972).

Schroeder, Paul W., *The Transformation of European Politics, 1763–1848* (Oxford: Oxford University Press, 1994).

Shlapentokh, Dmitry, *The Counter-Revolution in Revolution: Images of Thermidor and Napoleon at the Time of the Russian Revolution and Civil War* (New York: St Martin's Press, 1999).

Sieburg, Friedrich, *Robespierre*, traduit de l'allemand par Pierre Klossowski, Preface by Michel Vovelle (Paris: Mémoire du livre, 2003).

Skocpol, Theda, *States and Social Revolution: A Comparative Analysis of France, Russia, and China* (New York: Cambridge University Press, 1979).

Soboul, Albert, *La Civilisation et la France napoléonienne* (Paris: Arthaud, 1983).

Solomon, Maynard, *Beethoven* (London: Shirmer Trade Books, 2001).

Sorel, Albert, 'Tolstoï-Historien', *Revue bleu* (1888): 460–499.

Spielman, John, *Leopold of Austria* (London: Thames and Hudson, 1977).

Staël, Madame de, *Dix années d'exil* (Paris: Fayard, 1966).

——, *Considérations sur la Révolution française* (Paris: Tallandier, 2000).

Stendhal, *Napoléon* (Paris: Editions Climats, 1998).

Stoye, John, *The Siege of Vienna: The Last Great Trial between Cross and Crescent* (New York: Pegasus, 2006).

Sydenham, M. J., *The First French Republic, 1792–1804* (Berkeley: University of California Press, 1973).

——, 'Le Crime de 3 Nivôse (24 December 1800)', in J. F. Bosher (ed.), *French Government and Society, 1500–1800: Essays in Memory of Alfred Cobban* (London: Athlone Press, 1973): 295–320.

Talleyrand, Charles Maurice de, *Mémoires: L'époque Napoléonienne*, ed. Georges Duby (Paris: L'Imprimerie nationale, 1996).

Thayer, Alexander Wheelock, *Thayer's Life of Beethoven*, rev. and ed. Elliot Forbes, 2 vols (Princeton: Princeton University Press, 1964).

Thibaudeau, Antoine-Clair, *Mémoires de A. C. Thibaudeau (1799–1815)* (Paris: Plon, 1913).

Tomiche, Nicole, *Napoléon écrivain* (Paris: Colin, 1952).

Treue, Wilhelm, *Art Plunder: The Fate of Works of Art in War and Unrest*, trans. Basil Creighton (New York: John Day Company, 1961).

Tripier le France, J., *Histoire de la vie et de la mort du Baron Gros* (Paris: J. Martin, 1880).

Trotsky, Leon, *History of the Russian Revolution*, trans. Max Eastman, 3 vols (London: Victor Gollancz, 1934).

Tulard, Jean, *Des Français sous Napoléon: La Vie Quotidienne* (Paris: Hachette 1978).

——, *Napoléon à Sainte-Hélène: Texts préfacés, choisis et commentés par Jean Tulard* (Paris: Robert Laffont [Bouquins], 1981).

——, *Le Consulat et l'Empire, 1800–1815. Nouvelle Histoire de Paris* (Paris: Hachette, 1983).

——, *Napoléon, ou le mythe du sauveur* (Paris: Fayard, 1987).

——, *Nouvelle bibliographie critique des Mémoires sur l'époque napoléonienne écrits ou traduits en français* (Geneva: Droz, 1991).

——, *Joseph Fouché* (Paris: Fayard, 1999).

——, *Les Thermidoriens* (Paris: Fayard, 2005).

——, Fierro, Alfred and Leri, Jean-Marc, *Histoire de Napoléon par la peinture* (Paris: l'Archipel, 1991).

—— and Garros, Louis, *Itinéraire de Napoléon au jour le jour, 1769–1821* (Paris: Tallandier, 1998).

Vigny, Alfred de, *Servitude et grandeur militaire* (Paris: J. de Bonnet, 1972).

Walter, Jakob, *The Diary of a Napoleonic Foot Soldier*, trans. Otto Springer (London: Penguin, 1993).

Weider, Ben and Hapgood, David, *The Murder of Napoleon* (New York: Congdon & Lattès, 1982).

Whitcomb, E., 'Napoleon's Prefects', *American Historical Review*, LXXIX: 1089–1118.

Wilson, Stephen, *Feuding, Conflict, and Banditry in Nineteenth-century Corsica* (Cambridge: Cambridge University Press, 1988).

Wilson-Smith, Timothy, *Napoleon and His Artists* (London: Constable, 1996).

Woloch, Isser, *Napoleon and His Collaborators, the Making of a Dictatorship* (New York: W.W. Norton, 2001).

——, *The New Regime: Transformations of the French Civic Order, 1789–1820* (New York: W.W. Norton, 1994).

Woolf, Stuart, *Napoleon's Integration of Europe* (London: Routledge, 1991).

Zamoyski, Adam, *Rites of Peace: The Fall of Napoleon and the Congress of Vienna* (London: HarperCollins, 2007).

——, *Moscow 1812: Napoleon's Fatal March* (New York: HarperCollins, 2004).

Zieseniss, Charles-Otto, *Napoléon et la cour impériale* (Paris: Tallandier, 1980).

——, *Napoléon et les peintres de son temps* (Paris: Palais de l'Institut, 1986).

Index